SHARING POWER

Sharing Power

Women, Parliament, Democracy

Edited by
YVONNE GALLIGAN
Queens University Belfast, Northern Ireland

MANON TREMBLAY
University of Ottawa, Canada

Routledge
Taylor & Francis Group
LONDON AND NEW YORK

First published 2005 by Ashgate Publishing

Published 2016 by Routledge
2 Park Square, Milton Park, Abingdon, Oxfordshire OX14 4RN
711 Third Avenue, New York, NY 10017, USA

First issued in paperback 2016

Routledge is an imprint of the Taylor & Francis Group, an informa business

British Library Cataloguing in Publication Data
Sharing power : women, parliament, democracy
1. Women in politics 2. Legislators 3. Sex role
I. Galligan, Yvonne II. Tremblay, Manon
320'.082

Library of Congress Cataloging-in-Publication Data
Sharing power : women, parliament, democracy / [edited] by Yvonne Galligan and Manon Tremblay.
p. cm.
Includes bibliographical references and index.
ISBN 0-7546-4089-2
1. Women in politics. 2. Legislators. 3. Sex role. I. Tremblay, Manon.

HQ1390.S53 2005
320'.082--dc22

2004025165

ISBN 13: 978-1-138-27643-7 (pbk)
ISBN 13: 978-0-7546-4089-9 (hbk)

Contents

List of Tables

List of Tables

List of Contributors

Thanh-Huyen Ballmer-Cao is Professor of Political Science at the University of Geneva and the University of Zurich where she teaches comparative political behaviour. She has directed several research projects, in particular the National Research Programme 'Women, law and society: paths towards equality' initiated and funded by the Swiss government (1991-1996). She is director of the Department of Political Science at the University of Geneva and director of the doctoral programme 'Gender, social regulation and globalisation'. Her publications are mainly in the areas of political behaviour, electoral systems and political elites, with a particular focus on gender.

Sharon Bessell is Senior Lecturer in the Asia Pacific School of Economics and Government at The Australian National University. Her research interests include gender and political participation; social policy for vulnerable children; child labour and children's rights; and human rights and policy. She teaches courses on gender and policy and children and social policy. Dr Bessell has experience in academia, as a consultant working on development and social policy and in the non-government sector and has worked extensively throughout Southeast Asia, particularly Indonesia and the Philippines.

Jill M. Bystydzienski directs the Women's Studies Program and is Professor of Sociology and Women's Studies at Iowa State University. She is the author of numerous articles and book chapters on women in politics and cross-cultural comparisons of women, as well as several books, including *Women Transforming Politics: Worldwide Strategies for Empowerment* (1992), *Women in Cross-Cultural Transitions* (edited with Estelle Resnik; 1994), *Women in Electoral Politics: Lessons from Norway* (1995), *Democratization and Women's Grassroots Movements* (edited with Joti Sekhon; 1999), and *Forging Radical Alliances across Difference: Coalition Politics for the New Millennium* (edited with Steven Schacht; 2001). She is currently working on a book on intercultural couples.

Alisa Del Re teaches Political Science at the University of Padua (Department. of Political and Historical Studies) where she also teaches courses on equal ppportunities. She has also taught at the University of Paris VIII, and at the Institut d'études Politiques (IEP). She is one of the founders of the international research group 'Etat et Rapports Sociaux de Sexe', based in Paris, and continues to participate in its activities. Her research interests address gender-related themes, with special attention to social and family policies and to the question of reconciling work and family. She is particularly interested in political citizenship and women's representation at national, European, and local level.

Yvonne Galligan is Director of the Centre for Advancement of Women in Politics and Reader in Politics at Queen's University Belfast. She teaches and researches on gender politics, and directs an eleven-country comparative study, funded by the European Commission, on the gender impact of democratisation and European Union membership in Central and Eastern Europe. She has written extensively on women and politics in Ireland, and among her publications are *Women and Politics in Contemporary Ireland* (1998) and *Contesting Politics: Women in Ireland, North and South* (1999, edited with E. Ward and R. Wilford).

Sandra Grey is a lecturer in Social Policy at Victoria University of Wellington, where she teaches courses on family policy, changes in political values and policy administration in New Zealand. Her research focus has been on the discursive impact of the women's movements of Australia and New Zealand particularly in relation to 'work' and family. Sandra is also interested in ways of evaluating the influence of women in legislative assemblies and has published on the topic of 'critical mass' in the New Zealand House of Representatives.

Elisabeth Kardos-Kaponyi is Associate Professor of Sciences, Economic and Public Administration at Budapest University. Her teaching and research activity has been in two distinct fields: international public law and human rights, and international business law. She has run several courses and diploma-seminars on human rights and gender issues. In 1990 she was nominated by the Hungarian government as a delegate to the Council of Europe and began to work there on the international protection of human rights, with a particular focus on equality between women and men. She has presented Hungary's last three periodic reports on the CEDAW Convention to the United Nations. She is the author of several academic articles.

Monique Leyenaar is Professor (UHD) of Political Science, University of Nijmegen, Netherlands, specialising in gender and politics; political influence of citizens; local politics and comparative political systems. She also works as a consultant and advises the Netherlands government on policies concerning participation and mobilization of citizens as well as on the application of gender mainstreaming. She published *Empowerment of Women: The Netherlands and other European Countries* (2004) and other recent publications include 'Netherlands: Political Careers between Central Party Dominance and New Pressures', in: J. Borchert and J. Zeis (eds.), *The Political Class in Advanced Democracies, A Comparative Handbook* (2003, with B. Niemoller) and *'Lokale beleidsbeïnvloeding in 2003: een genderanalyse van de participatie van burgers'*, Werkdocument no. 297, Ministerie van Sociale Zaken en Werkgelegenheid, (2003, with B. Niemoller).

Laura Morales (MSc at LSE, MA Juan March Institute, Ph.D. Universidad Autónoma de Madrid) is Assistant Professor of Political Science at the Universidad de Murcia. She has previously lectured at the universities Autónoma and

Complutense in Madrid. Her interests lie especially in the areas of electoral behaviour and political participation. Among her most recent publications in English are 'Political Participation: Exploring the Gender Gap in Spain', in Gender Inequalities in Southern Europe, M.J. González, T. Jurado and M. Naldini (eds.), London: Frank Cass, 2000; *Citizens in Polities: the Individual and Contextual Determinants of Political Membership in Western Countries*, Working Paper no. 164, Madrid: CEACS, 2001; and 'Associational Membership and Social Capital in Comparative Perspective: the Problem of Measurement', *Politics and Society*, vol. 30 (1), 2002.

Luis Ramiro (Ph.D. European University Institute, Florence) is Associate Professor of Political Science at the Universidad de Murcia. He has previously lectured at the Universidad Carlos III de Madrid. He has published extensively on Spanish political parties. Some of his most recent publications in English are *The Crisis of Communism and Party Change. The Evolution of Communists and Post-Communists Parties in Western Europe*, Barcelona: ICPS (2003); 'Electoral competition, organizational constraints, and party change: the Communist Party of Spain (PCE) and United Left (IU), 1986-2000', *Journal of Communist Studies and Transition Politics*, vol. 20 (2), pp. 1-29 (2004); "Latecomers but 'early-adapters'. The Adaptation and Response of Spanish Parties to Social Changes" (with Laura Morales), in Kay Lawson and Thomas Pooguntke (eds.), *How Parties Respond to Voters. Interest Aggregation Revisited*. London: Routledge (2004).

Stéphanie Rousseau has a PhD in Political Science from McGill University (Montreal, Canada). She is currently a Post-Doctoral Fellow at the Institute of Latin American Studies at the University of North Carolina at Chapel Hill (USA). She works on gender, social movements and citizenship, human rights, and social policy and development in Latin America, and has published several pieces on these issues.

Marian Sawer is Professor and former Head of the Political Science Program, Research School of Social Sciences at the Australian National University. She is a former President of the Australasian Political Studies Association and is Chair of Research Committee 19 (Gender, Politics and Policy), of the International Political Science Association. She was made an Officer of the Order of Australia (AO) in 1994 and is a Fellow of the Academy of Social Sciences in Australia. Marian is currently leading the Democratic Audit of Australia, which involves some 35 academics, and is also writing a history of Women's Electoral Lobby. She has published 11 books, including *Elections: Full, Free and Fair* (2001), *Speaking for the People: Representation in Australian Politics* (2001, with Gianni Zappalà), *The Ethical State? Social Liberalism in Australia* (2003) and *Us and Them: Anti-Elitism in Australia* (with Barry Hindess, 2004).

Mariette Sineau, political scientist, research director of the Centre National de la Recherche Scientifique (CNRS), works in Paris, at Centre de Recherches

Politiques de Sciences Po (CEVIPOF). Her main research fields are women's political behaviour and women politicians. Her work is also concerned with family policy and the child care system. Her recent publications include *Profession: femme politique. Sexe et pouvoir sous la Cinquième République* (2001), *Who Cares? Women's Work, Childcare, and Welfare State Redesign* (2001, with Jane Jenson), and *Mitterrand et les Françaises: un rendez-vous manqué* (1995, with J. Jenson).

Manon Tremblay is Professor of Political Science and director of the Research Centre on Women and Politics at the University of Ottawa. She has written extensively on Canadian women and politics. Her articles have appeared in the *Australian Journal of Political Science, Canadian Journal of Political Science, International Political Science Review, Journal of Legislative Studies*, and *Party Politics*.

Celia Valiente is Associate Professor at the Department of Political Science and Sociology of the Universidad Carlos III de Madrid, Spain. Her research is on public policy and social movements in Spain with a perspective of gender. Among her recent publications she is the author of 'State Feminism and Central State Debates on Prostitution in Post-Authoritarian Spain in *The Politics of Prostitution*, (2004, ed. Joyce Outshoorn), 'The Feminist Movement and the Reconfigured State in Spain (1970s-2000)' in *Women's Movements Facing the Reconfigured State*, (2003, eds. Lee Ann Banaszak, Karen Beckwith, and Dieter Rucht); and 'Mobilizing for Recognition and Redistribution on behalf of Others? The Case of Mothers Against Drugs in Spain' in *Recognition Struggles and Social Movements* (2003, ed. Barbara Hobson, 2003).

Mi Yung Yoon is an Associate Professor of International Studies at Hanover College in Hanover, Indiana. She currently chairs the International Studies Department. She received a Ph.D. in political science from Florida State University. Her areas of research include women's political representation, democratization, and cross-border military interventions in internal conflicts in sub-Saharan Africa. Her articles appear in the *Journal of Conflict Resolution*, the *Legislative Studies Quarterly*, and *Democratization*. For her research, she visits sub-Saharan Africa almost every summer. She is currently working on an article about women's political representation in Mauritius.

Chapter 1

Introduction

Yvonne Galligan and Manon Tremblay

Worldwide, women hold just under 16 per cent of all parliamentary seats. This global figure masks great divergences between countries. In the Netherlands women comprise 36 per cent of national assembly members, while in Indonesia, they make up only 11 per cent of parliamentarians. In Spain, 36 per cent of legislators are women, while in Peru women's parliamentary representation stands at 18 per cent. Established democracies such as the United Kingdom and Canada have surprisingly low levels of women in parliament with 18 per cent and 21 per cent respectively. Women's presence in the national assemblies of some emerging democracies such as Hungary (10 per cent) is even more scant, although in Croatia 22 per cent of legislators are women.

This book seeks to explain these wide variations in women's parliamentary presence through a series of closely investigated country case studies carried out within a common framework. The 15 substantive chapters cover over 20 cases chosen to represent democracies at various stages of development, ranging from the post-Communist transition democracies of Eastern Europe and the emerging democracies in Asia and Africa to the long-established liberal democratic states in Europe, North America and the Antipodes. Our cases cover five continents, presidential and parliamentary regimes, and political cultures where religion influences public attitudes along with cultures where secular views predominate.

The Right to Vote and Run

We have noted above that the proportion of women in parliament varies greatly from one country to another, ranging from quasi-parity in Rwanda to the total absence of female parliamentarians in certain countries of the Arab peninsula. The differences between the countries suggest that the descriptive representation of women in parliaments constitutes a complex phenomenon that is forged by a combination of diverse forces which serve to both facilitate and limit women's access to the parliaments. These forces shape the path to the parliamentary sphere, which essentially consists of four phases: eligibility, recruitment, selection, and election (United Nations, 1992, 30). As Table 1.1 shows, these steps in political representation do not always follow in a smooth sequence. Although women gained the vote and the right to run for election in Indonesia in 1945, the first woman to hold political office was appointed (not elected) to parliament in 1950. In the vast majority of countries around the world, eligibility, defined as the right to stand for election, does not constitute an obstacle to women's access to parliament; the laws of most countries recognize the formal right of women to present their candidacy in legislative elections. This acquired right does not, however, imply that women are in fact capable of seeking a mandate as a legislative representative, or in other words, that eligibility is free from the influence of systemic discrimination. For example, the candidacy requirements for many countries are coupled with a monetary bond, which can limit the practical ability of women to stand for election. Holding the formal right to stand for election in legislative elections does not therefore suffice.

Table 1.1 Women's political rights (selected countries)

Country	Women's Suffrage	Women's eligibility to run for election	First woman elected/appointed
Australia	1902, 1962	1902	1943 E
Canada	1917, 1950	1920, 1960	1921 E
Croatia	1945	1945	1992 E
France	1944	1944	1945 E
Hungary	1918	1918	1920 E
Indonesia	1945	1945	1950 A
Ireland	1918	1918	1918 E
Italy	1946	1946	1946 E
Netherlands	1919	1917	1918 E
New Zealand	1893	1919	1933 E
Norway	1907, 1913	1907, 1913	1911 A
Peru	1955	1955	1956 E
Spain	1931	1931	1931 E
Switzerland	1971	1971	1971 E
United Kingdom	1918	1918	1918 E

Source: United Nations (2003), Human Development Report

To be successfully elected to parliament, an individual must both demonstrate certain strengths and convince key political actors of her ability to fulfil an electoral mandate. The former challenge corresponds with the recruitment phase, and the latter with the selection phase. Recruitment consists of the identification of individuals who, within the population, are capable of holding a representative function, and this is linked to the possession of key resources: knowledge, social prestige, time, expertise and finance. Of course the nature of these resources and their influence on women's access to parliamentary assemblies varies from one country to another. For example, the definition of social prestige depends upon the political community to which one belongs. Nonetheless, parliamentarians are, on the whole, more educated than the general population, they are employed in positions that reflect the upper echelons of society, they have privileged access to vast networks of knowledge and expertise, and they often benefit from an advantageous financial situation relative to their fellow citizens.

The Role of Parties

The selection of candidates consists of formally designating the individuals who will carry the party banner into an election. Although one may stand as an independent candidate, most often political parties play an important behind-the-scenes role in determining the candidates for legislative elections. Several authors (such as some contributors to this volume) view political parties as holding the primary responsibility for the weak presence of women in parliaments; parties are often more resistant to the candidacy of a woman than to that of a man, and for a variety of different reasons: despite their efforts to identify female candidates, they may be unable to find any women willing to declare their candidacy, the electorate might not vote for women because of a general view that women's primary role is in the private sphere, or women may not have the necessary resources to participate in a political sphere. What's more, parties may further restrict women's political opportunities by virtue of the fact that, as parties, they are in a position to interpret the electoral rules. If proportional representation systems are largely recognized as facilitating women's election when compared with majoritarian systems, this positive outcome is generally due to party interventions designed to redress historical gender discrimination, such as quotas or favourable positioning on electoral lists. That many countries with proportional representation have a low proportion of women in their parliament forces us to consider the role of parties in shaping the limited access of women to the parliamentary sphere.

Finally, elections also pose a number of difficulties for women who wish to sit in parliamentary assemblies. As concerns the preferences of voters, research has generally shown that the electorate does not discriminate either positively or negatively against women who seek a parliamentary mandate, however other variables such as the influence of religious leaders and strongly-held patriarchal attitudes can jeopardize the veracity of this general observation.

The Role of the Electoral System

The influence of the electoral system upon the election of women to parliaments generates a greater consensus in the literature. An idea that has gained significant currency is that electoral systems based on proportionality are more sympathetic to the election of women to parliament than those based on majoritarianism (Norris, 1987; Bystydzienski, 1992; Rule and Norris, 1992; Paxton, 1997; Matland, 1998; Sawer, 1997, 1998). It is true that, roughly speaking, countries which employ a proportional formula in the election of their representatives boast a higher proportion of female parliamentarians than countries with a mixed system, which in turn yield higher levels of women than countries with a majoritarian system (Squires and Wickham-Jones, 2001). That said, this remains a very general affirmation. In fact, electoral systems do not exist in isolation, but rather function within a framework and context that is shaped by a multitude of forces.

As mentioned earlier, the role of political parties cannot be overlooked when attempting to understand the descriptive representation of women in parliaments; it is political parties who control the flux of candidates, in terms of identities and numbers. Moreover, it would seem that in order to serve as a springboard for the election of women, a proportional system must incorporate certain elements: it must be a proportional system with lists, the political parties must be in a position to elect several of their candidates per electoral district, the lists must be closed, the electoral threshold must be reasonably high (Matland, 1998; Laver *et al*., 1997). In short, if electoral systems with proportional representation seem to contribute to the election of women more so than majoritarian systems, this cannot be taken as a universal rule to be applied to political contexts worldwide.

Aside from the electoral system, elections present other difficulties for women aspiring to public office, notably the treatment by the media of female candidates, as well as the rules that determine the seat turnover rate and the influence of incumbency. Several studies suggest that the media may contribute in limiting the election of female candidates, either because they convey a sexist depiction of female candidates, because they present them according to a media frame that has been designed for men, or because they receive less coverage in airtime and in print, not to mention the fact that the coverage is less favourable than that given to male candidates (Kahn, 1996; Norris, 1997). The rules affecting the turnover rate in politics could also limit the entrance of women into parliaments, be it due to the fact that the same person may simultaneously hold several positions or because there is no limit to the number of times a representative may be re-elected (Sineau, 2000). There is no consensus, however, as to the influence of these factors upon the weak presence of women in parliaments (Caress, 1999; Carroll and Jenkins, 2001).

Strategies for Equal Representation

Calls from women for equal political representation combined with either constitutional change or party electoral strategies have brought the issue of bringing more women into the legislature onto the agenda of many countries, including the countries in this book. Although countries differ in terms of political culture, political institutional landscape, and perceptions of women's political citizenship, the common thread uniting party stances on women's representation is their level of recognition that targeted measures are necessary to support women into political life. Not surprisingly, given the diversity of democratic practices and cultural norms regarding women's citizenship, a wide variety of strategies for improving women's political presence have been employed, with greater or lesser effect, over the last two decades. Soft measures, such as skill training, are widespread and are conducted by both non-governmental organisations and political parties. More robust interventions, such as quotas, are the subject of political initiative, either through voluntary party quotas or binding quotas prescribed by law (Bergqvist, 1999), but are not easy to bring into effect. In addition, and as noted above, electoral rules have come under scrutiny for their contribution to the perpetuation of gender imbalanced parliaments.

Clearly, the choice of interventionist measure is influenced by the political culture: juridical political systems, such as France, and systems where constitutional arrangements are being renegotiated, such as in many African states, are more open to enacting fundamental rule changes than political systems where liberal individualism predominates decision making. However, Matland and Montgomery (2003, 32) make the vital point that instituting supportive rules or procedures to increase women's seatholding need to be implemented to have any effect. Otherwise, such rules are little more than empty rhetoric. Thus, in assessing the capacity of political systems to address and accommodate demands for gender parity in the legislature, the influence of the hegemonic political culture cannot be ignored. Nor can the difficulties of implementing gender power-sharing initiatives be under-estimated.

Do Women in Politics Make a Difference?

There is a general expectation in the literature on women in politics that female legislators will impact on politics in a number of distinct ways. At one level, there is the expectation that elected women will provide role models for other women and that their presence is symbolically important in conveying the message that political decision making is an arena where women can contribute as fully as men. The level of symbolic, or descriptive, representation is further taken as a measure of the status of women in a society, signifying the degree to which patriarchal norms govern gender relations. In addition, it serves as a powerful indicator of the inclusiveness or otherwise of a democratically elected ruling elite.

At another level, there is an expectation that parliamentary women will seek to influence the political culture, parliamentary agenda and policy outcomes (Lijphart, 1991; Dahlerup, 1988, 275-6; Norris, 1996, 93-101). In other words, not only will women seek to represent their constituents' interests in parliament, but that they will also bring a different perspective to bear on public issues and ways of working that springs from their gendered understanding of the world. Closely allied to this expectation is the view that elected women will represent women, whose interests, voices, and perspectives are not generally included in decision-making processes. These are high demands to have of any group of legislators, and indeed, they presuppose that there is a reasonable level of gendered consciousness among elected women. Yet, the empirical evidence shows that such is not always the case, and indeed that women, especially women MPs from conservative parties, are either unaware of, or deliberately reject, a gendered analysis of political issues (Krupavièius and Matonytë, 2003, 101).

How women work within parliamentary instutitons is a growing area of research (Reingold, 2000; Acker, 1990; Duerst-Lahti and Kelly, 1995; Cowell-Meyers, 2002, 2003; Childs, 2004), with a particular focus on the extent to which parliamentary agendas and institutional arrangments are 'feminised' and the effect of 'feminine' styles of political leadership on the processes of parliamentary decision-making. Perhaps the ultimate effect of having more women in legislatures removes the exotic novelty of their participation and normalises political decision making as an activity with an equal appeal for both women and men. However, the question must be whether having more women engaging in parliamentary politics contributes to business as usual, or makes a qualitatively distinctive impact on legislative processes and outcomes. Can a critical mass of women MPs have a long-term effect on the parliamentary process, and if so, can one measure and evaluate the extent of that effect? If women's participation brings little by way of extra insights into political life, then the challenge is to explain why this may be the case – perhaps it is a function of low numbers and inability to influence legislative deliberations, perhaps it is a reluctance to express gender identity politics, or perhaps it is an expression of a political ideology that does not focus on the gendered nature of political issues. These hypotheses point out the inherent tension between women as representatives of their party, their constituents and for gender group issues that also arise for ethnic, religious and representatives of other social groups not conforming to the conventional MP profile.

The chapters in this book contribute to discussing and expanding on the ideas raised in this introduction. In general, the tone of the chapters is optimistic, while acknowledging the real limitations each political culture, party system, and parliamentary tradition places on the scope and capacity for bringing about an equal sharing of legislative power between women and men. Together, they provide a snapshot of gendered democracy across various regions of the world at the beginning of the 21st century. The chapters set out each country's particular institutional landscape before rooting women's political history within that landscape. Following a discussion of the obstacles to women's political representation bringing out individual nuances of women's political participation, each chapter turns to a consideration of the strategies employed to counter these inhibitors. The authors then evaluate women's contributions in parliament with a particular emphasis on whether women sought to represent women as well as their party and constituency. Finally, each chapter concludes with reflections on what the future holds for political women and for democratic politics in general through women's active and continued participation.

Chapter 2

Indonesia

Sharon Bessell

Introduction

On 21 May 1998 Indonesia's President Suharto resigned, ending more than three decades of authoritarian rule known as the New Order. During Suharto's New Order, parliament existed, but exercised little decision-making power. Indeed, few beyond a relatively small circle of men had any share in power. The military played a 'dual role' (dwi fungsi) that went beyond issues of national defence. The military had an institutional role in politics with 75 seats within the National Parliament reserved for unelected military officers. The military also played a lucrative role in the economy. The New Order regime placed great emphasis on national stability and economic growth. The price for national stability was the imposition of a national identity on a country made up of peoples with different histories, languages, cultures and religions. Indonesian national identity, as constructed by the New Order, was homogenous and highly gendered. Economic growth was the centrepiece of the New Order's achievements. Indonesia was often presented as a show-case of good economic management. While the benefits of economic growth were not shared equally across the population, there were marked improvements in the quality of life during the New Order period. Education enrolment rates increased, with equal numbers of boys and girls enrolled in and completing primary school by the late 1980s. Access to health care improved and infant mortality rates and deaths from preventable diseases fell. Income per capita increased.

In 1997 with the onset of the Asian economic crisis, the two pillars of President Suharto's success – national stability and economic improvement – were shattered. The rupiah plunged against the United States dollar and the price of basic commodities increased dramatically. Both white collar and factory workers faced widespread retrenchments. As the nation faced economic devastation, national unity and stability began to fracture. In May 1998 massive student demonstrations were held across the country. On 12 May four students from Trisakti University in Jakarta were shot and killed by security forces. On 13 and 14 May riots broke out in Jakarta, destroying large areas of the city's business precinct. Jakarta's ethnic Chinese community was a primary target of the riots, which took on a highly gendered dimension with extreme sexual violence and gang rape against (primarily ethnic Chinese) women. Indonesia's long awaited political transition was, as John McBeth pointed out in late 1998, seriously flawed (McBeth, 1999, p.23). Given the particular consequences of the economic crises for women and the gendered violence of the May riots, the transition appeared especially flawed for women.

Upon Suharto's resignation, Vice President Habibie stepped into the Presidency, in line with the nation's Constitution. General elections, announced for June 1999, were duly held, and widely heralded as the first free and fair elections held in Indonesia since 1955. As part of the political transition that followed the resignation of Suharto, the Habibie administration introduced a wide range of political reforms including new electoral laws and a program of radical decentralisation, which was the antithesis of the heavily centralised and authoritarian state of the New Order. Within Indonesia, decentralisation was widely considered to be central to democratic consolidation. It is also an immensely ambitious task. The 1999 elections were held after rapid and extensive revision of the electoral system, whereby a complex hybrid of proportional representation and district quotas was agreed upon for the new elections. Under the 1999 regional autonomy laws, substantial responsibility for decision-making and service delivery – previously concentrated in the national government – will be devolved to district (kabupaten/kota) level. Thus, while the focus of this chapter is on the national parliament, the role of district level assemblies – and the extent to which women share in decision-making within those arenas – will become increasingly important in coming years.

At the national level, the reforms undertaken following the resignation of Suharto gave rise to more active legislatures, with considerably greater scope to influence and indeed shape the political agenda than was possible during the New Order, when parliament was essentially the rubber stamp of the executive. Significantly, the early initiatives of the legislature following the 1999 elections sought to limit the power of the President, initially by placing two-term limits on the offices of both the President and Vice-President. Subsequent constitutional and legislative changes strengthened parliament's powers to monitor and demand accountability from the executive. Initial steps were also taken towards ending the political role of the military, with the number of parliamentary seats reserved for military officers reduced from 75 under the New Order to 38 (just under eight per cent) following the 1999 elections. In 2003, all reserved seats for the military were abolished.

Indonesia's transition towards democracy in 1998 and the general elections of 1999 were welcomed by democrats around the world as significant for several reasons. First, with a population of some 210 million Indonesia is one of the world's most populous nations. Second, prior to 1998 Indonesia's leadership played an important role in the politics of Southeast Asia, particularly within ASEAN, and had long championed the Asian Values perspective that rejected the relevance of democracy and human rights discourses to Asia. Political transition in Indonesia was regarded by many as critical to the shift away from authoritarianism in Southeast Asia and the emergence of a liberal wing within ASEAN. Finally, as the world's largest Muslim nation, Indonesia's political transition provides a potential example of the compatibility between parliamentary democracy and Islam.

For these reasons, Indonesia's transition towards democracy received a great deal of attention from scholars, the media and donor agencies and governments. The problems that accompanied transition – including deep-rooted and ongoing corruption, severe communal violence, and questionable leadership – and Indonesia's bold experiment with decentralisation have all been the focus of detailed commentary and analysis. A critical question is whether political transformation will result in the establishment of a parliamentary process that is both accountable to and representative of the people. Throughout the nation's independent history, parliament has not been genuinely representative, with the most obvious shortcoming being the very small numbers of women. In exploring the question of whether transition will open the way to greater numbers of women in parliament, this chapter examines the history of exclusion and the serious obstacles that remain.

The Emergence of the Women's Movement

The women's movement grew markedly during the late colonial period, as nationalist aspirations intertwined with concern about so-called 'women's issues' such as education for girls, child marriage and polygamy. A primary concern of women's groups was that the interests of women would be advanced in an independent Indonesia. The first in a series of Indonesian Women's Congresses was held in 1928, and the Federation of Indonesian Women's Associations was formed the following year at the 1929 Congress. The Federation adopted a stance of non-involvement in politics, but in reality issues of nationalism and the struggle for independence could not be avoided. If women's groups were concerned to secure certain rights and protections for women in an independent nation, the nationalist movement could see the value in winning the support of the women's groups. Women were urged to inspire patriotism in their children and their duty as mothers of the people was invoked (Jayawardena, 1986, p.151). These images of woman-mother have since been a consistent theme of gender relations in Indonesia, with important implications for women's political roles. The 1930s brought the emergence of Isteri Sedar (Alert Women) which was openly political and nationalist. The movement encouraged women to participate actively in politics (Jayawardena, 1986, p.151). In 1932, Isteri Sedar's conference was addressed by a young, male nationalist leader who delivered a speech entitled 'The Political Movement and the Emancipation of Women'. The speech drew an explicit link between the struggle for nationalism and the struggle for women's rights. The speaker was Sukarno, who would become Indonesia's first President. While the focus of women's movements in the 1920s and 1930s continued to be on girls' education, polygamy and child marriage – with some intertwining of these issues with nationalism – the issue of women's franchise did feature of the agenda, often in a nationalist context. For example, the 1941 proposal that Dutch women, but not Indonesian women, be granted municipal voting rights was met with considerable protest. Indonesian women finally won the right to vote in the final years of Dutch rule. The right of women to vote and stand for election in the new independent nation was enshrined in the 1945 Constitution.

Women and Parliament in Independent Indonesia

Upon independence in 1949, Indonesia adopted a system of parliamentary democracy and established the Konstituante (Constitutional Assembly), which was tasked with providing a framework for governance in the newly independent nation. Women were among the representatives who took part in the Konstituante debates of the 1950s, and discussions included the role of women within independent Indonesia. While women were guaranteed certain rights and protections, these debates failed to provide the basis for equal opportunities for women in political life. Early in the independent life of the nation, some political parties developed women's organisations, such as Nahdalatul Ulama's Muslimat, which lobbied for women to be put forward as parliamentary candidates. Nevertheless, political parties failed to preselect women. Other ostensibly 'representative' organisations – such as trade unions – remained male dominated, as did the leadership of religious organisations. Despite the linkages that had been drawn between women's emancipation and political independence – not least by the male leaders of the nationalist movement – women did not gain anything close to an equal share in the parliament of the new nation.

Between 1950 and 1955 only nine of the 272 members of parliament were women (less than four per cent). The first national election was held in 1955, with women turning out to vote in large numbers. This did not, however, translate into significantly greater numbers of women in parliament. Following the 1955 general election, the number of women increased to 17 (less than seven per cent). As Blackburn has noted the 'lack of women is taken so much for granted that most commentators on Indonesian elections do not bother to mention it' (1994, p.272). During the 1950s no women were appointed to cabinet.

By 1957 Indonesia's party system was disintegrating and by the end of the decade the new nation had abandoned its short experiment with parliamentary democracy. The shift away from parliamentary democracy stifled the potential for debate about the parliamentary representation of women (and of many other groups). With the rise of the New Order under President Suharto in the late 1960s, Indonesia's shift to authoritarianism was consolidated. Women were included in successive parliaments under the New Order regime, but the percentage remained low. Like their male counterparts, female parliamentarians had limited space to advance issues beyond those approved by President Suharto and the ruling elite. Debates about the rights and roles of women that did not accord with New Order political and gender ideology were explicitly excluded from the parliamentary agenda. There was a conspicuous absence of women from each of Suharto's cabinets until 1978. The few women who were appointed to cabinets during the 1980s and 1990s were inevitably limited to those ministries and responsibilities associated with women, such as social welfare and the role of women (see Blackburn, 2001a, p.278).

While the absence of women in successive Indonesian Parliaments and Cabinets gained relatively little attention, the accession in 1996 of a woman to the leadership of one of New Order Indonesia's three officially sanctioned political parties attracted widespread comment. As leader of the Indonesian Democratic Party of Struggle (Partai Demokrasi Indonesia - Perjuangan, PDI-P), Megawati Sukarnoputri – daughter of Indonesia's charismatic first President who presided over the transition away from parliamentary democracy in the late 1950s – attracted an enormous following and prompted widespread debate about female leadership. Megawati's popularity was, in large part, a result of the fact that she was her father's child, which was of more significance for her supporters than the fact that she was her father's daughter. Among her opponents, however, her sex was a political weapon to be used against her.

In May 1998, amidst a collapsing economy, mass demonstrations against Suharto and the political elite, riots in several major cities and violent attacks against ethnic Chinese (particularly women), Suharto announced his resignation and Vice-President Habibie was sworn in as President. A week after taking power, Habibie – with the agreement of parliament – announced that general elections should be held in mid-1999. On 7 June 1999 the nation held its first democratic elections in more than forty years. In the weeks leading up to the election, non-government organisations ran campaigns to encourage women to vote, impressing on them their right to cast their vote as they wished, without pressure from husbands or male relatives. On election day, women demonstrated an enthusiasm for the democratic process and – like men – turned out to vote in large numbers. As will be discussed below, the party that won the largest number of votes was Megawati's Democratic Party of Struggle; an outcome that was to provoke considerable debate about female political leadership. Yet the percentage of women in parliament decreased from 16 per cent to 8.8 per cent.

In addition to the National Parliament (DPR), Indonesia has the People's Consultative Assembly (Majelis Permusyawaratan Rakyat, MPR). During the New Order, the MPR was the supreme political body and central to Suharto's control of the political landscape, with half of the 1000 members appointed. The MPR has undergone several changes since 1998. Changes prior to the 2004 elections resulted in the MPR becoming fully elected, consisting of members of the DPR and members of the Regional Representatives Council. The MPR no longer elects the President, as was the case in 1999, but has responsibility for issues such as constitutional amendments and the impeachment of the president. Over the past decade, the number of women in the MPR has remained consistently low. In the period 1992-97, 60 of the then 1000 members of the MPR were women (six per cent). This number declined to 56 in the 1997-99 period. Following the transition towards democracy, the number of women in the MPR stood at 59. In October 1999, the new President, Abdurrahman Wahid, announced his cabinet, which included two women. Khofifah Indar Parawansa was appointed to the traditional cabinet post for women: Minister for the Role of Women. In a break with traditional stereotypes, Erna Witoelar was appointed Minister for Housing and Regional Development. Two years later, Megawati replaced Abdurrahman Wahid as President. Her Cabinet of National Unity included two women: Rini Suwandi was given the non-traditional portfolio of Trade and Industry, while Sri Rejeki Sumaryoto replaced the outspoken feminist Khofifah Indar Parawansa as Minister for Women's Empowerment.

Women have been politically active through Indonesia's history, both prior to and since independence, yet this activity has not translated into parliamentary representation. The fall of Suharto's authoritarian New Order was not accompanied by greater representation of women in the nation's parliament and the opportunities for women to engage in the formal processes of decision making are as limited as ever. Overcoming the barriers to women's parliamentary representation presents a major challenge for Indonesia, but one that must be met if democratisation is to have substantive meaning and include that 51 per cent of the population who are female. As the following discussion indicates the barriers are formidable.

Obstacles to Women's Political Representation

New Order Ideology

With Indonesia's transition towards democracy, New Order ideology is being openly challenged and fundamentally revised. Nevertheless, aspects of that ideology – developed and reinforced over more than three decades – remain highly influential in shaping social and political relations in Indonesia. This is particularly true in regard to gender relations. The image of the domesticated woman – central to New Order ideology if not to the reality of most women – remains strong and is a major barrier to women gaining an equal share of political power.

The New Order state was highly gendered, as were the roles promoted by the state as acceptable. As I have argued elsewhere, the construction of 'ideal types' was central to New Order ideology and control (Bessell, 1998). Within these constructions, citizens, families, children and, particularly, women were allocated specific roles and attributes. While women were not formally excluded from political life or parliamentary representation, the dominant ideology militated against it. Moreover, while the 1945 Constitution guarantees women's right to vote, it does not contain provisions on gender equality or non-discrimination in political representation (Katyasungkana, 2000, p.262). Indeed, it would have been somewhat extraordinary for a document adopted more than five decades ago – in Indonesia or elsewhere – to have addressed such issues.

Julia Suryakusuma has argued that during the New Order period, Indonesian social organisation and relationships were infused with paternalism, with President Suharto portrayed as the father of the nation. Suryakusuma argues that strong paternalist strains in Javanese political culture – characterised by deference to power and authority – coincided with military norms of hierarchy and obedience to command (Suryakusuma, 1996, pp.92-102). These highly gendered characteristics were translated into key features of the New Order State. The concept of azas kekeluargaan – or the family principle – was central to New Order philosophy, with the state itself conceptualised as a family. If building families was to be central to building the nation, then it was necessary to build the right kind of family. This meant extending state control into the family. Within the carefully structured official power hierarchies of the New Order, the family was the smallest administrative unit and women's roles within it were carefully defined and utilised by the state.

The depoliticisation of the women's movement was one aspect of the New Order's overall strategy of social and political control. The mass-based organisation, the

Family Guidance Welfare Movement or PKK (Pembinaan Kesejahteraan Keluarga) was central to this strategy. Apart from religious groups, the PKK was the only mass organisation that village women were permitted to join. PKK had a central role to play in promoting and implementing official development plans at the local level and sought to harness women's support for the national development agenda. The state also exerted considerable control over Kowani (the Federation of Women's Organisations), the official umbrella body of women's organisations. Rather than representing women's interests, Kowani has been criticised (most vehemently by Indonesian women activists) as contributing to the domestication of women and excluding them from the public sphere (Sadli, 2002, p.83).

Through the activities of these women's organisations, and the policies and rhetoric of the New Order regime, women were constructed first and foremost as mothers and secondly as instruments for national development. Law number 5 of 1974 defined the relationship between the women's movement and the state, allocating five roles to women: wife; household manager; child bearer; educator; citizen (Nadia, 1996, p.240). It is somewhat ironic that while this law severely curtailed women's public and political roles, Law number 4 of the same year provided women's groups with what they had demanded for so long: a national marriage code, providing some protections to women in relation to marriage – particularly polygamy, consent and age of marriage. While some of the rights and protections to which women were entitled within marriage and the domestic sphere were now codified, their scope to act outside of that sphere had been curtailed in law.

Julia Suryakusuma has dubbed the New Order's construction of the role of women 'State Ibuism'. The term Ibu literally means mother, but is also used in a variety of contexts including as a respectful form of address for women. Suryakusuma argues that the New Order State co-opted the term and used it in a very narrow way that emphasised the biological meaning (Suryakusuma, 1996, p.101). Thus the New Order state sought to present motherhood as the primary, predetermined and natural role for women.

Within New Order ideology, there was little scope for the ideal woman to enter the masculine world of politics, parliament and formal decision-making. In her study of an urban community in Java, Norma Sullivan has noted that despite New Order ideology women did engage in politics at the community level and often exerted considerable power. Sullivan argues, however, that 'the decisions women make in this female dominated realm do not have the same consequences for others as do decisions made in the mainstream of public affairs which is characterised...by male dominance' (1994, p.114). Given the ideological constructs imposed by the New Order it is not surprising that few women entered the national parliament, and even fewer gained a place in cabinets. While the constructs of the New Order are now being challenged and often cast aside, their legacy – particularly in relation to the politics of gender – remains influential. Ibusim is likely to remain a barrier to the representation of women in the national (and local) parliaments for many years to come.

Religion

While New Order ideology remains a barrier to women's parliamentary representation in the post-New Order era, additional barriers are evident. One potential obstacle is opposition to women's parliamentary representation, and more precisely women's political leadership, on religious (Islamic) grounds. The position of women within Islam has long been the topic of debate. These debates are often complex and nuanced, weaving together the teachings of the Prophet, interpretations of religious jurisprudence and local custom. At the simplest level, there is stark contrast between those who see a sex-based hierarchy as inherent, legitimate and divined by God and those who emphasise the egalitarian nature of Islam. The latter group argue that inequality between men and women is shaped not so much by Islam as by particular social, cultural or political contexts (see Platzdasch 2000 for an excellent overview of the issues).

In Indonesia, the possibility of a female president saw these debates erupt with vigour and passion. In the wake of the 1999 general elections, debates were no longer theoretical and the possibility that the country would have a female leader was very real. Megawati Sukarnoputri's Democratic Party of Struggle had won the largest number of votes and held 153 – or 35 per cent – of the 462 seats contested. Given her leadership of the party and her substantial personal following, Megawati had a strong claim to the presidency. Under the 1945 Constitution the President is elected by the then 700-member People's Consultative Assembly (Majelis Permusyawaratan Rakyat, MPR). As noted above, the MPR – like the Parliament itself – is a heavily male dominated institution. The MPR met in October 1999, some four months after the general election, allowing ample time for speculation and debate about the presidency. Much of this debate played out in an ostensibly Islamic context.

The deep divisions among Islamic scholars and Muslims on what Islam defines as the appropriate 'place' for women and, more specifically, on the legitimacy of women taking up positions of political leadership, came to the fore. Bernard Platzdasch has succinctly captured the debate as follows:

> On the question of women and political leadership, there is a general lack of clarity. There is no statement in the Islamic tradition to prohibit a woman from becoming a rajah, caliph, sultan or president. But neither is this explicitly permitted (Platzdacsh, 2000, p.341).

In February 1999 the kiai (Muslim scholars) of Nadatul Ulama, Indonesia's largest Muslim organisation, declared that a female president would be acceptable to the umat (Muslim community). This did not, however, end the debates – largely because they were fuelled not only by varying interpretations of religious doctrine, but also by political self-interest. The month after the declaration of the kiai, Abdurrahman Wahid argued that a woman president would be unacceptable to the majority of Muslims (McIntyre, 2001, p.94). As a potential presidential candidate, Abdurrahman Wahid's objection to women in positions of national leadership must be understood in the context of a political power struggle.

Another political leader, Hamzah Haz also expressed strong opposition to the idea of a female president in 1999, declaring that it would be contrary to Islamic teaching. As leader of the Muslim United Development Party (Partai Persatuan Pembangunanm, PPP), Hamzah had a strong stake, not only in Islamic teachings but also – perhaps more so – in the far more secular world of politics. In the lead-up to the MPR sitting, Amien Rais (leader of the National Mandate Party – Partai Amanat Nasional, PAN – and speaker of the MPR), Hamzah Haz and other leading Muslim politicians formed the so-called central axis (poros tengah). This was an alliance of Muslim parties, designed to capture the majority of votes within the MPR and ensure that Muslim parties maintained a strong stake in power. The agreed candidate of the central axis was Abdurrahman Wahid, who was duly elected to the presidency (Bourchier, 2000, p.23). Megawati's claim to the presidency had been overcome, and her sex was a useful weapon in the campaign to keep her out of the presidential palace. As president, Abdurrahman Wahid was able to overcome his misgivings about female leaders sufficiently to appoint Megawati to the position of Vice President. By 2001, Hamzah Haz also appeared to have overcome his aversion to a female president, as he accepted the Vice Presidency under President Megawati.

Prevailing Stereotypes and Ideology

While some opposition to the possibility of a female president was based on various interpretations of religious principles, the ensuing debates suggested that prevailing stereotypes, about not only the role but also the 'nature' of women, act as an implicit barrier to the political representation of women. Such stereotypes pre-existed Suharto's accession to power, but reinforced and were reinforced by New Order ideology, which sought to harness gender stereotypes for political ends. The New Order construction of women drew on particular aspects of Islamic and Javanese traditions that define women's roles as limited to the domestic or private sphere and secondary to those of men. At the same time, traditions whereby women acted in public roles were studiously excluded from the official discourse. Barbara Hatley has suggested that the influence of patriarchal Hindu ideology, which slowly spread across Southeast Asia from the second and third centuries AD, resulted in the emergence of 'polarised images of dependent, devoted wife and wild temptress/widow-witch' (Hatley, 2002, p.132). There is little scope for women to be cast as autonomous political actors within such stereotypes, which provided fertile ideological soil in which the New Order could plant its own gender ideology of 'State Ibuism'. Aspects of traditional belief systems, Islam and New Order ideology – which are contradictory on many issues – have all served to construct an ideal of womanhood that is centred on notions of wife and mother. Woman as political leader and decision-maker outside the realm of the household does not sit easily with this ideal.

Strategies to Increase Women's Parliamentary Representation

During the New Order, strategies to increase the parliamentary representation of women were extremely limited. The disappointingly, but not unexpectedly, low number of women elected to parliament in the 1999 general election focused the attention of those supporting greater parliamentary representation of women on how that objective might be achieved. Many women's groups, which had previously given comparatively little attention to women's political rights, have taken up the challenge. These groups have found an ally within policy making circles in the form of the Ministry for Women's Empowerment. Formally called the Ministry for the Role of Women, and charged with implementing the New Order's gender policies, the Ministry has now emerged as a champion of women's rights and gender equity.

The Role of Women's Groups

Despite the relatively few women who have entered Indonesia's National Parliament, the considerable barriers to women's parliamentary representation, and official ideology that seeks to define women's roles in the private sphere, women have been important within the broad political scene in Indonesia. Throughout the New Order, women's groups were significant political actors – either as state sponsored advocates of official policy or as critics and opponents of the repressive regime. In post-Suharto Indonesia, both women's organisations and individual women staked a political claim – albeit largely outside the formal decision-making arena. As Oey-Gardiner has pointed out, several of Indonesia's largest and most influential non-government organisations – including the Centre for Electoral Reform; the International NGO Forum on Indonesian Development; the Urban Poor Consortium; and the Environmental Forum – are headed by women (2002, p.111).

Non-government organisations provide an avenue through which women can engage in the politics of the nation, and in the post-New Order these groups have far greater space in which to operate. The political transition and the debates around the possibility of a woman president has alerted some non-government organisations – particularly women's organisations – to the need to confront the relative absence of women from formal decision-making processes. As Susan Blackburn has noted, women's organisations entered the debate on the merits of a female president rather late. However, by 2001 the issue of women's political representation had gained momentum (Blackburn, 2001a, pp. 278-9) and strategies to improve what is considered an unacceptable and undemocratic situation are being actively explored and debated.

Quotas, Women's Caucuses and Electoral Reform

Gender quotas, women's caucuses within parliament and electoral reform are considered strategies to increase women's parliamentary representation. The Ministry for Women's Empowerment has identified its role in post-Suharto Indonesia as achieving 'more equitable treatment for women in the family, society and nation' (Parawansa, 2002, p.73). To this end, the Ministry has stated the need to increase women's involvement in decision-making processes, both within parliament and the bureaucracy. The Ministry supports a quota of thirty per cent for women in parliaments – as well as at the senior levels of the civil service – as one strategy for achieving this.

The notion of adopting quotas received support from a broad constituency, including parliamentarians, senior officials, non-government organisations, labour unions and activists. In April 2001, advocates of women's political rights came together at a workshop hosted by the Centre for Electoral Reform, the Indonesian Women's Political Caucus, the Indonesian Women's Coalition for Justice and Democracy and the Indonesian Centre for Women in Politics. The workshop, held in Jakarta, was part of the Asia Pacific 50-50 campaign, which aims – somewhat ambitiously – to achieve thirty per cent representation of women in parliaments, cabinets and local decision making bodies by 2003 and equal representation by 2005. The participants at the Jakarta workshop agreed that quotas are a necessary strategy if the number of women in national, provincial and district legislatures is to increase. Debate focused not on the necessity of quotas, but on the percentage required and the form that quotas might take (Report of the Jakarta Workshop of the Asia Pacific 50/50 Campaign). While there was no consensus on the precise nature of quotas, there was firm agreement that political parties should be lobbied to support a quota system. The Ministry for Women's Empowerment reconfirmed its support for quotas.

The notion of quotas remained contentious, but support was building. In Indonesia, one of the most influential opponents of a quota system is herself a women – President Megawati Sukarnoputri. Megawati argued that quotas are counterproductive and undermine the dignity of women; any advancement secured as a result of quotas would be neither genuine nor sustainable. Instead the President, who came to power in no small part as a result of her family pedigree, argued that accession to political office must be based on merit alone (see Jakarta Post, 2 March 2002). Despite the controversy, however, some parties have adopted at least a rhetorical commitment to quotas. Interestingly, one of these is Megawati's Democratic Party of Struggle, which requires one women be represented for every five men on local executive boards.

In 2003 advocates of quotas won a significant victory. The 2003 electoral reform bill mandated that women must make up thirty percent of candidates for the 2004 parliamentary elections. The reform does not go so far as some would have liked. Importantly, the quota applies to candidates, not to seats – or even winnable seats. Nevertheless it was hailed by Indonesian activists and some international organisations as an important step forward.

While the question of quotas provoked particular debate, it is only one strategy promoted by advocates for greater representation of women in parliament. In addition to supporting quotas, the Ministry for the Empowerment of Women has promoted the development of networks between women engaged in party politics – both within parliament and beyond (Parawansa, 2002, p.76). The Indonesian Women's Political Caucus – one of the co-organisers of the Jakarta workshop on women's political participation – now operates across party lines, with some 200 members from seventeen parties. The agreed need to increase the number of female candidates and the number of women in parliament galvanises women of very different political, religious and ideological persuasions.

A third potential strategy that has received limited attention to date is the need to make the electoral system more 'woman friendly'. Advocates of greater parliamentary representation for women have pointed out that experience elsewhere around the world shows that proportional representation and mixed systems are more likely to produce parliaments with a better gender balance. During the revision of electoral laws in 2002 and early 2003, debates about the relative merits of electoral systems raged, this included discussion of open- versus closed-list proportional representation. These debates focused on the implications for political parties, with concern for gender equity largely relegated to women's groups.

The 2004 Elections

Indonesia's second democratic parliamentary elections were held in April 2004. This was a little more than twelve months after the adoption of the requirement that 30 percent of candidates be women. The 2004 elections saw an increase in the number of women elected to the DPR – but the increase was small. In 1999, 43 women had won seats, meaning that women made up just under nine percent of the parliament. In 2004, that figure increased to just 11.1 percent, with 61 women elected. Only 12 sitting female candidates were re-elected. No party achieved 30 percent representation of women in the parliament. This result suggests that a quota for candidates is not a sufficient tool to redress the barriers to women's parliamentary representation in Indonesia. 2004 also brought Indonesia's first direct Presidential election. In that contest, Megawati lost office to Susilo Bambang Yudhoyono. In the lead-up to that election debates about female political leadership were not as prominent as in 1998-99. President Megawati's defeat can be attributed to her political performance, rather than to her sex.

Democracy and Decentralisation: Opening Opportunities or Closing Doors?

In her study of the consequences of political liberalisation on women in Jordan, Tunisia and Morocco, Laurie Brand concludes that 'shock transitions appear to offer the greatest opportunities and the most serious challenges to women' (Brand, 1998, p.256). In Indonesia, the onset of the economic crisis and the fall of Suharto represent a severe 'shock transition', and indeed there are both new opportunities and enormous barriers to women's parliamentary representation in the new political environment. Opportunities arise from new freedoms of expression and association, a free media and international support for a transition to democracy. But, as discussed earlier, barriers of sizeable magnitude remain. These barriers are reinforced by the nature of party politics in post-New Order Indonesia and by the decentralisation that has accompanied democratisation.

A striking feature of Indonesia's political transition is the proliferation of political parties. During the New Order period, only three political parties were officially recognised and permitted to contest elections. In contrast, 48 parties fielded candidates in the 1999 general election. The 1999 Law on Political Parties identifies three roles that are expected of parties. First, to provide political education to enhance people's awareness of their political rights and obligations. Second, to promote and champion community interests in policy through deliberative bodies; and third, to prepare community members to fill political positions in accordance with democratic principles and institutions (Fealy, 2001, p.99). This gives parties considerable responsibility to foster popular participation in the processes of democracy. Such a responsibility should include fostering and ensuring the participation of both women and men in the political processes – and guaranteeing women's access to party membership, pre-selection on equal terms and opportunity to enter parliament. To date, few parties have risen to the challenge of ensuring these opportunities for women.

Political parties in Indonesia, while often having a women's branch, are for the most part heavily male dominated and highly patriarchal in structure. Even when women reach positions of authority within party structures, they tend to be excluded from the informal power structures where 'real' decisions are made. The reluctance of political parties to take up issues of gender equity in any serious way acts as a significant barrier to women's parliamentary representation. Perhaps more importantly, the prevailing attitudes within the majority of political parties prevent women from substantially influencing their policy agenda.

Indonesia's political transition has been accompanied by a programme of far-reaching decentralisation. The highly centralised nature of Suharto's New Order is seen as antithetical to democracy and participation. Consequently, decentralisation is widely considered to be critical to democratisation. Is it possible that the process of decentralisation and the devolution of substantial powers to local parliaments will create space for women to enter local parliaments in greater numbers? It has been suggested that there is greater opportunity for women to enter local level parliament, where higher levels of education, literacy and 'political knowledge' are arguably less important than at national level. India provides an example of relative success in increasing the numbers of women in local parliaments (see Jain). Yet in India, where a democratic system was adopted upon independence, it took several decades, legislative intervention in the form of quotas, and resolute determination on the part of female candidates for the number of women to increase significantly. In Indonesia, an early assessment provides little optimism that decentralisation will increase women's representation in local parliament, at least in the short to medium term. As discussed earlier, the 1999 general elections included elections for parliaments at provincial and district (kabupaten/kota) levels. As at national level, women fared particularly poorly in the local elections, with the absence of women particularly noteworthy at the highest levels of decision-making. Only one of the thirty provincial parliaments is chaired by a woman (approximately three per cent), while a mere six of the 245 regency parliaments are chaired by a woman (around two per cent) (Oey Gardiner, 2002, p. 106).

Resistance to women's parliamentary representation is – in some areas – stronger at local level than at national level. While New Order ideology, some interpretations of Islam and prevailing stereotypes continue to obstruct greater parliamentary representation of women, there is nevertheless some rhetorical commitment to promoting opportunities for women to enter politics at the national level. In part this commitment responds to the rhetoric of donor agencies (including bilateral donors who themselves have a rather poor record in terms of women's parliamentary representation) which demands attention be paid to this issue. The Indonesian government ratified the United Nations Convention on the Political Rights of Women in 1968 and the Convention on the Elimination of All Forms of Discrimination Against Women in 1984. The extent to which these commitments were translated into practice is open to question – particularly in regard to women's political representation. Nevertheless, these instruments provide a potentially important source of pressure for reform, both from within Indonesia and from outside. Yet if the national government failed to act to advance women's equal access to the parliamentary processes, it is likely that local governments will be even less active. Early indications suggest that decentralisation will result in a diminishing commitment in many districts to an international discourse that advocates equal access to political representation.

Laurie Brand has argued that in periods of political liberalisation, 'political and social conservatives of various stripes – and in some cases even so-called progressives…construct similar programs for women when given free rein and voice: glorification of motherhood, promotion of women as repositories of family honor and societal values, the retreat of women from the work place, restriction to various forms of public space….' (Brand, 1998, p.263). In Indonesia, such developments appear to be particularly problematic in some local areas and have serious implications for women's representation in local (and national) parliaments – and indeed for all aspects of women's lives. Edriana Noerdin has argued that the opportunity for the formation of village councils and customary institutions, provided under the Law Number 22/1999 on decentralisation, is likely to be deleterious for women because there is no accompanying regulation to 'prevent the revitalisation of feudal and patriarchal values embedded in many of these customary institutions' (Noerdin, 2002, p.182). Noerdin identifies the Nagari system of West Sumatra, which excludes women from the formal decision making processes by restricting participation to (male) clan chiefs (2002, p.182), and the revival of syariah law in some areas, as examples of re-emerging structural barriers to women's representation in local and regional decision making bodies.

Do Women Make a Difference?

The question of whether women parliamentarians can make a difference in post-Suharto Indonesia is an open question. Any collective influence of women, in terms of progressing particular issues or impacting on the culture of the institution, is necessarily limited by their small numbers and the ongoing barriers to greater representation. Democratisation will not necessarily be accompanied by greater representation of women in parliament. The accession to power of a female president sent a clear signal that women can engage in political decision-making at the highest level. Yet Megawati herself demonstrated no enthusiasm for a feminist agenda.

While Indonesia's history over the past century is characterised by the absence of women from the parliamentary life of the nation, recent examples show that individual women are able to make a substantial difference to policy. Since the fall of Suharto there have been substantial changes to policy at the national level that have practical and symbolic significance for gender equity. Prior to 1999, the Indonesian Government adopted aspects of the international agenda for women, for example the Convention for the Elimination of All Forms of Discrimination Against Women was ratified and the government committed itself to the principles of various international conferences including the Beijing Platform for Action. Yet commitment remained shallow and was overshadowed by the essentially patriarchal ideology of the regime. Political transition has brought potential threats to gender equality, but has also resulted in notable advances for women.

As noted earlier, the Ministry for the Role of Women changed its name to the State Ministry for the Empowerment of Women in 1999. Susan Blackburn has suggested that the change went far beyond the name. According to Blackburn, '[I]t marked the end of women's affairs being seen as issues restricted to wives and mothers; the approach is now to tackle the construction of gender in Indonesian society that limits women's rights to equity and equality' (2001b, p.78). Significantly, the Ministry began to agitate for greater parliamentary representation of women, supporting women's political networks and the establishment of women's caucuses at national and provincial level, and advocating the introduction of quotas (Parawansa, 2002, p.76). The Ministry has played a crucial role in seeking to transform the role of the state sponsored women's organisations of the New Order period from perpetuators of the status quo into forces for women's empowerment. The New Order's 'Women in Development Management Teams', designed to co-ordinate the government's women's programmes and promote women's role in contributing to national development, became 'Women's Empowerment Teams'. In a similar vein, the Ministry has proposed that the 1974 Marriage Law be amended to redefine women's roles beyond the domestic sphere (Parawansa, 2002, pp.76-7).

The National Plan of Action for Women (2000-2004) was a result of collaboration between the Ministry and a range of political, religious and community organisations. The Plan identifies five key areas for action:

- Improving women's equality of life;
- Raising awareness of justice and equity issues across the nation;
- Eliminating violence against women;
- Protecting the human rights of women; and
- Strengthening women's institution (including increasing women's parliamentary representation).

The changes that have taken place within the Ministry – and the new agenda that it is advocating – should not be romanticised or idealised. Shifting from the rhetoric to the actuality of empowerment will require an abundant supply of resources, political will and determination; as will influencing the agenda beyond the Ministry. Nevertheless, it is clear that a new era has dawned.

The change of name and focus of the Ministry was ushered in by Kofifah Indar Parawansa, who was elected to parliament as a member of Nadatul Ulama (the party of Abdurrahman Wahid) and appointed Minister for Women's Empowerment and head of the National Family Planning Coordination Agency (Badan Koordinasi Keluarga Berencana Nasional, BKKBN). Under the stewardship of Kofifah, the Ministry was transformed. Similarly, the aims and approach of the National Family Planning Coordination Agency changed markedly, as issues of quality, choice and empowerment were given prominence over reduction in the number of births. Both Megawati and Kofifah demonstrate the potential for women to take on the mantle of political leadership in Indonesia and dramatically influence the policy agenda. The particular ways in which each has wielded power demonstrate the very different agendas that women parliamentarians will have. Notably, Kofifah was replaced as Minister for Women's Empowerment when Megawati acceded to the Presidency. During her tenure as Minister for Women's Empowerment, Kofifah pursued an agenda that focused specifically and explicitly on the empowerment of women and the promotion of gender justice and equity. While the obstacles to fully achieving these goals remain enormous, Kofifah did indeed 'make a difference'. Megawati, too, made a difference. The very fact of her presidency has placed the issue of women's parliamentary representation on the public agenda and demonstrated in the most practical way that political office is not the preserve of men. Yet Megawati did not have a directly positive impact on issues of gender justice and equity. Not unlike other notable female heads of government, Megawati not only resists, but appears to reject, a feminist agenda.

Kofifah and Megawati can also been seen as individual embodiments of the general principal that has been well demonstrated. Women can and do make a difference within parliaments – both individually and en masse. But the nature of that difference is determined by a range of factors, including the opportunities and restrictions women parliamentarians face, the degree of support or hostility from parliamentary colleagues (both male and female) and their constituencies, their political allegiances, and their personal ideologies and belief systems. Female parliamentarians, like their male counterparts, pursue a range of agendas and bring a range of qualities – both positive and negative – to parliament. Unlike their male counterparts, however, female parliamentarians are conspicuous by their low numbers.

Conclusion

As the foregoing discussion indicates, women have actively engaged with democracy throughout Indonesia's history. This is evident in the campaigns of the women's movement prior to independence, in women's involvement in the Constitutional debates of the 1950s, in the numbers of women that voted in the 1955 and 1999 elections, and in the role of women's non-government organisations in the protests that led to the fall of Suharto and since 1998. Historically, women's groups have also sought to influence the policy agenda and have has some success in doing so. This is apparent during the Constitutional Debates of the 1950s and in relation to marriage laws. Yet this success has been limited and largely from outside parliament. The small number of women within parliament during the New Order period had extremely limited space to influence the policy agenda within the authoritarian political environment that prevailed. However, the same could be said for men. While the ruling elite in New Order Indonesia was both largely male and heavily masculinist, neither women nor men outside this elite were able to exert significant influence over the parliamentary agenda. With the fall of Suharto and the subsequent political transition, women have openly agitated for representation within the formal processes of decision-making, and a very small number – including Megawati Sukarnoputri and Kofifah Indar Parawansa – have successfully taken up the mantle of political power. For the most part, however, political transition has not opened up greater space for women to share in the formal political life of the nation. Indeed, in some districts the space for women to engage in parliament appears to have been closed down in recent years.

The obstacles to Indonesian women entering parliament arise from a combination of historical legacy, a particular interpretation of Islam, the patriarchal ideology fostered by the New Order regime, gendered stereotypes, and political self-interest on the part of some male power brokers. Political transition has not wrought immediate benefits for women in terms of parliamentary representation, while decentralisation appears to be creating new barriers for women. In the new political environment, women's groups are adopting and lobbying for a range of strategies to increase the numbers of women in parliament. The demand for greater representation of women in both national and local parliaments is now on the political agenda. The path towards a greater – let alone equal – share in power for Indonesian women looks set to be a long and difficult one. It is a path being pursued by women and men who envisage a genuinely representative and equitable political system for their nation, and consider that such a system can only exist when women gain an equal share in the formal processes of decision-making.

Chapter 3

Hungary

Elisabeth Kardos-Kaponyi

Introduction

The recent history of Hungarian politics needs to be divided into three stages in order to understand the scope for women's participation in parliamentary, and more generally, political life. From 1949 to 1989, although there were parliamentary elections to the national assembly, Hungary was not a parliamentary democracy. The main political institution, the communist party – known initially as the Hungarian Workers' Party, MDP, and from 1956 called the Hungarian Socialist Workers' Party, MSZMP – wielded centralised power. The national assembly met for between one and three days each year. Decision-making rested with the central committee of the party and lawmaking was conducted through the Presidential Council. Although a 30 per cent quota for women existed, it was not honoured. Only in the 1970s did women's representation hover around 24 per cent, and finally in 1980, women made up 30 per cent of the national assembly (Table 3.1).

These female representatives, were chosen for parliamentary seats by communist party leaders, 'legitimised' through elections that were a façade rather than true democratic contests. Between 1989 and 1990, Hungary moved from being a centralised one-party state to a democratic multi-party system. This peaceful transition had its roots in the mid-1980s as the political regime began to liberalise. Parliamentary reforms in 1988 meant that the legislature began to operate as a place of scrutiny and debate. In 1989 Hungary was proclaimed a parliamentary republic and the first free elections took place in March 1990. In the third period, from 1990 onwards, Hungary consolidated liberal democratic institutions and practices and in 2004 became a full member of the enlarged European Union. In the midst of these monumental political changes over a relatively short period of time, women's representation in the national assembly declined to a low of seven per cent. The story of the marginalization of women from political power is inextricably bound up with Hungary's social traditions and political practices.

Table 3.1 Women in the Hungarian parliament, 1941-2002

Year	Total Seats	Males	Females	% Female
1941	421	409	12	2.9
1947	411	389	22	5.4
1949	402	331	71	17.7
1953	298	246	52	17.4
1958	338	276	62	18.3
1963	340	278	62	18.2
1967	349	280	69	19.8
1971	352	268	84	23.9
1975	352	251	101	28.7
1980	352	246	106	30.1
1985	386	306	80	20.7
1990	386	358	28	7.3
1994	386	344	43	11.1
1998	386	361	27	7.0

Source: 1945-94, Inter-Parliamentary Union (1995); 1998, Montgomery and Ilonszki (2003, p. 124); 2002, www.ipu.org/parline

Hungary's Political System

The desire of individuals for freedom, self-determination and full participation in political and public decision-making gave rise to political changes in Central and Eastern Europe in the late 1980s from which Hungary was not immune. A new election law enacted in 1985 (1983/III, Law) instituted a national list along with multiple candidacies at district level. The candidates, still nominated by the communist party, were obliged to sign a statement saying that they fully agreed with the party programme. The national list was put together from notables nominated by non-governmental organisations and trade unions whose independence from the party was illusory. Nonetheless, although these reforms were designed to give an impression of democracy to the socialist system, political change proceeded, and the last Hungarian parliament played an important role in the peaceful transition to democracy. Essential aspects of the 1949 constitution were amended. The principle of unity of power along with a centralised state structure was replaced by a system of institutions based on the separation of powers and the protection of human rights.

A change in the parliamentary rules in 1988 fostered lobbying activities, while MPs began to form parliamentary groups, forecasting the formation of new parties. First the Independent Group was formed, followed by the Dissident Democratic Group, which later split into two – the Hungarian Democratic Forum (MDF) and the Alliance of Free Democrats (SzDSz). Days before the declaration of Hungary as a parliamentary republic, the Hungarian Socialist Party, MSzP, was formed from the old communist party. After 1990, other parties emerged to represent sectional interests: the Party of Hungarian Justice and Life (MIÉP) was formed in 1993 and gained parliamentary representation in 1998. Fidesz, a liberal youth party, was also formed in the early years of democracy and initially attracted a sizeable membership from young Hungarian intellectuals, many of them women. In 1993, as the party moved to centre-right, this liberal wing became a casualty of the party's shifting ideological positioning. The position of its predominantly male leadership on women's issues became more conservative: it joined with other parties in opposing abortion, emphasised women's role in preserving and transmitting national identity, and expressed anxiety over the falling birthrate among ethnic Hungarians. The Independent Smallholders' Party (FKgP), also conservative in orientation, sought to represent Hungary's extensive agricultural small-holder interests. On the left of the political spectrum, the small Workers' Party and the Green Party emerged, but have not to date cleared the five per cent electoral threshold to gain parliamentary seats. Since 1990, then, Hungary has evolved a multi-party political system where competition for power takes place at four-year intervals.

The Hungarian Electoral System

In 1989 round-table negotiations resulted in a new electoral act (1989/XXXIV, Law) which combined local individual candidates elected by majority vote in constituencies, party lists at regional level (20 regions) and party lists elected by proportional representation. A two-round election system was instituted and the first free democratic elections took place on 25 March and 8 April 1990. Almost one half (176) of the seats are filled through single member districts where a candidate may become an MP by winning the majority of votes. The other 210 seats are filled through a proportional party list system, based on territory (152 seats) and national list (58 seats).

The three ways of winning seats means that while representatives of minor parties and independent candidates can win parliamentary seats in the constituencies, national list seats go to parties with considerable political weight and voter support. In other words, there is an inbuilt majoritarian bias in the electoral system, designed to produce an easily identifiable winner so that a solid majority can be created for a stable government. Not surprisingly, as we shall see below, this electoral system does not favour women's parliamentary representation.

Women in Parliament and in Government

As a result of social changes brought about by World War I, the People's Act 1 of 1918 ensured that women gained the right to vote at the same time as men. The consolidation of a communist system after World War II not only centralised all political power, it also resulted in controlled elections and the elimination of all political opposition. Candidates for parliamentary elections were nominated by the state party, with quotas allocated to regions and certain demographic and professional groups. During this period the formal representation of women in parliament reached nearly 30 per cent.

However, in the first democratic elections in 1990, women's presence in parliament dropped to seven per cent and has averaged around ten per cent since then. The left-wing MSzP had most women MPs in its ranks following the 2002 elections, at 12.9 per cent. Although few women have been elected to parliament since the first democratic elections in 1990, female MPs have nonetheless participated in the business of the legislature. They have consistently taken part in the committees on social affairs, employment, culture, local government, and constitutional matters along with having a presence on a range of other committees. However, in 1998, there were no women MPs on six of the 21 parliamentary committees, including the committees for the budget, the court of auditors, and impeachment. By 2002, women's participation in parliamentary committees had grown, although the social and family affairs committee and the employment and labour committee had most women, constituting 41 per cent and 27 per cent of the membership respectively. Nonetheless, women were also members of a wide range of other committees, many of them dealing with policies not traditionally associated with women, such as the economy, defence, EU integration, and constitutional matters. Women also constituted 12 per cent of committee chairpersons and 6 per cent of deputy chairpersons. Despite this progress, one-third of the committees in 2002 had no women members.

Governments since 1990 have been almost all-male affairs. One woman minister was appointed in each of the three governments formed during the 1990s. Their portfolios covered justice (1998-2002) and labour (1994-1998), while one woman was a minister without a portfolio (1990-1994). When women ministers were appointed in previous governments, they were given caring-type portfolios such as social affairs, education, health, and the 'soft' economic portfolio of light industry. However, in 2002 the socialist-liberal government appointed four female ministers, giving them responsibility for social, family affairs and health; environment and water; the interior, and equal opportunities. Women's parliamentary visibility also increased after the 2002 elections, even though their presence remained low: women held the offices of speaker and deputy speaker, and the leader of the largest parliamentary party, the socialist party, was also a woman. Thus, after long years of being marginalised from power, women made important breakthroughs in cabinet and legislative post-holding in 2002.

Obstacles to Women's Political Representation

The findings of research on women's political representation would suggest that single member districts would inhibit women's political representation while multi-member PR lists would provide more opportunities for gender-balancing party seatholding. However, a close examination of the 1990, 1994 and 1998 election results indicates that these assumptions do not fully hold for Hungary. In 1990, women were twice as likely to come to parliament through the national list than the single member district and county lists combined. However, by the 1998 election, the pattern of women's recruitment to parliament was more evenly dispersed across the three entry channels. This in itself does not explain women's low representation in what is arguably the most consolidated democracy in former Eastern Europe. Instead, to understand women's exclusion from political power we must look to the behaviour of parties in constructing their lists.

The Hungarian electoral law allows candidates to have more than one opportunity for election. A party notable, for instance, can contest for a seat in a single member district and also be included on the party's national list. If she wins the district election, her name is struck from the national list. Multiple contests by individual party members introduce uncertainty as to the outcome, and this unpredictability is exacerbated by the manner in which the national seats are allocated. In essence, there are no predictable 'safe' seats in Hungarian politics. Therefore party managers play safe by nominating male leaders and notables to win district and county seats, and place women in low positions on the national list. Along with the low proportionality of the county seats and the high party seat change post-communism, it is not surprising that parties seek to ensure election of their predominantly male leadership (Montgomery and Ilonszki, 2003, 108-113). Women candidates lose out in party decisions on the order of candidates in party lists as their names are generally placed well down the lists. They lose out a second time on multiple nominations – women are more likely to run on regional lists only, thereby reducing their chances of gaining a parliamentary seat. Thus, women political hopefuls have considerable structural obstacles to negotiate in seeking a parliamentary career.

The electoral behaviour of parties, however, is a vote-maximising response to what they construe as voter preferences. Indeed, there is considerable evidence pointing to a highly masculinist culture in Hungarian society. Public opinion surveys show Hungarians to hold highly traditional assumptions on gender roles that can be attributed in part to a reaction against social conditions during communism (Montgomery and Ilonszki, 2003, 106-8; Eberhardt, 2003). The return of democracy also brought patriarchal attitudes towards women as voters and candidates to the fore. Eberhardt (2003, p.13), in a summary of Tóth's campaign findings, notes that:

> The image of women in the first three election campaigns was essentialist: when addressed as voters, women always appeared as housewives, mothers making emotional decisions for their families. The leaflets and publicity materials of women candidates expressed a similar view, and often they were depicted with their child/ren in their arms. The media debates at election times hardly ever showed or asked women, but if they did they were called in as experts of education or social affairs, and were totally outnumbered and often talked over by their male colleagues. The interests of women were equalled with that of the family and children, and the issues addressed to women were only details of family policy or child protection.

In addition, there is some evidence to indicate that women voters are more conservative than men: in the 1994 election, liberal and conservative parties drew more support from women than from men This conservative conception of gender relations translates into a politics which prohibits an acknowledgement of women's interests, as Eberhardt (2003, p. 13) notes:

> The general gender blindness of Hungarian society, academia and politics explains why even female politicians find it pointless to talk about 'special women's interests' – they believe in the general unisex nature of politics. Party politics is based on general political, economic, patriotic or symbolic messages, not considering, and thus excluding, women's issues.

Indeed, there is considerable evidence of a highly masculinist culture in Hungarian politics. The transition from communist rule was dominated by men as the new party system was formed and electoral system put in place. Party programmes did not touch on women's issues, or did so in very traditional terms – presenting women as mothers, and in a family context. As a consequence of this male bias in party attitudes, women political hopefuls were, and are, less favourably situated in seeking a parliamentary career than their male colleagues. To begin, they usually lack the family support provided by a caring spouse, and are in a less financially advantageous position than men to engage in a political career. Indeed, statistical data point to female candidates more frequently claiming a non-traditional family arrangement than men, with fewer children (or none) compared to male candidates (Montgomery and Ilonszki, 2003, 107).

Yet, on the surface, women's political experience would suggest that they have the capacity to hold national office. Again, statistics indicate that women come to the nomination process with more extensive political backgrounds, especially in local party politics, than men. However, the low selection rates for women aspirants and their poor positioning on party lists suggests that party strategists fear that women are not as effective vote-getters as men. These discriminatory attitudes are internalised by women political hopefuls, who do not feel comfortable in openly declaring their political ambitions, especially if they belong to the major parties (Montgomery and Ilonszki, 2003, 114). Nonetheless, in spite of a considerable array of personal, attitudinal and systemic barriers, women's share of nominations is gradually increasing.

These systemic and structural inhibitors to women's participation in Hungarian electoral politics stems from, and is an expression of, a wider cultural reluctance to afford women realistic opportunities for political involvement. Attitudinal surveys highlight the dominance of a highly traditional conception of gender roles, with women seen as the primary care-givers. It is estimated that women spend on average triple the amount of time on household tasks and childrearing than do men (Koncz, 2001, 35). Women's participation in the paid workforce decreased significantly after 1990, thereby pushing them into financial dependency within the family. For those who stayed in the workforce, the structure of women's employment began to change, with women moving into the lower-paid sectors of the economy and experiencing a deterioriation in working conditions (Government of Hungary, 2000, 33).

Table 3.2 Hungarian women candidates by party (%), 1990-2002

Party	1990	1994	1998	2002
Fidez	12.3	7.9	9.1	7.4[a]
MSzP	10.0	0.8	8.9	12.6
FKgP	7.0	8.8	12.2	0.0
SzKSz	11.9	12.0	14.1	19.6
MIÉP	0.0	10.2	11.6	14.9
MDF	5.9	8.3	6.1	0.0[b]
Munkáspárt	9.5	17.7	17.0	21.7
KDNP	6.4	9.1	19.9	0.0
Independent	7.9	10.7	3.9	13.8
TOTAL	8.5	10.0	12.5	14.0

Notes: *a. Joint candidates with MDF; b. Joint candidates with Fidez*
Source: Eberhardt (2003, p. 12)

Women's opportunities for economic advancement, and in particular their participation in economic decision-making, are more restricted in the transition economy than before, and this is seen as having a negative impact on their chances for getting into political decision-making. In addition, the problems of combining paid labour with family responsibilities is exacerbated by the dismantling of child-care supports (creches, kindergartens, day nurseries) previously available under state socialism. Thus, the low paid and unfavourable structure of women's employment, their disadvantaged position in the labour market, long working hours, combined with the shouldering of the major share of home duties act to inhibit, and even depress, women's political engagement. These are the tangible consequences of a patriarchal view of women's social role, where women's greater political participation is supported only by one-third of the population. It is not surprising, then, to find few women in political life in Hungary.

Opportunities for Increasing Women's Representation

Parties are the gatekeepers to political power, and this is as true in Hungary as in other countries. Although political parties have been reluctant to admit women's interests and recognise gender equality in political affairs, there were some signs of parties taking women as political actors more seriously in the 2002 general election. The strongly-supported Hungarian Socialist Party (MSzP) introduced a 20 per cent quota before the 2002 elections as a result of a campaign by the women's caucus within the party. However, it did not succeed in filling this quota, and managed to field only 13 per cent women candidates. Although this party maintains an ideological commitment to women's representation dating from the communist era, its implementation of gender equality initiatives stems as much from pressures deriving from EU equal opportunity requirements as from progressive thinking within the party. In the 2002 elections, the party made a point of integrating gender equality and equal opportunities into their campaign strategy.

In addition, their international connections with other social democratic parties provided equality-oriented party members with further support in advocating women's issues within its ranks.

The Alliance of Free Democrats Party (SzDSz), a liberal party, led the way in recognising that women were under-represented in parliament and faced specific obstacles in pursuing a political career. This party also recognised the legitimacy of women's issues, placing them in a human rights framework. However, for all of its early espousal of women's rights and women's political advancement, the SzDSz has rejected affirmative action as a strategy for redressing gender discrimination, preferring instead to focus on individual merit and talent as the basis of candidate selection. Not surprisingly, the party does not have a women's caucus. Nonetheless, during the 2003 EU referendum campaign the party used women's issues (along with child poverty and discrimination against the Roma people) to highlight the extent of the social policy agenda that needed to be addressed before joining Europe.

Women were very much part of the early life of the Young Democrats-Civic Party (Fidesz-MMP), but as the organisation became formally constituted as a political party, a masculinist perspective dominated and women's participation in the party's affairs declined. The migration of women out of the party after 1993 coincided with a shift in the party's orientation from liberal to right-wing politics. In 2003, the party constituted a women's caucus, but this did not indicate a return to liberal or even centrist politics. In a speech inaugurating the women's group, party president and ex-prime minister, Orban, expressly warned the group not to coduct their gender policy on a feminist basis, but instead to preserve the more traditional value system in which women are seen as mothers, church-goers and preservers of the national identity (Eberhardt, 2003, p.14).

The Hungarian Democratic Forum (MDF) appears on the surface to offer opportunities for women's political advancement, given the high profile of its female president, Ibolya Dávid. However, its rightist policies prevent the party from considering affirmative action in its candidate selection policies, and this has led to a decline in the proportion of strong female candidates put forward by the party (Montgomery and Ilonski, 2003, p.121).

The Independent Smallholders Party (FKgP), the strongest of the parties seeking to represent Hungary's agricultural interests, has a women's organisation led by the wife of the party president, József Torgyán. Adept at mobilising conservative, rural voters, the party did not field any women candidates in the 2002 general election. In a similar vein to other right-leaning Hungarian parties, there is a significant resistance to the adoption of gender quotas for political recruitment while party policies on women's issues are very much in the traditional mould.

Of the minor parties in Hungarian politics, only the Green Party and the Workers' Party (Munkáspárt) have a serious commitment to women's representation and women's politics. However, their marginal electoral status prevents them from making any significant influence on the political scene.

In summary, then, the most hopeful prospects for women's parliamentary representation in Hungary at the time of writing rest with the Hungarian Socialist Party and the liberal Alliance of Free Democrats. The strong resistance towards affirmative action strategies is a legacy from past communist experience, with the quota having highly negative connotations. However, there is little evidence of parties adopting alternative supportive measures such as training programmes for women political hopefuls. Where women's sections exist within parties, their objectives are not necessarily directed at promoting gender equality, and scope for a feminist influence is largely determined by party ideology. Let us now examine civil society to determine the extent to which there is an orientation towards feminist politics within the women's movement.

The Women's Movement

During the period of state socialism, from after World War II until 1989, the Patriotic People's Front (PPF) was the only mass-based organisation in Hungary and worked closely with the socialist regime. In 1970, it absorbed the women's organisation, the Hungarian Women's Democratic Alliance (MNDSZ) and replaced it with a new grouping, the National Council of Hungarian Women. This Council became another branch of the socialist government and its leaders were members of the party's central committee. Socialism in Hungary was of a more benevolent brand than in other countries in former Eastern Europe, and from 1970-89 a civil society dialogue on pressing environmental, financial and economic problems was fostered by the PPF. In the mid-1980s, women's groups also became active, particularly after the 1985 UN Nairobi conference on women. The Hungarian government and its women's organisation were unable to follow up on the commitments on women's emancipation and women began to pressure the government to implement change. In 1987 a new law on associations allowed the formation of groups and organisations independent from both party and government, and with this reform women's groups began to flourish alongside other NGOs. Many international women's organisations set up 'sister' groups in Hungary and in the first flush of democracy in 1989. Today, there are 350 women's organisations in Hungary, covering a wide range of interests from anti-conscription to enterprise creation. However, only a small number could be called 'feminist' and feminist politics in Hungary is still at an early stage of development. In addition, the women's sector is divided among itself. Many women's NGOs will not work with European Union women's groups to further equal opportunities at home and across the Union. Those organisations who have worked – mainly bilaterally – with EU-based groups have done so in order to secure funds for their organisation. Only in recent times have women's groups in Hungary come to understand that they must work together, domestically and internationally, to influence national and EU policies on women. However, women's groups have some difficulty in making common cause with one another due to the newness of feminist activism and the competitive funding environment in which they operate. The two main tasks facing Hungarian women's groups in 2003 is to set up a national co-operative structure involving all women's organisations and to formulate a strategic plan for women's rights that attracts support from all groups. One of the leading organisations in this process is the

Hungarian Women's Alliance, a national organisation with 40 affiliated member groups that has been working successfully since 1990.

A burgeoning women's sector, however, does not constitute a feminist movement. A feminist perspective on political issues is still a secondary form of analysis, while the representation of women's interests is in early stages. Although recent times have seen many advances towards understanding the gender implications, and possibilities, of equal opportunities feminism, and the issues of domestic violence and trafficking of women and girls have prompted a range of responses from feminist groups, these developments presage a nascent, rather than a fully-formed, women's movement. The perspectives coming from this early feminist thinking have yet to infuse the women's sector, let alone enter the consciousness of political party members. Therefore, one must conclude that for the time being, the gender agenda is not fully accepted and established among women's groups, let alone in Hungarian civil society organisations which remain resolutely unaware of the gender dimension to their concerns. On a more positive note, the prospect of entry to the European Union has acted as a catalyst for women's groups to begin working together around gender issues. Thus, while women's emancipation is not yet a discourse rooted in civil society, much less in political parties, there are hopeful signs of a growing awareness of women's rights and the gender aspect of public policymaking.

Trade Unions and Women

One arena where the gendered dimensions of public policy have found a foothold is in the trade union movement. The collapse of the old socialist regime had negative consequences for the old-style trade unions associated with communism. In 1988, an independent trade union organisation, the Democratic Union of Scientific Workers, was established and soon was followed by several other independent organisations representing workers' interests. However, the transformation of Hungary from a command to a market economy resulted in the closure of many manufacturing industries and a dramatic rise in unemployment. As a result, the level of union membership dropped from 96 per cent to 61 per cent in 1992 (Eberhardt, 2003, pp.17-18). Women's union membership is about equal to that of men, and the largest labour federated union, MszOSz, has an active women's committee with branches among its extensive network of 87 affiliated unions. The main activities of the women's committee focus on improving the employment conditions of working mothers, highlighting equal opportunities and working to end gender-based discrimination, and providing training on EU directives on women's rights and equal opportunities. The work of the women's committee, along with a high level of women's unionisation, has resulted in many women trade unionists reaching the middle levels of decision making within the union hierarchy. Across all decision making structures in the confederation, women's presence is 38 per cent – a reasonable record, and one from which many women can gain experience for political life. At the highest level, women are less evident: of the 87 unions affiliated to MSzOSz, only 22 (25 per cent) are led by women. Nevertheless, it is clear that the trade union movement has the potential to supply experienced female decision-makers for political office.

Women's Policy Machinery

In spite of the stony soil of party politics and the shifting sands of women's NGOs on gender equality, women's interests are institutionalised within the bureaucracy – if rather marginally. For a start, the Hungarian constitution prohibits sex discrimination in a range of articles, as do the labour and civil codes of law. Women's affairs were the concern of the Ministry of People's Welfare on transition to democratic rule. In 1995, the government established the Hungarian National Mechanism Assuring Equal Status of Women in the Ministry of Social and Family Affairs, subsequent to the UN World Conference on Women. In 1996, it was renamed the Office for Equal Opportunities and transferred to the ministry for Labour. The small secretariat worked hard to raise awareness of equal opportunities issues, with some success. In 1998, following a change of government, the unit was named the Office for Women's Issues in the Ministry for Social and Family Affairs. This office builds on the work of its predecessor in extending its relations with civil society, researchers and experts in equal opportunities. It actively gathers data and disseminates information for use by equality advocates. In October 1999 it established the Council for Women's Issues to enable women's interests secure organised representation in policy making. A year previously, the parliamentary committee on human rights, minorities and religion created a sub-committee on women (Hungary, 2000, p.31). Hungarian anti- discrimination law was strengthened in 2003 with the enactment of a single equal opportunities act permitting the adoption of positive action measures to remove discriminatory practices. Thus, in a relatively short period of time, a legal and institutional structure for women's rights has been created in Hungary, giving effect to international commitments and to implementation of EU equality directives. Without these external drivers, it is quite possible that the equality framework now in existence would not have come about, given the low visibility of women's issues as concerns in both civil society and among public policy-makers.

Conclusion

Tentative signs of promise for gender equality in political representation are thus evident in a range of areas. However, they co-exist with countervailing forces, leading us to agree with Montgomery and Ilonszki's conclusion (2003, 126) that 'persistent female under-representation in post-communist Hungary results from a confluence of electoral, cultural, and party system factors'. Some political parties are open to the issue of gender equality, but as we have seen, the electoral system favour major parties, while cultural attitudes offer parties little incentive to increase the proportion of women candidates or place them in winnable list positions. In general, the resistance of parties towards gender representation both within party structures and as winning candidates constitutes one of the most significant challenges for feminists in the coming years.

Since 1990, an extensive framework for representing gender interests in policy-making has been created, including a new equal opportunities law, and these institutional initiatives offer the possibility of nurturing a stronger presence of women in parliament. Yet, the women's movement itself is weak at present and cannot influence the dominant political discourse to reflect women's interests and concerns. The gender-blindness of Hungarian politics also makes it difficult for women in parliament to give voice to gender concerns, and indeed their very low numbers makes it almost impossible in such circumstances for them to begin articulating a political feminism. However, the existence of the women's sub-committee of parliament has the potential to bring women-focused issues to the attention of elected representatives, thereby raising awareness of a gendered perspective and creating the political space for a discussion of women-centred issues between parliamentarians and women's organisations. The public, however, does not engage with politics from a gendered point of view at present, and women's civic and political persona is still constructed around traditional social roles. Nonetheless, a gendered perspective on politics and public policy matters is fostered within the trade union movement, and as Hungary's democratic politics deepens, it is likely that the issue of women's representation will emerge as part of a wider debate on women's role in society.

Chapter 4

Italy

Alisa del Re

Introduction

The Republic of Italy was established on 2 June 1946 following a constitutional referendum in which women voted for the first time. The head of state is the president of the Republic who acts as a representative of national unity. The democratic structure of the state allows for a division of powers: the government has executive power whereby the prime minister and ministers are nominated by the president of the Republic on the basis of electoral results. Ministers can be both elected in parliament or non-elected 'experts'. Legislative power falls within the realm of parliament which is divided into the Chamber of Deputies and the Senate; both chambers are responsible for putting forward and approving bills or laws. The Chamber of Deputies is composed of 630 deputies (71 or 11.3 per cent of which were women in 2001); the Senate is composed of 321 senators (26 or 8.1 per cent of which were women in 2001).

The Senate also consists of life-long senators such as former presidents of the Republic and senators who have been nominated for the presidency: these include the only woman, the Nobel Prize winner Rita Levi Montalcini. An unusual feature of the Italian parliamentary system is the power of the Senate – the government is equally responsible to the upper and lower house and a bill must pass the Senate as well as the lower house in order to become law. Thus, the Italian parliament is more truly bicameral than most two-house parliaments. The average number of women elected to the Chamber of Deputies over the fourteen legislatures has been 7.6 per cent, with an all-time low of 2.7 per cent in 1968 and an all-time high of 15.1 per cent in 1994 (Table 4.1). Women's representation in the Senate has been significantly lower, averaging 4.6 per cent across this period.

Up until the 1990s, the Italian political system was entirely dominated by one major party, the Christian Democrats (DC), with left or right wing swings, depending on the formation of the governing coalition. In the early 1990s, a series of political events further eroded the already slim chances that women had of reaching positions of political authority. The fall of the Berlin Wall led to an internal crisis in the Italian Communist party (PCI) resulting in its exclusion from governmental decision-making (a position it had otherwise held since 1946). Subsequently, the party fragmented, reforming in 1991 as the Party of Democratic Socialism (PDS) which later became Democrats of the Left (DS).

In addition, the party system underwent a major period of crisis which took two forms: a corruption scandal that rocked the political system and the emergence of new right parties. The 'Clean Hands' (Mani Pulite) corruption scandal touched all the major parties, leading to the virtual disintegration of the DC and the Socialist party (PS). Many believed that the 1992-1993 'Clean Hands' judicial enquiry into political corruption would renew the political class, perceived by the general public as inadequate and untrustworthy. However, new political personnel were not recruited from the scandal-free circles of female politicians. Rather, changes were made by recruiting new male political leaders from different social, professional and political categories. These included industry leaders, representatives of Italy's north-east 'local' movements, businessmen and politicians, who entered the political scene and secured political success simply by virtue of not being under investigation for corruption. Despite the fact that very few women were being investigated at the time, the gender prejudice remained firmly in place and was used to prevent women from climbing the political ladder. Had this not been so, it is fair to assume that they would have been considerably well represented.

Table 4.1 Women in the Italian Chamber of Deputies, 1946-2001

Year	Total seats	Male MPs	Female MPs	% Female
1946	556	535	21	3.8
1948	574	530	44	7.8
1953	590	557	33	5.6
1958	596	571	25	4.2
1963	630	601	29	4.6
1968	630	613	17	2.7
1972	630	606	24	3.8
1976	630	583	47	7.5
1979	630	577	53	8.4
1983	630	582	48	7.6
1987	630	549	81	12.9
1992	630	579	51	8.1
1994	630	535	95	15.1
1996	630	560	70	11.1
2001	630	559	71	11.3

Source: 1945-95, Inter-Parliamentary Union (1995, p. 149); 1996, Inter-Parliamentary Union (1997, p. 16); 2001, www.ipu.org/parline

Second, a series of newly formed parties of the right, fundamentally uninterested in promoting women's political participation, entered the political arena. These included Lega Nord (*Northern League*), Forza Italia (*Go Italy*) and Alleanza Nazionale (*National Alliance*) which have been part of the 'Casa delle Libertà', Italy's governing coalition, since 2001. These three new entries to Italian politics differ only in degree in terms of their negative attitudes towards the gender issue: Forza Italia dismisses the gender debate on the basis that the social and political systems of discrimination no longer exist; Alleanza Nazionale reduces the gender issue to the role of the family and emphasises women's reproductive role within the family; Lega Nord's positions are ambiguous: it frequently and openly uses sexist language and discourse, yet initially it could boast of a relatively high degree of female participation. Some of its female members had political authority: for example, Irene Pivetti chaired the Chamber of Deputies from 1994 to 1996. Today, however, the number of women in positions of authority in the Lega is considerably lower.

In addition to the above crises confronting the political system, changes made to the electoral system, particularly to the majority system, also contributed to women's under-representation. In 1993, Italy adopted a mixed electoral system comprising of proportional and majority elements. In the Chamber of Deputies, 75 per cent of deputies are elected by means of majority voting in single-seat constituencies; the remaining 25 per cent are elected by proportional representation. In the Senate, representatives are elected to single-seat constituencies. The effect of changing the electoral rules meant that parties belonging to the same coalition became more competitive. In an effort to secure electoral success, parties turned to their older and more established representatives to maximise their votes. Inevitably, this old political cadre was made up of men. As a result, women did not feature in any significant way and were not put forward as party candidates with realistic opportunities for winning seats.

Historical Facts of Women's Representation

The issue of women's right to vote in Italy was raised by some of the first women's emancipation movements and a handful of scholars, jurists and politicians following the nation's unification in 1860. Campaigns seeking the extension of male voting rights (achieved in 1912) also included a significant number of proposals to extend suffrage to women, too: Anna Maria Mozzoni and the socialist Anna Kuliscioff are two of the suffragettes whose petitions were used to back up such proposals. As the Fascist era loomed, the right to vote, including the issue of women's suffrage, was suspended following the implementation of the regime's 'exceptional' laws. With the end of Fascism the women who had taken part in the liberation movement joined forces to claim their right to partake in the choices now facing the liberated country. On the morning of 30 January 1945, Ministers De Gasperi (Christian Democrats) and Togliatti (Communist Party) proposed that the right to vote be extended to women and that women also be elected to Parliament, this proposal being part of each party's strategy for mass consensus. As a result, Italian women have had the right to vote and stand for election since 1 February 1945. The first elections in which women exercised their suffrage took place on 2 June 1946 in a referendum to choose between the monarchy and a republic and to elect the Constituent Assembly. This election resulted in 21 (3.8 per cent) women being elected to the 556-seat Chamber of Deputies. However, it was only in 1987 that women's parliamentary seat-holding broke the ten per cent threshold, and it has hovered around eleven per cent since the mid-1990s.

Three decades were to pass after women's enfranchisement before women held cabinet office. The first female government minister was Tina Anselmi in 1976 (Employment Minister). Twenty years on, the D'Alema government (1998) boasted the highest number of female ministers: six in all. Four women were given cabinet portfolios under premier D'Amato in 1998 and two women served in cabinet in the Berlusconi government elected in 2001.

Obstacles to Women's Political Representation

Studies of Italian women's political participation highlight the scarcity of opportunity for women to be considered as potential politicians. While in some measure this can be explained by party ideology, this barrier is also due to the dominant cultural climate. Following a European research project (2000-2003) researching local government, interviews with Italian local representatives revealed that each candidate profoundly believed that women are indeed bound to their domestic environments, they remain 'mothers' whose primary duties are family-oriented (del Re, 2004). Being politically active, regardless of the ability and expertise with which this occurs, is, for women, an extra activity added to their primary family concerns. Women's opinion of women, of themselves and other elected politicians, is more developed: they recognise their own ability to be more meticulous in their everyday doings which arises from having been more exposed to interpersonal relationships and being responsible for others. As newcomers to the political stage, on the one hand they have been exempt from any allegations of corruption which emerged in the 1990s and have therefore remained unscathed by any 'negative press'; on the other, they appear to be more careful and practical given that they have no precedents. However, there is a widespread belief that voters do not favour women candidates and that, as a result, any position of power which women reach is achieved and maintained by working much harder than their male colleagues.

In Italy, as elsewhere, political parties are gatekeepers to elected office. In order to understand the under-representation of women in Italian politics, we have analyzed gender attitudes in Italy's three main parties during the first ten legislatures, 1946-1987 (changes since 1992 do not allow for a full analysis). From a historical perspective, the percentage of women parliamentarians is not entirely consistent over this period in time: in four legislatures (1948, 1979, 1983 and 1987) women's presence matched or exceeded the average 7.6 per cent, while in the other six legislatures it fell considerably short of this measure. This confirms the fact that at certain moments in history, (female) gender representation was more significant than at other times (see Table 4.1).

Of the three major parties, the left-wing Communist party has the highest degree of female representation. The other two parties, the Socialists (PSI) and Christian Democrats (DC) have far fewer women among their parliamentary ranks (Table 4.2) in the 1946-87 period. This low representation of women among MPs from the PS and DC is not related to female party membership. Indeed, women's party membership in the DC and PCI shows that the DC had a much larger proportion of women members which did not, in turn, translate into a proportional number of seats. On the contrary, the PCI had a much smaller proportion of women members yet it elected a larger percentage of women than the DC. It therefore seems clear that female representation is not related in any positive sense to the level of women's party membership.

Table 4.2 Women in the Chamber of Deputies by major party (%), 1948-1992

Year	DC	PCI	PSI
1948	5.4	14.8	3.7
1953	4.3	11.1	5.2
1958	3.6	7.4	3.4
1963	4.1	8.1	2.2
1968	2.9	5.5	1.0
1972	2.9	9.2	1.6
1976	3.4	16.5	1.6
1979	3.3	17.6	1.6
1983	3.0	20.0	3.9
1987	4.5	27.8	5.2
1992	4.8	20.5	4.3

Source: Del Re, A (1999)

Could increased gender representation be due to the effectiveness of the system of recruitment rather than pressure from grassroots members, thus explaining why there were more women in the PCI? Or perhaps representation stemmed from the need to portray a political image linked to the process of electoral competition rather than from pressure from below? In this case it could be explained in terms of 'promotion' from above, i.e. as the result of a parliamentary recruitment process controlled by party leaders rather than by spontaneous political forces. Paradoxically, it would seem that achieving a balanced representation of gender requires 'artificial' interventions in the political process (Cotta, 1979, pp. 132-33).

The data relating to the PCI provide some interesting trends: during the elections of the first legislature, the number of elected women members was relatively high (14.8 per cent); a progressive drop took place in the run-up to the fifth legislature in 1968 (5.5 per cent) followed by a sharp increase, reaching its peak by the tenth legislature in 1987 (27.8 per cent). These figures clearly suggest that factors other than the effectiveness of recruitment methods and party organisation were responsible for determining the extent to which women were represented in parliament. If such representation did indeed depend on the openness of the Communist party to women's political ambitions there would be much more numerical continuity over time. The same can be said to apply to the pattern of women's parliamentary seat-holding in the case of the Christian Democrat and

Socialist parties. Instead, there appears to be another factor influencing women's opportunities for candidate selection and election. It seems that the degree of female representation depended on each party's response to the needs of electoral competition. Let us now examine this proposition more closely.

The PCI needed to prevent the DC from obtaining a large proportion of the female vote during the campaign for the first legislature and this would explain the relatively high percentage of communist women elected in 1948. Indeed, the PCI's increase in female representation amongst its MPs would seem to be an attempt to redress the political balance by portraying a more female-friendly image in view of the DC's chances (due to cultural and social reasons) of successfully representing a large proportion of women.

The subsequent reduction of PCI female members in subsequent legislatures could be due to the fact that the Communist party failed to effectively undermine the DC's hold on the female electorate. This could, therefore, explain why the PCI became less committed to portraying itself in favor of female representation. Similarly, the trend in increased female representation in the PCI which started during the 1972 general election campaign could be put down to an electoral strategy which acknowledged both the feminist movements of the time and the fact that women had become more politically active. At the time, however, there were no explicit demands coming from civil society for more female representatives. By 1976, the PCI's strategy was to portray an image of itself as a modern party, and on this basis it appealed to a wider range of voters, including women. In addition, the DC had lost some of its traditional female support, while, de facto feminist movements (or ideologically similar parties, such as the Radical Party) did not have the resources to seriously compete against the PCI. Thus, the PCI was able to capitalise on a weaker opposition than before and, along with its own broader appeal, it secured the election of increased numbers of women. At the same time it came closer than ever before (or after) to challenging the hegemony of the Christian Democrats.

Neither the Christian Democrats (DC) nor the Socialist Party (PSI) have implemented specific mechanisms to compensate for the lack of female political participation. For the DC, this is probably due to the fact that the party was strongly linked to sectors dominated by women and consequently, the problem of gaining female support was not seriously taken into consideration. Despite the fact that the DC mainly appealed to the middle classes, it was strongly linked to the Catholic Church (and its activities) which typically attracted women who were not necessarily from the middle classes, but who nonetheless were likely to be party members.

As far as the PSI is concerned, female representation remained low because it did not seem to be linked to so-called 'female sectors', unlike the DC. Moreover, it seemed to lack the organisational facilities and control of the Communist Party (PCI) in managing the recruitment process. Giovanna Zincone (1985) claims that 'progressive' parties, as opposed to more moderate ones, opened their doors to women in order to either improve their party image or swing the balance of consensus in their favour during an election campaign. Nevertheless, she adds, parties are generally more or less favourable to promoting female membership depending on factors such as party 'culture'; the tendency in certain parties to be more or less female-friendly also depends on how much pressure feminist groups are exerting at any given time.

Strategies for Increasing Women's Political Representation

Although party recruitment practices remained resistant to women's political aspirations, feminist activists began to take an interest in institutional politics from the late 1980s and began to forge alliances with party women. In November 1986, female members of the PCI and non-party feminists put forward a 'Travelling Women's Charter' in which they laid out an agreed women's agenda focusing on increasing the number of women political representatives. Feminists began to realise how few women had been elected over time and the negative consequences this had in terms of empowerment. As a result, political schools for women were founded across the country and, following the examples of Britain and France, there was a surge in political initiatives aimed at increasing the numbers of elected women. The schools provided training courses in political effectiveness, and also taught women how to mediate between different forms of traditional politics. The women attending these schools learnt to see themselves as different subjects and agents who were 'new' to the decision-making processes of society: they used the schools to experiment and invent new ways of being politically active. Moreover, they became aware that one could not simply 'add on' her new, political identity to the political scene until policies had been significantly changed; as a result, these schools helped pave the way for the transition from a 'neutral' concept of politics to a gender-based one. This meant recognising the legitimacy and authority of both men and women as political agents responsible for the way in which male and female lives were organised.

However, these initiatives went largely unnoticed by most political parties, with no 'official' acknowledgement of the degree of gender-specific political know-how coming out of these schools. Thus parties were unable, or unwilling, to tap into a reservoir of politicised and politically-skilled women when seeking to renew representative politics. The exception was the PCI, where in 1986 feminists within the party were successful in achieving a minimum 25 per cent quota for women in the party's executive boards. In 1989, the PCI adopted the principle of equal representation of men and women on all internal boards and congress delegations and provided that 33 per cent of candidates for internal party positions should be women (Guadagnini, 2001).

The problem of gender imbalance in political decision-making was heightened during the course of the 1990s due to international pressures, such as the Platform for Action agreed by governments at the UN fourth world conference on women in 1995, recommendations issued by the European Commission, and the Amsterdam Treaty which emphasised the EU commitment to equal opportunities. These influences, along with internal pressure from feminists, led government to a degree of new-found sensitivity to gender issues and an increase in policies promoting positive actions.

Yet, there was some dissonance within the feminist movement as to the form and nature of female representation in institutional politics. Culturally strong factions of the movement such as the *Libreria delle Donne* (Women's Bookstore) in Milan and those in support of the theory of 'difference' claimed women should dissociate themselves from the political games of the time. This feminist tendency examined hidden forms of political strategies and social practices known as 'politica prima' (literally, 'before politics', when political representation as such did not exist). Ultimately, such an approach offered the opportunity of scrutinising the link between the creation of a political demand and a new form of political management capable of providing an adequate gender-sensitive response. Other women's groups, such as the Anglo-American Emily's List, which were ideologically compatible with left-wing parties, were unable to introduce influential and widespread practices to integrate women in traditional politics.

As new electoral laws were being debated in 1993, a guideline was introduced by some women Senators to ensure some degree of equality for both sexes elected on the basis of proportional representation in the Chamber of Deputies (which applies to just 25 per cent of seats). This guideline stated that 'neither sex can, as a rule, be represented by more than two thirds in the candidate lists' and was approved almost unanimously by Parliament. For local and regional elections, the provision ensured that a maximum of two-thirds of candidates in a list could be drawn from one sex. In local constituencies with less than 15,000 inhabitants, the maximum threshold for one sex was set at three-quarters of the list candidates. Under the proportional system for election to the Chamber of Deputies, the law stated that for each list with more than one name, candidates should alternate according to gender (man-woman; woman-man).

This guideline was mistakenly referred to as 'electoral quotas which favor women'. The adoption of the guideline evoked heated debate among women parliamentarians, it divided the women's movement and gave rise to an extensive media debate which cast the issue as a quarrel between women. Shortly thereafter, in the course of the 1993 local elections, the clause was revised to state that 'neither sex may account for more than three quarters of the councillors in the lists of candidates', turning the guideline into a compulsory rule (Guadagnini, 2001). The rule was subsequently abolished by the Constitutional Court because it was deemed harmful to the principle of gender equality. Nonetheless, the provision did ensure the number of women elected in the different assemblies increased (although not proportionally) during both the 1994 general elections and the 1995 local elections. In 2000, a bill (A.C. 5758) providing a constitutional basis for positive actions to guarantee gender equality for women and men entering the civil service, and particularly for those standing for election was proposed by Claudia Mancina of the Parliamentary Committee on Constitutional reforms. This bill was approved by Parliament. The amendment to the first paragraph of article 51 of the Italian Constitution (which states 'The Republic promotes equal opportunities between men and women, with this aim') became law on May 30, 2003 (LC 1/03). Although regional legislators do not appear inclined to amend the regional statutes according to this Constitutional amendment, it is likely that they will do so in time. On the other hand, the national political agenda does not include consideration of a necessary amendment to electoral laws which would implement the substance of this constitutional provision.

Women in Parliament – Influencing Change

Although there is an absence of significant female representation in parliament, it is worth noting that behind every equal opportunity policy (which is innovative by its very nature) there is the initiative of women who have been elected or of women's civil pressure groups.

In Italy, the 1990s heralded the introduction of an important political-legal initiative promoted by women's movements and women parliamentarians. The initiative consisted of a new bill relating to significant changes in working hours. it arose from popular demand and was put forward by Nilde Iotti, Senate chairwoman. This bill had, up until then, never been discussed in Parliament. It later became the archetype of innovative governance policies in many local and regional governments across Italy. Eventually, it became Law 53/00 (presented by the Social Policies Minister, Livia Turco) on community care policies and working hours.

In the mid 1990s, women parliamentarians formed active cross-party lobbies, something which had never happened previously and which hasn't been repeated since, to gain approval for a bill to outlaw sexual violence. Yet, in 2002, a parliamentary debate on human fertilisation found little support among women from different political backgrounds: rather, these women seemed to accept the moral or ideological views of their political group.

To try to overcome gender inequality, in 1997 former premier Romano Prodi and Equal Opportunities Minister Anna Finocchiaro introduced a directive addressed to all government members. Its objective was to promote a higher distribution of power and responsibilities among women as well as ensuring that both men and women could enjoy more freedom of choice and social equality. The directive was in the form of an invitation to create a national plan of action; it also provided political recommendations for local governments committing them to reach certain objectives through individual actions. Minister Laura Balbo provided a 'competence' database (to show that competent women do, in fact, exist) which also provided information on women's availability (to show that, contrary to the beliefs of party leaders, women are indeed free to take on political responsibilities). Moreover, the directive aimed at providing gender statistics. Law 157/99, art. 3 is also a case in point: it states that parties are entitled to a five per cent election refund if they use their financial resources to encourage active female participation. However, none of these politically significant initiatives has been followed up in practical terms or tested for effectiveness in achieving equal opportunities.

Political change is not only due to the activism of women parliamentarians. Rather, it could be argued that the feminist movement is a major influencer of legislative reform. Between 1970 and 1978 it succeeded in altering laws to facilitate the introduction of abortion, divorce, contraception and family planning clinics (Del Re, 1996, 43-4). However, in recent times parliamentarians and feminist activists have contributed to introducing woman-friendly reforms to policies and political practices.

Conclusion

Undoubtedly, this discussion on the numbers of women elected to Italy's parliament paints a somewhat bleak picture that highlights a serious distortion in the country's democratic system. Despite this, however, neither the government nor other political parties are giving the issue priority on their political agendas. Political debate on gender representation is both scarce and feeble; no practical issues are addressed and there is no follow-up when solutions or recommendations are provided. Moreover, disinterest in gender equality issues, and in women's representation in particular, is common to all parties across the political spectrum.

The Italian nation was created as a unified state although it has maintained the constitutional possibility of opting for administrative decentralisation in its regions. In this respect, since the 1990s, considerable debate has taken place over the issue of federalism. Indeed, many parties have included a form of regional federalism in their election programs. In 2002, regional statutes were modified and measures taken to introduce regional election legislation. The introduction of equal opportunity clauses was discussed following approval of the amendment to art. 51 of the Constitution to promote equal entry opportunities to the civil service for both men and women. However, these debates lacked passion and a real sense of drive. Women parliamentarians or ministers were not particularly engaged and showed either indifference or reluctance in addressing these issues.

In Europe, many favour balanced and equal political participation which is seen as the expression of a need to achieve real – and not merely formal – equality between men and women; there is agreement that the political systems in which women are under-represented are in fact incomplete democratic systems in that they are male-dominated; many also believe that female under-representation deprives existing decision-makers of an essential and different form of political input. Although these views are voiced by many theorists, they are far from being part of the language or substance of Italy's policies.

Fundamentally, the problem in Italian politics is that gender analysis swings between egalitarianism, which banishes and irons out gender differences, and difference, which recognises the fact that women are oppressed, yet denies their individuality.

There are two possible ways around this dilemma. One is by introducing a form of corporate representation (dealing with specific interest areas such as abortion) which means reducing general interest in a specific area. This would mean redistributing policies amongst different social groups. The second option relies on ensuring a more egalitarian distribution of power, particularly in terms of political representation, such as equal opportunities for men and women. This option is less predictable in terms of the effects of equal opportunities and of managing the gender perspective in political issues, yet it would probably turn out to be a less disruptive challenge to the political system. It is also clear that for Italy to be fully a part of Europe it must also increase the number of its women parliamentarians. Moreover, a political class made up of both men and women increases the country's chances of being truly democratic.

For such change to come about, a first step might be to resolve Italy's problem of obtaining statistics on gender representation. The problems encountered in gathering this basic data makes it very difficult for researchers to carry out political gender analyses and forces analysts to either cover up gender issues or to underestimate the problems of equal opportunity. As a consequence, politicians feel more justified in falling back on gender prejudices which help them avoid the crucial questions they need to address to achieve a fully democratic system. If one of the conditions for reducing this democratic deficit is to change our cultural reference points, solving this data problem would be a good starting point. Having clear, objective statistical evidence of gender trends in social arenas and political office-holding would enable us to improve the quality of political management and share out responsibilities amongst both men and women.

part of Europe it must also increase the number of its women parliamentarians. Moreover, a political class made up of both men and women increases the country's chances of being truly democratic.

For such change to come about, a first step might be to resolve Italy's problem of obtaining statistics on gender representation. The problems encountered in gathering the basic data makes it very difficult for researchers to carry out political gender analyses and forces analysts to either cover up gender issues or to underestimate the problems of equal opportunity. As a consequence, politicians feel more justified in falling back on gender prejudices which help them avoid the crucial questions they need to address to achieve quality democratic system. If one of the conditions for reducing this democratic deficit is to change our cultural reference points, solving this data problem could be a good starting point. Having access to objective statistical evidence of gender trends in social arenas and political office-holding would enable us to improve the quality of political management and share out responsibilities amongst both men and women.

Chapter 5

France

Mariette Sineau

Introduction

France has a Jacobin tradition, in other words a strong central state that regularly intervenes in public affairs. The decentralisation laws of 1982-83 that transferred certain state powers to local government bodies only partially reduced political centralisation. The constitutional regime designed for the Fifth Republic in 1958 is semi-presidential. It is characterised by the predominance of a more powerful executive branch than is usually found in other democracies. Election of the head of state (President) by universal suffrage (since 1962) bestows on this figure considerable popular legitimacy, while the Constitution confers broad powers on the office. Senior civil servants trained in the major state institutes play a crucial role in the executive. The overwhelming power of the president is achieved to the detriment of that of the parliament, which is bicameral. The National Assembly (577 members), elected by direct suffrage, is less powerful than was the Chamber of Deputies under the Fourth Republic (1946-1958). The Senate (321 members) represents local territorial units as well as the French abroad. It is elected by a college made up of deputies, regional and departmental councilors and municipal council delegates. This 'second' chamber must yield to the first in the event of political discord, and cannot dismiss the government. One specific feature of this arrangement is that it has made ministerial and parliamentary functions incompatible. Due to this rule, established in order to limit the power of the two chambers, it is primarily senior civil servants who are called upon to exercise executive and even parliamentary functions.

Political parties in France are characterized by their weakness: their numbers are scant by comparison to many of their European counterparts. Less than three per cent of the voting population is estimated to belong to a political party. The party system is organized around two poles, the left and the right, each divided into two subsets. The right is separated into a moderate liberal wing, the Union pour la Démocratie française (UDF, Union for French Democracy) and the Gaullist authoritarian branch, mainly formed by the former Rassemblement pour la République (RPR, Rally for the Republic). The left is also split between a revolutionary left embodied by the French Communist Party (PC) and a moderate, reformist left represented by the Socialist Party (PS). 'This "bipolar quadrille" constitutes the basic structure of the party system, its genetic imprint, so to speak' (Mény, 1999, p. 56). The expansion of the Front National (FN, National Front) electoral base beginning in 1984 and that of Les Verts (the Greens), starting in 1989, has disrupted the traditional interplay among parties.

Whereas under the Fourth Republic the deputies were elected by a system of proportional representation, under the Fifth they are elected by a two-round uninominal majority vote (except for the 1986 elections which used the proportional system). Senators are elected in two ways: by uninominal majority vote in the smaller departments, by proportional representation in the larger departments. Already latecomers to full citizenship, French women were denied access to parliament through practices designed by the Fifth Republic. To get them out of this trap, the system had to be reformed from on high.

Tardy Access to Parliamentary Representation

The Last to Become Citizens

In retracing the history of women's suffrage in France, it soon becomes clear that the country that conceived of the Rights of Man omitted those of women. Subsequent historical events have led to women's political citizenship being imbued with three significant paradox. The first paradox: France, which led Europe in establishing universal male suffrage in 1848, was far behind, along with Belgium and Italy, in acknowledging women's right to vote. Nearly a century separates these two events that extended political rights, making the 'daughters of Marianne' wait until 1944 to enjoy the full rights of citizenship.

A second paradox: French women had the rare privilege of entering the government before enjoying the rights of mere citizens. In 1936, Léon Blum, head of the Front Populaire government appointed three women as undersecretaries of state. Irène Joliot-Curie, Suzanne Lacore and Cécile Brunschvicg had the peculiar experience of being part of the government without being either voters or eligible candidates. Léon Blum rather hastily believed that the Socialist Party had 'virtually achieved gender equality'. This was, however, a meager symbolic compensation for those whose political enfranchisement was not even part of the Front Populaire platform.

The third paradox of French democracy, women's political rights were not the result of a vote in parliament but were granted by decree. The ordinance of 21 April 1944, drafted by the French Committee of National Liberation and signed by General de Gaulle, recognized them as 'voters and eligible citizens under the same conditions as men'. The number of voters thus more than doubled from 1936 to 1945, from 11.7 to 24.6 million. French women obtained all of their political rights in one go. They voted for the first time on 29 April 1945 in the municipal elections and on 21 October 1945 to elect deputies to the Constituent Assembly. Within this body, the nation's first female representatives numbered 33 out of 586, or 5.6 per cent.

Can this delay in access to representation be attributed to a 'weakness' of the feminist movement? Actually, the movement was divided into three factions (reformist, moderate with a Catholic bent and radical). The suffrage movement to some extent failed to form a mass organization capable of political lobbying. Although the vigour of feminism was manifest in 1900, this was no longer the case in the interwar period. Movements bogged down in political feuds lost their following, and were no match for the extreme misogyny of the parties, the Communist Party excepted. The Radical Party did not allow women to join until 1924. In the SFIO (socialist), the party leadership tightly controlled the few women who joined the party (Bard, 1995, p.240). Only the Communist Party clearly pronounced itself in favor of sexual equality and fielded women candidates for office the municipal elections between the two wars.

Furthermore, strong political reasons played in favor of continuing to deny full citizenship rights to women. Between the two world wars, the Senate, dominated by the Radical Party, symbol of the Third Republic (1870-1940), was strongly opposed to women's suffrage, rejecting three bills passed by the Chamber of Deputies. The radical senators blocked women's political enfranchisement because they were afraid the women's vote would lean to the right, toward clerical reactionarism, and thus endanger the Republic, in other words their very power. Just as they were for a long time excluded from political citizenship, married women were also excluded from civil citizenship. Up until 1938, the Napoleonic Code (1804) viewed them as incompetent (along with minors and the insane). French women therefore enjoyed no legal freedoms until the second half of the 20th century (Sineau, 1994).

A Cautious Entry into Parliamentary Careers

It was thus under the Fourth Republic that French women first entered parliament. The history of the first women politicians began favourably. In the postwar period, their arrival was all the more looked forward to since they embodied a dual change with respect to the disqualified Third Republic politicians: many of the female candidates were chosen from the ranks of Resistance workers, and so symbolized both a renewal of the elites and the triumph over the occupying force. All the major parties except the RPF, the Gaullist party, fielded women in key positions on their lists. The most feminist lists were first the Communist Party, followed by the Christian-inspired Mouvement Républicain Populaire. In the Chamber of Deputies, elected in November 1946 and which totaled 619 representatives, 35 women were elected to office (23 communists, 9 MRP and 3 SFIO socialists). This initial score of 5.6 per cent of women in the lower house was modest but promising. In the top European countries for female representation, France then was ahead of the Scandinavian countries, despite the latter being a trailblazer in women's rights.

The advent of the Fifth Republic was to mark the end of great expectations for women and the beginning of a long journey through the desert. In fact, the right to be elected was to be removed from them by practices inaugurated with the new institutions. The 1958 elections, the first to take place by uninominal vote, were laden with significance: only 68 out of the 2,809 candidates were women, in other words a ludicrous proportion of 2.4 per cent (table 5.1). That was a significant setback. A correlative drop occurred from one Republic to the next, in the proportion of female candidates elected, which went from 3.2 per cent in 1956 to 1.6 per cent in 1958. During the first twenty years of the Fifth Republic, women were a minority of about two per cent to hold office in the Assembly. With the exception of the first legislature, the Communist Party (yet which had few members in Parliament) had the highest percentage of women deputies. At the other end of the spectrum, the Gaullist party, with overabundant numbers, showed a percentage of women hovering around one per cent (with a peak at 2.5 per cent in 1967). It was not until the 1978 legislative elections, under President Valéry Giscard d'Estaing's term, that the share of women elected registered a slight increase (3.7 per cent), due, once again, to the Communist Party.

Oddly enough, the left's victory in 1981, bringing to an end 23 years of right-wing rule, kept the overwhelming male domination of the Assembly nearly intact: almost 95 per cent of the deputies were men. Usually favored by election landslides, women were left by the wayside in the socialist administration. The PS fielded only 8.5 per cent women, getting even fewer elected. In the 285-member strong socialist group, making up nearly 60 per cent of the house, women were scarce (6.6 per cent). The feminist and socialist sympathizer Gisèle Halimi, spoke of the 'unpleasant dizziness' she felt when she was 'confronted for the first time with the flood of men that had swept through the hemicycle'. (Halimi, 1997, p.107).

The 1988 legislative elections was virtually a rerun of this confiscation of representation by men: only 5.7 women were elected to sit in parliament. From François Mitterrand's first seven-year term to the second, women's representation in the Palais Bourbon increased by a mere 0.4 percentage points. The PS, which fielded 9.4 per cent women candidates, only saw 6.2 per cent women elected. With a group 275 deputies strong, it had proportionally fewer women than the RPR (7.5 per cent).

Between these two high points of success for the socialists, the 1986 legislative elections, lost by the left, had awakened great hopes among women activists because they were to take place according to the proportional system, which supposedly had the potential for 'interrupting the systematic elimination of women', to quote former President, François Mitterrand. Although a record number of female candidates ran for office, a record number of them were defeated. Out of the 656 female candidates fielded by the major parties, only 5 per cent of them were elected, whereas 20 per cent of the male candidates managed to enter the Palais Bourbon. Female socialist deputies (21) made up 9.9 per cent of the socialist group. As for the right, with a majority in the National Assembly, it only had nine women in office, or three per cent of the RPR and UDFgroups! Although the proportional system played into the hands of the FN which, with ten per cent of the votes cast, obtained 35 seats, one of them held by a woman, it failed to help women (Mayer/Sineau, 2002). After the 1993 legislative elections, lost by the left, the proportion of women among the deputies continued to stagnate at 5.9 per cent: a shameful record that put France in last place among European countries and ranked it 72nd in the world.

The negative record was to be reversed in the early elections of 1997, which the left won. For the first time in the history of the Republic, the proportion of women deputies crossed the symbolic threshold of ten per cent (Table 5.1). The socialists, who had enforced a quota of 30 per cent female candidates, elected the most women (17.2 per cent), followed by the communists (13.9 per cent). The right-wing parties (RPR and UDF) lagged behind, with 4.7 per cent women elected. An indication of their rise in power, women deputies managed to obtain official recognition for the feminization of their parliamentary title.

The results of the 2002 legislative elections, to which the law of 6 June 2000, known as the law on parity (cf. infra), applied, did not deliver the expected wave of feminization. The major parties preferred to pay fines rather than feminize their nominations, because that would have meant 'sacrificing' incumbent deputies. On the right, the two main parties, the Union pour la Majorité Présidentielle (UMP, 'Union for the Presidential Majority', a new formation grouping the main right-wing parties) and the UDF fielded fewer than 20 per cent women.

Table 5.1 Women candidates and MPs in the French National Assembly, 1958-2002

Year	Total Candidates	Women candidates	% Women	Total MPs	Women MPs	% Women
1958	2809	68	2.4	552	9	1.6
1962	2172	55	2.5	482	8	1.6
1967	2190	70	3.2	487	10	2.0
1968	2265	75	3.3	487	8	1.6
1973	3023	200	6.6	490	8	1.6
1978	4266	706	16.5	491	18	3.7
1981	2715	323	11.9	491	26	5.3
1986*	6804	1680	24.7	577	34	5.9
1988	2896	336	11.6	577	33	5.7
1993	5139	1003	19.5	577	34	5.9
1997	6360	1464	23.0	577	63	10.9
2002	8456	3257	38.5	577	71	12.3

* proportional voting system

Source: Interior Ministry

On the left, the PC did much better, with 44 per cent women candidates, the PS just 36 per cent. Only the small parties, which did not have incumbents to consider, and the Greens, respected the parity of candidacies. With the right gaining a political victory, women occupied only 71 seats out of the 577 (12.3 per cent, compared to 62 seats or 10.7 per cent in 1997) in the National Assembly. The UMP, by far the majority, returned only 10.4 per cent of women deputies, the UDF claimed 6.8 per cent. As for the PS, it returned 16.3 per cent women, while women MPs made up 19 per cent of PC representatives. In all, the proportion of women in the National Assembly has gone from 10.7 per cent in 1997 to 12.3 per cent in 2002, in other words a miniscule increase of 1.6 per cent, symptomatic of the failure of the law on parity, in any case as regards its application to the legislative elections.

In the Senate, the marginal role of women has been just as manifest for many years. It was not until the 1989 elections that their proportion exceeded three per cent, reaching a mere five per cent in 1992. The change came with the 2001 renewal of the

Senate: due to the law on parity, women made some headway in the upper house, with 35 senators out of 321, or 10.9 per cent. Once again, the communist group has the most women in its ranks (43 per cent), followed at some considerable distance by the socialist group (14 per cent).

Climbing the Upper Echelons of the State

In France, it is easier for women to become ministers than deputies. Since the route of universal suffrage was so long barred to them, women chose to assert their political ambitions through nomination and technocratic competence rather than through elections. Distinctions can be made depending on the period. In 1958, Charles de Gaulle wanted to govern among men, perceiving women as destabilizing factors in politics (Sineau, 2001, pp.30-33). Although 61 per cent of women votes supported him in the second round ballot, securing his re-election in 1965, he in no way felt any urgency to bring more women into government. For the eleven years he remained in power, only two women took part in government as deputy ministers in the departments of welfare and education. The period following the events of May 1968, marked by De Gaulle's resignation as head of state and the arrival of Georges Pompidou (April 1969), did not stimulate any reflection on the unequal sharing of power between the sexes. Jacques Chaban-Delmas' cabinet (1969-1972) included only one woman. Not until Pierre Messmer's second cabinet (April 1973) did two women participate in government together.

It was Valéry Giscard d'Estaing, in 1974, who broke with the masculinist culture of the Fifth Republic. He was the first president to use the power of nomination invested in the head of state to bring more women into government. It was his response to the strongly-articulated feminist critique of the traditional male order in politics. Acting as a precursor, he set a precedent that would be imposed on all his successors. During his term, the proportion of women in the government rose to 9.5 per cent, compared with 2.4 per cent under de Gaulle and 3 per cent under Pompidou. Jacques Chirac's cabinet in May 1974 first had three, then five women out of 42 members, or 12 per cent, including a full-fledged minister (Simone Veil, Ministry of Health). Although Giscard d'Estaing gave a high profile to women's participation in government, he long kept them in second rank of the hierarchy: out of 21 ministerial positions attributed to women in seven years, only four were full ministers, one a delegate minister, all the others deputy ministers. Not only were they given secondary roles, but female ministers were relegated to the social sectors, confined to a maternal mould.

During his two presidential terms, François Mitterrand did more than his predecessor to promote women in politics: he oversaw the creation of a full ministry for Women's Rights, the appointment of women to two important government positions, the feminization of ministerial offices, heads of civil services and major state institutions (Conseil d'État, Cour des Comptes). Lastly, he appointed two women to the highest position of the Republic. In 1992, he had the president of the National Assembly designate the first women among the nine 'sages' of the Conseil Constitutionnel, equivalent to the Supreme Court. Prior to that, in May 1991, he appointed Édith Cresson as Prime Minister of the Fifth Republic. Under François

Mitterrand's presidency, the proportion of women ministers was higher under a left-wing government than that of the right and increased between his first and his second term.

This cooptation at the highest level of the state, which favored young alumnae from the grandes écoles, particularly the École Nationale d'Administration (ENA), did a great deal to change mind sets. Yet without the presence of a critical mass in Parliament, the situation in which the few women promoted found themselves was, and remains, unstable. Their true status is apparent: they have been handpicked by the head of state and have no democratic legitimacy. Édith Cresson tasted this bitter experience, the political press tearing her to pieces while she was Prime Minister, and hastening her fall (she remained in office for only 10 months and 18 days).

The feminisation of the executive has by no means been halted; it is now a well ingrained process: during Jacques Chirac's term 26 per cent of cabinet ministers were women and Lionel Jospin's 1997 left-wing government was composed of 30 per cent women. In an unprecedented situation, there were more women at that date in the upper echelons of the hierarchy than in the lower (five full-fledged ministers, one delegate minister, and two deputy ministers). Two prime positions were attributed to them: the key ministry of Employment and Solidarity (assigned to Martine Aubry) and the Justice Ministry (assigned to Élisabeth Guigou). Women exemplified the pluralistic composition of the cabinet (three socialists, two communists, one from the Green party), and symbolized youth (they were on average only 46.7 years old, compared to 51.5 years old for the members of government on the whole). Their profile confirmed the technocratic nature of the recruitment: three of them, Martine Aubry, Élisabeth Guigou and Ségolène Royal were ENA alumnae. The feminization of the government won favor with public opinion: surveys showed that the women ministers were popular. June 1997 marked a turning point: the beginning of real power held jointly by women both in the executive and in legislative bodies.

Obstacles to Full Representation

At the foundation of democratic culture is the principle of the people's sovereignty, reserved for male individuals, for it was the French Revolution in 1789 that made women's political incapacity an absolute principle. This was not the case under the ancien régime, some women having voted in the Estates General in 1789. In the eyes of successive generations of republicans it thus legitimated the belief in women's incompetence in public affairs. Parliamentary democracy was built from the start, if not against women, certainly without them, on the following precept: women were confined to the role of reproduction, men retained a monopoly on power. On the basis of these premises, any incursion of women into the political sphere was thought to threaten the foundations of the social order by abolishing the barrier between the private and the public sphere.

The dominance of Catholic culture in France, 'the eldest daughter of the Church', merely ratified the traditional division of labour between the sexes in mentalities and beliefs. The Church for a long time taught a dual moral code: men were to command

and take care of public affairs, it was women's duty to procreate and keep house under the husband's authority, which ordered them to keep away from all political and public life.

Men also found support in the Fifth Republic institutions to perpetuate their power, because many rules laid down in 1958 to modernise politics long kept women out of contention for political office. The institution of the majority vote to elect deputies is one example of the barriers faced by women when seeking a place in political life. Presented as a more effective method by which to come up with a majority, it penalised female candidacies because it significantly personalises an election. Lacking experience, women were perceived by political parties as less competitive, and so the parties were less willing to nominate them. In addition, the highly local nature of the election, taking place in small voting districts, gave the advantage to the well-established male representative. It encourages individuals to collect multiple mandates by which electoral strongholds are constituted and maintained. This practice, which has become irrepressible under the Fifth Republic, has further contributed to disadvantaging women, who got a late start in the race for office.

The majority voting system also limited women's access to the Senate. Statistics show that most of the women elected to the upper house since 1958 have been put in office thanks to the proportional system. This system has thus proved more favourable to female candidacies, especially when parties, the Communist Party, for instance, were determined to impose them. Indirect suffrage has also harmed women. The senatorial college is in charge of most of the delegates of small rural communes and is 80 per cent male. It tends to curb the election of anyone who does not have the profile of a local notability. By filtering popular representation, along with other modus operandi (nine-year term, renewal by thirds), the Senate remains a conservative chamber that has little inclination to accord women a place, any more than it is inclined to pass laws enlarging their rights. The institutional reforms pushed by the left after 1997, to 'open up' recruitment (parity, increased restriction on multiple mandates) came up against strong opposition in the Senate.

The political importance given to the senior civil servants from the ENA not only in government but also in the National Assembly has been another penalizing factor for women. The ENA, although co-educational since its inception, long remained a men's school (until the 1970s, they made up over 90 per cent of each graduating class).

Cheated by political institutions, women have also been just as badly shortchanged by the political parties. Underrepresented in leadership positions, they hardly have the means of making their voices heard. The PC is an exception, being the only party since 1945 to reserve nominations for women. More recently, the Greens have included parity in their regulations. In the past, the parties' means of designating candidates depended both on the type of party organisation (centralised or decentralised) and the type of voting system used. For elections using the proportional representation system, the lists were generally made up by the national party leadership. Thus, the PS leadership instituted a quota of 30 per cent women as early as the 1979 European elections, before drawing up a parity list for the 1994 European elections. (The PC, the Mouvement des Citoyens and the Greens also presented parity lists in these elections). The uninominal vote lends itself more to a decentralized procedure and depends less on the national leadership. However, in a very centralized party such as the PC, the leadership has always practiced quotas for candidates, though without stating so openly (quota for young candidates, women, workers, etc.). In 1996, the PS likewise demonstrated political will by imposing 30 per cent female candidates in the 1997 legislative elections. Henceforth, all practices for designating candidates are going to change radically due to the new legislation.

Lastly, the feminist movement of the 1970 has its share of responsibility in the political underrepresentation of women, for it long advocated a militant anti-parliamentarianism. 'It expected change to come from the social movement, not from greater participation of women in the system of representation' (Picq, 2002). The 1981 presidential election was the opportunity for a belated turnaround. After years of not engaging in dialogue with the parties and accusing politicians of being patriarchal, many feminists called for a vote for François Mitterrand in the 1981 presidential election, acknowledging that the left represented a chance for women.

As for public opinion, beginning with the second half of the 1970s, it was less and less hostile to women holding high political office (deputy, minister, Prime Minister). The popularity of the two women ministers under Giscard's term, Françoise Giroud and Simone Veil, did a lot to change the image of women in power. History would remember the name of Simone Veil, who embodied the law legalizing abortion. The direct broadcast of parliamentary debates on television helped to establish her popularity. The dignity with which she faced attacks, confronting an Assembly that was almost exclusively male, won her the esteem of public opinion for many years.

Strategies to Feminize the Parliament

Most European countries with the exception of Belgium leave it up to the good will of the parties to ensure women's access to political representation. France, by having recourse to legislative obligation, is an exception to this general rule. In reality, the situation was blocked to such an extent that the system had to be pressured from on high. There were institutional and party reasons for the blockage, as we have seen, but legal reasons as well. Indeed, the *Conseil* handed down a decision on 18 November 1982 invalidating a 1982 municipal law that set up a maximum of 75 per cent for the representation of each sex on the list of candidates in the municipal elections in towns over 3,500 inhabitants. Invalidation was justified in the name of citizens' equality before the law, guaranteed by article 3 of the 1958 Constitution and article 6 of the Declaration of the Rights of Man and the Citizen. This decision, which constituted a precedent, blocked the perspective of reform.

The radical idea of parity, in other words guaranteed equality of numbers for access to elected office, emerged at the end of the 1980s, backed by feminists and feminist movements who put pressure on the constitutional bodies. The goal of parity reflects a radical change in the feminist issue, which shifted from social questions to matters of political representation (Collin, 1999). The conversion of feminists to the requirements of legal reformism was hastened by the analysis of certain intellectuals. While the publication of the book *Au pouvoir citoyennes! Liberté, Egalité, Parité* in 1992, helped to popularise the idea of parity, some legal experts challenged the legitimacy of making law on the basis of gender. Francine Demichel, author of a column on parity in the *Recueil Dalloz*, showed that women, because of their legally 'unanalyzed and invisible', status, were the 'minor sex of legal theory'. Condemning the rigid conception of 'abstract' citizenship, she argued that gender should be integrated into the theory of representation. She concluded that only parity could 'replace this unilateral identification of one sex with the other by true equality in the relations between the sexes'.

Female politicians also encouraged the demand for parity. In June 1996, ten former women ministers, both on the left and the right, published a manifesto in favour of parity in the magazine *L'Express* (6 June issue), which had a strong impact on the outcome of the debate. Gradually taken up by political actors of all colours, parity became a decisive issue during the 1995 presidential campaign and the 1997 legislative campaign. In a context of a crisis of in political representation, the idea was spreading that a democracy without women was a warped democracy. Opinion polls, moreover, revealed that public opinion aspired to see a new, more feminine elite. The political changeover that brought the socialists to power in June 1997, hastened the reforms because their leader, Lionel Jospin, had made the renovation of political institutions (parity and limiting the number of mandates held at one time) a focal theme of his campaign.

The constitutional amendment of 8 July 1999 designed to establish equality between men and women allows Parliament to take affirmative action measures in favour of women. The new wording of article 3 of the Constitution (regarding national sovereignty) provides 'The law fosters equal access of men and women to elected office and functions'. Article 4 stipulates that political parties 'contribute to implementing [this principle] in conditions determined by the law'. For political reasons, the term 'parity' did not appear in the text, although it was the very object of the reform.

This new constitutional arrangement led to the law of 6 June 2000, known as the law on parity which, for all elections by list, requires all parties to field 50 per cent of the candidates of each sex (give or take one digit). Alternating parity (one man/one woman) is required for one-ballot elections (European and senatorial), and parity by group of six for two-ballot elections (regional, municipal). If the parties do not obey these injunctions, the list is deemed invalid. For the legislative elections, the law is more lenient, providing only for financial penalties for parties that do not field 50 per cent female candidates (within a range of two per cent). These reforms signalled a break with the republican culture, substituting a gendered order for the old order based on the neutrality of citizenship.

In addition to the legislative elections, two other elections have taken place under this new law: the September 2001 senatorial elections (cf. supra) and the March 2001 municipals in which 47.5 per cent women were elected in towns of over 3,500 inhabitants, compared with 25.7 per cent previously. The new law has thus proved to be an effective tool to produce equality. The enforcement of parity, and to a lesser extent the holding of multiple mandates (made more restrictive by the law of 5 April 2000), have set off an in-depth renewal of French elites.

However, the instrument has room for improvement, for it has certain loopholes. The law not only neglected the municipal executive (mayors and deputy mayors) and intercommunal structures, but departmental assemblies as well (elected by uninominal vote). As long as these institutions remain male strongholds, this will have negative repercussions on the distribution of candidacies in the legislative elections. Indeed, parties prefer to assign the good voting districts to the 'notables', in other words departmental elected officials (often mayors), whose voters are familiar with, thereby excluding women yet again from opportunities to build the necessary profile for high political office.

The Role of Women in Parliament

Since 1945, the numerical weakness of women in Parliament has left them to play a minor political role: they have seldom been in positions of power, and have therefore been, and continue to be, relegated to the social fields, less sought after by men.

The make-up of the National Assembly 'Bureau', the seat of parliamentary power, is revealing of gender inequality. In June 2002, in the twelfth legislature, women were assigned only modest functions, occupying only one of the six vice-president positions and two of the twelve posts of secretary. The three questeurs (in charge of administration at the Assembly) are men. Since 1958, only one woman has occupied this function, and for a very brief time at that. The president of the National Assembly is traditionally a man. Of the fifteen countries in the European Union, France is one of the rare countries that has never had a women preside either house of Parliament. Knowing that the European Parliament has already been presided over by a woman on two occasions, that the two houses of the Spanish Parliament elected in 1999 are presided over by women, it is easy to measure how far behind France is in this area.

The four political groups of the new Assembly elected in June 2002 are all led by men. Even fewer women deputies than in the previous legislature have positions of power in the six National Assembly permanent commissions. None is president, a single one is vice-president (Cultural, Family and Social Affairs), and only one is secretary (Production and Trade). As for the distribution of women among these various commissions, it reflects the more traditional division of political tasks between the sexes. Women are overrepresented in the Commission of Cultural, Family and Social Affairs: in June 2002, 37 women deputies were on it (nearly one out of two), representing over a quarter of the members of this commission. On the prestigious Foreign Affairs Commission, women lost the beginning of influence they had in the preceding legislature (5.5 per cent compared to 11.4 per cent). Other commissions involving the powers of the state are once again nearly entirely made up of men. The Defense and Armed Forces Commission has only four women out of its 69 members (5.8 per cent). Likewise, the Finance, Economy and Planning Commission remains a male stronghold (3 women out of 73). The specialization of women in the social domain can have a positive dimension. In the eleventh legislature, women parliamentarians lent particular expertise on a number of bills and reforms that came under the Ministry of Employment and Solidarity, regarding matters of exclusion, family allowances, childcare allowances, male/female inequality in the workplace and other related issues. On the whole, female participation in parliamentary life was proportionally a respectable average since, during the 1998-1999 session, they asked 12.2 per cent of the questions of the government.

The Fifth Republic reduced the number of parliamentary commissions from twenty to six to avoid the difficulties of governance experienced in the Fourth Republic. Today the system seems out of step with social realities. While waiting for reform, two delegations have been created that are likely to transform into commissions. Within them, women's presence is clearly strong. First, in 1999, a parliamentary delegation on women's rights and equal opportunities for men and women was formed. Made up of 36 members, it included 19 women and 16 men, and it was presided over by a woman. Secondly, a European Union delegation at the National Assembly was formed, the role of which is to examine Community legislation from Brussels. In 1999, six out of its 36 members were women, or nearly 20 per cent, and one of the three vice-presidents was a woman.

Though it is difficult to predict the consequences of a more massive influx of women into Parliament, the actual sharing of power between the sexes is likely to be more effective in reorienting political priorities than the granting of political rights in was 1944, which remained purely formal. In any event, the deputies themselves are deeply convinced that women will bring about great changes. Questioned in 1999, nearly 70 per cent of the people's representatives believed that 'if there were a third women at the National Assembly... politics would change in form' 49 per cent that it would 'change in substance' (Sineau, 2001, p. 248). Due to the differences in their life experience, women are well placed to influence the content of political programmes and fill gaps in a common good previously defined without them. Because they have a different understanding of the relationship between private and political life, women are in an ideal position to rethink the business of politics, to bridge the gap between the public and the private domains. They can therefore forge another model of actor, more in touch with daily reality, giving a central and credible role to politics. This is basically what the French expect from the feminisation of power.

In future, women in France will only truly influence the political debate if two conditions are met. The first is that they must fight to obtain a reform on the law of parity. As much as this law is exemplary in the requirements it imposes on the parties to establish a parity of candidates in elections by list, it is ineffective when it comes to the norms decreed for candidacies in legislative elections that take place by uninominal vote. In fact, it leaves the choice open to political parties: either they field 50 per cent of the candidates from each sex or they face financial penalties. In a voting system that gives the advantage to incumbent notables, parliamentary groups prefer to pay fines than to eliminate incumbents by nominating women.

The second challenge female politicians will have to meet is not to miss the opportunity offered by the building of Europe. For today the source of law is more in European institutions than in national parliaments. Sixty per cent of national legislation is already European, and it is at the European level that the important political decisions will be made in future. French women are in a good position to be prominent actors in this new entity, because Europe provides them with an important access route to politics. Failing to be elected in their countries' assemblies, they have sought their fortune elsewhere, in the Parliament in Strasbourg. As early as 1979 and in the first election by universal suffrage (and by the proportional system by list), they made up over 20 per cent of the French delegation. Today, they make up over 40 per cent. This European route to political achievement for women has had a great inspirational figure in Simone Veil, who was elected president of the European Parliament in 1979 and who has contributed to establishing the commission on women's rights. She has been a model figure and has inspired followers. Twenty years later, in 1999, the French woman Nicole Fontaine was elected to this same office. Although French women are in a good position to make their voice heard in the European Parliament, they are underrepresented (like other European women) at every level of the Convention on the Future of the European Union, the new structure in charge of remodelling its institutional architecture. A disturbing sign for the future of women in politics.

Chapter 6

Ireland

Yvonne Galligan

Introduction

The Republic of Ireland is a unitary state covering around four-fifths of the land area on the island of Ireland. The remaining one-fifth, known variously as the 'six counties', 'Northern Ireland', or the 'north of Ireland', is part of the United Kingdom. The existence of two sovereign jurisdictions on this small island is a consequence of an early 20th century political settlement that gave the Republic of Ireland independence from British rule in 1922, leading to the creation of a republic in 1949. Despite the turbulent history of Anglo-Irish relations, Irish politicians, nationalist and unionist, worked within the Westminster political system and their understanding of parliamentary politics was shaped by this experience. When it came to establishing new political institutions in 1922, the rules and procedures of the House of Commons were adopted by the new parliament, as was the general parliamentary framework, with a popularly-elected lower house (Dáil) and an upper house (Seanad). However, there is some departure from conventional political institution-building at this point, for, as Coakley (1998, p.195-9) points out, the 60-seat upper house became quite unique in its composition. Second chambers generally represent either the population of a state or regions within a state and are either elected (directly or indirectly) or appointed. The Irish Seanad, however, was primarily designed to represent the views of interests such as business, labour, agriculture, administration, cultural and educational interests and others. In keeping with this quite exclusive selection of public interests, the route to a Seanad seat is through election by a restricted group of voters - local and national politicians determine the outcome of 43 seats, university graduates can vote to fill six seats and the Prime Minister (Taoiseach) appoints an additional eleven persons. Complex rules govern the nomination process and the vote counting procedures, the latter being conducted under rules similar to those governing general elections.

This brings us to the second major deviation from British politics. The plurality electoral system was not adopted for the newly independent state. Instead, Irish political elites favoured a variant of proportional representation advocated by the British Electoral Reform Society known as proportional representation by means of the single transferable vote (PR-STV). The unrepresentative outcomes of the plurality system were much criticised by British electoral reformers at the turn of the 20th century and PR-STV was devised as a counter to its disproportional effects. The new system placed a focus on the choice of individual voters and the highly proportional outcomes in terms of party strength made PR-STV particularly attractive to Irish politicians. The electoral system was strongly supported by Sinn Fein, whose founder, Arthur Griffith, was an early member of the Proportional Representation Society of Ireland. In 1918, PR-STV was enacted for one town council election and put into effect the following year. The proportionality of the result it delivered, with party representation closely mirroring voter support, excited considerable interest among reformers and Irish politicians. Shortly thereafter the British government decided to implement this new electoral system for the 1920 local elections in Ireland and then for the 1921 election securing Irish independence. Thus, as Sinnott notes, 'By 1921, PR-STV had not only been endorsed by a significant section of the nationalist movement but had actually reached the statute books' (1999, p.101). This form of PR was included in the 1922 constitution and specified in the Electoral Act of 1923. The fledgling independent state had opted for multi-member districts and maximising the representation of voter preferences over single-member districts and one-party dominance. Two attempts to change from PR-STV to a simple plurality system, in 1959 and again in 1968, were soundly defeated by the electorate in referendums. While there have been occasional discussions on changing the electoral system to single member districts and party lists put forward chiefly by Fine Gael, these suggestions have not found particular favour with elected representatives or the public. Indeed, the technical alteration of ballot casting and counting from a manual to an electronic process provoked heated debate in 2004, underlining public and political attachment to customary electoral practices.

Party politics is historically dominated by two major parties that emerged from Sinn Fein in the 1920s. Fianna Fail ('Soldiers of Destiny') came to represent small farmers, industrial workers and small business owners and traditionally draws support from all social classes and economic segments of society. The party evolved a broad mass appeal from an early stage (it was formed in 1926) and on average commands the support of around 40 per cent of the electorate. Fine Gael ('Family of the Irish') formed the first post-independence government and has drawn support from wealthier sections of the Irish electorate – large farmers, professionals and large business owners. Its fortunes have fluctuated over the years, ranging from 23-40 per cent electoral support. The Irish Labour Party is the third long-lasting party, founded in 1918 as the political voice of the trade union movement. With the dominance of the nationalist agenda in Irish politics at the critical point of state formation, the Labour Party has long been the minor party in Irish politics, attracting between nine and twenty per cent of the popular vote.

The last two decades have seen a fragmentation of the long-enduring three-party system with the rise and consolidation of new parties in the electoral arena. The Progressive Democrats, a neo-liberal party, was formed in 1985-6; Democratic Left emerged in the 1990s as an offshoot of a republican-socialist party and later merged with the Labour Party; while the Green Party also made its political mark in the 1990s. More recently, Sinn Fein ('Ourselves Alone') has come to pose an electoral challenge to both Fianna Fail and Labour with its left-of-centre and republican appeal. Also represented in parliament is the tiny Socialist Party and a range of independent parliamentarians, some of whom are disaffected former members of Fianna Fail, others are non-party representatives.

Fianna Fail was sufficiently strong to form single-party governments from the time it came to power in 1932 until 1992. Its dominance of politics and government was interspersed by occasional coalitions headed by Fine Gael and including the Labour party. Between 1979 and 1997, instability in the party system resulted in more frequent changes of government. Since 1997, a broadly right-of-centre coalition comprising Fianna Fail and the Progressive Democrats has held office (Gallagher, Marsh and Mitchell, 2003).

Women's Suffrage and Parliamentary Representation

The vote for women in Ireland was closely tied to the franchise campaign in Britain in the late 19th and early 20th centuries as Irish and English feminists worked together to win political rights for women from a strongly resistant British government and parliament. From the 1870s onwards, Irish women sought political equality with men, expressing their aim through the extensive organisation of suffrage societies, active lobbying of Irish parliamentarians and, ultimately, militant action against government property. In 1876, Anna Haslam, who, with family wealth and connections actively supported women's economic independence, formed the first Irish suffrage society, the Dublin Women's Suffrage Association. For the next twenty years the Association tirelessly petitioned the House of Commons and Irish MPs on the suffrage issue. Its efforts at grass-roots mobilisation was, however, constrained by the volatile political environment in Ireland arising from the demand for land law reform, and the Association's campaigns on other woman-related issues such as reform of the Married Women's Property Acts.

At the turn of the century, the rise in nationalist sentiment along with an Irish cultural revival led to the founding of Sinn Fein (1905) which held out the promise of independence as a more radical alternative to the modest home rule demand of the Irish Parliamentary Party. The growing radicalism of politics influenced the direction of the suffrage movement. In 1908, Hanna Sheehy Skeffington and Margaret Cousins founded the militant Irish Women's Franchise League modelled on Emmeline Pankhurst's Women's Social and Political Union. This was soon followed by the formation of a number of other smaller suffrage societies and in an effort to co-ordinate energy and activities, an umbrella group, the Irish Women's Suffrage Federation was established by socialists and trade union activists Louie Bennett and Helen Chenevix in 1911. These suffragists, along with many others, actively lobbied for extension of the franchise to women, but the politics of Home Rule in the House of Commons and strong opposition to the cause of women's equality by the leader of the Irish Parliamentary Party, John Redmond, among others, led to the defeat of a suffrage bill in 1912. Irish suffragists resorted to militant action, while militancy was renewed in England. Marches, and public demonstrations and confrontations were organised by the IWFL and supported by many women prominent in Sinn Fein politics.

Between 1912-14, 35 Irish women were convicted for vandalising public and government property, and many of them went on hunger strike while in prison in support of their suffrage demands. From 1914 onwards, the cohesiveness of the suffrage movement in Ireland came under strain from two developments – the outbreak of World War I and the rise of nationalist separatism. While the WSPU in Britain ceased its militancy and became involved in activities supporting the war, suffrage societies in Ireland initially concentrated on war-relief work, but later the mood shifted to opposing the war on pacifist grounds. Yet, the context in Ireland was one of rising militarism for the purpose of obtaining independence and increasingly suffragists divided on the locus of their primary loyalties – feminist pacifism or nationalist militarism. In January 1918, the Representation of the People Act was passed by the House of Commons and extended the vote to all men over 21 years and women of 30 years and over despite opposition by the Irish Parliamentary Party to its application in Ireland. The outcome of the 1918 election gave Sinn Fein complete dominance of Irish politics and the party's subsequent negotiations with the British government led to independence for the greater part of the island in 1922. As with many suffrage societies, the IWFL and its sister organisations faded away once suffrage was partially obtained (Cullen Owens, 1984). The new Irish government provided for suffrage for all adults over 21 years in the 1922 constitution and in 1923 enacted legislation to that end. The victory was hollow, for, despite gaining the vote, women were generally excluded from political affairs thereafter.

Although many prominent Irish women were centrally involved in the nationalist movement in the early 20th century, women were largely absent from the political life of the state for over fifty years following independence. The new nationalist leaders, while revolutionary in their politics of Anglo-Irish relations, held highly conservative views on gender relations and were reinforced in this thinking by a traditionalist social culture influenced by authoritarian Catholic social teaching and practice (Randall and Smyth 1987). The symbolic appointment of revolutionary nationalist Countess Markievicz to the Ministry of Labour in the nationalist government-in-waiting in 1919 remained the only instance of female cabinet office-holding until 1979. Of the eleven administrations formed since 1979, women have held on average thirteen per cent of cabinet posts and ten per cent of junior ministerial positions. Women's inclusion in cabinet is tokenist, and women's ministerial responsibilities are predominantly in policy areas associated with women – education and social affairs – but this pattern appears to be changing somewhat (Table 6.1). Nonetheless, the office of Prime Minister (Taoiseach) remains resolutely in male hands, as do the influential ministries of Finance and Foreign Affairs.

Table 6.1 Cabinet membership in Ireland by gender, 1979-2002

Year	Government	Men	Women	%Women	Portfolio
1979	Fianna Fail	14	1	6.6	Gaeltacht*
1981a	Fine Gael-Labour	13	1	7.7	Health
1982a	Fianna Fail	15	0	0.0	-
1982b	Fine Gael-Labour	14	1	6.6	Education
1987	Fianna Fail	14	1	6.6	Education
1989	Fianna Fail	14	1	6.6	Education
1992	Fianna Fail-Prog. Democrats	14	1	6.6	Tourism
1993	Fianna Fail-Labour	13	2	13.3	Education; Justice
1997	Fianna Fail-PD	12	3	20.0	Employment; Arts; Enterprise
2002	Fianna Fail-PD	13	2	13.0	Employment; Social Affairs

*Gaelic-speaking regions

Source: Author's calculation

Women's parliamentary presence is as sparse as their cabinet participation, partly because of the reluctance of parties to field women candidates in any substantial number. Between 1922 and 1977 the average Dáil contained only four women (three per cent) compared with 143 men. Over that 55 year period, only 25 individual women held seats in the lower house. Since 1977, women's parliamentary representation has moved into double-digit figures, rising to 22 (13 per cent) in 2002 (Table 6.2). This increase coincides with Fine Gael's placement of women candidates in winnable seats in the course of the 1980s and a similar initiative by Labour and the Progressive Democrats in the 1990s.

The pattern of women's representation in the upper house (Seanad) reflects that of the lower house: a total of 19 female senators were elected or appointed between 1937 (when the upper house was re-constituted in its current form) and 1977. In 2002, ten women (16 per cent) gained seats in the upper house. At local level, women's presence, at 15 per cent, is markedly similar to that in the higher political echelons. The overall level of women's political representation, then, is a poor reflection of women's activism in civil society. Indeed, the 1990 election of the first woman head of state, Mary Robinson, was anecdotally perceived as the outcome of a successful mobilisation of women voters. This result was all the more remarkable in a predominantly conservative culture with little evidence of gender gaps in voting preferences. Her successor, Mary McAleese, has consolidated the place of women in high political office. Despite the outstanding success of both women's presidential term, parties remain reluctant to put women forward for electoral contests.

Table 6.2 Women in the Irish Dáil, 1977-2002

	Total Candidates	Women Candidates	% Women	Total MPs	Women MPs	% Women
1977	376	25	6.6	148	6	6.6
1981	404	41	10.1	166	11	6.6
1982a	366	35	9.6	166	8	4.8
1982b	365	31	8.5	166	14	8.4
1987	466	65	13.9	166	14	8.4
1989	371	52	14.0	166	13	7.8
1992	482	89	18.5	166	20	12.0
1997	484	96	19.8	166	20	12.0
2002	463	84	18.1	166	22	13.2

Source: Author's calculations

Obstacles to Women's Political Representation

Social Attitudes

The main factor inhibiting women's participation in decision-making is generally recognised as being the degree to which a society holds negative attitudes towards the involvement of women in politics. In a study of obstacles to women's political participation in Ireland, Randall and Smyth (1987, p. 200) noted that:

> Irish women have until the very recent past been subject to a particularly intense, if complex, process of socialisation, through the agency of family, school and the Church, into an acceptance of an extremely traditional division of labour between the sexes and its implications for women's political role.

Thus, as Randall and Smyth graphically present, the socialisation process, which transmits traditional assumptions about women's role in society has been reinforced in Ireland through the Roman Catholic church which prioritised a home and family-based role for women. Although Irish Catholics today are less attached to religious observance than in the past, social attitudes remain heavily influenced by traditionalist assumptions regarding women's place in society. This becomes very evident in the responses to a 1997 European equal opportunity survey. Irish men were among the most reluctant in the EU to interrupt their careers to bring up a child (20 per cent in favour) and the difference in Irish gender attitudes on this measure (30 per cent) was among the largest in the EU (European Commission, 1997, pp. 42-7). Irish women favoured more childcare facilities and additional financial help with childcare in about equal amounts, broadly in line with the European women's average of 49 per cent and 46 per cent respectively, while Irish men indicated a preference for financial supports (45 per cent) over additional childcare facilities (40 per cent). Significantly, the survey revealed a significant gap in political interest between men and women in Ireland: 66 per cent of men and 49 per cent of women regularly discussed political affairs with family and close friends, indicating that politics is viewed as a male preserve. This disengagement of women from public issues carries over into workplace decision-making, where more women (45 per cent) than men (33 per cent) believed that the workplace was dominated by men who did not trust women to take appropriate decisions (European Commission, 1997, pp. 49-57). Furthermore, more women (66 per cent) than men (56 per cent) felt that their family responsibilities prevented them from taking on decision-making positions.

Thus, it appears that in general social attitudes in Ireland continue to expect women to pursue a traditional family role while balancing the obligations flowing from this role with job and career demands. It is not surprising, therefore, to find the public sphere dominated by men. For women with political ambitions, the practicality of pursuing this time-consuming career in tandem with child-rearing is an issue of greater significance than it is for their male colleagues. Data from a comprehensive survey of women legislators pointed to family responsibilities as the most significant source of difficulty in pursuing a political career – demands that are exacerbated when a politician is from a constituency outside the capital city of Dublin (Galligan *et al.*, 2000, pp. 41-2). This point is indicative of the weight of traditional cultural attitudes in Ireland, even among women who have managed to get elected to the highest legislative office. It suggests that in Ireland, as elsewhere, 'culture continues to be a significant influence on the proportion of women parliamentarians' (Norris and Inglehart , 2001, p. 32).

Local Base

If, as research has repeatedly shown, both education and occupation are relevant factors in the development of a political career for both women and men then one must ask in what way they are significant. The standard of education of the average parliamentarian has increased over time, and the business of being a member of parliament has become a full-time occupation in its own right. Women members of parliament are mainly drawn from the professions or service sector employment while their male colleagues come from more varied employment backgrounds. This employment pattern indicates that women are at least as well educated as their male counterparts and are therefore equally competent to undertake the task of legislating.

Educational achievement alone does not ensure electoral success for either women or men. Indeed, in an Irish context, one of the most important determinants of political success continues to be the strength of a candidate's local support. One of the most effective methods of establishing this is through local government service. However, as we have seen, there are relatively few women in local government due to the persistence of conservative party selection practices. One way of overcoming this disadvantage is through the development of local networks based on occupation. Professions such as teaching, medicine, law and business are generally seen as conferring status within a local community. They involved extensive interaction with the local electorate, and can be used as a foundation for personal bailiwick-building. In addition, these occupations bring economic independence and relative flexibility of time, two additional advantages for a person ambitious to hold political office. It was no accident that teaching was the occupation of the majority of women in the Dáil in the 1990s. While it still provides women political aspirants with a very significant local networking base, women parliametarians' working lives have diversified to include other occupations with the potential to generate a high local profile such as social work, law and business. These employments combine three important factors facilitating political career-building: income security and financial independence, opportunities for local contact, and time in which to pursue support-building activities.

Local voluntary activity presents another method of building a public profile, either or its own or combined with work-related activities. Previous research suggested that women's participation in organised voluntary and community groups and activities did not necessarily bring women into political life, and this finding remains substantially true (O'Donovan and Ward, 1999). However, more detailed research into the backgrounds of political women indicates that, for them, involvement in voluntary and community initiatives played an important part in their political socialisation. This 'grassroots' route to political office was identified as an important factor by almost half (45 per cent) of women parliamentarians (Galligan *et al*., 2000, p. 40).

It appears that women with political ambitions try to follow the common routes of entry to political life and if these routes are closed to them, they seek alternative ways to gain credibility as a potential candidate. The influence of localism is one that many aspiring women politicians find difficult to counteract if they have not had the opportunity to break into a brokerage network through local authority service, occupational activity, or grassroots involvement. In other words, the opportunities for building recognition and credibility as a candidate are more limited for women than for men. Women political hopefuls are more likely to look to their party leaders for 'sponsorship' at the candidate selection stage in order to compensate for a lower access to local networks.

Finally, while family connections have been important in determining routes to political power in Ireland, this has traditionally been a more significant factor for women than for men. From 1927 to 1973 the majority of women elected to the Dáil were related through family or marriage to former legislators. This trend broadly continues, with 41 per cent of women elected in 2002 having a family connection with national politics (Gallagher, 2003, p. 114). More specifically, one can observe the trend over time where the 'widow's seat' has been replaced by a father-daughter succession, with no widows elected to the Dáil after the 1970s (Galligan *et al.* , 2000, p. 35).

Candidate Selection

However, the above explanations, which focus on social and economic factors, do not fully account for the small number of women in politics. We must also look at the barriers embedded in the political system itself, and particularly at the selection processes of the political parties. There is now an extensive appreciation of the central role played by parties in helping or hindering women's electoral opportunities. Specific aspects of party behaviour and ideology have been found to impact on women's chances of selection for parliament. Caul's study (1999) of 68 parties in twelve advanced democracies found that women are more successful in getting to parliament when they belong to left (especially new left) parties, when there is a solid number of women serving in party national executives, when the rules of selection are clearly stated and complied with, and when gender targets or quotas are in effect. Complementary research providing explanations for women's political under-representation have focused on internal party selection processes as the single most important obstacle to women's political participation (Norris and Lovenduski, 1993, Russell, 2000). In the 2002 election, women comprised 19 per cent of all candidates, with Fianna Fail fielding 13 women candidates (12 per cent) and Fine Gael selecting 15 women (18 per cent). Research in the UK indicates a growing awareness of the important role discriminatory attitudes among party activists play in curtailing women's opportunities for selection (Shepherd-Robinson and Lovenduski, 2002). Although Irish party central organisations are now more directly involved in the candidate selection process, and indeed make rhetorical remarks about the need for more women candidates, parties have not yet rectified a gender imbalance in candidate tickets, indicating that similar attitudes prevail among Irish selectors (Galligan, 2003, p. 49-50). Nonetheless, given the importance of the electoral system in structuring political opportunities, the multiple-seat districting leads to intense internal party rivalry for a place on the party's constituency ticket. Local party units jealously guard their right to choose the persons to carry the party banner into an election, and local selectorates favour male candidates, given that men are likely to be office-holders or 'favoured sons' of incumbents. Across parties, with the exception of the small and relatively new Progressive Democrats, women have a more up-hill route to nomination and selection than men, as traditionally politics has been cast in a male image. Many women who make it through the selection process have had the support of their party national headquarters in their struggle to convince local party members of their credibility as candidates – a condition that is less than essential for male selection opportunities.

One of the reasons for the low selection rate of women candidates traditionally put forward by party activists has been that they perceive male candidates as being more available for electoral contests than female candidates. There is a developing strand of research investigating party members' attitudes towards women candidates that seems to highlight a view among party members that women appear to prefer family over politics. There are mixed reactions to this explanation among women and men party members, with women in Fine Gael more inclined than men to agree that women's family commitments keep them out of electoral politics (Gallagher and Marsh, 2002, p 133). The significant time demands of a family are also perceived by women legislators as an important inhibitor to women's political careers, and this finding is supported by a worldwide survey of women legislators that found balancing the amount of time devoted to family and public activities to be the single most cited inhibitor (67 per cent) of office-seeking (Interparliamentary Union, 2000).

The same strands of research also investigate demand-side explanations for women's under-representation, for instance that selectors fear that women will lose votes and therefore are not attractive candidates to put forward. This proposition is strongly rejected by Fine Gael party members (Gallagher and Marsh, 2002, p. 133). When asked the fundamental question of whether women and men have equal opportunity to participate or be selected as candidates within their party, women in Fine Gael were less likely than men to agree that their party provided equal opportunities to women and men. Thus, the perception of obstacles to women's political participation recognises that the problem of supply is not the sole explanation for the few women coming forward for selection. Instead, there is a general awareness of the structural and attitudinal barriers to women's participation, with women, not surprisingly, being more acutely aware of this impediment.

Other research tackles the question of women candidates from another perspective – that of voter preference. There are no clear conclusions arising from this research, partly because of the few numbers of women going forward for election. An analysis of voter choice at the 1997 election indicated that voter attitudes had become more positive than before towards women as parliamentary representatives. When factors such as age, incumbency and previous political experience were controlled, no significant gender bias was found among voters. The factors that really mattered in winning election were party and incumbency. Thus, it would be expected that male TDs from the larger parties would have a greater chance of being re-elected than a female TD or female newcomer (Galligan, Laver and Carney, 1999). A study of the 2002 election results confirmed this general finding. Overall, men won around 600 more votes than women candidates and male incumbents were much more successful in getting elected than all female candidates (incumbent and newcomer). However, all women candidates had the edge on newcomer men (Gallagher, 2003, pp. 90-1). These findings must remain tentative until significantly more women contest Dáil elections.

Strategies for Increasing Women's Political Presence

Following a courting of women's votes in the 1977 general election, some women's organisations began to raise awareness of the absence of women from decision making During the 1980s, campaigns to support women candidates in general and European elections were led by the Women's Political Association. The National Women's Council of Ireland (NWCI) directed attention to the scarcity of women on public boards. Women's groups in Fine Gael and Labour sought to improve women's participation at senior party levels and in political life. Looking back, one can identify some success from these campaigns. In the 1980s, leading feminists were elected to the Dáil, some of whom went on to hold ministerial office and exert a long-term influence on the policy agenda in their ministries. Persistent pressure from the NWCI and the second Commission on the Status of Women finally resulted in a 1993 government commitment to a target of 40:60 gender balance on public boards. Gradually, new legislation involving the creation of an overseeing agency incorporated provisions for gender balance on the agency board. Thus, the Irish Sports Council, for example, is required to have three women on its ten-member board. In addition, government made a serious attempt to implement the 40:60 gender balance in appointments to public boards under its control. These efforts paid some, if modest, dividends. By 1998, women's representation on state boards and boards of public interest had risen to 27 per cent, but this level of participation rose only slightly, to 29 per cent, by 2004. Women's representation on the national executives of political parties also improved from the 1980s, although, with rare exception, women were unable to turn participation in national party affairs to their electoral advantage. Thus, despite considerable effort from women's groups and some genuine commitment from government, the barriers to women's political representation seemed insurmountable.

The continuing dearth of women in electoral politics generated a renewed degree of concern among the women's movement as the new century dawned. It was also identified by policy makers as an issue for action, given the need to account for progress on women's rights under Convention for the Elimination of Discrimination Against Women (CEDAW) and the Beijing Platform for Action. The National Women's Council of Ireland adopted women's political participation as one of four major areas of action between 2002 and 2007. In 2002 it was funded by government to investigate the participation of women across political and public life and develop recommendations for change. The resultant publication, *Irish politics: jobs for the boys!* and an accompanying photographic exhibition of gender imbalance in decision making demonstrated the deep political disadvantage experienced by Irish women and provided evidence, if such were needed, for government action. The official response has been disappointing. Although government has funded an awareness-raising campaign based on the publication and photographic exhibition that has travelled to local communities across the country, it has not followed up with more concrete initiatives supporting opportunities for women's involvement in political and public decision-making.

Parties, too, have begun to pay new attention to the absence of women from their ranks. Financed by public funds earmarked for gender equality, Fianna Fail, Fine Gael, Labour and Sinn Fein have developed party-focused strategies for encouraging more women into political careers and supporting emerging women political hopefuls. In the case of Sinn Fein and Labour, party commitment is reasonably comprehensive, linking the empowerment of women members with selection strategies that go some way to redressing the male-gender bias among grass-roots members. Both parties strive to attract ambitious women and work to achieve a gender balance in their candidate list. Sinn Fein indicates a particular commitment to advancing women in electoral politics, given their poor record in 2002 and their place as challenger in the party system. Fianna Fail, the largest party, remains ambiguous about its commitment to promoting women electorally and, while willing to foster a more woman-friendly party culture, is less anxious to steer the locally-based selection process in women's favour. Fine Gael must come to terms with its plummeting voter support and, in the process, women are less likely to be seen as being important partners in the revival of party fortunes.

In sum, then, the scope for implementing strategies for improving women's political participation are limited. A neo-liberal government, in office since 1997, is reluctant to interfere in the 'free market' of electoral competition by legislating for gender equal representation. Although criticised in 2003 in a UN report for the low representation of women in elected office, and urged to adopt 'temporary special measures' to address the gender deficit in the legislature, the Irish government has firmly resisted instituting any initiatives to redress this problem. Instead, it provides support for individual party awareness-raising projects and is also willing to encourage a wider societal debate on gender equality in political life and public decision-making. Opportunities for campaign training are welcomed by party women, and the additional infrastructural support in the form of women's officer enables the co-ordination and delivery of development programmes of this kind. However, many party women are now questioning the value of training programmes if their opportunities for selection are not improved.

Women's Parliamentary Influence

Although research to date has paid little attention to women's political work once they achieve office, a study of the profile and careers of political women made some interesting observations on the subject (Galligan *et al*, 2000). In essence, the question being asked was if Irish female parliamentarians gave primary importance to their legislative tasks or did constituency duties figure more prominently in their understanding of parliamentary representation? In a famous phrase, Chubb (1963) described the activities of elected representatives as being one of 'going about persecuting civil servants', suggesting that the majority of Irish politicians spent the bulk of their time on constituency business. Gallagher and Komito (1999) also point to the extensive constituency case-load borne by Irish parliamentarians, but point out that this level of brokerage is not unique to Ireland and that it is an integral part of the job of being a public representative. When one examines the extent to which women engage in constituency work, it is clear that this form of public work is as important for political women as it is for political men. Yet, when asked to identify their most significant parliamentary achievement, only three (five per cent) mentioned constituency related activities. Over half (56 per cent) of parliamentarians identified specific policy and legislative initiatives as their most important contribution to Irish political life. An additional one-fifth (20 per cent) measured their achievement in terms of career progression, moving from being a backbencher to ministerial office or other leadership position (Galligan *et al*, 2000, pp. 46-8). Thus, women parliamentarians are mindful of their dual role of being a constituency representative and a legislator.

Studies of women parliamentarians appear to indicate that women legislators seek in some way to speak and act for women in the community and also show that there is some expectation among women voters that women politicians will share their concerns (Sawer, 2002, pp. 8-9, Childs, 2002, p. 143). Indeed, many of the discriminatory policies enacted against women in Ireland from 1937 onwards are seen as the product of a male-dominated political order. It is clear that during the 1970s, when women's parliamentary representation was almost negligible, government and parliament was only partially responsive to the growing voice of gender reform. The articulation and representation of women's rights fell to the emerging feminist movement, a reform-minded judiciary and the European Commission. According to Scannell (1988, pp. 129-30), these agencies were more important catalysts in the initiation of change in the status of women than either politicians or parliament, suggesting that the political system was forced to respond to external pressures rather than being prepared to initiate change. While European directives on employment and judicial decisions on individual rights acted as an important spur to specific legislative changes, the re-emergence of the women's movement in the early 1970s prompted a public discussion of discrimination against women in law and public policy.

Evidence suggests that women's lobby groups have had a more immediate influence on specific aspects of public policy than the efforts of women parliamentarians (Galligan, 1998). In 1972, the Commission on the Status of Women, established by government two years earlier on foot of lobbying from women's groups, recommended that action be taken to remove discrimination against women in the areas of the home, employment, social welfare, taxation, family law, jury service, public life and education. Twenty years later, the report of the Second Commission on the Status of Women – again a government response to women's groups' demands for gender equality – made a further 211 recommendations in broadly similar areas. Both reports provided important blueprints for gender equality and raised many important issues with respect to women's lives that had not previously, or had only marginally, been the subject of political attention. In addition to the policy changes advocated in these documents, the women's movement became effective lobbyists for legislative reform on specific issues such as family law (AIM – Action, Information, Motivation), domestic abuse (Women's Aid), sexual violence against women (Rape Crisis Centres). The political voice of women became represented by the Council for the Status of Women, later known as the National Women's Council of Ireland (NWCI), to which over 200 women's groups were affiliated in 2002. In the 1990s, NWCI representatives were admitted to the highly corporatised economic and social decision-making social partnership as one of a number of representatives from the community and voluntary sector, thus giving women's interests an entry – although little more – into a highly influential, primarily economic interest-based, elite. The resulting three-year economic and social programmes that shaped the allocation of Ireland's financial resources throughout the 1990s contained relatively minor provisions for gender equality, mainly in the area of equal pay.

If lobbying efforts were not sufficient to secure change, national and European judicial systems served as agencies of progress. The McGee (1973), de Burca (1976) and Airey (1979) cases, which respectively established the right of married couples to import contraceptives for their personal use, the right of women to serve on juries, and the right of women to free legal aid, are seen as important cases leading to legislative reform of benefit to women. The principle of equality for women in social welfare entitlements was conceded by the government in 1990 following a judgement from the European Court of Justice in a case brought by two women, Cotter and McDermott, against the state. The contentious issue of abortion was also placed on the political agenda through court findings – from the European Court of Justice in 1991, the European Court of Human Rights in 1992 and the Irish Supreme Court in 1992 (Connelly, 1999, pp. 20-2). In particular, the Supreme Court judgement in the 'X' case brought about three referendums in November 1992 that sought to clarify public policy on the abortion issue. The results were indeed clear, if not to the taste of many politicians – there was a clear majority against an absolute ban on abortion and in favour of affirming the right of a woman to travel to procure an abortion. There was also a majority in favour of information being made available on abortion services outside the state (Kennelly and Ward, 1993). As Kennedy (2002, p. 115) observes, the outcome of the 1992 referenda meant that the position on abortion remained that as ruled by the Supreme Court – abortion was lawful where there was a real and substantial risk to the life of the mother. A further referendum was sought by 'pro-life' groups wishing to institute a complete ban on abortion in the state, and in 2002 a further three-part effort by the government to restrict the implications of the Supreme Court ruling was defeated.

Although the representation of women's interests has largely been conducted by voices outside the legislative system through lobbying and legal challenges, there have been feminist voices within the Dáil – mainly from the ranks of Fine Gael and Labour – seeking to address women-specific issues. The first minister for women's affairs, Nuala Fennell, oversaw important legislative changes in women's family status in the mid-1980s (Galligan, 1998). Women with connections to the feminist movement (Monica Barnes, Gemma Hussey and Frances Fitzgerald of Fine Gael) and social democratic politics (Eithne FitzGerald, Niamh Bhreathnach, Joan Burton) consistently advocated and promoted woman-friendly policies, while Liz O'Donnell of the Progressive Democrats also adopted a woman-centred view on public policy issues. Her party leader, Mary Harney, has consistently supported women's political participation, and has acted as a powerful role model for women. Most of these individual women belonged to women's organisations before moving into politics, and consequently brought an awareness of gender and gender-related issues into their political perspectives. However, these singular voices over a 25-year period cannot be said to amount to a strong, coherent feminist voice within the Dáil. Indeed, in the survey of women parliamentarians mentioned above, advocacy of women's issues was ranked seventh in a list of fourteen policy areas. However, before rushing to judgement on women politicians, it is important to note that they ranked education, health, social affairs and equality in their top five priorities – policy areas with particular implications for women's lives (Galligan *et al.*, 2000, pp. 49-50). Reluctant to be over-identified (or, in some cases, associated with) feminist issues, and unwilling to be type-cast as speaking for women, the few women TDs in parliament favour interest in more general 'soft' policy concerns as a substitute for articulation of a feminist view on wide-ranging policy issues. They cannot be overly criticised for taking this stance, for, as a visible minority in parliament and in a political context where party discipline is strong, women parliamentarians have little option but to moderate their views to fit with the masculinist culture and norms pervading Dáil business.

Conclusion

The relationship between women and politics in Ireland has become more complex over time. Women considering a career in public life continue to do so in a cultural environment that expects them also to fulfil traditional home-based duties. In partial response to these pressures, women are postponing having their first child until later in life and one-child families are becoming increasingly common. Ireland ranks low on the European scale in terms of women's representation in political life, yet there is no significant bias among the electorate against women candidates: incumbency is the main criteria of further success in electoral politics. Women remain under-represented as election candidates and although parties are developing some initiatives to redress this imbalance there remains an important obstacle at the 'gatekeeping' candidate selection stage. Given this analysis, and despite the strong role models presented by Mary Robinson, Mary McAleese and others, the likelihood of a substantially increased presence of women in political life is slim without the adoption of strong affirmative action measures by parties. Put into an international context, the conditions for expanding women's electoral opportunities are slim. Left parties in Ireland attract only a small proportion of the overall vote; party national executives have less than 30 per cent female members; selection rules may be transparent, but do not necessarily fulfil equal opportunity guidelines; while there is continued resistance to targets and quotas within the major parties. The continuing absence of women from parliament poses challenges to the context, style and substance of political representation as Ireland's democratic structures move into the 21st century.

Note: This chapter draws significantly on Y. Galligan (2004), 'Women in politics' in John Coakley and Michael Gallagher (eds) *Politics in the Republic of Ireland*, 4th edition, London: Routledge.

Chapter 7

Sub-Saharan Africa

Mi Yung Yoon

Introduction

The countries in sub-Saharan Africa are relatively new. They became independent after the late 1950s following the independence of Ghana (1957) and Guinea (1958), respectively. Only Liberia and Ethiopia were spared from the European colonialism in Africa. During the colonial rule, women in many African countries played an active role in the liberation struggle, but their contribution to the liberation struggle did not bring a gender balance in new governments. Women were absent in political decision-making positions at the time of independence and have remained under-represented since then. Today there is no female head of state in Africa. There is only one female Prime Minister (Maria das Neves Batista de Sousa in São Tomé and Príncipe), one female vice president (Isatou Njie-Saidy in The Gambia), and five female presidents of assemblies (Frene Ginwala and Naledi Pandor in South Africa, Mulatu Toshome in Ethiopia, Grace Beatrice Minor in Liberia, and Ntlhoboi Motsamai in Lesotho). They occupy only 14.1 per cent of single-house or lower-house seats (Inter-Parliamentary Union 2003). In the executive, women accounted for 15.4 per cent of ministerial and vice ministerial positions in 2000 (United Nations Development Program 2003).

The marginalisation of women in politics today can be traced back to the colonial period. Women in pre-colonial African societies by no means had equal rights with men, but they exercised political and economic rights of their own. In some pre-colonial societies, women held high political positions although men usually occupied top positions (Parpart 1988, p. 209; Foster 1993, p.104). They also had control over economic resources (e.g., access to the land, budgetary independence within the household, trade, etc.) (Waylen 1996, p.51). European colonialism, however, took away these rights.

Women who held political positions in pre-colonial societies lost their positions when colonial powers recognized men as chiefs or intermediaries to meet their administrative needs. The exclusion of women in the political domain was solidified by the colonial education that taught skills and European languages mostly to boys to fill low-level administrative positions (Waylen 1996, p.62). Because of these colonial practices, women virtually had no participation in the colonial administration and at the time of independence, males who received higher education during colonialism and had experience in the colonial administration took government positions in most countries (Parpart 1988, p.214; Foster 1993, p.107). Women were further marginalized by customary laws the colonial powers introduced to 'govern personal matters of Africans' (Cawthorne 1999, p.63). For example, in pre-colonial Africa, the land was communally owned. When colonial powers individualized property rights, men generally got the land titles (Parpart 1988, p.211; Waylen 1996, p.57). Customary laws also regarded women as minors under the authority of males (Foster 1993, p.106; Cawthorne 1999, p.66). As a result of these laws, women in many African countries still cannot own and inherit the land, travel without the permission of their husbands, have legal guardianship of their children, enter into contracts, and obtain bank loans (Geisler 1995, p.547; Cawthorne 1999, p.66).

Given that laws are enacted and repealed in the legislature, women's under-representation in African parliaments warrants some serious concern. Although women's parliamentary representation has increased over time since their first entry into the legislature, the severe gender gap has remained. The recent political change toward democracy in Africa that began in the early 1990s generated some optimism for greater women's legislative representation, but failed to deliver the expected outcome and instead lowered their representation (Yoon 2001a, p.177).

Of 43 sub-Saharan African countries examined in this study, only Ethiopia, Nigeria, and Sudan have federal systems. Presidentialism is the most common form of political system with 37 countries in sub-Saharan Africa practicing this type of system; five countries have parliamentary systems, and one has a monarchy in which the king exercises executive and legislative power. Except for Uganda and Swaziland, each of which has a 'no party' system, all other countries have multiparty systems although only one or two parties tend to occupy an overwhelming majority of parliamentary seats (Yoon 2001b). For legislative elections, 13 countries use proportional representation systems, 21 use majority or plurality systems, and eight use mixed systems. This study examines women's legislative representation in this context.

This chapter is a general overview of women's legislative representation in sub-Saharan Africa. After the introduction come historical facts about women's legislative representation. This part examines whether women's legislative representation has improved since their first entry into the legislature. Next is a discussion on the barriers to women's parliamentary representation to understand the persistent under-representation of women in parliament despite some improvement over the years. With the recent democratization, gender inequality in politics has received much attention. Therefore, the following section examines what efforts have been made in sub-Saharan Africa to increase women's political representation. As Table 7.1 shows, women in some countries occupy a significant portion of parliamentary seats. Does a critical mass of women in parliament make a difference in the lives of women? The remaining part of the chapter, therefore, turns to this question by focusing on the impact of women's parliamentary representation on legislative outcomes in Senegal, South Africa, Tanzania, and Uganda.

Women's Legislative Representation over Time

The constitutions of African countries guarantee the rights to vote and to hold offices to all adult citizens, both men and women (Ochwada 1997, p.124). While women in the West and in other parts of the developing world attained these political rights after a long and tumultuous struggle, women in most sub-Saharan African countries received these rights before independence or at the time of independence. Women in Benin, Comoros, Côte d'Ivoire, Djibouti, Equatorial Guinea, Gabon, The Gambia, Mauritius, Senegal, Seychelles, Sierra Leone, and Tanzania received these rights long before independence (Inter-Parliamentary Union, 1992, pp.6-7), whereas women in Angola, Botswana, Cape Verde, Kenya, Madagascar, Mozambique, Namibia, Rwanda, São Tomé and Príncipe, and Uganda received these rights near, or at the time of, independence (Inter-Parliamentary Union 1992, p.6). However, women in some countries did not obtain these rights even long after independence. For example, women in predominantly Muslim northern Nigeria were denied the right to vote until the new constitution of 1979 (Howard 1985, p.292). In Central African Republic, which became independent in 1960, women gained their suffrage and right to stand for election in 1986. Black women in South Africa received these rights when the black majority took power in 1994. In most African countries, women gained these two political rights at the same time. However, women in some countries (e.g., Djibouti and Zimbabwe) gained the right to stand for election after they had gained the right to vote.

Women in sub-Saharan Africa are latecomers to the parliamentary politics. As Table 7.1 demonstrates, women's right to stand for election was not immediately followed by their entry into the national legislature in most countries. Women were elected or appointed into parliament long after they had gained the right to stand for election, in many cases much more than a decade later. Although women's legislative representation has fluctuated over the years in most countries, the overall women's representation appears to be higher today than when they first entered into parliament.

The 1990s became a turning point in African politics as more than 40 countries began a transition from single-party authoritarian rule to multiparty democracy and held multiparty presidential and parliamentary elections. Many of them already held second or third multiparty elections over the past decade. However, as was reported in other democratizing regions of the world (e.g., Latin America, Eastern and Central Europe, and the former republics of the Soviet Union), democratization has also decreased the overall female legislative representation in Africa (Yoon 2001a, p.177). If so, what prevents women from entering into the national legislature? This is the question to which the chapter now turns.

Table 7.1 Women's political participation in sub-Saharan Africa

Country	Year of Independence	Right to Vote	Right to Run	First elected/ Appointed(%)	% women MPs	% women Cabinet
Angola	1975	1975	1975	1980E (8.3)	15.5	14.7
Benin	1960	1956	1956	1979E (8.3)	6.0	10.5
Botswana	1966	1965	1965	1979E (5.4)	17.0	26.7
Burkina Faso	1960	1958	1958	1978E (1.8)	11.7	8.6
Burundi	1962	1961	1961	1982E (9.2)	18.4	4.5
Cameroon	1960	1946	1946	1960E (1.0)	8.9	5.8
Cape Verde	1975	1975	1975	1975E (1.8)	11.1	35.0
Central African Republic	1960	1986	1986	1987E (3.8)	7.3	NA
Chad	1960	1958	1958	1962E (1.3)	5.8	NA
Congo	1960	1963	1963	1963E (5.5)	8.5	NA
Côte d'Ivoire	1960	1952	1952	1965E (3.5)	8.5	9.1
Djibouti	1977	1946	1986	2003E (10.8)	10.8	5.0
Equatorial Guinea	1968	1963	1963	1968E (5.7)	5.0	NA
Ethiopia	-	1955	1955	1957E (1.0)	7.7	22.2
Gabon	1960	1956	1956	1961E (1.5)	9.2	12.1
Gambia	1965	1960	1960	1982E (6.1)	13.2	30.8
Ghana	1957	1954	1954	1960A (9.6)	9.0	8.6
Guinea	1958	1958	1958	1963E (18.7)	19.3	11.1
Guinea-Bisseau	1974	1977	1977	1972A (8.3)	7.8	8.3
Kenya	1963	1963	1963	1969E/A(1.2)	7.1	1.4
Lesotho	1966	1965	1965	1965A (9.1)	11.7	NA
Liberia	-	NA	NA	NA	7.8	NA
Madagascar	1960	1959	1959	1965E (0.9)	3.8	12.5
Malawi	1964	1961	1961	1964E (2.0)	9.3	11.8
Mali	1960	1956	1956	1964E (1.3)	10.2	33.3
Mauritania	1960	1961	1961	1975E (2.9)	3.7	13.6
Mauritius	1968	1956	1956	1976E (4.3)	5.7	9.1
Mozamique	1975	1975	1975	1977E (12.4)	30.0	NA
Namibia	1990	1989	1989	1989E (6.9)	26.4	16.3
Niger	1960	1948	1948	1989E (5.4)	1.2	10.0
Nigeria	1960	1958	1958	NA	NA	22.6
São Tomé and Príncipe	1975	1975	1975	1975E (18.2)	9.1	NA
Senegal	1960	1945	1945	1963E (1.3)	19.2	15.6
Seychelles	1976	1948	1948	1976E/A(4.0)	29.4	23.1
Sierra Leone	1961	1961	1961	NA	14.5	8.1
South Africa	1961	1933/94	1933/94	1933E (0.7)	29.8	8.1
Sudan	1956	1964	1964	1964E (0.4)	9.7	5.1
Swaziland	1968	1968	1968	1972E/A(1.8)	3.1	12.5
Tanzania	1961	1959	1959	NA	22.3	NA
Togo	1960	1945	1945	1961E (2.0)	7.4	7.4
Uganda	1962	1962	1962	1962A (NA)	24.7	27.1
Zambia	1964	1962	1962	1964E/A(5.3)	12.0	6.2
Zimbabwe	1980	1957	1978	1980E/A(7.5)	10.0	36.0

Sources: Chazan et al. (1999), UN Human Development Report (2003), Inter-Parliamentary Union (1995), Inter-Parliamentary Union (2003). NA = not available; MPs 2003 figures, Cabinet figures 2000.

Barriers to Women's Parliamentary Representations

Unequal Access to Education

Women's education is an important resource for their political representation (Foster 1993, p.111). It not only expands the pool of women eligible for elective offices, but also increases the number of women willing to participate in politics by enhancing their self-confidence. In sub-Saharan Africa, the gender gap in education widens as the level of education goes up. It is more serious in the rural areas, where many women have little or no access to education (Global Coalition for Africa 1998, p.75). Multiple factors limit girls' access to education. Girls are not enrolled in schools due to domestic responsibilities, income-generating activities, pregnancies, and early marriages in some communities (Otunga 1997, p.46). The belief that women's role as wives and mothers do not need formal schooling also has negatively affected women's chances for education. In addition, most parents do not regard education for female children as an investment, because female children will become a part of another family once they marry while male children will stay within the family (Ochwada 1997, p.135; Otunga 1997, p.47). Therefore, when resources are limited, parents tend to choose the education of male children (Otunga 1997, p.47).

Lack of Financial Resources

Women cannot run for elective offices, in large part, due to a lack of financial resources. For example, in Tanzania the majority of women aspirants were unable to pay the fees set by their own political parties for filling out forms to stand for parliamentary and local elections in 2000 (Temu and Kassim 2001). In Ghana more women desired to run for parliamentary seats in the 2000 elections than before, but the fee to be paid to the Electoral Commission for qualification discouraged them from running (Aubrey 2001). Women's unequal access to well-paying jobs and lack of control over productive resources such as the land and credit are mainly responsible for their lack of funds. In sub-Saharan Africa, the majority of the female work force is either in farming or in the informal sectors, which offer little by way of resources needed to pursue elective offices; because men are the owners of their family properties, women have fewer family resources to generate finance and lack the collateral banks require to secure bank loans.

Patriarchal Culture

A patriarchal culture favors sexually segregated roles (Ochwada 1997, p.124). The expected roles of women in a patriarchal culture are as wives and mothers, and politics is not a female domain. This cultural view on women's roles influences not only women's decision to run for elective offices but also the electorate's voting decisions. Women are unwilling to run for elective offices because they do not view themselves as politicians. Voters do not vote for female candidates because of their stereotypical view of women, deeply embedded in the male dominant culture. Women who decide to run often face intimidation, violence, ostracism, and verbal abuse throughout their campaigns as was seen in the 1997 Kenyan elections in such constituencies as Kitui Central, Westlands, Nakuru Town, Dagorett, and Lugari and in the 1992 Zambian elections (Geisler 1995, p.56; Nation Reporter 1998). Some women also face opposition from their own families, particularly from their husbands.

Socialization

Karl (1995, p.12) states that 'in nearly all societies, girls are socialized to identify with the family and the private sphere, while boys are brought up to act in the public sphere'. This gender-biased socialization, according to her, makes it difficult for women to have the self-confidence and skills necessary to pursue political offices. Family, education, and the media are identified as the major agents of such socialization. Children acquire social and cultural values including gender identity and gender roles at home (Moshi 1998, p.xi). In schools, girls are educated to become mothers and housewives or to take traditionally female occupations such as nurses, secretaries, and teachers, while boys learn subjects that will help them become leaders (Parpart 1988, p.217; Gordon 1991, p.33; Otunga 1997, p.44). Textbooks and the media reinforce the stereotypical images of women by portraying them as performing those specific roles (Ufomata 1998, p.68). Moreover, the media often depict women as 'dependent, helpless, and irrational' (National Assembly of Malawi and UNESCO 1996, p.16).

Household Responsibilities

Rai (1994, p.210) states that women generally have limited time 'at their disposal to cross the boundary of their private lives into the public sphere'. It is because of the multiple roles women play in their private sphere. In Africa, domestic tasks (e.g., childcare, fetching water and fire wood, preparing and processing foods, house cleaning, washing clothes, and caring for the elderly and the sick) are women's primary responsibilities (Nzomo 1993, p.69). Their household responsibilities become heavier when economic conditions deteriorate, because they have to work harder and longer hours to make up the difference.

Unfavorable Electoral System

Women in single-member majority or plurality systems are less successful in getting parliamentary seats than in proportional representation systems (Norris 1985; Rule 1987, 1994; Matland 1998). In single-member majority or plurality systems, political parties are more cautious and hesitant to nominate female candidates because of the voter prejudice against female candidates (Rule 1994, p.690). However, in multi-member proportional representation systems, political parties have an incentive to include more women to appeal to a broader segment of voters (Rule 1994; Matland

and Studlar 1996). As was found in consolidated democracies, majority-plurality systems also negatively affect women's legislative representation in sub-Saharan Africa. The average percentage of women in parliament is much lower in majority-plurality systems than in proportional representation systems (Yoon 2001a, p.180).

Strategies to Increase Women's Legislative Representation

Efforts have been made to enhance women's representation in parliament at various levels. At the societal level, women's non-governmental organizations (NGOs) have been instrumental in improving women's representation at all levels of the government. Their roles include mobilizing women to stand for elections, lobbying political parties and politicians to include more women in their party slates and in government, leadership training and financial support for candidates, and voter education. For example, the National Council of Women in Kenya sponsors programs to help women 'gain experience in public speaking and campaign finance' (Lawless and Fox 1999, p.53). In South Africa, it was the National Coalition of Women, formed in 1992, that played the significant role in getting the African National Congress (ANC) to nominate women for 30 per cent of its slate for the 1994 legislative elections (Humarau 1996, p.38). In Zambia, the National Women's Lobby Group established a campaign support fund for female candidates contesting the 1996 parliamentary elections and contributed significantly to increasing the number of women elected to the parliament from seven to fifteen (SADC Gender Monitor, 1999). In Botswana, *Emang Basadi* (Stand Up Women) has conducted workshops in lobbying, advocacy, and campaign management for prospective women political candidates since 1994 (SADC Gender Monitor 1999). It has also held political education campaigns to persuade women voters to vote for women candidates (Geisler 1995, p.566).

In Namibia, the Namibian Women's Manifesto Network, a coalition of NGOs, launched a '50/50 campaign' in 1999 to achieve gender balance in all elected government positions. Specifically, it proposes the 50/50 Bill, which states that all party lists for future National Assembly elections must be gender-balanced and the names of female and male candidates must alternate 'zebra style' on the lists (Namibian Women's Manifesto Network 2002). In Nigeria, some NGOs (e.g., Gender and Development Action, Women's Empowerment Movement, the National Council for Women's Societies, etc.) have demanded reserved seats for women in parliament and more appointments of women for government positions (Tripp 2001, p.145).

At the governmental level, several African countries have used gender quotas to increase female representation in parliament. While Sudan, Uganda, and Tanzania have reserved seats for women, Botswana, Equatorial Guinea, Mozambique, Namibia, Senegal, and South Africa have party quotas voluntarily established by political parties (Inter-Parliamentary Union 2003). In Uganda, 56 of 74 women in parliament are reserved seat members, while in Tanzania 48 of 62 women in parliament hold reserved seats (Amongi 2002a; Kassim 2003). Thus, the women elected to reserved seats in these countries far exceed in numbers the women elected in constituencies. In the case of Sudan, where all of the 35 women are reserved seats members, there would be no women in parliament without reserved seats for women (Inter-Parliamentary Union 2003). The high percentage of women in the parliament of Mozambique, Namibia, and South Africa is mainly due to the substantial gender quota of the Front for the Liberation of Mozambique (30 per cent), the South West African People's Organization (30 per cent), and the ANC (33 per cent), the ruling party in Mozambique, Namibia, and South Africa, respectively.

According to Caul (2001, p.1225), when one party in a system adopts a quota for women, competing parties match its policy to avoid losing women's votes. This diffusion, however, has not yet taken place in sub-Saharan Africa. Except in Botswana, where two minor parties have quotas, only a single political party practices a gender quota in other countries with party quotas. As of today, only Djibouti mandates gender quotas to all political parties for national legislative elections. Djibouti had never had a woman in its parliament until 2003. Women's parliamentary representation rose from zero to 10.8 per cent in 2003 due to the new legislation that mandated a certain number of women on each party list, giving women seven of the 65 seats (Africa Online 2003, *Women and Ruling Party Win Djibouti Elections*).

At the sub-regional level, following the recommendation of the 1995 World Conference on Women in Beijing, heads of state of the Southern African Development Community (SADC) passed the Declaration on Gender and Development in Blantyre, Malawi in 1997 to increase women's representation at all levels of decision-making structures to 30 per cent by 2005. In 1999, a conference that the SADC Gender Department convened adopted an 'Action Plan for Women in Politics and Decision-Making in SADC' (Women in Development-Southern African Awareness 2000). Of 14 member countries of the SADC, only Mozambique (30 per cent) and South Africa (29.8 per cent) meet the 30 per cent expectation to date. At the regional level, no earnest and noticeable continent-wide effort has been made to increase women's representation in national governments.

Does a Critical Mass of Women in Parliament Make a Difference?

As Table 7.1 shows, although almost one half (49 per cent) of parliaments in sub-Saharan Africa have less than ten per cent women MPs, women in six African parliaments occupy more than 20 per cent of parliamentary seats. Does a critical mass of women in those parliaments have any significant impact on passing laws for women? To address this question, the study chooses Senegal, South Africa, Tanzania, and Uganda, where women account for 19.2 per cent, 29.8 per cent, 22.3 per cent, and 24.7 per cent of parliamentary seats, respectively. Women also occupy more than 20 per cent of legislative seats in Mozambique, Namibia, and Seychelles, but the data for these countries are unavailable. This study includes Senegal because its female legislative representation is close to 20 per cent.

Senegal

Female legislators formed *Le Reseau des Femmes Parlementaires*, a non-partisan network of female parliamentarians, to press for women's issues such as parental authority, outlawing female circumcision, and greater female representation in parliament. The collective work of female legislators and women's organizations led to the passage of the legislation that banned female circumcision in December 1998. Female members of parliament (MPs) freely express their views but do not have enough women to pass the laws they support because of their minority status in the legislature.

Similarly, women's concerns are difficult to prioritise because of women's poor representation in the parliamentary executive. Of eight vice presidents, one is female; of two treasuries, one is female; of six elected secretaries, three are women; and of 11 parliamentary committees, only one is led by a woman. Women legislators also lack unity for several reasons: female MPs from polygamous families do not agree with other female MPs on certain women's issues; some do not understand or are unable to analyze clearly the issues other female MPs press for because of the lack of education; and they sometimes have divergent interests.

South Africa

In the South African National Assembly, both the Speaker and the Deputy Speaker are women. Of 41 parliamentary committees, women chair ten (Parliament of South Africa 2003). Female MPs played a significant role in establishing the Parliamentary Committee on Improvement of Quality of Life and Status of Women and the Commission of Gender Equality. Since 1994, they have worked to pass dozens of laws that directly affect the lives of women. Examples of their legislative accomplishments include:

a) the ratification of the United Nations Convention for the Elimination of All Forms of Discrimination against Women;
b) the Termination of Pregnancy Act of 1997, which legalizes abortion;
c) the Domestic Violence Act of 1998, which criminalizes perpetrators and allows abused women to obtain a remedy;
d) the Labour Relations Act of 1996, which includes women's maternity rights and codes against sexual harassment in the work place;
e) the Customary Marriages Act of 1998, which grants customary marriage partners equal status as well as equal rights to property; and
f) the Equity Act of 1998, which bans discrimination in the work-place and mandates implementation of affirmative-action plans to employers (Parliamentary Joint Standing Committee on the Improvement of the Quality of Life and Status of Women 1999; Morna 1999).

To put the women's agenda forward, female MPs established the Parliamentary Women's Group within the National Assembly and women's caucuses within all nine provincial parliaments (Budlender *et al.*, 1999, p.38). They also formed women's caucuses within political parties (e.g., the African National Congress Parliamentary Women's Caucus). Women's caucuses have been instrumental in ensuring female legislators' views are reflected in setting priorities and drafting legislation (Budlender *et al.*, 1999, p.39).

However, female MPs also have been constrained by party disciplinary codes, sexism among male MPs, and the lack of professional skills needed for their jobs (MacGregor 2000, p.31). When their party's interests are different from the women's interests they are pressing for, it is difficult for them to oppose their party's positions (Van Donk and Maceba 1999, p.20). This constraint is more serious in list proportional representation systems, where candidates are elected on party lists and political parties decide who will be on their lists. South Africa uses a list proportional representation system for national legislative elections.

Tanzania

As is the case in other African countries, sexual violence against women has been one of the serious problems in Tanzania. In response to this problem, the parliament passed the Sexual Offences Special Provisions Act of 1998, 'which provides for life imprisonment for persons convicted of rape and child molestation' (Africa Online, *Gender Profiles: Tanzania*). To give women an equal right with men in land ownership, the parliament enacted the New Land Act of 1999 and the Village Land Act of 1999 (Social Watch 2001). Women parliamentarians and women's NGOs were instrumental in formulating and passing these laws (Morna 1999; Social Watch 2001).

As noted previously, an overwhelming majority of female MPs in Tanzania hold reserved seats. According to Killian (1996, p.22), recruitment methods for reserved seats for women 'limit the extent to which women are able to make a distinctive impact on gender-related public policy'. Under the new multi-party constitution, each political party nominates and ranks female candidates for women's special seats and elects a certain number of women on the basis of proportional representation among the political parties represented in the parliament (Killian 1996, p.28). These mechanisms, as in South Africa, reduce women MPs' ability to advocate women's interests different from those of their party.

Uganda

The Uganda Women Parliamentary Association (UWOPA), which includes all female MPs, made a significant contribution to adding Articles 32, 33, and 40 to the 1995 Constitution and to establishing the Ministry of Gender. Specifically, Article 32 stipulates the affirmative action in favor of groups marginalized on the basis of gender, age, disability or any other reasons. Article 33 addresses women's rights to equal treatment with men. Article 40 mandates women's right to maternity leave (Amongi 2002a). The UWOPA also played a vital role in passing the amendment that makes a rape a crime subject to capital punishment in the penal code and the amendment to the

Land Act of 1998 granting legally married women co-ownership of land with their husbands (Amongi 2002b).

The UWOPA has used diverse strategies to integrate women's issues in legislation and government policies. It has worked with gender-sensitive male MPs, has fought to place female MPs on parliamentary committees as chairpersons or as members and in executive positions of the several parliamentary caucuses, has lobbied for the appointment of more female ministers, and has formed a partnership with NGOs (Amongi 2002a). As a result of its efforts, women are relatively well represented in parliamentary executive positions. Women lead the Committee on Budgeting, the Committee on Social Services, and the Committee on Local Governments and Public Services as chairpersons. Women also serve the Committee on Legal and Parliamentary Affairs, the Committee on Natural Resources, and the Committee on Presidential and Foreign Affairs as deputy chairpersons. In 2004, UWOPA's priorities include passing the Domestic Relations Bill that deals with the issues of women's inheritance rights and the right to divorce. The Domestic Relations Bill faces much opposition from men because it includes domestic violence as one of the grounds for divorce.

Although female MPs have made some positive changes for women, according to Goetz (1998, p.249) and Amogi (2002a), only a small number of women MPs are truly committed to women's interests. For example, some female MPs elected in constituencies oppose women's issue bills such as the Domestic Relations Bill in order not to anger male voters in their constituencies (Amongi 2002a). On the other hand, female reserved-seat members lack independence in making legislative decisions. They tend to support President Yoweri Musevini's positions, because without his commitment to enhancing women's political representation, they would not be in the parliament. Therefore, ironically, the reserved-seat system established to improve women's representation in parliament has constrained women's capacity to influence legislative decision-making for women (Tripp 2000, p.25). Besides these constraints, most female MPs have difficulties in understanding parliamentary practices and procedures because of their lack of education and experience. For these reasons, many of them do not participate in parliamentary debates. They also experience discrimination and sexual harassment by male MPs, who do not perceive female MPs as serious about and capable of political business. Sometimes, male MPs caucus alone because they believe that women MPs do not have much to contribute. They also tend to dominate key decision-making because they are the majority (Amongi 2002b).

Conclusion

This study discussed the obstacles to women's legislative representation in sub-Saharan Africa and the strategies used to enhance women's representation with a brief historical overview of women's legislative representation in the region. It also examined the impact of a critical mass of women in parliament on legislative outcomes focusing on four cases where women occupy almost or more than 20 per cent of parliamentary seats. Women's legislative representation has improved since their first entry into the legislature, but has remained severely low. Women's unequal access to education, lack of financial resources, and domestic responsibilities as well as the male dominant culture, socialization, and the unfavourable electoral system have been the major barriers to women's full representation in parliament. Women's NGOs, political parties, and governments in some African countries have used various strategies to improve women's legislative representation and their strategies indeed have significantly contributed to improving women's representation in their legislatures.

It is difficult to assess how effectively a critical mass of female legislators represents women's interests, mainly because of the paucity of data. A critical mass of women has existed for such a short time period only in less than a dozen of African parliaments. Therefore, very little information is available for analysis. Nonetheless, the four cases examined in this study suggest a positive impact. The progress female MPs have made in those countries has been visible. Female MPs formed women's caucuses across party lines to put women's concerns on the agenda, have worked closely with women's NGOs, and have influenced their parliaments to pass laws for women. The laws against sexual violence, outlawing female genital mutilation, and the laws that grant women the right to own and inherit the land, to mention just some, might have not been possible without a critical mass of women in those parliaments.

However, those four cases also suggest that the number of female parliamentarians alone is not sufficient to make substantive changes in favour of women. The male dominant culture in both parliament and constituencies, female MPs' lack of understanding of parliamentary rules and procedures, the mechanisms used to increase women's legislative representation, domestic responsibilities, the minority status of women in parliament, and the language used for debates have negatively affected their effectiveness. Some parliaments in Southern Africa conduct business in English only. This practice undermines the efficiency of female MPs who lack proficiency in English (National Assembly of Malawi and UNESCO 1996, p.11). In addition, not all female MPs are committed to women's issues. The barriers women face in their path to parliament and in parliament will not easily disappear. However, the commitments of women's NGOs, some governments and political parties, and the SADC to greater representation of women in politics lead us to believe that women's legislative representation in sub-Saharan Africa is more likely to increase in the future. Thus, on the basis of preliminary findings, the study cautiously predicts that more laws will be enacted, amended, or repealed to improve the lives of women in sub-Saharan Africa, although it is uncertain how soon those laws will be implemented.

Chapter 8

Peru

Stéphanie Rousseau

Introduction

Within the Latin American region, Peru comes out as an example of the progress in women's representation in parliament, even if the gains have come only recently and remain fragile. As one of the dozen Latin American countries who have so far adopted quota legislation for elections at the national legislature, Peru offers an interesting case for exploring the political dynamics which can lead to such measures, the impact that Congresswomen have once elected, as well as practical lessons deriving from the experience of two elections where quotas have been used at the level of the legislature. Moreover, the deterioration of its democratic regime at the same time that women were entering the realm of electoral politics in greater numbers presents an interesting paradox.

A republic with a unitary state structure like the majority of Latin American countries, Peru has a presidential regime with a unicameral proportional representation electoral system with a preferential vote based on closed-lists for the members of the national Congress. Its political party system has been radically renewed since the early 1990s, with the demise of the democratic Left and the incapacity of traditional parties to retain public support in light of the multiple crises faced by Peruvian society at the time. Since the election of the political outsider Alberto Fujimori in 1990, the proliferation of political 'movements' – rather than parties in the strict sense of the term – has been the norm. Some of the older parties managed to survive, but the new political panorama was made only more difficult by the fact that the decade-long regime of President Alberto Fujimori (1990-2000) was characterized by a centralization of power in the hands of the executive and increasing control over the judiciary and the electoral authorities.

The greater presence of women in electoral politics is connected to a broader trend of women's participation in the political sphere, which can be traced back to the 1980s but has much more forcefully materialized in the second half of the 1990s. Peruvian women decided to enter the realm of institutional politics in greater numbers in a period when the regime in place – that of Fujimori – was neither democratic nor purely authoritarian, which is why analysing their experience generates interesting questions on the relationship between democracy and women's parliamentary representation. This new political protagonism corresponded to a strategy of relatively powerful women's organizations in civil society to invest in the formal political terrain. It was also facilitated by the fact that the Fujimori regime was willing to build a political constituency among women and be seen as a modern leader promoting women's participation. As a result of the social-structural changes of the preceding decades, a greater availability of well-educated, professional women looking for leadership positions only made it more feasible, especially in a context where women had gained a positive reputation as social leaders taking care of their communities.

The claim of this chapter is that Peruvian women have been able to gain greater access to electoral politics and parliamentary representation because of a coincidence of interests between the women's movement and the government of Fujimori, in the context of a very limited democratic regime with strong authoritarian features (Levitsky and Way, 2002). A second point which will be made is that even a modest number of women in parliament can have positive repercussions on the advancement of women's rights when there is a balance of forces in civil society and within the State that allow for such progress to be made. Peruvian political culture has made significant leaps in less than a decade in how it portrays and values women's political contribution, which also plays a significant part in the story.

The main features of the contemporary Peruvian political process, particularly Alberto Fujimori's regime in the last decade, will first be summarized to present the framework in which women's entry into institutional politics and the strategies they have put forward have unfolded. A summary of Peruvian women's history of political participation will follow and the main facilitating factors and obstacles to greater gender equality in parliamentary representation will be presented. This will allow for an explanation of the dynamics behind women's use of political channels and institutions to further their agenda of legislative reforms in favour of women's rights. Some discussion of the Fujimori regime's interest in promoting women's access to the public sphere will be made. Finally, there will be an assessment of the space taken by women in Congress, with examples of some of their legislative victories, to conclude on the paradoxes of women's advances in the troubled political panorama of the 1990s in Peru.

Fujimori's Peru

Contrary to most countries in the region which were led by reactionary, right-wing military regimes from the late 1960s up to the mid-1980s, Peru had a reformist military regime taking over in 1968 and leading the country's modernization and social reforms until the creation of the first full-fledged democratic regime with universal suffrage in 1980. The mobilization of popular sectors and parties of the Left grew significantly during that period, in part because of the military regime's explicit policy of promoting lower classes' organization in the first half of its rule. The eventual exhaustion of the economic model implemented by the reformists, pressure from conservative sectors, the more radical and independent Leftist organizations and some of the regime's own social base, led to the end of military rule in 1980. The Left and socially progressive sectors had a critical or ambivalent view of what they called 'bourgeois democracy' at that time. Yet the majority of the Peruvian Left accepted to play by the new rules of the game in the 1980s and actually managed to perform very well in municipal and national elections, enough so that Peru was seen in those days as one of the rare Latin American countries where the Left had some capacity of winning control over the state through electoral means. Yet acute divisions within the Democratic Left, the growing strength of violent Maoist and Guevarist guerillas and an unprecedented economic crisis all led to the collapse of the party system in the late 1980s-early 1990s and to a profound crisis of governance. It is in this context that Alberto Fujimori was elected democratically in 1990 (McClintock and Lowenthal, 1983; Cameron and Mauceri,1997).

A political outsider leading a 'party' with no roots in society, Fujimori won by appealing to the poorest sectors of Peru through a populist discourse and false promises of not engaging the country in a neoliberal structural adjustment process. The Peruvian state in the early 1990s was close to collapsing, paralysed by a political dead-end with the strength and intensity of insurgent attacks now reaching the capital Lima. The political class was unable to manage its conflicts to face the causes and consequences of violent Leftist mobilization. Soon after being elected, Fujimori created an alliance with the military and the secret police and perpetrated what has been labelled a 'self-coup' (*auto-golpe*), closing down the Congress in 1992, rewriting the Constitution and organizing elections for a Constituent Assembly that were held without the majority of opposition parties and with low voter turn-out. This period saw drastic security and military operations, enlarged powers given to secret services, control of the executive over the judiciary, as well as the implementation of a structural adjustment program which hit the poorest but managed to put the economy back on track (Roberts, 1995; Tuesta Soldevilla, 1999).

Fujimori's grip on power did not end with his re-election in 1995. Many attributed his second victory to his ability to control insurgent violence and redress the economy, but also to the opposition's incapacity to organize itself efficiently. The crisis was substantially resolved as his second term began, thus making it difficult for the regime to sustain itself only on the basis of the same discourse of fear and memories of hunger. The constitution drafted by Fujimori in 1993 did not allow for a third consecutive presidential term. But as his second term unfolded, Fujimori imposed in a blatantly authoritarian fashion his willingness to run for a third time. First, the three judges of the Supreme Court who opposed his unconstitutional candidacy were dismissed by the executive in clear violation of the principle of independence of the judiciary. Then, control over the judiciary and the electoral institutions by the executive was reinforced. The majority of the media became instruments in the hands of Fujimori's government, through blackmail or negotiated deals between media owners and the regime. The few independent press that remained received regular threats and was pointed out by regime authorities as radical and potentially pro-terrorist. The authoritarian nature of the regime became all the more obvious, partly because of but also leading to the opposition in civil society and in the party system recovering some of its capacity to voice dissent and mobilize in the late 1990s.

The electoral process in 2000 reflected the legalistic façade and corruption on which the regime was based. The greater scandal involved the revelations by witnesses that Fujimori's party had organised a 'manufacture' for forging signatures in order to meet the requirements to register as an official party running for office. But due to some organisations in civil society, some key political opposition figures, and the active presence of international electoral observers, Fujimori's intent on keeping power failed a few months after supposedly fraudulent electoral results had been imposed. Alberto Fujimori and Vladimiro Montesinos, the head of the secret services, both flew out of the country in disgrace. The Congress elected in 2000 had very little legitimacy and the government parliamentary group soon fragmented in light of the public revelations of the buying off of some Congress members by Montesinos. This allowed opposition Congress members to lead the transition by first appointing one of them as transitional President. New elections were held in June 2001 and power was transferred to the new President Alejandro Toledo and to a new Congress.

Women in Peruvian Political Life

Peru is one of the Latin American countries where women were granted political rights the latest, in 1955. As points of comparison, Ecuador granted the right to vote to women in 1929, Brazil in 1932, Argentina in 1947, Mexico in 1953. Early on at the beginning of the twentieth century, small feminist groups such as Evolución Femenina, led by a few intellectual women, challenged the common belief in women's inferiority and claimed the need to grant women access to education and employment. Their demands included equal civil and political rights, of which equal suffrage rights were central. Women's suffrage rights were also discussed within the Constituent Assembly of 1932, as part of the debate between the landowning oligarchy and the workers. The APRA party (Alianza Popular Revolucionaria Americana) presented a law project in 1931 to extend suffrage to illiterate people and to working class women, making a clear distinction between the women who were part of the working class and therefore had a legitimate right to participate politically, and those 'bourgeois' women who were influenced by their husbands and the Church. The struggle went on for years between conservative and labor sectors on the legitimacy of broadening suffrage rights to include women and/or to the illiterate population, in what was perceived by each sector as a way to gain more votes, rather than a genuine concern for equality (Villar, 1994).

Peruvian President General Manuel Odria finally decided to give literate women the right to vote in 1955. This move did not correspond to a sustained struggle by an organized women's movement to demand suffrage, but rather to an opportunistic political calculation on the part of a dictator who wanted to legitimize his power (Villar, 1994). At that time only literate males over 21 had the right to vote. As could be expected, the majority of the population was illiterate by then, and within this group, women formed the majority. Most literate women in fact belonged to elite families that were usually supportive of the oligarchic regime.

The first women parliamentarians were elected in 1956, one to the Senate and eight to the Chamber of Representatives. In 1963, this number was reduced to two, for no reason other than the limited participation of women by that time. Again at the Constituent Assembly elections of 1979, only two women got elected (Villar, 1994, pp. 51-2). Then at every elections since 1980 up to and including the ones held in 1995, women managed to win between six per cent and eleven per cent of the parliamentary seats (Promujer, 1998, p.30; Movimiento Manuela Ramos, 1996, p.26; Foromujer, 1995, p. 18). At the time of the self-coup in 1992, four out of 60 Senators (6.7 per cent) were women, and twelve out of 180 deputies (6.7 per cent). At the election of the Constituent Congress of 1992 they got only 8.8 per cent of the seats. The new 1993 Constitution created a single Congress, thus eliminating the bicameral system. This institutional change did not affect significantly the prospects for women to win seats, since they represented 10.8 per cent of the 120 Congress members in the 1995-2000 legislature.

In terms of women's participation in the lists of candidates, their numbers actually decreased slightly between 1980 and the first half of the 1990s. For the Senate, there were almost 15 per cent of women candidates in the 1980 and 1985 elections, whereas in 1990 it lowered to 12 per cent. For the Chamber of Representatives, in 1980 15.7 per cent of the candidates for the Lima department were women, and in 1990 they were 16.9 per cent, which compensated a little for the decrease in the Senate. Yet in 1995, about 13 per cent of the candidates for the unicameral Congress were women (Foromujer, 1995, pp.19-20). No specific policy was adopted by any party to position women candidates favourably in the lists, and as a result, except for some very popular individual women, the majority of them were actually not running in a 'winner' position.

The second half of the 1990s saw a breakthrough in women's participation in institutional and electoral politics. Their numerical presence more than doubled at the Congress in 2000. To be more precise, in 1995 the lists of candidates to the Congress included 12.4 per cent of women, with 10.8 per cent of the seats ending up being held by a female Congress member. In contrast, in the 2000 legislative elections, 26 per cent of candidates were female, and 21.6 per cent of the seats were filled by women. In the 2001 legislative elections, 36 per cent of the candidates were women, a significant increase, but the number of elected women declined to 18 per cent of the seats, mainly because of significant changes made in the electoral system. At the municipal elections of 1998, 25 per cent of candidates were female, and about 25 per cent got elected. This contrasted with the preceding results whereby women formed only 9.7 per cent of the municipal authorities after the 1995-1996 elections (Promujer, 1998, p.131).

An important explanation for the notable increase in women's parliamentary representation is to be found in the 'quota laws' approved by the Congress in 1997. Among the dozen of women elected in the 1995 Congress, some of them are to be especially credited for these legislative victories, although as we will see further, other variables played a key role. The 'quota laws' are in fact two different sets of clauses introduced in the electoral laws regulating elections at the national and municipal levels, which made mandatory a minimum of 25 per cent of female or male candidates in the party lists for the Congress and municipal elections, increased to 30 per cent in 2000. As such, these legislative measures have played an important role in increasing the number of women elected, not to mention of course the number of women who participate as candidates, since so far the electoral supervisory body and political parties have abided by the quotas in the electoral processes which took place in 1998 (at the municipal level), 2000 and 2001.

The first nominations of women to the cabinet date back to the APRA government of Alan García (1985-1990), with two women being appointed minister, one Minister of Education and the other Minister of Health (Vargas and Olea, 1997, p.32). In 1998, during the second mandate of Alberto Fujimori, women represented 22.7 per cent of the total of deputy ministers, while only one woman was minister (7.14 per cent). At the beginning of 1999, Fujimori made an historic move by appointing a woman to each of the portfolios of Justice, Women and Human Development, and the Ministry of the Presidency, and accounting for 20 per cent of cabinet ministries. In 2003, in the new government of Alejandro Toledo, one woman headed the ministry of Women and Human Development, while another held the prestigious and powerful position of President of the Council of Ministers.

Facilitating Factors and Obstacles to Greater Gender Balance in Congress

In addition to the mandatory quotas, some factors can be identified that explain the relatively better performance of women as candidates in recent years. One such factor seems to be the evolution of public opinion in favour of women politicians. Women's role in the public sphere as administrators, political representatives, and leaders of social organizations, has become increasingly accepted and valued by Peruvians. Surveys in the late 1990s have shown that, especially within the capital Lima where one third of all Peruvians live, women were seen as having as much to offer or even more than men in terms of public leadership and responsibilities (Blondet, 1999a; Alfaro, 1998; Calandria, 2000). This may explain why the quota laws have received a high level of popular support. In a survey commissioned by the non-governmental organization Calandria in 1998, 75.6 per cent of the population approved them, while in 2000 80.9 per cent indicated their support (Calandria, 2000, p.20). These figures show not only that Peruvians see women's contribution to political affairs as valuable, but that the intervention of the State is legitimate or necessary to provide women with greater access to political office.

Generally speaking, regular surveys since 1996 have revealed a constant increase in the percentage of Peruvians supporting women's active role in politics and measures to promote gender equality (Calandria, 2000). That support is so strong that, for the first time in Peruvian history, a woman running as presidential candidate in the 2001 elections got very close to winning. Lourdes Flores Nano, a distinguished career politician, came within one per cent of the second most favoured candidate, former President Alan García. Many later argued that, had she taken part in the run-off elections, she would have won over President Toledo and would have been the first Latin American woman to win a presidential election based on her own merits and not on family connections to famous male politicians.

An interesting observation emerging from the Peruvian case is that some of the traditional gender characteristics attributed to women have in fact become one of the basis for supporting their contribution to political leadership. In a context where politicians in general were perceived to be corrupt, authoritarian, lazy and self-centered, electing women became perceived as a worthy alternative. When asked to compare male and female mayors, respondents in a survey in 1998 indicated that while men work more and are more efficient, women are more honest, loyal, just and sensitive to social and human issues (Alfaro, 1998, pp.24-5).

The mothering and caring characteristics which the average Peruvian values in women were seen as necessary to clean up the political sphere and provide more trustworthy political leadership. Seeing women and men as having different attributes and political skills did, in this case, lead to favorable public opinion towards women's involvement in political affairs, even if some prominent women played a key role within the corrupt web of the Fujimori regime. On the other hand, public polls have also revealed that in Lima, there is a general 'spirit of equality and respect for gender equity ... which reflects a process of modernization of citizenship'(Alfaro, 1997, p.29). However, gender roles and responsibilities in the household remain traditional and unequal, even if this is also changing with the youngest generation (Alfaro, 1998b, p.27).

These findings would seem to nuance the argument put forward by Pippa Norris and Ronald Inglehart according to which 'there are substantial differences in attitudes toward women's leadership in postindustrial, postcommunist, and developing societies'; 'traditional attitudes are a major barrier to the election of women in parliament'; and 'as a result of the process of modernization and value change, these cultural barriers have been fading most rapidly among younger generations in postindustrial societies' (Norris and Inglehart, 2001, p.132). What these authors claim is that traditional culture would be the main explanatory factor for the low level of women's representation in elected legislatures. Yet in light of the above, we can see that traditional attitudes towards gender roles in the household are not necessarily contrary to a culture that favours women's equal access to the political sphere, even if based on distinct gender attributes. Moreover, cultural change may be more rapid than predicted by the indicators of economic development and democratization, considering that younger generations in Peru are more favorable to gender equality in the household and in public life, thus revealing similar patterns of generational attitudinal change in developing countries – at least some of them – and postindustrial societies.

If some features of the Peruvian political system clearly present obstacles to women seeking political office, others are more ambiguous or even favorable to a fuller inclusion of women. One noticeable feature of Peruvian politics in the 1990s was the lack of internal democratic elections for filling positions within most political parties, and the absence of legal requirements in that regard. As there was no legislation regulating political parties up to 2003, parties were generally devoid of regular procedures for selecting their internal authorities as well as their candidates, not to mention the lack of mechanisms to control party finances and spending. Very often since the early 1990s, political parties or 'movements' were created for an election and disappeared or changed drastically when the next election was called. The phenomenon of the 'political outsider', represented most forcefully by Alberto Fujimori, became the norm in Peruvian politics in the 1990s. As a result, politicians invested very little in the institutionalization of the political organization which they created mainly to pursue their political ambitions rather than to follow a political platform endorsed by a wide membership. The selection of candidates was a process guided by informal criteria rather than established, democratic mechanisms. No accountability mechanisms existed within parties. In that context, it is not surprising that no political party has so far implemented on its own initiative a program to promote women's active participation as candidates, or women's greater access to parties' internal positions.

In terms of the electoral system, the double preferential vote with closed party lists which has been in place since the creation of the unicameral Congress in 1993 seems to have encouraged women's electoral success. This system allows voters to select, among the list of the party that they support, up to two individual candidates to which they give their 'preferential vote', irrespective of the particular position which these candidates occupy in the list. The greater number of preferential votes a candidate obtains, the more likely he or she is to get a seat from the total number of seats given to each party according to the percentage of total votes the party received. This system in effect renders positioning in the list not exclusively important for a candidate's likelihood of being elected, although the prestige associated with occupying the first ten or twenty ranks may have an impact on some voters' choices.

In the 2000 elections, the double preferential voting system allowed 16 women to be elected to a position higher than the one they were assigned in their party list, but it also resulted in ten women being elected to positions lower than the one they occupied in the list. Overall then, it would seem that the preferential voting system allows voters to bypass the ranking determined by political party leaderships, expressing a higher support for some women candidates than that given by their parties. However, a high proportion of voters did not use the opportunity to cast one or two preferential votes, as it remained optional. They limited their choice to the party in general. In the end, therefore, the order of the lists often determined who got a seat. In that regard, the statistics for the 2000 elections reveal that parties were still not very inclined to grant women a proportion of the winner positions equal to their proportion of candidates, that is 25 per cent. In 2000, the first 10 positions of all parties' lists – out of 120 – had 17 per cent of women, and the first 20 positions had 18.5 per cent of women. The majority of women, that is 59 per cent, were positioned in the last half of the lists (El Cuarto Feminino, 2000, pp. 4-5).

Another important aspect to consider in the Peruvian electoral system is the single national electoral district which was put in place with the 1993 Constitution, which created a unicameral Congress. The electoral reform introduced in 2001 maintained the unicameral Congress but abolished the single national district and reintroduced the multiple, department-based districts. Prior to 1993, the Senate was elected according to a single national district, whereas the Chamber of Representatives was elected according to departmental districts, thus providing for regional representation. Aside from the clear centralizing effect of the installation of a parliament without regional representation in the 1993 Constitution, it is interesting to see what consequence this had on women's electoral opportunities.

The impact seems to have been null in the context where there was no quota law such as during the 1995 elections, as the number of elected women remained as low but constant. However, comparing the 2000 and 2001 elections provides another perspective. The effect of the 2001 electoral reform is noticeable since the number of women elected went down from 26 in 2000 to 22 in 2001, with the total number of

Congressional seats remaining the same. Considering that 11 per cent more women ran as candidates in 2001 compared to 2000 (36 per cent versus 25 per cent), this difference in the results cannot totally be disconnected from the change in the electoral system. Some early explanations provided by Peruvian analysts point to the lower level of women's leadership and the greater prevalence of traditional gender roles outside of Lima, which would make voters less likely to support women candidates in their district. The findings in the literature on the correlation between greater district magnitude and better opportunities for women to be elected seem to be confirmed by this case (Rule, 1994).

Women's Strategies and Political Institutions

The high level of public approval of women's contribution to public affairs can be explained in great part by Peruvian women's massive entry into social organizations from the early 1980s onwards. Faced with the need to respond to the basic necessities of their family and community, lower class women have created grassroots organizations to maximize the use of scarce resources and the time they spend in attending these needs. As successful organizations and networks emerged around survival activities like the preparation and delivery of meals, they gradually claimed greater recognition from the state as well as material support. Parallel to that, non-governmental organizations (NGOs) funded by international aid have increasingly taken a central role in the social and political life of Peru because of the weakness of state institutions and the lack of state resources in attending social needs. Women have always been key players in that process, and the first feminist groups of the 1970s grew into sophisticated and relatively powerful NGOs with wide national and international networks.

The end of the 1980s and the 1990s saw this process of consolidation of women's NGOs together with a shift in feminist practice and discourse, focussing increasingly on formulating policy proposals, using legal strategies and engaging state institutions in addressing women's needs and rights. The agenda and resources of international aid agencies, which are the main and sometimes the only source of financial support for the various women's NGOs, contributed to this new orientation. The development of the international human rights agenda, including the recognition that 'women's rights are human rights' at the international level through the World Conference on Human Rights in 1993 and the World Conference on Women in 1995, also provided tools and frameworks used by Latin American women to articulate their demands and strategies.

Women's decision to invest in the mainstream political scene and call on state institutions to address their claims is a general trend which has taken place throughout Latin America in the 1990s (Rodríguez, 1998). In the case of Peru, this move can be traced back to 1990 when Foro-Mujer (Woman's Forum) was created. A forum made up of six women's non-governmental organizations, Foro-Mujer was born to address explicitly the question of women's political participation. It became a focal point for the elaboration and development of strategies for increasing women's access to politics. The efforts of Foro-Mujer led to the creation of the first inter-party coalition of Congresswomen in 1991, but the political turmoil in which the country was enmeshed at the time did not facilitate any type of sustained coordination between them. The coalition aimed at advancing certain issues which were identified as key for improving women's status, but the self-coup of 1992 destroyed this initial impetus with the dissolution of the Parliament by President Fujimori. Yet Foro-Mujer continued to function until 1995 as a non-governmental and non-partisan consortium dedicated to promoting women's political participation. It organized a 'Campaign of Women for a Vote of Conscience' around the referendum on the Constitution drafted by Fujimori in 1993, raising the fact that this new Constitution erased some key articles promoting women's equality.

Foro-Mujer was the first to propose that a quota system be included in a law on political parties, that would make mandatory a minimum of 30 per cent of female candidates in the lists for internal party elections as well as for general elections at the municipal and national levels. The initiative was presented to the Constituent Congress in March 1994 but did not receive enough support to become legislation at that time. The forum disappeared after the 1995 elections because of divergent views within the member organizations. One of the latter, the Movimiento Manuela Ramos, one of the pioneer and largest women's organizations, continued the work by creating a monthly newsletter for members of Congress at the time of the installation of the Congress elected in 1995. The objective was to circulate information on women's issues, promote legislative proposals and educate members of Congress so that they would be willing to take on legislative initiatives that addressed women's claims and points of view. The newsletter generated sustained interest on specific legislative initiatives directly connected to the agenda of the women's movement, especially among a group of Congresswomen.

The World Conference on Women took place in Beijing, China, a few months after the installation of the Congress in 1995. A number of Peruvian Congresswomen participated either with the official government delegation or at the parallel NGO meeting. As a result of the discussions which took place, a few Congresswomen came back to Peru with new ideas in mind, such as the creation of a Permanent Congressional Commission on Women. Proposed by Beatriz Merino, a prominent opposition member, and supported by most Congresswomen, this Commission rapidly became an important vehicle for women's collaboration and legislative innovation. It was the first Commission to organize public hearings inside and outside of Congress, which allowed Congresswomen to make contacts with various organizations and individuals in civil society. It invited experts and stakeholders in order to give profile to its legislative initiatives and develop more solid arguments to defend them in plenary assembly.

The quotas included in national and municipal electoral laws were also a topic of interest at the Beijing Conference, to the point that it was included in the Declaration and Program of Action adopted by the participating member States. This inspired some of the Peruvian Congresswomen who were present, and reinforced the case made by women from civil society who had lobbied for such measure to be discussed at the Congress. The legislative measure presented by Congresswoman Lourdes Flores Nano in 1995 launched the debate which lasted two years before leading to the adoption of the quota.

The Fujimori Regime's Interest in 'Promoting' Women

A central part of the puzzle to understand women's advances in the mainstream political sphere in the 1990s is the favorable attitude of the highest political authorities, starting with the President himself. The Fujimori regime, in need of political support to maintain its power amidst growing opposition, put forward a strategy to develop its popularity among women as of 1995. The steps taken by Fujimori to create an image of leading a 'women-friendly' regime coincided with the international momentum created by the Beijing Conference, but were fundamentally connected to the need for the regime to develop new support bases. In fact, a number of women had already started to play key roles as spokespersons defending the regime from its initial days. This is particularly true of a little group of Congresswomen who had become central to the Fujimori regime's image (Blondet, 1999b; 2002). The main ideas conveyed by these politicians were the need to protect the nation against terrorism, which they often mixed with indiscriminate accusations against the Left in general, the discrediting of traditional political parties, and the emphasis on the paternalistic figure of Fujimori as a provider of food aid and security to the majority of poor women.

The period 1995-1996 corresponded to some kind of 'honeymoon' between women and the Fujimori regime, although the majority of women's organizations remained cautious in their willingness to collaborate with it. Right after the 1995 elections, Fujimori attracted the attention of the women's movement by being the only president to attend the closing session of the Beijing World Conference on Women, and making a speech in favour of women and the importance of family planning. A few months later, another surprise occurred when Fujimori came back from an international meeting with donors in Germany and announced the creation of a Ministry of Women's Affairs and Human Development, the first of its kind in Latin America. In the same period, a national policy on family planning was launched and the Ministry of Health introduced for the first time a range of contraceptive methods within the services offered by public health clinics, amongst which were free tubal ligation or vasectomy surgery. The gender quotas to be inserted into the electoral laws were also supported by the President.

Yet this strategy of buying women's support by granting them greater presence within the state and political institutions was overshadowed by a number of scandals which revealed the true nature of Fujimori's 'feminism'. The most brutal was the revelation of the existence of incentives for public health clinics to perform a certain number of tubal sterilization surgeries. Some of the women who went through surgery died because of deficient medical care, others complained of having been pressured into the operation, or of not having been informed that they would be sterilized immediately after a caesarian section. Another major area where women's rights were violated consisted in the political manipulation of state-provided food aid programs, especially during electoral campaigns. Threats, blackmail and gifts were used by public servants to coerce lower class women into voting for Fujimori and his party. In light of these abuses, a gradual yet increasing process of mobilization of women in civil society who denounced the regime's authoritarianism became one of the features of the opposition to the Fujimori regime through organizations such as Mujeres por la Democracia (Women for Democracy) and the Movimiento Amplio de Mujeres (literally, Large Movement of Women).

This opposition developed in parallel with continuing efforts by some organizations in the women's movement to promote women's political participation. Movimiento Manuela Ramos and four other NGOs joined under the Project Promujer (Pro-Woman) financed by the United States Agency for International Development (USAID), which started in 1998 around the municipal elections and continued as of 2001. Promujer sought to promote women's political participation by disseminating information around gender quotas, monitoring their implementation by electoral bodies and political parties, providing assistance and training to women candidates, lobbying for a women's agenda in the Congress, and educating the population about the importance of gender equality in public affairs.

Promujer took a protagonist role by launching public campaigns in favor of voting for women candidates, and raising public attention in favour of the quotas. It became a resource center for political parties who looked desperately for women candidates at the time of making up their lists, and for women who looked for parties with which to run for elections. Yet Promujer and its activities were soon accused of contributing to legitimizing a regime which was under serious attack especially from 1997 onwards when Fujimori's intention to run for a third term was confirmed. Increased tensions emerged within the women's movement, as some organizations that were not part of the Promujer project opposed the fact of promoting women's electoral participation for the 2000 elections in a context where the conditions for the holding of genuine democratic elections did not prevail.

The Congress elected in the controversial elections of 2000 was initially led by four women, in an unprecedented move by the regime to try to give legitimacy to an otherwise questionable electoral result. In this context, some prominent Peruvian women were quoted as saying that 'it's better to have four authoritarian women than four authoritarian men', a somewhat shocking yet very revealing statement (cited in Vargas, 2000, p.3). This statement mirrored some of the discourse used in the years around and following the passing of the quota law, which emphasized the ethical integrity of women's leadership. The contradiction was evident when the nomination of these Congresswomen was so directly used for the regime's desperate attempt to keep hold of power. The victory of seeing so many women at the top of the Congress was a bitter one, and indeed it was seen by some feminists as another development likely to lead to a backlash against women politicians among the sectors who were critical of the regime.

Women at the Congress under Fujimori

The increase in the number of elected women in Congress as of 2000 did not have a measurable repercussion on the legislative agenda because of the political turmoil generated by the fraudulent elections, the subsequent escape of Fujimori and Montesinos, and the installation of a transitional government at the end of 2000. The

Congress elected in 2000 was abrogated and lasted only one year, and as such was totally absorbed by the tasks involved in investigating and sanctioning the corrupt authorities of the Fujimori regime. In the 1995-2000 legislature though, even a small number of women in Congress made a difference in developing innovative legislative advances regarding women's rights. The combination of the activism of some of these Congresswomen with the support from women's organizations and the space granted by the regime for some issues led to significant steps being taken to advance the agenda of women's rights.

A strong constraint under the Fujimori regime was that the government party exercised a very tight control over the Congress, not hesitating to redesign parliamentary procedures, or interpret them in a very questionable fashion, in order to maintain full powers over the legislative process. Through constant control over the nomination of the presidents of all the specialized Commissions with legislative authority, the government party limited significantly the impact that opposition members could have within the Congress. This did not, however, influence negatively on Congresswomen as women, as shown for example by the fact that some women were appointed as President of the Congress. It did, however, complicate the procedures for some legislative initiatives to be approved, because of the fact that most often the legislative initiatives that were approved were those proposed by a member of the government party. Opposition Congresswomen understood the game and accepted that some of their key legislative proposals would be repackaged and proposed again by members of Congress from the government side, in order to see their agenda on women's rights be implemented to the greatest extent possible.

The creation of the Comisión de la Mujer (Commission on Women) of the Congress in October 1995 came from a motion presented by several Congresswomen from both opposition and government parties. Not all Congresswomen became active within it – in fact not all of them could be appointed to it at the same time because of the limited number of seats – and a few of them actually became strong critics. The Commission was initially created as a special Commission without the authority to present legislative initiatives, but after one year of impressive work, it was granted full authority as a regular Permanent Commission of the Congress, with Members of Congress appointed from both opposition and government parties. While it did not reach the level of prominence that the Finance Commission or the Commission on the Constitution always enjoyed, the Commission on Women managed to become a central instrument for those Congresswomen and some women in civil society who sought to advance the women's movement's legislative agenda.

Among the laws which resulted from the work of Congresswomen, those creating electoral gender quotas are the most symbolic. These were discussed within the many projects to reform the electoral code presented by various Members of Congress in 1995 and 1996. Of the 39 reforms discussed by the Commission on the Constitution, four included some clauses establishing quotas for parliamentary lists. Two of these were projects presented by female members of Congress, the other two by male members of Congress. When the Commission rendered its opinion, it recommended adopting a measure which did not introduce quotas (a proposal from a Congresswoman from Fujimori's party, Martha Chávez). At the time of the discussion in plenary in

1997, Chávez tried to sustain her proposal by discrediting the opinion of the Commission on Women on the matter, which prompted a lively discussion resulting in the adoption of a clause included in the measure presented by an opposition Congresswoman, Lourdes Flores Nano. The latter proposal had the advantage of introducing a gender-blind quota through establishing a required minimum of candidates in both sexes, thus bypassing the critics saying that the notion of quota was discriminatory. The adopted legislation however set the quota to 25 per cent, which was the base-line advocated by the government party, and not 30 per cent as stated in the legislative initiatives presented by opposition members of Congress.

The modification of the Penal Code was another central objective pursued by the women's movement from the late 1980s onwards, as it identified serious problems relating to the definition of the crime of rape, the status of women as victims of rape and sexual violence, and the responsibility of the State in protecting victims and punishing perpetrators. An early reform in 1991 provided some corrections, yet some important areas were left untouched. One such area was the existence of a norm that absolved a perpetrator of rape from penal sanction if he subsequently married the victim. A reform presented by Beatriz Merino in March 1996 sought to eradicate such a norm and was finally adopted in April 1997. Another significant modification of the penal code introduced the obligation for public prosecution in cases of sexual violence. Prior to this, the prosecution of rapists was left to the victims themselves. Two legislative initiatives were presented by opposition Congresswomen Beatriz Merino and Ana-Elena Townsend in 1998. A law was adopted in May 1999 as a result of an extensive campaign jointly run by feminist NGOs, women in key positions in the State and the media, and the Congresswomen who put the proposal forward, together with Members of Congress who were sitting on the Comisión de la Mujer, headed during that period by a women from the government side (Dador, 2000).

Conclusion

This chapter has shown that the presence of women in the Peruvian Congress in the last decade has delivered positive results in terms of legislative initiatives in favour of women's rights, notably on the question of introducing gender quotas for legislative and municipal elections. The number of women elected was not so relevant for these advances as much as the institutional weight they have been able to achieve through the Commission on Women at the Congress. Moreover, it seems that an equally crucial factor was the strength of organized women in civil society, which was manifest in the expertise and networks which women in non-governmental organizations used strategically throughout the 1990s. The resources that women's organizations mobilized in support of and parallel to Congresswomen's own efforts were facilitated by the availability of international funding and the pressure set by worldwide women's rights activists. Last but not least, the willingness of the Fujimori government to use women as an object and subject for political support and legitimacy is also fundamental in explaining women's political and legislative advances in Peru.

However, the Fujimori regime was not devoid of dangers for women participating in politics. To mention only a few of the dilemmas and difficulties involved, the critical distance which some sectors of the women's movement had to take increasingly to oppose the arbitrary, corrupt and authoritarian features of the regime generated tensions. The project Promujer, dedicated to promoting women's political participation, came to be seen as an irresponsible or at least highly questionable move by a sector of the women's NGOs. The division raised by Promujer within the women's movement highlighted the question of the validity of promoting a greater political participation of women in political institutions within a relatively authoritarian context. What was at stake was whether it was meaningful to promote the participation of all women candidates from all parties, when some were clearly the advocates and supporters of an authoritarian regime, and more generally whether it was worth at all supporting political participation in an electoral process that was clearly not fair nor free. Women's greater inclusion in the political sphere and the democratization of the political system in general experienced some temporary divorce in Peru, yet most of the advances remain in the current post-Fujimori regime.

Chapter 9

United Kingdom

Fiona Mackay

Introduction

Until recently, the UK has been presented as a textbook case of a highly centralised unitary state. A parliamentary system, its representatives are elected under a simple plurality system and governments are formed from the majority party in the parliament.[1] The polity is characterised by single-party government, executive dominance of the legislature, and adversarial two-party politics. Within this framework, women have traditionally fared poorly: the UK has had one of the worst records in terms of female representation in parliament

However, the political system of the UK has recently undergone rapid change with far-reaching constitutional and institutional restructuring. By far the most important developments are the creation of devolved legislatures in Scotland and Northern Ireland and a devolved assembly in Wales in the late 1990s. As a result substantial power has been devolved from the centre to the sub-state level and Britain has moved from being a highly centralised unitary state to a quasi-federal model of governance. Another defining – but under-reported – feature of this reconfiguration of the political landscape has been the historic shift that has occurred in terms of the gendered distribution of political power. The first elections to the new devolved institutions in Scotland and Wales resulted in a gender coup with high levels of female representation at 37 per cent and 42 per cent respectively – all the more dramatic given the poor track record of the UK. In Northern Ireland, although women make up a relatively modest 14 per cent of assembly members, this represents a considerable improvement upon past records in the Province. The second Welsh and Scottish elections in 2003 broke new ground. In Wales women achieved their goal of equal representation, taking up 50 per cent of the seats in the National Assembly for Wales – believed to be a world first. In Scotland, women edged closer to the top of global league tables and now make up 39.5 per cent of members of the Scottish Parliament (Mackay, 2003).The implications for women and politics from these moves towards a multi-level polity form a key theme of this chapter.

Political System Past and Present

Before focussing upon the gender dimensions of the UK case, we first provide more institutional context. Textbook simplicity has masked a more complex institutional reality. The UK is perhaps more accurately classified as a Union state (Rokkan and Urwin, 1982; Holliday, 1999) rather than a unitary state because, although domestic sovereignty is formally concentrated in the Westminster Parliament, political and administrative structures have always existed in the constituent parts of the UK. That reality has become yet more complicated since devolution. This complexity is illustrated by developments in the electoral system where we see a move from relative electoral uniformity to one of variation. Elections to different levels of government in mainland Britain have traditionally been conducted by 'first past the post' contests for single constituency seats: a single-member simple plurality majoritarian electoral system. However since the election of a Labour government in 1997, a number of new systems have been implemented and other reforms proposed. At time of writing (2003), elections at national UK and local government levels were still conducted by plurality.

The Scottish Parliament and National Assembly for Wales, elected for the first time in 1999, uses a modified majoritarian system, the Additional Member System (AMS). Under AMS a certain proportion of single member constituency seats are elected using FPTP and a certain proportion of seats, known as List or Additional Members, are allocated through a regional party list system to achieve greater proportionality in terms of the relationship between party support and number of seats gained. This system is similar to those operating in Germany and New Zealand. The Northern Ireland Assembly, created in 1998, is elected using the Single Transferable Vote similar to that in the Republic of Ireland (see chapter 6). The elections to the Parliament of the European Union were conducted using a party list system with multi-member constituencies for the first time in 1999. This presents the current complex framework within which the political recruitment process takes place in contemporary Britain and suggests there are now multiple pathways to power in a multi-level polity.

History of Women's Parliamentary Representation

Demands for women's suffrage began in the 19th century but took a militant turn in the early 20thcentury after the failure of numerous attempts to secure votes for women. From 1903-14, Emmeline Pankhurst's Women's Social and Political Union (known as the suffragettes) engaged in a campaign of both peaceful and violent political confrontation which engendered massive publicity for the cause and put the government under intense pressure until the campaign was halted by the outbreak of World War I. Women gained partial enfranchisement in 1918 in the 4th Reform Act, which extended the vote to women over 30 and all men over the age of 21. It was not until 1928 that the franchise was equalised to all men and women over the age of 21. The first woman Member of Parliament, the Irish revolutionary Countess Markievicz, was elected in 1918 but refused to take up her seat. Lady Nancy Astor, elected in a by-election in 1919 became the first female MP to sit in the House of Commons (Vallance, 1979). However this breakthrough led not to a flood but rather a trickle of women into Westminster. For most of the post-suffrage period, the percentage of women MPs at Westminster fluctuated at between two and five per cent, one of the poorest records amongst liberal democracies (along with France and the US). It was not until 1987 that the proportion of female MPs broke through the five per cent barrier (6.3 per cent). This figure increased to 9.2 per cent in the 1992 General Election and doubled to 18.2 per cent in 1997 falling back to 17.9 per cent 2001. These increases were primarily as a result of improvements in one party – the Labour Party – and the use of controversial gender quotas in the 1997 General Election.

Women in the Executive

Between 1929 when the first woman was appointed as a Cabinet Minister and 1979, when the first female Prime Minister was elected, a mere seven women had served as Cabinet Ministers. In the eighteen years of Conservative administration between 1979 and 1997 a further three women held Cabinet posts (in addition to Margaret Thatcher who served as Prime Minister from 1979 to 1990). In contrast, between 1997 and 2002 eleven women held Cabinet positions in successive Labour administrations.

As elsewhere women have tended to be appointed to 'soft' portfolios in areas of social policy, for example there have been six female Education ministers. However the status of these positions heading high spending ministries should not be underestimated. Women have also served in non-traditional areas such as transport, employment, agriculture, and trade and industry. Whilst, famously, the UK has had a female Prime Minister, there has to date never been a woman in the other top posts such as Chancellor of the Exchequer, Home Secretary or Foreign Secretary. Whilst some female cabinet ministers have progressed the women's agenda in government, most notably Barbara Castle who drove through the equal pay and sex discrimination legislation in the 1970s, others have displayed little interest in pursuing policy in such areas.

The Obstacles to Women's (Full) Parliamentary Representation

The comparative literature suggests a range of factors that present barriers to women's full participation in electoral politics and representative office. Systematic factors relate to the legal system, the electoral system, the party system and the general structure of political opportunities. Party political factors relate to issues such as party organisation, recruitment practices, party rules, party ideology and the strength of internal women's lobbies. Individual factors relate to social, economic and personal constraints that confront potential female candidates (see, for example, Norris and Lovenduski, 1995; Norris, 1998).

The UK is a relatively secular society with broadly progressive attitudes with respect to women's status. There are high levels of public support for the increased presence of women in politics and little evidence to suggest that voters discriminate against female candidates. However these generally enabling contexts are outweighed by a complex set of constraints that operate at systematic, party political and individual level.

An important but often neglected systematic factor is the dominant liberal ideology and relatively individualistic culture of the UK as compared with much of Europe. This narrow understanding of equal opportunities, with its focus on the individual and the protection of rights, is illustrated by sex discrimination and other equalities legislation. Compared to strong affirmative action policies on gender equality that can be found in other countries, British legislation is limited and weak. For example, affirmative action in employment or access to education as understood in US contexts is classed as positive discrimination and is illegal under UK law (Breitenbach *et al.*, 2002). Although political candidacy has not been conventionally understood to constitute employment under sex discrimination legislation, these definitions have in part shaped what is seen to be acceptable (Mackay, 2001).

The specifics of the UK political and electoral systems are unfavourable in respect of women's representation. Comparative studies demonstrate women are least likely to progress in single member simple plurality majoritarian systems (Norris, 1996; Caul, 1999; Rule and Zimmerman, 1994). First, the opportunity to fight winnable seats is restricted in a majoritarian system without term limits which advantages sitting MPs, this is known as the 'incumbency problem'. Second, because the system means that 'the winner takes all', selectors are encouraged to choose standard or 'ideal' candidates who have traditionally been white males, rather than risk non-standard candidates such as women (Norris 1996; Caul 1999).

Party Political Factors

Parties are the primary gatekeepers to political office. Parties in the UK have been characterised as 'centralised parties with decentralised candidate selection' (Denver, 1998). In all the major parties, selection procedures are largely decentralised to local constituency parties who guard their independence jealously. Party leadership retain some control over approved 'lists' of nominees from which local parties can invite potential candidates for selection and can apply targets. This decentralisation makes it difficult for party leaders to respond to external pressures to promote women and it is at local level that resistance can be entrenched. This means that formal changes to rules may be required because the leadership's powers of persuasion and influence may be limited. Until 1999 parties differed to the extent that selection and recruitment procedures were transparent and criteria for selection institutionalised. Lack of transparency and the persistence of informal suitability criteria as well as formal eligibility criteria may all act to deter outsiders, such as women and minority ethnic persons, from presenting themselves as aspirant candidates (Caul, 1999, Bradbury *et al.*, 2000, Russell *et al.*, 2002).

Party ideology plays a role in enabling or inhibiting women as parliamentary candidates. It is well documented that parties of the left are more favourably disposed to women's demands for greater access to political positions than are parties of the right. This general trend is borne out in the UK, where the Labour Party has made considerably more progress on the issue than its counterparts. The presence of well-organised and well-placed female party activists within political parties is also highlighted as an enabling factor: acting as an internal lobby, a pool of politically experienced women and a link with autonomous women's movements. Conversely, lack of organisation presents a further barrier. The next section describes the growth of a female lobby inside the Labour Party which correlates with the increasing action on the issue. Organisation within the other parties is less prominent, especially explicit feminist groupings (Lovenduski and Randall, 1993).

The impact of individual and structural social factors to disadvantage women as potential politicians cannot be underestimated, particularly the implications of the gendered division of domestic labour and women's lower socio-economic status relative to men (see, for example, Randall, 1987, Norris and Lovenduski, 1995, Squires and Wickham-Jones, 2000, Mackay, 2001). 'Supply' problems can be identified in some circumstances (ie. not enough women put themselves forward for consideration). However the weight of the evidence suggests that it is a lack of 'demand' by political party 'selectorates' that poses the greatest obstacle to women (Squires and Wickham-Jones 2000). Overall, it is systematic and party political factors and opportunity structures that provide better explanations for the relative under representation of women in the UK. Institutional rigidities are compounded by a marked lack of political appetite, as compared to international counterparts, for gender party rules on candidate selection such as quotas (Russell 2000).

Strategies for Improving Women's Representation

Until 2002 and the introduction of permissive legislation to enable parties to adopt positive discrimination without fear of legal challenge, the state has not intervened on the issue of women's representation. Constitutionally-mandated quotas or quotas enshrined in electoral law have not been seriously contemplated in the UK. If the matter has been seen to require action, then it has been for political parties as the primary players to implement such reforms as they see fit.

There is a range of possible party measures: reforms to selection procedures to make them fairer and more transparent; 'promotional' measures such as active encouragement, the targeting of potential women candidates and the establishment of informal or formal mentoring and shadowing schemes; and 'soft' or 'weak' positive action measures such as training or the provision of resources to sponsor individual women. Further along the continuum are 'weak' positive discrimination measures such as guaranteed places for women on short lists and balanced selection panels. The strongest measures involve mandatory guaranteed quotas such as all-women short lists, constituency 'twinning' and the 'zipping' or 'alternating' of female and male candidates on regional lists (Lovenduski, 1993).

Since the early 1980s all the major parties have made some attempt to improve their performance, responding to pressure from a number of sources. The social salience of the issue has increased over the past twenty years or so and opinion polls and other social surveys now consistently register high degrees of public support for more women in politics and support for parties to take special measures to increase their numbers. The establishment of an all-party 300 Group (which campaigned to get 300 women MPs into the Westminster Parliament by 2000) acted as a lobby and a training, publicity and resource group. Most crucially, feminists who had first moved into mainstream politics, particularly the Labour Party after 1979, began to organise around the issue, and to build and maintain internal pressure (Lovenduski and Randall, 1993, Perrigo, 1996, Lovenduski, 1999).

During the 1980s, all the political parties stated their commitment to improving the levels of women parliamentarians. Most encouraged women candidates to come forward and exhorted local constituency parties to give them fair consideration. However these rhetorical and promotional strategies had negligible results.

In the 1990s, a sea-change occurred in the Labour Party in response to concerted demands from women party activists and office-holders. Campaigners linked arguments to the Labour Party's wider programme of modernisation, the need to appeal to women voters and the promotion of social inclusion (Perrigo, 1996). In Scotland, and Wales (and to a lesser extent Northern Ireland), the issue of women's under representation became a high profile element of broader civil society campaigns and processes of constitutional reform (Brown, 1998; Breitenbach and Mackay, 2001; Mackay *et al.*, 2002).

The Labour Party began to implement internal quotas for party posts in the late 1980s and early 1990s but had failed to agree on candidate quotas, although targets were set and a weak rule introduced whereby women nominees were guaranteed a place on constituency short lists. However it soon became clear, that, 'without some mechanism to secure improvement, progress in women's representation would be glacial' (Lovenduski, 1999, p. 204). In response to the particular difficulties of securing change in the context of the UK electoral system (see above), a policy was agreed in 1993 whereby compulsory all-women short lists were to be introduced in constituency contests for half of all 'inheritor' seats (where the sitting MP had stood down) and half of Labour's target seats (marginal seats held by other parties which Labour assessed were winnable). It began to be implemented in 1994/5 in the run up to the 1997 General Election. However, the policy was challenged in 1996 and subsequently ruled to constitute unlawful discrimination under the Sex Discrimination Act 1975. Until then it had not been thought that political candidate selection and recruitment came within the remit of the Sex Discrimination Act. Despite legal opinion that it was likely the judgement would be overturned on appeal, the party leadership chose not to challenge the ruling and dropped the policy; although selections already made under the system stood (Eagle and Lovenduski 1998, Lovenduski 1999, Russell 2003).

The success of the all-women short list policy, although only partially implemented, was demonstrated by the 1997 General Election results which saw the number of women in the House of Commons double from the 1992 figure of 60 to a total of 120. At 18.2 per cent the representation of women at Westminster reached an all-time high and brought Britain into line with many other European Union member countries, although still well below levels achieved in Scandinavian polities. All but eighteen of the female MPs were elected from the Labour Party. Women accounted for almost one-quarter of Labour's MPs as compared with only 7.8 per cent of Conservative MPs and 6.5 per cent of Liberal Democrat members.

To summarise so far, concerted strategic action by well-organised women activists inside the Labour Party created the momentum to change party rules. In the first instance, internal party quotas increased the proportion of women as office holders at different levels of the Labour Party including the key bodies of the National Executive Committee and the Shadow Cabinet. Well-positioned women then provided a further springboard for the successful promotion of candidate quotas with guaranteed results. As noted above, female activists used a range of discursive and political opportunities to press home their case. In particular they were successful in linking calls for more women MPs with programmes of party modernisation and electoral competition for female voters. Although there were female party members active on the issue within the other main UK parties, their campaigns have been less organised and effective which reflects, at least in part, relatively weaker influence and organisational capacity within their respective parties.

It is difficult to discern a direct influence of the wider women's movement on campaigns for equal representation at Westminster, although feminist lobby groups such as the Fawcett Society have been active. As noted earlier the influence has been primarily indirect through the entry of feminists into the Labour Party. The UK women's movement has been characterised as having peaked as a mass movement in the mid 1970s before fragmenting in the 1980s and no longer representing a cohesive social force, although individual feminists entered political and social institutions (Lovenduski and Randall, 1993). However the pattern of organisation and the degree of fragmentation is geographically varied. We move now to examples where the women's movement has played a crucial and direct role in campaigns for women's representation: in Scotland and Wales, and in Northern Ireland.

Constitutional Change and Women's Political Representation in Scotland, Wales and Northern Ireland

We have already noted the high levels of women's representation in the new devolved political institutions of Scotland and Wales, and the modest though significant improvements in Northern Ireland. These achievements were not an inevitable by-product of devolution, rather they were the outcome of determined action by different alliances of women in the three jurisdictions. These gender campaigns took advantage of the institutional, political and discursive opportunities that the devolution debate and subsequent restructuring process presented (Brown *et al.*, 2002; Mackay *et al.*, 2002).

Scotland

In Scotland, a broad coalition of women's organisations, grassroots activists, female trade unionists, party women, key insiders and gender experts came together under the umbrella of the 50:50 campaign. Over a period of about ten years they worked to build a public and political consensus around the key aims of improving the representation of women in political office and institutionalising gender concerns in any new Scottish Parliament through policy machinery and channels for consultation and participation.[2]

Party measures to improve women's representation In the run up to the first elections to the Scottish parliament in 1999, internal and external pressure was brought to bear on the political parties, particularly the Labour Party. All the parties stated their concern to see more women in politics and their intention to encourage women to come forward for selection. In addition, some the parties improved their recruitment and selection procedures. However, in the final event, the Scottish Labour Party was the only party to operate a mechanism to guarantee gender balance in representation. Women had gained significant positional influence inside the Labour Party as a result of UK-wide internal party quotas (see above) and had been active in UK-wide campaigns for candidate quotas. They were supported in their campaigning by some key men and by the vocal groundswell of grassroots women activists. In addition to the modernisation and women's votes arguments that had been well-rehearsed at UK level, activists argued that gender balance would provide a powerful and visible symbol of 'new politics' and a modern, relevant and democratic Scotland (Mackay *et al.*, 2003).

Under the AMS system adopted in Scotland, 73 of the 129 MSPs are elected from constituencies. The remaining 56 members are selected from eight regional party lists. As Labour was likely to get the majority of its seats from the FPTP constituency contests, a positive action scheme was designed to 'twin' constituencies. Under this scheme, constituencies were matched in terms of a variety of indicators, including winnability.[3] Both men and women could stand for selection for a pair of constituencies. This mechanism was devised by Labour women activists and academics as a means to avoid a possible legal challenge under the Sex Discrimination Act 1975.

The Scottish National Party (SNP) was likely to get the majority of its seats in the regional or 'top-up' lists under the new electoral system and had proposed to use 'zipping' in their party lists as a way of ensuring gender balance. However, this proposal was narrowly defeated by rank-and-file members at a special party conference in May 1998. Nevertheless, as the main contender to Labour, the SNP could not afford to appear to be lukewarm on the issue of gender balance when the issue was so prominent in public debate. In practice, informal measures resulted in the high ranking of women candidates on party lists.

The Conservative Party and Scottish Liberal Democrats did not institute positive action, although the Liberal Democrats had signed an electoral agreement with Labour, brokered by women activists, in which they committed the party to the principle of gender equality in the first elections. Positive action proposals failed to gain support because of fears that the party might be vulnerable to legal challenge.

Although campaigners did not achieve everything they wanted they had ensured a high profile for the issue of women's representation as a matter of electoral competition (Brown, 1999 Mackay *et al.*, 2002). In 1999, women comprised 37 per cent of MSPs in the new Scottish parliament. They were half of the Labour parliamentary group and 42 per cent of the SNP parliamentary group. Women made up around a third of the Scottish Cabinet ministers and convened around a third of the powerful all-purpose parliamentary committees.

The influence of women campaigners also can be discerned in a number of the institutional features of the post-devolution Scotland, including the 'new politics' key principles of the Parliament: the sharing of power, accountability, access and participation, and equal opportunities.[4] Family-friendly working hours are in operation in the parliament, a parliamentary Equal Opportunities Committee has been established and an Equality Unit has been set up within the Scottish Executive. A number of new channels and mechanisms for consultation have been created, which provide opportunities for women's organisations to be represented and to engage with the policy-making process. The Executive has adopted a 'mainstreaming' approach, endorsed by the parliament and championed by the Equal Opportunities Commission in Scotland, whereby equalities considerations, including gender, are integrated into the everyday work of government including policy development and the drafting of legislation.

Wales

In Wales, opportunities were constrained by the relative lack of public and political debate on constitutional reform and the prevailing ambivalence about the devolution project but nevertheless women were able to press for significant concrete gains. Against a backdrop of political division and public indifference, a small group of key women activists struggled to incorporate a gender perspective and to link devolution debates with arguments for gender balance of political representation and improved channels for women to voice their concerns (Mackay *et al.*, 2002).

Many of these strategic women – high ranking bureaucrats, academics, feminist policy advocates, elected politicians and trade unionists – held positions of influence in the Labour Party in Wales and the Welsh nationalist party, Plaid Cymru. They therefore worked within their respective parties to push for positive action to promote women candidates and to link gender equality with internal programmes of party modernisation and arguments about winning female votes (Russell *et al.*, 2002).

Party measures to improve women's representation In many senses developments in Wales represented a politics of 'catch-up' with Scotland. Ironically, this resulted in outcomes that not only caught up but, in many respects, overtook Scottish achievements. Both the main parties, the Welsh Labour Party and Plaid Cymru operated specific mechanisms to try to achieve gender balance in representation. They also improved their selection and recruitment procedures for candidates seeking to join the national panel of candidates.

The results of the first elections to the National Assembly for Wales illustrate the success of the positive action strategies with women comprising 40 per cent members of the Assembly (which shortly afterwards rose to 42 per cent). Twinning delivered more than 50 per cent of Labour's seats for women and Plaid Cymru's 'gender template' on the regional lists delivered 30 per cent. There were no serious moves to adopt positive action for the selection of Liberal Democrat or Conservative candidates in Wales.

Women in the National Assembly for Wales Women achieved prominent positions in the assembly – comprising half of the first Welsh Cabinet, including the Health, Education and Finance Ministries. One of the five deputy minister appointments was female and women comprised around 40 per cent of committee convenors. As in Scotland, family friendly working hours are observed in the Assembly. In 2003 women held five out of nine seats in the Welsh Cabinet – second only to New Zealand.

In addition, gender concerns have been further institutionalised through a statutory equality positive duty (Chaney and Fevre, 2002), the establishment of an Equality of Opportunity Committee and the creation of an Equality Policy Unit. Equality mainstreaming, including gender equality, is being promoted in the Assembly and is also being rolled out into public bodies that receive their funding from NAW such as Health Boards. There is statutory annual reporting on the progress NAW and public bodies have made with respect to promoting equality and an annual debate. (Chaney *et al.*, 2005 forthcoming).

Northern Ireland

In Northern Ireland the concern to end violent conflict was the primary motivating factor for the most powerful players and it was only at the last stage of the peace process that women were able to effectively intervene in debates and promote broader ideas of inclusion into political dialogue (Mackay *et al.*, 2002). Proposals in the mid-1990s for a Forum and multi-party talks to negotiate a new political settlement in the province opened up a window of opportunity for women activists seeking a role in the process (Galligan *et al.*, 1999). However faced with unresponsive and indifferent political parties, women activists from trade unions, academia and grassroots women's sector organisations came together to create the Women's Coalition (NIWC) to contest the Forum elections in May 1996 (Fearon, 1999, Roulston, 1999). At the subsequent elections they were ranked the ninth most popular party out of 24, which gave them two elected Forum members and a team at the multi-party talks.

The Women's Coalition struggled in the talks to insert a gender perspective in difficult circumstances (Fearon, 1999, Ward, 2000, 2001). However the negotiated agreement, which paved the way for the new Assembly, reflected their contribution in, for example, its declaration of women's right to participate in political life and its recommendations to establish a civic forum to bring civil society voices into the new political institutions (Mackay *et al.*, 2002).

The creation of a women's party had little discernible impact on the main parties and their candidate procedures in the run up to the Assembly elections. A total of 14 women (13 per cent) were elected to the Assembly (later rising to 18 per cent), this included two women from the Coalition. Women held three ministerial positions and 17 out of 110 places on assembly committees (15.5 per cent) in the first assembly (currently suspended), including three deputy chair positions. However, it must be noted that no female chairs were appointed and several committees had no women members at all. In the 2003 Assembly elections, the Women's Coalition lost both its seats.

Women are less visible as elected members of the Assembly and the stop-go nature of the peace process has left little room for gender politics. However individual women are seen to be influential. There are also important ways in which gender concerns have been institutionalised. As in Scotland and Wales, the Northern Ireland

Assembly has promoted more family-friendly working practices. An extensive equality mainstreaming programme is also underway which centres around a powerful statutory duty (Section 75) placed upon all public bodies, including government departments, to have due regard to promote equality of opportunity and to draw up equality schemes. The duty is enforced by the Northern Ireland Equality Commission. Although primarily driven from a community and 'fair employment' perspective, it does allow the opportunity for gender equality concerns to be integrated into the work of government and public authorities in the province (Donaghy, 2003). As in Scotland, a Civic Forum has been established by the Assembly as a consultative body. It was proposed by Women's Coalition as a means of preserving the policy expertise and commitment of community actors, including women, built up over the period of direct rule and women comprise 37 per cent of the membership.

Constitutional change opened up opportunities in Scotland, Wales and Northern Ireland for women to mobilise around the issues of political representation in its broadest sense. Women's agency has been significant in shaping reform agendas but the opportunity to do so has been shaped by markedly different political conditions in general and in respect of the situations of women.

Women's Influence in Parliament

It is difficult to reach firm conclusions about the impact of women on politics in the UK context because, until recently, their numbers have been so small. In this section we briefly review the literature on women at Westminster. We then make some preliminary observations about women in the devolved institutions, drawing in particular upon current research on the Scottish parliament.

Westminster

Historic studies of MPs have yielded little evidence of sex differences in the House of Commons (Currell, 1974; Vallance, 1979). Virtually all the women MPs interviewed by Vallance in the late 1970s saw themselves as party politicians first and foremost and displayed little solidarity with other women MPs. This led Vallance to state, 'The women are too interested in and too divided by politics to contemplate any sort of a corporate identity'. (Vallance, 1979, p. 96). Although Hills (1981) found evidence that female Labour MPs were more radical than their male counterparts, and Norris and Lovenduski (1989, 1995) found female parliamentary candidates in the 1987 and 1992 General Elections to be more liberal than male, party still proved to be the strongest predictor of attitudes.

And yet that is not the whole picture. Vallance (1979) noted that women MPs had always accepted, albeit reluctantly, that women expected them to represent their interests and that as such, they represented two constituencies: their geographical constituency, and the constituency of women. They also agreed that they tended to act more often than their male colleagues when sex equality issues arose. No formal caucus existed although Labour women worked closely together to combat the various challenges to abortion legislation during the 1970s (Vallance, 1979, pp. 83-90) and the 1980s (Coote and Patullo, 1990). Banks (1993) study of the legislative activities of female MPs from 1918 to 1970 reached the conclusion that, whereas women operated for the most part along party lines, there were some gender related issues about which women MPs would campaign as women: abortion, the marriage bar, sexual abuse and child abuse. Currell (1974), Vallance (1979) and Pugh (1992) have all noted that most, though by no means all, women MPs' activities were concentrated in traditional 'feminine' areas such as education, social welfare and health.

Evidence from the 1992 British Candidate Study (Norris and Lovenduski, 1995; Norris, 1996) into candidate attitudes and priorities found that, within each party grouping, women candidates were more feminist, more liberal and more left wing in their attitudes than male candidates. There was also a gender gap within each party in terms of policy priorities with women candidates expressing stronger concern than men for social policy issues. Modest gender differences were evident across a range of issues but party still remained the best predictor of attitudes. However in respect of women's rights, particularly in the fields of reproductive rights and domestic violence, clear gender gaps emerged which went beyond party. For example, Conservative women were more supportive of women's rights in respect of abortion and domestic violence than were male Liberal Democrats (Norris, 1996, p. 95). The successor 1997 British Representation Study reinforced the findings that 'women politicians are more likely to take a pro-woman line than men' (Lovenduski, 1977, p. 719).

The number of women MPs doubled in the 1997 General Election to 18.2 per cent. With this increase came renewed interest in women's role in parliament: would they think and act in gender-distinctive ways; would they have gendered attitudes and interests; would they have an impact on the political agenda?

Post 1997, there are far more Labour women in the House of Commons than there are female MPs from any other party. Labour women are generally more pro-women, more interested in women's issues, and more likely to prioritise equal representation than Conservative women. Labour women are overwhelmingly self-defined feminists compared to women from other parties. However when the attitudes of all women MPs are aggregated they are generally closer to the attitudes of Labour women than to the MPs of any other party. (Stephenson, 1997, Lovenduski and Norris, 2003).

Labour women MPs perceive themselves to have worked to promote gender issues and to insert gender perspectives into the work of parliament through select committees and parliamentary procedures and through an emphasis on constituency work. In this respect, Labour women see such work as playing an important part in the responsive representation of women's concerns (Childs, 2001-2002; Mactaggart, 2000) and claim 'the fine detail of government policy reflects much greater sensitivity to the needs of women' (Mactaggart, 2000, p. 7). However the promotion of women's concerns may be highly contingent upon arena, issue and political circumstances. Such action is potential rather than guaranteed as starkly illustrated in a landmark case, early in the 1997 government, when Labour women did not act to protect the interests of lone mothers and voted with their party to cut social security benefits (Childs, 2002, Mactaggart, 2000, Ward, 2000).

The constraints upon working in gender distinctive ways within the UK system remain strong and the costs of promoting feminist issues are perceived by women MPs to be high (Stephenson, 1997, Lovenduski, 1999, Childs, 2002). Women are still less than one in every five MPs, strict party discipline allows little room for manoeuvre, and political culture remains resolutely macho. Parliament is 'a male institution with silly rules and secret conventions, managed by men, for men' (female MP cited in Stephenson, 1997). In the above survey of women MPs across party, two-thirds of respondents felt it was harder to be a woman than a man in Parliament.

The Scottish Parliament

The proportions of women in the new devolved political institutions of Scotland and Wales eclipse those at Westminster and are well above levels that commentators refer to as a 'critical mass'. Turning first to Scotland: it is too early in the life of the new parliament and executive to make definitive judgements of what devolution – and female parliamentarians in particular – have delivered for women in terms of concrete outcomes. The policy and legislative process is lengthy and complex and it is particularly tricky trying to determine specific influences and causal links. However we draw here on research that captured the first two years of the operation of the Scottish parliament and explored the question: what difference does a substantial proportion of women politicians make to political institutions, political practices and policy agenda? This is framed within a wider comparative study of gender and constitutional change.

It is worth noting the different institutional context in which women parliamentarians are operating in Scotland as compared to women MPs at Westminster. For instance, as a consequence of the operation of a more proportional electoral system, AMS, there is multi-party representation in the Scottish parliament. Another difference relates to the role of the powerful parliamentary committees in a unicameral system with powers of scrutiny, investigation and the initiation of legislation. Thus the new system provides forums in which alternative political careers can be developed and in which politicians of all parties can make an impact on policy.

Overall there is a broad consensus amongst parliamentarians and commentators that the relatively large presence of women MSPs has made at least some 'difference' to political practices and political agenda in the Scottish parliament. A crucial impact has been the apparent 'normalising' of women politicians. In stark contrast to Westminster where women and minority ethnic MPs feel like 'space invaders' (Puwar, 2004) and are marginalised, patronised and exoticised (Puwar, 2004; Childs, 2001, 2002), women and men feel equally 'at home' in the Scottish Parliament. The visible presence of women acts as a powerful shorthand for 'new politics' and is seen to play a role in reinforcing – or underwriting – those aspirations. The high level of female representation therefore forms an important part of the nascent political culture (Mackay *et al.*, 2003).

Whilst the symbolic impact of women is widely recognised their substantive impact is more contested and seen to be highly conditioned by party politics and political context. However all the female parliamentarians and many of their male counterparts could point to examples of gender-related agenda setting, lobbying and policy innovation or modification. The issue of violence against women provides the clearest case of where the presence of female politicians has had an impact.[5] Spending on domestic abuse is proportionately higher than in England and a wide-ranging and radical national strategy is in place. Issues of domestic abuse and sexual violence have a strikingly high profile in both the parliament and the Scottish Executive. This is well-illustrated by the fact that the first piece of legislation to be initiated by a parliamentary committee was The Protection from Abuse Act 2000 which strengthened police and judicial safeguards for women abused by partners or expartners. It was driven forward by Labour and SNP women, with the support of key male colleagues.The broader equalities agenda has also been high profile in post-devolution Scottish politics. Women ministers are seen to have championed the agenda with its emphasis on consultation and the mainstreaming of equality perspectives into policy development and the drafting of legislative proposals. Female backbenchers are seen to have been more robust in their defence of the agenda, for example in their consistent support for the abolition of anti-gay legislation whilst many of their male colleagues wavered in the face of media hostility.

Perhaps the most striking finding is the apparent convergence in the working practices and policy priorities of women and men politicians and a move away from the gender stereotyping evident in many other political institutions. Whilst this trend can in part be explained by the constraints of party discipline and the pull of 'politics as usual' on women, it is more adequately explained by a subtle shift in men's attitudes, practices and policy agendas. The data suggest greater preparedness and willingness by men to raise issues traditionally reflective of women's interests and concerns. Some male politicians perceive that the mutually reinforcing influences of the new institution and the significant presence of women have enabled them to reform their own political practices: to think and act in different ways. As such the presence of women may have provoked a reconsideration of the masculine norms, values and behaviours traditionally played out in power politics (Mackay, Myers and Brown, 2003).

These processes of normalisation of women and their concerns can also be discerned in Wales, where the political agenda also gives weight to equality issues and gender concerns (Rees, 2002, Chaney and Fevre, 2002, Chaney, 2003, Chaney *et al.*, 2005 forthcoming). As in Scotland, some commentators have suggested that the strong presence of women in the National Assembly for Wales has had an impact upon male politicians and their politics (Feld, 2000).

Conclusion

Constitutional change and the move towards a multi-level polity has presented opportunities for women in the UK. The process of devolution resulted not only in the renegotiation of powers between centre and sub-state nation and region but also some redistribution of political power between the sexes. Building upon the progress made within the Labour Party at Westminster, significant proportions of women were elected to the Scottish Parliament and the Welsh Assembly. These advances were made by the Labour Party and by its main electoral contender in each country, the SNP and Plaid

Cymru. In these new institutions, women and their concerns are seen as a normal and unremarkable part of politics. In Northern Ireland, progress has been more modest but is nonetheless significant.

The reasons for success are complex but relate, in part, to the internal strength and persistence of women party activists, particularly in the Labour Party but also in the nationalist parties. The strategic mobilisation of the wider women's movement played a crucial role in both Scotland and Northern Ireland. In all three places, groupings of 'strategic women' highly placed and well-networked feminists within political parties, academia and women's organisations provided an important transmission mechanism by which gains made in one jurisdiction could be used in a politics of catch-up. So, Labour took seriously the threats of Scottish women activists that should their demands for gender quotas be frustrated they might set up a women's party because such a party was already in existence in Northern Ireland. In Wales, campaigners were able to use unfavourable comparisons with Scotland to press home their claims.

Party factors are important too: women's representation became a shorthand means to promote party modernisation and 'new politics'. In Scotland and Wales, it also became a feature of electoral competition in part as a proxy for the struggle for women's votes, although in Northern Ireland's fractured polity, constitutional politics drowned out gender politics in terms of electoral competition. Finally, within the Labour Party institutional factors relating to party organisation such as standard practices and centralisation contributed to the rationale for action.

What impact did the results in 1999 have on the wider political system? The international attention and plaudits that the gender coup in Scotland and Wales attracted served to keep the issue on the political agenda. These results heightened expectations of further progress although this optimism was tempered by the continuing uncertainty about the legality of positive action. As a consequence, none of the parties adopted quotas in the run up to the 2001 General Election. The fragility of developments was underscored by the result in which the number of women MPs dropped – albeit slightly – for the first time in 22 years. In turn, this caused the precedent of government intervention in the form of enabling legislation to remove legal obstacles to political parties adopting positive discrimination, including all-women shortlists. This, in turn, provided the momentum for further gains to be made in the 2003 elections in Scotland and Wales.

What we see happening is a complex dynamic between different levels of the polity: horizontally and vertically and between parties. There are now multiple pathways to power and multiple points at which women can lobby for change. Gains are fragile and changes in political culture slow, however the issue of women's representation in its broadest sense has been brought into the mainstream of politics and electoral competition.

Acknowledgements

This chapter draws upon two projects funded under the UK Economic and Social Research Council's Devolution and Constitutional Change Programme (L219252023 and ROO223281). The author gratefully acknowledges this support. Team members and associates include: Fiona Myers, Ann Henderson, Alice Brown and Haf Elgar (University of Edinburgh), Elizabeth Meehan and Tahyna Barnett Donaghy (Queen's University Belfast) and Paul Chaney (University of Cardiff).

Notes

[1] There is an Upper House (The House of Lords) and a Lower House (House of Commons). The House of Commons is the primary source of power and authority and will be referred to as parliament in this chapter. The House of Lords, which comprises hereditary peers, appointed life peers and the judiciary has scrutiny and revising functions but cannot indefinitely delay legislation that the House of Commons has approved. It is currently undergoing reform.

[2] For a detailed account of the 50:50 campaign – 'one of the most strategic campaigns for equality for women in Scotland' (McDonald *et al.*, 2001, p. 233) see the anthology Breitenbach and Mackay, 2001.

[3] Under twinning, the woman applicant with the highest number of votes was selected as the Labour candidate for one of the twinned seats, at the same time as the man with the highest number of votes was selected for the other. See Bradbury *et al.*, 2000; Russell *et al.*, 2002 for more detail.

[4] These principles were recommended by the Consultative Steering Group, a body set up by the incoming Secretary of State for Scotland to consult widely and make detailed recommendations on the parliament's standing orders and procedures (CSG, 1998). Women members of the CSG, backed by the Women's Co-ordination Group and the Equal Opportunities Commission, successfully put the case for equal opportunities to be included as a key principle (McDonald *et al.*, 2001).

[5] Working with, and building upon the considerable achievements of, grassroots women's anti-violence organisations such as Scottish Women's Aid, The Zero Tolerance campaign and Rape Crisis.

Chapter 10

Croatia

Smiljana Leinert Novosel

Introduction

Women's political representation in Croatia is similar to that of other former eastern European countries. It also has particular features not found in other socialist states that shaped the context and opportunities for women's participation in parliament. Croatia had a more liberal political culture than most communist countries, while the country's transition to democracy was marked by war. Both are consistent elements in Croatia's political history.

Croatia's strategic geopolitical position in central Europe with a Mediterranean coastline has delivered an historical legacy of political domination and strategic alliance-building along with periods of independence. In the Middle Ages Croatia was a powerful independent country, later it entered into political unions with some of its neighbors: with Hungary in the 12th century, Austria at the beginning of the 16th century, and Austro-Hungary from the second half of the 19th century through to 1918. After World War I, Croatia joined the Kingdom of Yugoslavia, which lasted until 1941, and after World War II Croatia became a republic within the Federal People's Republic of Yugoslavia, which later changed its name to the Socialist Federal Republic of Yugoslavia (1945-1991). Only at the end of the 20th century did Croatia achieve political independence again.

Independence took place within the context of massive transition changes in central and eastern Europe, replacing the communist regimes with democratic orders during a wave of democratization. But Croatia was not fortunate enough to go through the process in the manner of other central European countries with similar cultures and histories. Political system change in Croatia was accompanied by the disintegration of federal Yugoslavia. Following a referendum, Croatia declared independence on 25 June 1991. After an attempt to restructure the socialist Yugoslavia as a confederation (proposed by Croatia), Croatia's independence was followed by the occupation of one third of its territory by the Serbian forces of Slobodan Miloševic. The war, which lasted from June 1991 until May 1995, caused great human and material losses. During this period, Croatia simultaneously fought for international recognition (and recognition of its pre-war borders), as well as conducting a political and military struggle to gain control over all of its territory. The country was internationally recognized at the beginning of 1992, and its territory was returned gradually – part of it in a military action in 1995, and its easternmost part through a peaceful reintegration in 1998.Croatia was then the only post-communist country in which the parting with the communist totalitarian order was accompanied by war. 'In Croatia, war forcefully "interfered" with transition and nation-building processes, becoming a chief factor in those processes' (Kasapovic, 1996, p.153).

A New Political System

The first multiparty elections in the spring of 1990 marked the real beginning of the transition from a totalitarian political order to a democratic one. As in most transition countries, power was won by those who had not had it before – the Croatian bloc led by the most powerful party, the nationalist Croatian Democratic Union (HDZ). Conflicts between supporters of the old and new regimes, and conflicts about Croatia's secession from the Yugoslav federation and forming an independent state, combined to generate a two-party system following the elections (Kasapovic, 1996, pp.46-7). The electorate was extremely polarized into two camps – those who voted for the election winners, HDZ, (led by nationalist Franjo Tudman) and who supported a change of political regime and establishment of the nation-state, as against voters who supported the left grouping led by SKH-SDP,[1] the election losers, and favored retention of the status quo regarding the questions of statehood and the political system (Zakošek, 1991, pp.142-4).

The relationship between the governing HDZ and the opposition parties over the decade vacillated between cooperation and conflict (Zakošek, 2001, p.101). When the last source of outside threat to the country was gone at the end of 1998, as economic and social conditions in the country worsened, and when the opposition parties adopted a new coalition strategy, voter support for the HDZ and the parties close to it diminished. In the January 2000 parliamentary elections, the HDZ was replaced by a six-party opposing coalition, but was subsequently returned to power in the November 2003 elections. The gains made by women in the 2000 election (21 per cent of MPs) was not sustained in 2003, and women's share of Assembly seats fell to 18 per cent (Table 10.1).

In her analysis of transition processes Kasapovic points out that some authors viewed those processes negatively, labelling the political system in the 1990s an authoritarian regime, and assessing the index of democratization as very low (Kasapovic, 2001, 18). Nevertheless, she argues that one should distinguish between democratic changes at the level of social system and political subsystem from those that determined relations between the president, the parliament, and the government. For instance, James McGregor's analysis of the 1990 constitution clearly recognizes a constitutional commitment to parliamentary democracy, political pluralism, human and civil rights, free market and a unitary state. At the level of political subsystem he identifies regulations on division of power, a bicameral parliament, revision of bills and legislative and executive decisions in courts of law, direct presidential elections, and the right of referendum (McGregor, 1996). In practice, the system of government was semi-presidential, which favored authoritarian decision-making, and which promoted the president, Franjo Tudman as the chief agent of Croatian politics in the 1990-1999 period (Kasapovic, 2001, p.20).

The structure of the new polarization affected support for different kinds of electoral systems. The struggles to hold onto voter bases and to attract new voters were carried out under frequent changes of election rules. Almost all of the main models for parliamentary elections were tested in the four general elections held during the course of a decade: the absolute majority system (1990), a mixed system combining equal proportion of majority and election list mandates (1992), a mixed system with a predominant proportion of election list mandates (1995), and the list-proportional election system (2000) The list system adopted in 2000 allows for the election of 140 MPs from ten multi-member districts with 14 seats in each one. Additional seats are held by MPs representing national minorities (eight seats in 2003) and Croats abroad (six seats in 2003). A five per cent threshold limits the parliamentary presence of smaller parties and eliminates a winner-takes-all scenario. As Kasapovic notes 'Comparatively speaking, there is no other new democracy in Central and Eastern Europe in which election system changes during a single decade were so frequent and radical' (2001, p.27).

Along with frequent election system reforms, political transition in Croatia was characterized by a large number of elections for the House of Representatives (1990, 1992, 1995, 2000, 2003), two elections for the House of Counties (1993 and 1997), three presidential elections (1993, 1997, and 2000), and one plebiscite on national independence (1991). For the purposes of examining women's participation in the legislature, however, we will concentrate on the three post-communist elections to the House of Representatives (Sabor) in 1992, 1995 and 2000 respectively.The 2000 elections, based on a system of proportional representation, were won by a coalition of six parties, enabling a shift from a two-party system with a dominant party to a moderately pluralist system. However, the broad lines of a polarity between centre-left and centre-right parties continues. (Šiber, 2001, p.96). Constitutional reform carried out by the new government at the end of 2000 replaced the semi-presidential political system with a parliamentary one, and soon thereafter the House of Counties was abolished. Croatia is now a parliamentary democracy with a single chamber, the Sabor (Assembly).

Women's Politics in Croatia until 1990

Simultaneously with the development of capitalism and the processes of national integration, a middle-class women's movement emerged in southern Slavic countries around the mid-19th century. In the beginning, this movement took on the task of setting up independent women's organisations whose aim was to instruct and prepare women to care for others, nurture the deprived and transmit national identities. However, as early as the beginning of the 20th century, their activities moved into the political arena with a clear demand for women's suffrage and equality of women in law. For instance, at the founding convention of the 'Women's Movement' feminist society in Zagreb in 1925, women's suffrage was demanded as the necessary but not the only condition for equal participation of women in public life (Sklevicky, 1996, p.13). At the same time women were active in the workers' movement and in political parties. The founding of the Kingdom of Serbs, Croats and Slovenes after World War I created a new framework for already established models of women's organisations – middle-class women's organisations and the workers' movement. According to historian Lydia Sklevicky (1996, p.80), the two strongest women's organisations with a feminist orientation between the two world wars were the Yugoslav Women's Alliance and the Alliance of Women's Movements. As early as 1921 the former comprised 205 societies representing around 50,000 women, and its activities included broad cooperation with women's organisations such as the Association of University-Educated Women, the Alliance of Women's Movements, and others. The Alliance of Women's Movements comprised societies with the common goal of women's suffrage. It was especially active in the run-up to the parliamentary elections of 1927, in the passage of the new election law in 1935 and the drafting of the Yugoslav Civil Code in 1937, and especially in the organisation of the 1939 large-scale drive for women's suffrage (Sklevicky, 1996, p.80).

In the underdeveloped, poor and authoritarian country of the Kingdom of Yugoslavia, most women strove towards the same goal regardless of whether they belonged to the middle-class feminist movement or the Croatian proletarian women's movement.The common goal was fighting legalized inequality of the sexes that was inherited from a patriarchal social structure. However, it has to be added that the middle-class women's organisations and the proletarian women's movement had very different conceptions of how to achieve women's equality. The former sought to democratize society by reform, exerting continuous pressure on the government and its agencies and educating women in new social roles; the proletarian movement adhered to the idea that the women's question was to be solved through revolution and establishment of a new, classless society.

Fear of surging fascism resulted in the linking of these two movements and then the founding of a new mass organisation, the Popular Front. A youth chapter of the Women's Movement was founded under the auspices of the Communist Party of Yugoslavia in Zagreb in 1934. Its members interested in the women's question 'jumped into the institutional space opened by the feminists' (Sklevicky, 1996, p.80). As a result of the collaboration among feminists, who were mostly respectable professional middle-aged women and energetic young activists, this aspect of the Communist Party's work gained in importance and the number of women members increased. In 1925 women made up 0.8 per cent of Communist Party membership, rising to six per cent in 1940 (Sklevicky, 1996, p.141). In 1940 the highest rate of women members was in Slovenia, Serbia and Macedonia (ten per cent), followed by Montenegro (six per cent), Voivodina (five per cent), and Croatia (four per cent).

The period between the world wars was marked by strong activism on the part of women who no longer accepted social injustice or current political decision-making, whether the issue at stake was injustice in the workplace or the practice that decisions regarding war and peace were taken by others in their name. Women's dissatisfaction with the political order was expressed in protest politics. In 1934, 2,000 women took part in a miners' strike in Slovenia; in 1935, 5,000 women demonstrated for peace and against fascism in front of the German Consulate in Zagreb, while in 1936, 600,000 signatures were collected in a rally for peace and freedom. At the end of the 1940s the

Antifascist Women's Front (AFZ) became the sole heir to the tradition of struggles for women's rights. Founded in 1942, it was part of the Popular Front from the beginning, and controlled by the Communist Party, which directly determined its character and fate. During the war it mobilized a great number of women for fighting units, but also for the organisation of life behind the front lines, which became women's responsibility to a great extent. After 1945 the AFZ organisations extended all over the country. The AFZ represented the women of Yugoslavia in the international women's movement, and it was among the founders of the Women's International Democratic Federation. However, because of inadequate working conditions (especially in cities), and because of a constant striving to separate itself from the Popular Front, the organisation ceased to exist in 1953. Immediately thereafter, various organisations and societies which dealt with women's issues united into the League of Women's Societies of Yugoslavia, which was no longer an organisation of women, but which became an organisation of all citizens who wanted to contribute to solving all issues of concern to women.

In 1961 the Antifascist Front was replaced by a new social-political organisation, the Socialist League of the Working People of Yugoslavia (SSRNJ), within which the Conference for the Social Activity of Women was founded. The founding of the SSRNJ was meant to unite all social and interest groups (such as youth, women, etc.) into a single organisation. The Conference for the Social Activity of Women enjoyed a large degree of autonomy in its work, and it focused on national women's rights in an international context. The Conference extended over all of the then-Yugoslavia, involving an enormous number of women in all kinds of activities. Its operational autonomy was primarily the result of expertise in and familiarity with women's issues, as the Conference regularly coordinated its activities with outstanding experts in social policies, demography, political participation, law and health care, to name but a few.

A clear commitment to cooperation with everyone who could contribute to the improvement of the social position of women regardless of ideology testifies to the openness of this social organisation. The most interesting examples of its work include: publishing a journal for women, presentation of awards for contributions in the solving of women's issues, initiation of scholarly research about the social and political position of women, organisation of panel discussion and public talks, and running a contest for best literary works on women's subjects. The Conference played a very important role in the adoption of laws that affected the social position of women. One of the parliamentary committees was a Committee on Women's and Family Issues, whose objective was to intervene in the passage of laws that might threaten the achieved level of women's rights, based on expert opinions presented by the Conference. Using the Committee, the Conference managed to get a number of laws passed: for example, on family planning and on social care for preschool children. It was an active participant in the creation of labour laws, especially the law regulating the protection of women in the workplace (related to nightshift work, mothers with small children, and related matters.) In its last period, the Conference influenced the law on the required years of service for employed women, which provided that each woman could decide for herself whether she wanted to work as long as men or use the option of working fewer years. The Conference also secured financial support for infrastructural projects, such as the building of preschool care facilities and health care facilities for women. The breakdown of the socialist political system in the early 1990s put an end to the Conference's work. Its heir was the Alliance of Women of Croatia, a non-governmental organisation, which tried to preserve the positive legacies of almost thirty years of the Conference's work, with perceptibly less ambition and strength.

The effects of socialism become clearer in light of the fact that before World War II women were not equal with men in the political, legal, and economic senses, as well as in their private lives. The degree of inequality varied according to region, and differences between the city and the rural countryside were especially sharp. In the then-Yugoslavia women did not enjoy the right to vote and in some areas women were unable to access even primary education. The number of women in the workforce was less than a third (28 per cent), and women workers were concentrated in the textile industry, garment industry, food service industry, that is, the industries paying the lowest wages – as much as 30 per cent lower than men's. When there were restrictions in employment, women in the workforce were the first affected. Under such circumstances, the Communist Party of Yugoslavia (CP) offered a huge change with its concept of a radical change in the social position of women based on the ideas of equality between the sexes. The CP claimed that it recognized women's issues, that it was aware of their significance, and that it knew the solution to them – revolution with the goal of toppling class society and abolishing all forms of class inequality. The effects of the socialist system on women as a social group were twofold: an increase of women among the educated and the employed. They found employment mostly in non-capital-intensive industries, which caused women with the same qualifications to be paid perceptibly lower salaries than men, and to have lower representation in management.

A similar pattern was evident in the realm of politics: during World War II women got the right to vote as well as the opportunity to participate in political government but the 'pyramidal pattern' of men occupying the top decision making positions and women in the lower reaches of power was dominant here too. In order to at least formally establish equality between the sexes, quotas were introduced. When gender equality was taken seriously by political elites, this commitment was reflected in the higher representation of women in decision making. For instance, between 1958 and 1965, the proportion of women in the Sabor rose to 24.1 per cent. However, from 1965 to 1974, this figure fell to only 7.9 per cent. Between 1974 and 1990, the figure rose again to around 18 per cent (Leinert-Novosel, 1991, pp.34-5).

In the socialist era, 'innovations' in the realm of private life were a response to the family model of two working parents, and they included providing for women's reproductive rights, childcare provision, obligatory and paid maternity leave, support for pregnant women, and job security after childbirth. In practice however, women took on most of domestic work and the task of rearing children, The promised liberation from traditional roles that socialism held out to women did not become a reality.

Women's Politics During Transition, 1990-2000

The transition to democracy started on a note of disappointment for women who once more felt that they were 'victims' of political and social changes. Women experienced this period of 'delayed modernization' (Meznaric and Ule, 1994) as a formal worsening of their social position – the sudden loss of jobs, greater difficulty in getting jobs, material scarcity which often added to women's work within the family, and non-participation in political decision-making, especially at higher levels-all of which are among the most common characteristics of transition countries. Under the new conditions women no longer had the economic and social protections they formerly enjoyed and they practically disappeared from politics.

Table 10.1 Women in the Croatian parliament, 1992-2003

Year	Total Seats	Male MPs	Female MPs	% Female
1992	120	115	5	4.2
1995	108	101	7	6.5
2000	151	120	31	20.5
2003	152	125	27	17.8

Source: Glaurdic (2003, p.296); www.ipu.org/parline

The first multiparty elections in Croatia reduced the proportion of women at the highest levels of political decision-making to less than a quarter of what it was before (4.2 per cent). The representation of women in the Sabor then increased gradually and slowly – in 1992 women constituted four per cent of the members of the Sabor rising to 21 per cent in 2000, but falling back somewhat to 18 per cent in 2003 (Table10.1).Women's pattern of office-holding within the Assembly and in government is also mixed. In 2003, women chaired three parliamentary committees (12.5 per cent), and, while represented on each of the 24 committees, were a significant presence (35 per cent and over) on seven committees. A woman also held the position of vice-president of the Assembly. Four women (29 per cent) were appointed to positions in cabinet after the 2000 elections, with responsibility for the ministries of justice, the family, European integration, and environmental protection. The minister for the family, Jadranka Kosor, also filled one of the two deputy prime minister positions.

Obstacles to Women's Political Participation

A complex mixture of cultural and institutional bias accounts for the under-representation of women in Croatian political life. We will now examine these barriers more closely, considering social perspectives on women's role, political parties, women's attitude to politics and the media influence on images of women.

Social Attitudes Towards Women's Role

In spite of 40 years of socialism and a stated commitment to gender equality, a 1997 study shows very clearly that almost every other male respondent (49 per cent) and more than a third of female respondents (35 per cent) maintained a woman's place was in the home, where she should take care of the household and the upbringing of children. Among women respondents, those with lower education levels were more inclined to support a traditional role for women. About 40 per cent of respondents of both sexes were of the view that women were 'not born' to engage in politics. One third (33 per cent) of women and 39 per cent of men holding traditionalist values claimed that women do not belong in politics, while 67 per cent of women and 61 per cent of men holding modernist views claimed the opposite. An urban-rural divide in social attitudes was also observed, with traditionalist views on gender roles being more widely held among non-urban dwellers and 'modernist' views being held by a majority of those living in urban areas. Thus, while an overall majority of both women and men are supportive of a multi-dimensional view of women's citizenship, a significant minority holds a more conservative view of women's social roles. These attitudes have geographical and educational aspects: traditional thinking regarding women's place in society is more likely to be held by rural dwellers and by those with low levels of education, while modern attitudes are more likely to be found among those living in urban areas and those with higher educational attainments.

Political Parties and Women

Studies conducted in 1994 and 1999 show that the views of political parties on the position of women in society express particular combinations of modernism or traditionalism along with a position on social intervention or self-regulation.

The centre-right to far-right parties, HDZ (in power from 1990-1999), HSS, HKDU and HSP combine support for traditional values with a belief in personal free choice. In other words, they embrace values related to nation, family, and motherhood, but without restricting abortion rights; they endorse the right to education, employment, and professional career of women, but without special support for women. They endorse the participation of women in political decision-making, but without quotas for women; they favor more women in their parties, especially in the HDZ, but tolerate only small numbers of women in leadership positions, and have only recently begun to accept the need for separate women's organisations within parties.

On the more liberal part of the ideological spectrum, the HSLS, HNS, LS, SNS, IDS and SBHS favor free choice within a modern value system, with only negligible differences. In these parties concern for nation is replaced by concern for the individual. Family is an important category for these parties, but they embrace the modern idea of the 'partner' family. The right to abortion is viewed as a personal freedom. Women are desirable partners in public life, but there are few special support mechanisms for women, except for intra-party quotas for women and, more recently, intra-party women's organisations, and a more pronounced public interest in women's issues.

The SDP and ASH, as modern parties of the left, maintain that social intervention in favor of women is necessary. They advocate a modern family; they regard population problems as economic and social problems, and the right to abortion a fundamental human right; they consider employment outside the home a precondition of equality between the sexes; they see the insufficient participation of women in politics as a problem of the insufficient development of democracy, they have women's organisations in their parties and the highest percentage of women in the Sabor.

Although in recent years almost all parties showed more interest in women's problems – in part due to the pressure of the international community, in part due to the development of civil society and the activities of women's organisations in it – this growing interest was shaped in a conflict between two conceptions: a progressive centre-left view espoused by the opposition parties (up to 2000) and a traditionalist conservative view supported by the governing HSZ and parties of the right. Party attention (or lack thereof) to women's issues at the 2000 elections indicates that for even left of centre parties, the woman question was very much a peripheral issue. While it was to be expected that the conservative Peasants' Party (HSS) and nationalist Croatian Democratic Union (HDZ) would ascribe to a traditional family-related view of women's role in their manifestos, it was more surprising to find the joint manifesto of the left-oriented SDP and HSLS gave only a passing rhetorical commitment to women's equal access to power (Glaurdic 2003, pp.297-8).

Women's Attitudes Towards Politics

Why do Croatian women rarely get involved in politics? Earlier research on women's political activism pointed to a connection between a certain type of socialization in the family and certain personality characteristics (the 'activist' syndrome) as a precondition of political activism (Leinert Novosel, 1990). Disregarding genetic influence, the activist personality is in great measure formed by a modern type of socialization in the family that encourages and helps develop all forms of a child's active relationship with its surroundings, regardless of the child's sex. In addition, such families are usually characterized by a politically progressive orientation, all of which helps towards the formation of women activists ready to get involved in party politics. But, this kind of woman is still uncommon: some empirical findings show that 21 per cent of female respondents (as opposed to 12 per cent of male respondents) do not want to get involved in the solving of social problems. It is therefore understandable that at the beginning of 2000 only seven per cent of women, as compared to 15 per cent of men, were involved in the work of political parties. Although these figures do not deviate significantly from the indicators for the more developed democratic countries, they are less favorable than the comparable figures for the socialist era. It seems that family socialization, which was not under social control and which retained many conservative traits, seldom directed girls towards political activity.

A 1997 study confirmed women's lack of motivation to participate in politics, as well as the existence of some specific attitudes in comparison to other European countries. Croatian women respondents on the whole showed a perceptibly greater interest in politics than respondents from a chosen group of European Union countries: 86 per cent of Croatian women said they were moderately or strongly interested in politics. That is for example higher than men's interest in politics in Denmark (59 per cent), Germany (51 per cent), Great Britain (44 per cent), and elsewhere (Mossus-Lavau, 1991). Every other woman respondent in Croatia claimed to be close to a political party (almost the same number as men), but only four per cent of women wanted to get actively involved in politics. No significant difference was found with respect to women with different levels of education and different employment status: about 80 per cent of women with primary school education and 93 per cent of women with higher education showed an interest in politics (Leinert Novosel, 1998). The findings from December 1999 show a growing trend in women's interest in politics: as many as 91 per cent of women stated that they are moderately or strongly interested in politics. When analyzing women's interest in politics one should have in mind the 'phase of stagnation', which almost invariably begins around the age of 26 when family and work commitments begin to compete for women's time; the interest then grows again in the middle age and reaches a peak around the age of 50. Women who manage to transform a strong motivation and an inclination towards activism into political activity go on to become the rare women members of political parties. Generally, women are few in the membership and leadership of even the more modern parties.

Media Representations of Women

Given the polarised views on women's social responsibilities and the general resistance to women sharing power with men, it is interesting to examine whether media portrayals of women reinforce one or other dominant views of women's social roles. A study conducted in Croatia in January 1997 enabled an analysis of TV content, and specifically of the question of what kinds of stereotypes does TV present about women and men, and how it forms the minds of young people with regard to gender. The analysis showed that women were considerably represented in a formal sense in the creation of the shows (62 per cent of reporters were women, and 38 per cent men), but they had no considerable influence on TV content or on making programming decisions. In the period under study there were twice as many male figures as female figures; women primarily appeared in documentary, educational, and youth-oriented shows, while male characters dominated in news and current affairs programmes. The majority of female figures appeared in off-peak viewing times (54 per cent of men and 45 per cent of women in the afternoon), while in the prime time (evening) slot there were only 17 per cent of women in contrast with 83 per cent of men.

Women were featured in shows with no specific subject, and in those dealing with art, health, and related issues, while men participated in programmes dealing with politics, national defense, and sports. Similar differences were recorded with regard to representation in particular professions: women were mostly persons with no specific profession (16 per cent), followed by persons with professions related to arts and the media (25 per cent combined). Men were mostly politicians (35 per cent), then artists of all kinds (14 per cent), military personnel (nine per cent), and various experts (six per cent).

In short, the dominant television image of woman is as a dependent, confused, passive, and unsure person with a modest fund of knowledge, while men are represented as ambitious, dominant, courageous, strong, and smart. The content component of the analysis (focusing on topics and professions associated with women) showed that the social status of women is low, while men's social status is high, which can be recognized in the fact that men are connected with professions that by themselves denote strength and power. As a vehicle for socialising a population's views on gender, the media in Croatia are evidently a powerful vehicle for forming (or confirming existing) attitudes to gender relations.

Strategies for Increasing Women's Representation

The idea of quotas for women (Leinert Novosel, 1990, p.172), which has a long tradition in many developed democracies, provokes very different party reactions in Croatia. The more modern, left parties always favored quotas for women as the most effective method of intervention. The liberal parties, which later and very gradually started to introduce quotas in their party programs and practices, maintained that women's entrance into politics should be a result of personal ability, and not of sex. The traditionalist parties did not like the idea of quotas at all. Prior to the 2000 elections, the SDP, HSLS and HDZ claimed to have informal gender quotas, and the SDP manifesto explicitly supported mandatory quotas for women on party executive bodies (Glaurdic, 2003, 298-299). The fact that the gender quota was a relatively acceptable measure for giving women equal access to power for these three major parties suggests the existence of a strong and articulate women's presence within and outside party organisations.

The SDP's women's forum, formed in January 1995, has the objective of uniting women around improving gender equality within the party and society. The forum pays particular attention to training and promoting women candidates and lobbies for greater gender balance in candidate selection within the party. It is clear that the left parties SDP and HSLS have more woman-friendly recrutiment practices, with women in both parties constituting over one-quarter of their candidates in 2000.

The HDZ women's group has also played a role in influencing a more gender-balanced selection process. However, in this case, advances in women's selection and election are not based on ideological commitment, but instead are down to the personal influence of one powerful party woman, Jadranka Kosor, vice-president of the women's section and member of the party's executive council. In 2000, the proportion of HDZ women candidates more than doubled to 13 per cent, due to her efforts. However, the conservative outlook of the party suggests that such gains may not be sustainable in the future.

Similar to the goals of the other two women's intra-party groups, the Peasants' Party women's organisation, Croatian Heart, also has the aim of increasing the numbers of women in position of power within the party. Formed in 1998, it has had more success in organising educational and related activities for women than in getting women selected. Although the party has adopted a 30 per cent gender quota, HSS women have not been successful in getting it implemented.

The final major contributor to the debate on women's representation is BaBe (Be Active, Be Emancipated), a non-governmental organisation with roots in the women's movement. BaBe has raised the issue of women's absence from political power in public debates, campaigns and media-catching strategies at all elections in independent Croatia. It organises training programmes for women candidates from all parties and is credited by leading party women with making an important contribution to the dramatic increase in women's representation in 2000 (Glaurdic, 2003, 299-300). However appropriate is this anecdotal attribution of BaBe's success in empowering women, the increase in women's representation in the Sabor in 2000 is also due to the more mundane operation of the list system. Many women candidates got Sabor seats as substitutes for male candidates who took posts in the executive government.

Within the wider political system, gender equality in decision making has been accorded recognition in a number of different ways. Constitutional changes in December 2000 mention gender equality as a basic human right for the first time. A new national policy on equal rights of the sexes has been formulated and prepared for adoption, and the unclear concept of equality (*jednakost*) has been replaced by a new concept – equal gender rights (*ravnopravnost*). A draft law on equal gender rights, initiated by NGOs and outstanding experts, has been put forward for debate. On the eve of the local elections in the spring of 2001 legislation on the operation of political parties was enacted, and it introduced an incentive for women's candidacies – ten per cent higher financial support for women candidates of each political party that exceeded the five per cent election threshold. A requirement of the new electoral law regulating the local elections was that every political party include at least 30 per cent of women on their election candidate lists. These examples of affirmative action (i.e. the quota principle and funding incentives) are designed to reward those parties that include women in political decision-making.

To complement the governmental interdepartmental committee on equal gender rights (established in 1996), a new parliamentary committee has been set up – the Sabor Committee for equal gender rights. Composed of MPs of both sexes from different parties, its remit is to analyse new draft laws from the point of view of equal gender rights, and take action (by way of lobbying) for the adoption of a gender perspective in all laws debated in the Sabor.

Women in the Sabor: Making a Difference

The notion of 'critical actions', which in the developed democracies is increasingly supplanting the term 'critical mass', relies on a substitution of quantitative by qualitative indicators of women's political activity (Dahlerup, 1988). The idea of measuring the 'efficiency' of Assembly (Sabor) representatives emerged in 1999, on the eve of the election campaign, with the aim of determining who represents the interests of voters in the Sabor, and in what way, and how that role is carried out by women.

An analysis of the content of Sabor debates on laws, programs and reports (altogether 43 Sabor documents) showed that women were proportionately more active in the debates than men (Alliance, 2000). The activity index – the ratio between the number of instances of participation in debates and the numbers of women and men representatives in the Sabor – was 2.1 for women and 0.9 for men. The analysis also showed that the women representatives from the then-opposition (SDP, HSLS, LS, HSS, IDS, and HNS) were three times more active than their women colleagues from the HDZ. Sensitivity to social issues was measured on a scale of 1 to 5, where 1 meant insensitivity, and 5 meant maximum sensitivity. The representatives from the then-opposition parties also showed a greater social sensitivity than HDZ women representatives: the former got the average grade of 4.1, and the latter 3.0 (Alliance, 2000, 15, 29). In their participation in debates, women from the democratic opposition showed a perceptibly higher degree of modernism (2.8) than HDZ women representatives (2.4), which was also true in attitudes on women's questions. The few women in the Assembly became politically recognizable to the citizens of Croatia through their participation in Sabor debates. Their preference for traditionalism or modernism did not deviate from the ideological orientation of the parties to which they belonged.

In spite of the setting up of the parliamentary committee on equal gender rights, it is still not clear whether decisions taken by its members will be subordinate to party lines or take precedence over them. Committee members, even those from parties of the left, often speak of difficult battles in their own parties to get to an understanding of women's issues and to harmonize positions to be later defended in the committee and in the Sabor.

The behavior of representatives in the Sabor is in part motivated by a formal promotion of causes that facilitate Croatia's acceptance in Europe. Thus, considerable lip-service is paid to gender equality issues. However, some parliamentarians are resistant to ideas on gender equality, and seek to ridicule them during debates. This kind of behavior, characteristic of some male representatives, speaks of their traditionalist views on the position of woman in society.

Conclusion

Women's politics in Croatia, just like any other sphere of politics, is an indicator of the overall political climate in the country. The dominance of a social-democratic discourse today ensures that women's politics has a more modern character, defining it as part of the wider European women's politics. The emphasis on developing the public role of women is coupled with a reduction in support for women's private role. However, that does not mean that Croatian public opinion is of one voice when it comes to supporting modern conceptions of the role and position of woman in society.

There are still tendencies that cast women in traditional roles. The advocates of traditionalist ideas still cling to the idea of woman as mother who primarily takes care of children, and to the idea that families should be encouraged to have more children. While the supporters of these ideas are now in a minority, and while they now do not have the political power to realize their goals, their public statements are an indicator of the degree of people's social awareness of the position of woman in society. The conflict between the modern and traditional concepts is not surprising, especially in the context of the worsened economic situation in Croatia. However, the dominant modern concept of gender equality is the realistic future of Croatia. It can help explain the increase in women in political decision-making, while the influence on this increase, such as the proportional election system, quotas and affirmative action, is still not clear. The interests of women's NGOs range between traditional and modern understandings of women's role in society, with more progressive tendencies dominating. The NGO sector is important, as it provides an independent perspective on women's concerns, counterbalancing the views of government and party politicians. However, their actual influence on changing people's attitudes is very limited. There are many reasons for this, the most important being the way in which these associations are funded. Lack of dedicated, consistent funding leads to rivalry between many NGOs, lack of development of specialist expertise in aspects of women's rights, and an absence of co-ordination of activities.

Not surprisingly, NGOs are primarily concerned with their own survival, and only in second place with the issue for which they exist. The work of these associations is most often of the 'campaign' type, which means that they get more active on the eve of elections and anniversaries or on other special occasions. Their manner of work is not thought out in advance or proactive, they do not anticipate events or prepare to participate in them; instead they react, and most often too late, to incidents related to the treatment of women in public life. Their work is not coordinated consistently, but rather occasionally, and even then the coordination most often follows private connections or sympathies.

The relationship of the government to civil society is the second important factor in making a successful women's politics possible. While in the past decade the ruling authoritarian HDZ government had a resentful attitude towards NGOs, considering them biased in light of the sources of their funding, today NGOs are treated as partners, but with insufficient and only temporary cooperation. It follows therefore that the women's NGOs played a much greater role in the past decade (when they were the only alternative to the ruling policies) than today under conditions of a more developed democracy. For this reason, NGOs need to redefine a positive role for themselves under the changed political circumstances of the 21st century. The areas in which the women's NGOs have had success to date are free legal counseling for women, support for abused women, collection of information on women, and training of women for political activity.

Challenges still remain within the party system for women. Although the 2000 elections brought increased women into parliament, these gains are not necessarily sustainable without a stronger commitment to gender equality from Croatian parties, as the election results of 2003 demonstrates. Moreover, the continued, and extended, implementation of gender quotas and other forms of positive action in party lists are called for if current gains are to be preserved and increased. However, given the polarisation of the party system into modernist/left of centre and traditionalist/right of centre blocs, an across-the-board acceptance of women's equal right to share power with men will not be easily won.

Notes

1 SKH-SDP – Savez komunista Hrvatske – Socijaldemokratska partija (League of the Communists of Croatia – Social-Democratic Party). Other Croatian parties include HSS – Hrvatska seijacka stranka (Croatian Peasants' Party), HSLS – Hrvatska socijalno-liberalna stranka (Croatian Social-Democratic Party); LS – Liberalna stranka (Liberal Party).

Chapter 11

Canada

Manon Tremblay

Introduction

Canada is a constitutional monarchy. This means that Canada's head of state is not the Prime Minister, but the Queen of Canada (Elizabeth II), whose powers are defined and restricted by the constitution of Canada. The Queen is one of the three component parts of the Canadian Parliament (together with the Senate and the House of Commons). Among other things, she is invested with executive power and is commander in chief of the armed forces. In actual fact, however, the Queen no longer fulfils anything but highly symbolic purposes such as embodying the state beyond party politics. The Queen of Canada does not live on Canadian soil: she is represented here by the Governor General, who, under the constitution, has the same authority as the Queen and, in her absence, administers the government of Canada on her behalf. In 2004, the position of Governor General of Canada was held by a woman, Her Excellency the Right Honourable Adrienne Clarkson. She was appointed in 1999 by the Prime Minister of Canada, the Right Honourable Jean Chrétien. The first woman to become Governor General was Jean Sauvé, who served from 1984-1990.

Canada is not a unitary state. Like its neighbour to the south, it is a federation. The 1867 Constitution Act expressed the desire of the provinces of Canada, that is Lower and Upper Canada, (which roughly correspond to the Quebec and Ontario of today), Nova Scotia and New Brunswick, to enter into a federal union for the purposes of constituting a single country. Since that time, other provinces and territories have joined the ranks of the Canadian federation, the last being the Territory of Nunavut, which was officially constituted on 1 April 1999. According to the principle of federalism, there is a division of powers between the federal parliament and provincial legislatures. Under the Constitution Act, 1867, the Parliament of Canada wields exclusive legislative authority in matters pertaining to postal service, census and statistics, currency and coinage, marriage and divorce, and criminal law, to mention a few. The provincial legislatures have complete authority to make laws applying within their borders regulating, among other things, education, municipal institutions, the celebration of marriage, property and civil rights in the province and the exploitation, preservation and management of non-renewable natural resources and forest resources of the province. Certain jurisdictions, such as agriculture and immigration, are also shared between the federal government and the provinces. Over the years, Canadian federalism has become increasingly centralized (Pelletier, 2000).

In 1867, Canada adopted a British-style parliamentary system. In addition to the Queen, the Canadian parliament consists of two houses (bicameralism), the Senate and the House of Commons. Under the Constitution, the two houses of parliament have the same powers, except in financial matters, in which the Senate operates under certain restrictions. The Senate consists of 105 senators, who are appointed by the Governor General on the Prime Minister's recommendation, and represent the regions. The House of Commons is the chamber in which the people are represented: its 308 members are elected by the citizens of their respective constituencies to represent them in Parliament. The members play a number of roles, including that of passing legislation (which senators also perform), of course, but also that of representing their ridings, monitoring the executive and acting as ombudsmen. According to the constitution, the maximum length of a parliament is five years, after which members must obtain a new mandate from their electors. It is the Prime Minister's prerogative to decide on the election date.

The electoral system used to elect the members of the House of Commons of Canada is a single-member constituency plurality system (or the first-past-the-post system): following a single ballot, the person with the most votes is declared the winner, without it being necessary to have an absolute majority of ballots cast in the riding. Unlike the list system, in which each party elects a number of names by area of election, in a majority system such as Canada's, each party may put forward only one person per constituency. According to some, this electoral system is unfavourable to the election of women, a point to which we will return below.

The partisan system which animated the Canadian electoral scene in the 20th century may be characterized as a 'two-party plus' system – the Liberal and Progressive Conservative Parties plus the New Democratic Party of Canada (Erickson, 1997). This last, unlike the first two, has never formed the government, whereas the Liberal Party held power for more than 70 years during the 20th century. Throughout that period, the Progressive Conservative Party mainly occupied the right of the political spectrum, the Liberal Party the centre and the New Democratic Party the left. In the 1990s, however, there was a collapse of this 'two-party plus' system, which, in 1993, was replaced by a multi-party system, when new political parties, the Bloc Québécois and the Reform Party (which became the Canadian Alliance in 2000), were added to the House of Commons.[1] The Bloc, a left-of-centre party, promotes the defence of Quebec's rights and Quebec sovereignty. The (new) Conservative Party, most of whose support comes from Western Canada, clearly sits on the right of the political spectrum: its neo-conservative orientation is based on both an economic conservatism (eliminate the deficit, reduce debt and taxes, less state interference) and social conservatism (law and order, family values, protection of private property), while advocating a new style of representation based on the accountability of politicians. Despite their ideological differences, the five parties in the House of Commons have one point in common: they are reluctant to address the political representation of women.

Lastly, legislative and executive powers in Canada are intertwined, in that the latter emerges from the former: as a general rule, the leader of the party that elects the most members to the House of Commons is called upon to form the government, drawing upon the members of its party in the House of Commons. To remain in power, the government must have the confidence of a majority of members, which explains why Canadian political parties are very disciplined. Party discipline is based on a common position which is imposed on party members with respect to policies and voting in the House (Tremblay, Pelletier and Pelletier, 2000, p.447). The impact of party discipline on the political representation of women is not clear. However, if women could enter political parties, party discipline might help to improve their political representation (Tremblay, 1999, p.200-6; Young, 2002).

The purpose of this chapter is to sketch the broad outlines of the presence of women in the Canadian parliament, in particular the House of Commons. The first section provides a historical analysis of information on the descriptive representation of women in the lower house. This is followed by a review of the main problems encountered by women in getting elected to the House of Commons and a discussion of a number of strategies for increasing the presence of women in the Canadian Commons. The final section will assess the question whether women MPs are making a difference in parliament. In conclusion, a few of the challenges facing the representation of women in the Canadian House of Commons for the future will be considered.

Historical Portrait of Women in the Lower House

The first suffragist organizations saw the light of day in Canada in the late 1870s. The struggles for women's right to vote were punctuated by four bills, in 1885, 1898, 1917 and 1918, when the suffragists finally achieved success.[2] The debates on female suffrage included a broad range of arguments. On the one hand, granting women the right to vote was seen as causing a number of problems: family harmony would be undermined, women would not know how to vote and the balance of political forces would be destroyed. Some even went so far as to contend that women simply did not want the vote. On the other hand, granting women the right to vote was interpreted as an avant-garde decision, an act of modernization: women could employ their 'natural' abilities in the public sphere, thus helping to solve certain social problems such as alcoholism and the misery of poor families, abilities which society clearly needed at the dawn of the first social reforms.

In 1919, Canadian women won the right to run in federal elections. Two years later, they exercised for the first time their right to vote and stand for election, and as a result Agnes Macphail was elected to the House of Commons. However, as Table 11.1 shows, her election did not trigger an influx of women to the House of Commons: it was not until the 1970s that the overall proportion of female members exceeded one per cent, and not until 1988 that it rose above ten per cent. Another important observation to be made from Table 11.1 is that the 2000 election resulted in the stagnation of the number and percentage of women in the House of Commons of Canada. The 2004 election did not really improve this disappointing trend. Had a glass ceiling been reached in the representation of women?

Table 11.1 Women in the Canadian House of Commons, 1921-2004

Year	Total Seats	Women MPs	% Women MPs
1921-67*	3557	29	0.8
1968	264	1	0.4
1972	264	5	1.9
1974	264	9	3.4
1979	282	10	3.5
1980	282	14	5.0
1984	282	27	9.6
1988	295	39	13.2
1993	295	53	18.0
1997	301	62	20.6
2000	301	62	20.6
2004	308	65	21.1

* This global category includes the 14 federal general elections held from 1921-1965

Source: Author's calculations

With respect to executive duties, it was not until 1957 that the first woman joined the federal executive: that year, Ellen Fairclough became Secretary of State of Canada in the Progressive Conservative Diefenbaker government. The following year, she was appointed Minister of Citizenship and Immigration, then, in 1962, Post Office Minister, a position she held until she was defeated in the 1963 federal election. She was the only representative of her gender throughout her stay in government. Of the 175 women elected to the Canadian House of Commons from 1921 to June 2004, only 30 (17.1 per cent) were appointed to the executive as full ministers. That figure is low enough, but greater than the proportion of women elected to the Commons following the federal elections from 1968 to 2004: 11.1 per cent (347 females out of a total of 3138 MPs, see also Studlar and Moncrief, 1997). Of those 30 female MPs who were called upon to serve the Canadian government, 66.7 per cent(20 of 30) held more than one ministerial portfolio during their careers in Ottawa. However, only six (24 per cent) of those members who had ministerial responsibilities exercised them as senior ministers at least once in their political careers. The majority did not rise above the middle level of the ministerial hierarchy.

Table 11.2 provides a breakdown of the portfolios held by women in the federal government, by importance of the department and length of term in years. Apart from one woman Prime Minister (Kim Campbell from June to November 1993), the few women admitted to the pinnacle of federal power as senior ministers were responsible for a very limited range of portfolios: justice and health, two areas clearly associated with traditional female roles. On the other hand, women who acted as junior and intermediate ministers were responsible for non-traditional departments, such as foreign trade, consumer and corporate affairs, energy, forests, mines and natural resources, infrastructure, national revenue and employment. Ultimately, it appears that the idea that women are excluded from executive power must be revisited: although few have been senior ministers, they have been proportionally more numerous in the executive than in the legislative branch of state, and, in government, they have not been solely responsible for social matters.

Table 11.2 Federal Departments with women full ministers, 1958-2004

Senior Departments	Years
Health	1963-65; 1977-79; 1980-84; 1993; 1993-96; 2002-03.
Justice	1990-93; 1997-2002.
Intermediary Departments	
Canada Post	1962-63.
Citizenship and Immigration	1958-62; 1996-99; 1999-200; 2003-.
Communication	1975-79; 1986-88; 1993; 1996.
Consumer and Corporate Affairs	1983-84; 1984.
Defence	1993.
Environment	1974-75; 1984-85; 1993-96; 1997-99.
External Relations	1984-86; 1986-93; 1993.
Heritage	1996-97; 1997-2003; 2003-04; 2004 -.
Human Resources Development	1999-2003; 2003-04.
Industry	2003-04.
Intergovernmental Affairs	2004 -.
International Cooperation	1997-99;1999-2002; 2002-03; 2003-.
International Trade	1986-88.
Labour	1984-86; 1988-91; 1995-96; 1998-2003; 2003-04.
Multiculturalism	1996.
Natural Resources	1984-86; 1993; 1993-95; 1995-97.
Privy Council	2004-.
Public Safety and Emergency Preparedness	2003-.
Public Works and Government Services	1986-87; 1997.
Revenue	1976-77; 1996-97; 2002-03.
Treasury Board	1999-2003.
Junior Departments	
Indian Affairs	1993; 1997-99.
Sport Canada	1963-65; 1993-96; 1996-99.
Veteran Affairs	1993; 2004-..
Western Economic Diversification	1993.

Source: Author's calculations

Obstacles to Women's Political Representation

Access to the House of Commons of Canada is gained in four stages: eligibility, recruitment, selection and election. Each of the stages poses certain problems for women in getting themselves elected to the Parliament of Canada. As mentioned above, Canadian women won the right to vote in the federal election in 1918. In that respect, Canada was in the first wave of countries granting women the right to vote following World War I. The second wave occurred in the wake of the decolonization movement. Some studies have focused on the potential existence of a link between the year in which the right to vote and to run in elections was won and the percentage of women in parliaments, although no conclusive findings have been reached.

Recruitment is an informal process consisting of identifying in the population persons who may eventually enter the ranks of political personnel. It concerns a problem of supply: for reasons of socialization and gender roles, women do not have all the necessary assets (in terms of educational, occupational, temporal, social and other assets) to run in elections. Girls and women are said to be socialized in such a way that they do not consider politics as something possible for them, while gender-based social roles (in particular their family and domestic responsibilities) act as a real impediment to their political involvement. In support of this reading, the theory of countersocialization suggests that women involved in politics have experienced exceptional socialization for their gender, which has been confirmed by some Canadian research (Gingras, Maillé and Tardy, 1989, p.82; Tardy, *et al.,* 1982, p.38; Tremblay and Pelletier, 1995, pp.15-16). In Canada, this explanation, which draws on recruitment, has been explored inter alia by Bashevkin (1983a), Brodie (1985, pp.77-97, 1991), Gingras, Maillé and Tardy (1989, p.147), Kay, Lambert, Brown and Curtis (1987, 1988), Maillé (1990a, p.135; 1990b, p.4), Tremblay and Pelletier (1995, pp.17-37), Vickers and Brodie (1981).

Selection is the process used by political parties to designate their candidates. It entails a problem of demand: women purportedly do not meet the expectations of local political elites, who do not see them as winners. Not that the elites would knowingly dismiss female candidates, out of hand, but their understanding of what constitutes a winning candidate, as embodied in the *homo politicus* model, does not include women (Carroll, 1994, p.158-9, Norris and Lovenduski, 1989). However, in Canada, local elites are among the most important players in the selection process for candidates in a federal election, much more than national elites, because that selection is decentralized and informal (Carty and Erickson, 1991; Erickson, 1997, Sayers, 1999, pp.5-9). Thus, it is up to each party organization in the constituencies to name their candidate. In addition, the rules of the selection process are not defined by the state, which means that they vary from party to party, indeed from constituency to constituency for a single party.

The candidate selection process is a fundamental reason for the small number of female members of the House of Commons of Canada. Research has shown that it is more difficult for women to be selected as candidates by local elites than men (Erickson, 1991, 1993, 1997, 1998; Erickson and Carty, 1991, MacIvor, 1996, pp.261-7; Norris, Carty, Erickson, Lovenduski and Simms, 1990; Tremblay and Pelletier,

2001). A number of factors are apparently involved: women do not have the financial means to bear the cost of a nomination campaign (Bashevkin, 1993, pp.170-1; Brodie, 1991; Maillé, 1990b, pp.4-5), they do not have a network of contacts to support them (Bashevkin, 1982, 1991, 1993, pp.84-5; Brodie, 1991; Brodie and Vickers, 1981; Erickson, 1991, 1993; Gingras, Maillé and Tardy, 1989, pp.106-7; Tremblay and Pelletier, 1995, pp.27-32; Vickers ,1978; Vickers and Brodie, 1981), and, lastly, they face a large number of opponents for the nomination (Erickson, 1991).

While the candidate selection process appears to pose problems for women, it cannot be contended that it systematically excludes them because some do, in fact, run for office in federal elections. One belief suggests that women may be candidates in uncompetitive ridings. This explanation appears in many studies (Bashevkin, 1982, 1983b; Brodie and Vickers, 1981; Erickson, 1991; Kay, Lambert, Brown and Curtis, 1987; Vickers, 1978; Vickers and Brodie, 1981), although it has not led to a consensus: it is uncertain that women are candidates in less desirable constituencies than those where men campaign (Pelletier and Tremblay, 1992; Studlar and Matland, 1994, 1996).

Like the selection stage, the election process is not without difficulties for women. The first lies in Canada's electoral system, a single-member constituency plurality system, which a number of studies have shown does not favour the election of women (MacIvor, 2003; Matland, 1998; Norris, 2000; Rule, 1987; Rule and Norris, 1992). Multi-member proportional representation by list would do more to help women get elected (Darcy, Welch and Clark, 1994, pp.160-7; Kenworthy and Malami, 1999; Matland, 1998; Reynolds, 1999; Rule, 1992; Siaroff, 2000). And yet, apart from the electoral system, the will of political parties to open their doors to female candidates remains crucial in order to increase the number of women in politics (Matland and Montgomery, 2003). Besides, it appears that the parties' openness to women varies depending whether they are in power or in opposition: of the 175 female federal MPs from 1921 to June 2004, 122 (69.7 per cent) were elected for the first time under the banner of political parties that were not in power at the time the election was called. The parties interpret the opportunities that the electoral systems and electoral situation afford and then they act accordingly. Furthermore, electoral and partisan systems are part of a broader political context which reflects culture, values, attitudes and other factors. Relying on the fact that many proportional representation countries have fewer women in their parliaments than Canada, even with a proportional electoral system, if the parties are not determined to increase the presence of women in politics, there will be no more. France is a clear example of this.

The turnover rate in the House of Commons of Canada also appears to be a systemic barrier to the election of women. For the moment, there are no limits to the number of consecutive mandates a parliamentarian may seek. It is well known, however, that incumbents are more likely to succeed than candidates who have never sat in Parliament (Krashinsky and Milne, 1983, 1985, 1986; Pelletier and Tremblay, 1992). Since men occupy nearly 80 per cent of seats in the Commons, they thus have an advantage over women. In fact, the problem for women rests in getting elected the first time, since incumbent female members who seek a new mandate are equally competitive candidates as men (Tremblay, 2002a). That said, two points should be made for a full appreciation of the incumbent member's advantage. First, compared to other parliaments, the House of Commons of Canada has a high turnover rate, which is more of an asset than a barrier to the election of women in Canadian federal politics (Young, 1991). Second, the advantage of the incumbent member depends on the government's stability. By returning a Liberal government to power for a third consecutive mandate, the 2000 federal election not only resulted in the stagnation of the number of elected women, but more importantly it led to a significant reduction in the number of new female members: only eight women entered the Commons for the first time, compared to 19 in 1984, 21 in 1988, 39 in 1993, 25 in 1997 and 20 in 2004. In 2000, it was mainly incumbent female members who were reelected. The election of the Progressive Conservatives in 1984 and of the Liberals in 1993 marked significant advances in the representation of women in the House of Commons due to the success of new candidates who joined the ranks of female incumbents.

The problem women encounter in getting elected for the first time is less significant when they run for office in a constituency left vacant by a member from their party (Pelletier and Tremblay, 1992; Tremblay, 2002b). The problem is that women do not receive their fair share of these so called inherited constituencies, as was the case in the November 2000 federal election (Tremblay, 2002a). If the parties truly wanted to increase the presence of women in the House of Commons, they would offer them these inherited ridings on a priority basis.

Lastly, the third argument advanced to explain why so few women are reelected to the House of Commons of Canada is that the electorate resists female candidates. However, studies instead tend to suggest that women are not less competitive candidates than men in that they do not attract fewer votes (Hunter and Denton, 1984). Quite on the contrary, with respect to the federal elections held in Quebec between 1945 and 1993, Tremblay (1995) has shown that, given identical electoral status, women win more votes than men (see also Tremblay, 2002a).

In summary, women's under-representation in the House of Commons of Canada is explained by factors both short-term (such as the availability at the time of an election in inherited constituencies) and long-term (for example, gender-based socialization and social roles). Both have called for responses which, in the Canadian context, have not been forthcoming.

Strategies for Increasing the Presence of Women in the Canadian Commons

What strategies have been developed in Canada to increase the number of women in the House of Commons? Unlike other countries, the question of the representation of women in the Commons has scarcely mobilized the feminist movement, even less the federal government and political parties. To put it bluntly, the federal government has done nothing to improve the place women occupy in the Commons. This, moreover, does not mean that it has not been informed of the problem of women's exclusion from Parliament. In the early 1970s, the Royal Commission on the Status of Women (RCSW) lamented the absence of women from federal politics and argued not only for more women to be appointed to the Senate, but also for the political parties to run more female candidates.

One strategy available to parliament to induce the parties to head in this direction is financial in nature. Canada has a public financing system for campaigning political parties and candidates. If it truly wished to increase the presence of women in the House of Commons, it would act on one recommendation made by the Royal Commission on Electoral Reform and Party Financing (RCERPF), that the number of female candidates elected be one of the criteria for the refunding of political parties' election expenses. To date, this recommendation has remained a dead letter, although it was discussed in 1999-2000 in the context of the proceedings of the Standing Committee on Procedure and House Affairs when reforming the Elections Act was being considered. However, Parliament did not adopt it, and the Standing Committee merely expressed the wish, in its 22nd report, that policy and programs be put in place to increase the presence of women in the House of Commons, and that those provisions remain at the discretion of the parties. Until recently, the only provision of the Canada Elections Act that might promote an increase in the number of female members is that which recognizes child care expenses as an election campaign expense (not a nomination expense), which is definitely positive, but does not amount to much.

On 19 June 2003, Bill C-24 received royal assent. Amending the Canada Elections Act and the Income Tax Act, the Bill introduces spending limits for nomination contestants which is now fixed at one-fifth of the limit permitted for a candidate's election expenses in that electoral district during the immediately preceding general election. The recommendation echoed the findings of the RCSW and RCERPF that a party's nomination campaign could constitute a serious barrier to women's entry into the House of Commons of Canada. It will take several years before we can assess the genuine impact of this electoral change upon women's access to the Canadian House of Commons.

In the meantime, there is nothing to prevent the political parties from adopting measures to increase the number of female candidates in federal elections. And yet, in essence, they have scarcely made any particular efforts in this direction. The two new federal parties – the Bloc Québécois and the (new) Conservatives – have no plans to include more women in their candidate ranks. The New Democratic Party and the Liberal Party have a pool of funds to support the election campaigns of their female candidates. However, amounts allocated are still largely insufficient to cover the actual expenses of an election campaign. For example, average election campaign expenses reported by female candidates to conduct their 2000 federal election campaign were $18,778, whereas the average amount paid by the Judy LaMarsh Fund to female Liberal candidates was approximately $2,000 and by the Agnes Macphail Fund to female NDP candidates $1,200. Furthermore, although they have been in existence for a number of years now, support for these funds is far from unanimous within the parties. A survey recently conducted of female and male candidates to the 2000 federal election shows significant differences of opinion between women and men over the idea of allocating special and additional funds to aspiring female members: all female NDP respondents supported the initiative, compared to 72 per cent of male NDP respondents; 82.6 per cent of female Liberal respondents endorsed it compared to 53.4 per cent of male Liberal respondents who rejected it, while the corresponding figures for the Progressive Conservative Party were 55.6 per cent of women in favour and 78.6 per cent of men opposed.

The Liberal Party of Canada and the New Democratic Party are the two parties that have invested most to promote access for women to the Canadian House of Commons. At its 2000 biennial conference, the Liberal Party, under pressure from the National Women's Liberal Commission, resolved to urge the federal government to amend the Canada Elections Act so that day care expenses and other necessary family expenses incurred during the nomination and election campaigns could be included in election expenses. As noted above, for the moment, child care expenses are an election expense qualified for public reimbursement. The National Women's Liberal Commission succeeded in having the principle of spending limits for expenses incurred during nomination campaigns, a principle which is now part of the Canada Elections Act. Furthermore, the Women's Liberal Commission is also very active in encouraging women to seek nomination and preparing them to campaign, through information seminars, training sessions and mentoring programmess designed to establish relationships between new arrivals and women with experience in politics (Young, 2003).

A political philosophy that places it on the left of the Canadian political spectrum and a more intimate relationship with the feminist movement are likely not unrelated to the fact that the New Democratic Party has distinguished itself by its commitment to supporting women in politics, and even did so in the 1990s (Young, 2000, pp.136-140). One practice recently introduced by the NDP to foster the emergence of more diverse candidacies in the 1993, 1997, 2000 and 2004 federal elections was to divide Canada into clusters of constituencies, for each of which a targt (but not a quota) was set to achieve a balance of candidates in terms of the presence of women, persons with disabilities, visible minorities and Aboriginal persons. While this procedure spared the ridings where an incumbent member was seeking a new mandate (thus illustrating the barrier raised by the power of incumbents to renewing political personnel), a minimum of 60 per cent of constituencies where the NDP had reasonable chances of winning had to be allocated to women. At the same time as it invited more women to run in the nomination campaigns, the NDP also adopted a provision reimbursing child care expenses incurred during the nomination campaign, to a maximum of $500, effective for the 1997, 2000 and 2004 elections.

The Canadian feminist movement has not made women's political representation a priority on its agenda. This attitude may be explained in part by certain characteristics of the Canadian political system which scarcely stimulate any movement to elect women to parliament. These include the dominance of catch all parties, which, in the context of a majority electoral system, must negotiate extensive popular support and cannot adopt a form of representation identified with certain groups, and enforcement of party discipline which oversee parliamentarians' words and deeds and limit their independence. As a result, the feminist movement has expressed mixed and uneven interest in electoral politics. According to Young (2000, pp.54-81, pp.132-82), relations between the feminist movement and the federal government in this regard have gone through two phases. From 1970 to 1985, the liberal (or reformist) trend, which was at the time dominant within the feminist movement, saw the appropriateness of getting involved in electoral contests. The movement thus adopted a multi-partisan approach and maintained relations with the three major political parties then represented in the House. Since the mid-1980s, a transformation in the structure of political opportunities (in particular the 1984 election of a clearly neo-liberal government) as well as a consolidation of socialist and radical feminists within the movement led it to distance itself from the electoral scene and to adopt a non-partisan approach.

During the first period, the feminist movement's actions in the federal electoral field were to inform the political parties on women's issues, maintain informal ties with the three parties in Parliament and encourage them to present more female candidates (Young, 2000, pp.58-67). Two of the initiatives taken at the time clearly show the convictions of certain feminists about the appropriateness of getting involved in federal politics: the establishment of Women for Political Action (WPA) and the Feminist Party of Canada (FPC). The objective of the WPA, which was founded in 1972, was to increase the proportion of women in Canada's political institutions. In the 1972 federal election, two WPA members ran as independent candidates. The WPA subsequently reoriented its strategy: the idea was now to get involved in all established parties to make them more receptive to women, rather than to act as a separate party, an orientation which the Feminist Party of Canada adopted. The FPC, founded in 1979, pursued an objective of increasing the quantitative and qualitative representation of women on the federal political scene, in particular by promoting electoral participation more in harmony with feminist ideals. The FPC wound up its activities in 1982 (Zaborsky, 1987, 1988). Then as now, every electoralist strategy, such as those of the WPA and FPC, could scarcely produce results because of the Canadian electoral system, which, contrary to the proportional formulas, does not promote the election of female or male candidates from parties associated with a representation of interests which is perceived as too specific. In the absence of a gender gap as a result of which women would vote for women, and of a concentration of women in any part of the country, any plan by a feminist party (or women's party) in Canada is doomed to failure (at least if the idea is to have its candidates elected).

The second period, from the mid-1980s to the present, has been characterized by a distancing of the feminist movement from electoral politics. However, this does not mean that the movement – and its liberal (or reformist) component in particular – has entirely left the electoral scene. In fact, during that time, a whole series of strategies for increasing women's political representation has been deployed, including a leader's debate on women's issues and the introduction of groups dedicated to increasing the number of women in federal politics. Even the National Action Committee on the Status of Women (NAC), which was highly critical of electoral politics at the time, nevertheless thought it appropriate to develop voters' guides, at least for the 1993 and 1997 elections. In addition to the traditional leaders' debate on seemingly 'general' issues, the 1984 federal election witnessed a leaders' debate devoted specifically to women's issues. That event, which could not be repeated in subsequent federal elections (at least involving all party leaders), was probably not unrelated to the constitutional debates of 1980-1982, which not only effected a general mobilization of the feminist movement, but also put gender equality issues on the Canadian political agenda.

On the organizational side, the Committee for '94 was established in 1984 with the objective of achieving equal representation between women and men in the House of Commons by 1994. Until 1996, when it was dissolved, the Committee organized numerous activities to promote the election of women in federal politics, including conferences and an internship program so that women could familiarize themselves with political structures. Canadian Women for Political Representation (CWPR), a group based in Ottawa whose mission was to encourage women to take part in all forms of political involvement, was founded in 1986; it wound up its activities in 1989. Based in British Columbia, the Canadian Women Voters Congress (CWVC) is a non-partisan organization that is committed to encouraging women's political engagement within all levels of government. The CWVC established an annual Women's Campaign School, which includes three-day training and information sessions for women who wish to pursue elected office, or who wish to participate actively within a political campaign. At the end of 2004, the Women's Campaign School was still active.

More specifically on the Quebec political scene, Femmes regroupées pour l'accès au pouvoir politique et économique (FRAPPE) was founded in 1995. Like other organizations of its kind, FRAPPE was dedicated to promoting the participation of women in decision-making bodies by supporting the nomination of female candidates and providing them with training. Although FRAPPE still exists, its activities are quite limited. Conversely, two other organizations, the Groupe Femmes, Politique et Démocratie, and the Collectif Féminisme et Démocratie, have been seriously mobilizing over the course of the past few years. Founded in 1999, the mandate of the Groupe Femmes, Politique et Démocratie is to promote and support women pursuing political and democratic involvement. To that end, the group organizes educational activities that raise women's awareness of the importance of women's active participation in decision-making institutions. Additionally, training and information sessions are held for women who aspire to political office. The Collectif Féminisme et Démocratie, formed in March 2002, has been more specifically engaged in the campaign for reform of Quebec's democratic institutions. In particular, the Collectif is focusing on the adoption of a new electoral system, and the means by which specific conditions or proactive measures could be used to increase the number of women in the National Assembly of Quebec.

Encourage, inform, recruit, educate, train: these are the verbs that best describe the strategies deployed by the feminist movement in Canada – and particularly its liberal (or reformist) component – to increase the presence of women in the House of Commons. However, there is one verb that, until recently, was not part of the strategies used by liberal feminists to improve the political representation of women, and that is 'to finance'. Unlike other countries such as Australia and, in particular, the United States, the feminist movement in Canada has not a history of established funds (such as Emily's List) designed to support female candidates (or even male candidates with feminist positions). This may be explained in part by the very provisions of the Canada Elections Act under which only contributions to a political party or a candidate are tax deductible, which scarcely encourages donations to other players who may also perform important roles in Canadian political life. However, the absence of feminist financial support for women political hopefuls began to change in 2003 with the establishment of the *Fondation Femmes, Politique et Democratié*, which assists women running for political office.

Ultimately, the strategies developed by the Canadian feminist movement to increase the number of female members in the House of Commons have been more to adapt women to the electoral and parliamentary ground rules than to change the rules themselves. And yet increasing numbers of voices are being raised in Canadian society demanding a change from the majority electoral system to one favouring proportional representation. Although countries with a proportional or mixed electoral system generally have more women in their national parliaments than countries with majority systems (Squires and Wickham-Jones, 2001, p.9), proportional representation does not automatically guarantee more women in politics, as may be seen from the examples of Greece and Israel. In fact, the true source of any increase in the number of women in the House of Commons will stem from a genuine commitment by the parties to elect more women to it. This objective of having more women in the parliamentary arena is all the more necessary since some opinions suggest that women would make changes in politics.

Are Women Making a Difference in Canadian Politics?

The question of the presence of women in politics calls for two understandings of the word 'representation': descriptive and substantive. Descriptive representation favours the identity of the persons elected: in their composition, deliberative assemblies must be a reflection of the population, like a scale model or a microcosm. This reading of representation suggests that the female population is represented solely by the presence of women in political institutions. In this perspective, although the political representation of women remains deficient, it has nevertheless improved over the years: now that 20 per cent of the members of the House of Commons are women, Canadian women are better represented today than in 1921, when fewer than one per cent of parliamentarians were women. Nonetheless, women continue to suffer from the ongoing democratic deficit. Substantive representation is based on ideas: what is important is less the identities of the persons elected than their opinions and actions. Consequently, this reading of representation does not presuppose that the mere presence of women in parliamentary institutions is sufficient to represent women: to do that, they must express ideas and engage in actions to respond to the needs, demands and interests of women. In an informal manner, this perspective links the political representation of women with feminism: what is important is less the number of women in Parliament than their convictions and commitments, such that only a few feminist women would be sufficient to represent women (Trimble, 1993). More recently, Phillips (1995) has knowingly linked together presence and ideas: for symbolic reasons, it is important to have women in politics, but need we be concerned about their ideas? Since women and men have different collective experiences, women's access to national parliaments should affect their culture, rules and procedures, priorities, approaches to the decision-making process and public policies, their style and so on. In short, women's access to parliamentary institutions should transform the governance of those institutions in descriptive, of course, but also substantive ways.

In empirical studies focusing on Canada (of political staff at the federal level and in the provinces, territories and municipalities), there is no consensus as to whether women are making changes in politics. This lack of consensus is probably related to the diverse types of questioning, populations and methodologies used to explore this aspect of the political representation of women in Canada.

On the one hand, some studies show that women are not making a difference in Canadian politics. This is purportedly the case, for example, in how women understand the role of political representation and related activities. In their representation activity, elected persons may play a number of roles. They may be delegated and act not in accordance with their own judgment, but with the desires and wishes of their electorate and of what they consider to be in its interests (it is the delegate model). On the other hand, elected persons may play their representational role by relying on their own reading of the desires and interests of their electorate, notwithstanding the electorate's own judgement on the matter (the trustee model). Lastly, depending on the circumstances, representatives may embrace both these orientations (the politico model; Birch, 1964; Wahlke, Eulau, Buchanan and Ferguson, 1962).

Based on the idea that women appear to make a difference in Canadian politics as a result of collective experiences different from those of men, how then do they position themselves with regard to these roles as delegates, trustees and politicos? It may be hypothesized that they will favour the delegate model. As women have privileged relations with the domestic sphere and human reproduction, they should be more sensitive to people's day-to-day lives, their problems and aspirations, and more concerned as well with consulting them in a public decision-making context. In short, they should be closer to the people they represent. This reading does not hold. In virtually identical proportions, female and male members of the House of Commons saw themselves in January 1996 as trustees first of all.

However, the parliamentarian's role is more complex than a mere polarization between two alternatives. It implies a broad range of activities such as taking part in debates in the House, operating a riding office, developing party policies and working with interest groups, among other things. The idea that women are making a difference in politics implies that they maintain different relations from those of men with these activities which characterize the political representation role and, in particular, that they adopt a more people-oriented style. Some Canadian research supports this reasoning. Women questioned by Crow (1997) in Ontario and Tremblay (1996) in Quebec said they appreciated municipal politics precisely because of the proximity which that level of government afforded between them and their constituents. Yet other research conducted in the early 1990s of members from Quebec suggests that political men value exchanges with the public as much as their female counterparts. When asked what they preferred in their representational role, a very large majority of female and male parliamentarians said they enjoyed the sense of serving their community, which of course presupposes a certain proximity to people (Tremblay and Pelletier, 1995, pp.209-11).

As Table 11.3 shows, of the 14 activities evaluated by female and male members of the House of Commons in January 1996, none resulted in statistically significant differences between genders. What is more, contrary to what is suggested by the idea that women are making a difference in politics as a result of collective experiences different from those of men, female members do not attach more importance to activities that take place in their constituency (where they would thus be closer to people), such as operating their riding office, helping to solve specific problems, assisting in activities in their local communities or working with interest groups. And yet – and to add to the ambiguity – the same survey also shows that, while female and male members reported virtually the same areas of interests in politics, women attached slightly more importance to social topics (human rights, justice, the environment), thus substantiating the idea that they are closer to people.

Table 11.3 Canadian MP perceptions of importance of activities (%)

Activity	Important	
	Women	Men
Speaking in parliament	15.4	23.9
Holding regular constituency surgeries	4.0	1.1
Attending local party meetings	11.5	19.3
Parliamentary committee work	11.5	26.1
Representing regional interests	3.8	13.6
Helping with individual problems	0.0	0.0
Supporting the party leader	0.0	10.5
Developing party policy	0.0	10.3
Voting the party line in parliament	30.8	39.8
Speaking to the media	26.9	23.9
Attending local community functions	0.0	5.7
Representing the constituency in parliament	0.0	1.1
Working with interest groups	34.6	43.2
Defending party policy	15.4	25.3

Source: Author survey

On the other hand, some studies show the opposite – that women are making a difference in Canadian politics. Trimble (1997, pp.130-1) believes that female politicians can alter the direction of politics by speaking and acting on behalf of women, in at least five ways: (a) they can bring women's experiences to the political arena, those experiences previously considered as private under the traditional division of gender-based roles; (b) they can be in contact with the feminist movement and bring its demands into the political arena; (c) they can consider the criterion of gender when speaking out on legislation; (d) they can develop women's policies deliberately intended to change and improve the living conditions of the female population; (e) they can promote a different parliamentary style.

What is certain is that political women *feel* they are making a difference in Canadian politics. This 'mandate of difference', to borrow Skjeie's (1991) expression, is apparent from two studies of women elected to the Canadian House of Commons. The study by Tremblay and Pelletier (1995) was conducted on female and male Quebec members of the House of Commons and National Assembly in the late 1980s. It shows that a majority of female members felt that women and men managed political power in different ways, a judgement that was moreover shared by their male colleagues (Tremblay and Pelletier, 1995, pp.69-83). The second study, by Tremblay (1999, pp.173-210), was conducted on women elected to the Canadian House of Commons in October 1993. To the question, 'In your opinion, do women make a difference in politics?', 42 of the 44 female members interviewed answered in the affirmative. Those women felt they were making a difference in three areas: the political agenda, public policy and parliamentary style. These members contended that they had put certain issues on the political agenda which would have been ignored in their absence. They also affirmed that they were changing public policy, although less with regard to content than to form: women were more capable than men of grasping public policy through a humanistic, holistic, even feminist approach and more sensitive than men to the impact of public decisions on people's everyday lives (Brock, 1997; Carbert, 1997; Tardy, Tremblay and Legault, 1997, p.58-60). Lastly, with regard to parliamentary style, some female members contended that women were changing the parliamentary space (creating a parliament more sensitive to women's needs, for example) and time (changing the sitting schedules of the House, for example) and that they were altering the behaviour of their male colleagues in the House (by reducing, for example, the incidence of sexist jokes and the use of vulgar language; see also Desserud, 1997; Gingras, Maillé and Tardy, 1989, pp.228-9; Tremblay and Pelletier, 1995, p.64; Trimble, 1997).

Apart from the sense of making changes, do women actually alter the direction of politics – in other words do female members express ideas and engage in actions that can meet the needs, demands and interests of women? Some studies suggest they do. Considering speeches made in the House of Commons during the first session of the 35th Parliament, Tremblay (1998) made the following finding: female members were more inclined than male members to speak and act for the purpose of supporting women's issues, although that activity remained marginal with regard to the more general mandate of representation (see also Tremblay, 1993; Tremblay and Pelletier, 1993). In addition, at least once in the Parliament of Canada, the presence of women made a difference for the women in the population: in 1991, the mobilization of female senators made it possible to defeat Bill C 43, the purpose of which was to recriminalize the practice of abortion in Canada (Sharpe, 1994, pp.208-9, Tremblay and Boivin, 1990-1991).

Ultimately, are women making a difference in Canadian politics? By their presence alone, women are definitely altering the descriptive representation of the Commons, not to mention that they can be models and thus inspire young girls and women to make a commitment to politics. That said, with regard to substantive representation, the findings to date suggest the need for prudence. Some studies show that women are not making a difference in politics; women conceive of their representational role and related activities within the same parameters as men. Others suggest that female MPs feel they have a 'mandate of difference': female politicians contend that they are making a difference with regard to political agenda, style and public policy. Some empirical studies support this reading: female politicians more than their male counterparts express ideas and engage in actions that can meet the needs, demands and interests of women.

Any analysis of the substantive representation of women in Canadian federal politics must however be sensitive to the ground rules of Canadian parliamentarianism which can promote or limit women's ability to speak and act in favour of the female population. For the time being, women have not achieved a critical mass in the Canadian House of Commons. And, if the results of the 2004 federal election are a herald of things to come, then this critical mass should not be expected in the near future. Furthermore, female members are not organized in a multi-partisan caucus with a view to analyzing and promoting women's issues in Parliament even if the Liberal Party (which forms the government) has such a structure. And, even where a women's caucus exists, party discipline can greatly limit the ability of female members (particularly if they belong to the government party) to speak and act for women. However, once more numerous, influential and organized in a structure that can mobilize female parliamentarians, they may eventually take control of party discipline and put it at the service of the political representation of women. Unfortunately, for the moment, these conditions are far from being met.

Conclusion

The main challenge facing the political representation of women in Canada in the coming years is one of definition and action: that the low representation of women in the House of Commons be defined as a democratic deficit, and that it be part of a broader reform of federal political institutions. First of all, it is important that the public become aware that women have been excluded from descriptive representation in Canada, that this bypassing be defined as a deficiency of representative democracy, and that the will to correct the situation should arise. This public awareness can only come through an extensive social debate in which findings are made, objectives set, alliances set up and solutions reached. What is more, this kind of public debate is essential in order to encourage the political class and political parties to commit to change. The example of France speaks for itself: French political elites would never have accepted parity if they had not been compelled to do so by public opinion (Tremblay, 2000-2001).

Any reform of federal political institutions will be all the more accepted by the public, the political class and the parties if it maintains deeply-rooted links with the values which have hitherto animated Canadian political life. Equality is one of those values, as witness its inclusion in the Constitution, particularly in the Canadian Charter of Rights and Freedoms. An interesting way to understand equality is as parity: since humanity consists of women and men in roughly equal numbers, the precincts of power should be distributed equally between the two genders. Parity not only aims at diversity, but also imposes balance on representation, a quality which, for the moment, is strikingly lacking, as men account for about 80 per cent of political representation. Proceeding with a reform of federal political institutions on the basis of parity between women and men would entail reviewing the constitutional and institutional parameters which form the theatre of political representation. It is clear that no effort to achieve parity can be made without certain changes in the electoral system and without a genuine desire by the parties to make more room for women in their ranks.

Although, according to one trend of Canadian public opinion, changes should be made to the electoral system, such changes have not been the subject of public debate. Consequently, the first step in this direction would be to launch a social debate on political representation, a debate that would include the more specific issue of the political representation of women. In this regard, the example of Scotland is an important one: after a number of years of public discussion, the new Scots political community chose to maintain certain ties with its electoral traditions, while opening up to a form of representation more concerned to reflect social diversity. Scotland thus adopted a mixed electoral system combining majority representation and proportional representation. Some academics have suggested that Canada should adopt such a mixed electoral system (Milner, 1997, 1999).

Parity also leads one to imagine parties operating less as closed cliques and more as entities concerned with inclusion. Whether it be majority system or proportional representation, parity cannot be achieved without a genuine investment by the parties in the political representation of women. Proportional representation favours the election of women, provided it is based on lists on which female candidates are in an eligible position and where they alternate with men (the zipper system). However, women cannot be put in an eligible position unless the parties wish to make more room for them in their ranks. The majority system requires this will among the parties all the more since it offers resistance to the election of women. And yet, provided parties cooperate, certain strategies can be considered within the majority system in order to tend toward female/male parity. These include:

a) inviting the political parties to cast their net more widely when they recruit potential candidates by considering, for example, more customary female socialization areas such as community groups, socio-cultural organizations and women's groups;
b) ensuring that more women are in positions of power within the political parties, thereby encouraging them to develop a support base in order to carry nominations;
c) establishing data bases of potential female candidates on which candidate selection committees can draw, and update them regularly;
d) better defining the rule in effect during nomination campaigns and exercising better control over campaign finance;
e) making money available to aspiring female candidates in order to help them pay certain expenses incurred during nomination campaigns;
f) reserving for female candidates who are not incumbent members constituencies where they have real chances of being elected, namely constituencies left vacant by the departure of a member from their party;
g) providing training to female candidates to maximize the extent of their abilities and

personal resources;

h) assessing monetary penalties for parties that do not have a sufficient percentage of female candidates;

i) maintaining, increasing and supporting the money that certain political parties reserve for their female candidates;

j) promoting the establishment of private funds intended to support the election campaigns of female candidates.

Ultimately, the main challenge for the political representation of women in Canada over the next few years is to modernize federal political institutions: to shift from a democracy that endorses the confiscation of political power by a minority of men to a democracy that views the two genders as constituent principles of its representative institutions – in other words, a democracy of parity.

Notes

[1] The Reform Party became the Canadian Alliance in 2000. After merging with the Progressive Conservatives in 2004, they now form the Conservative Party and in this chapter are referred to as the (new) Conservatives.

[2] Women in the Canadian Armed Forces as well as certain women with close male relatives in the British or Canadian armies obtained the right to vote in 1917. The right to vote, an elementary attribute of citizenship, was denied to women and men of certain minorities (Chinese, Japanese and South Asians) until the 1950s, and it was not until 1960 that Parliament passed legislation granting the vote to all adult Aboriginals in Canada.

Chapter 12

Switzerland

Thanh-Huyen Ballmer-Cao

Introduction

Compared to other countries, the Swiss political system is characterized by the following elements: highly developed federalism that allows the management of a society traversed by divisions in religion, language and ethnicity; an equally widespread direct democracy that strongly integrates the various actors while dividing power among them; an electoral system organized as a function of the very important proportionality rule; a four-party government represented by a college of seven equal members; and a parliament composed of two chambers in which the National Council represents the people and the Council of States represents the regions (called cantons in Switzerland). In addition to these institutional elements, it is the way in which the political system functions in Switzerland that constitutes its distinctive mark, namely the concordance based on compromise and the division of power.

Quite paradoxically, in this very old democratic system that pretends to be attentive to political representation and the division of power, the participation of women in the making of decisions has a very young history. Formally, it goes back only to 1971 with the introduction of women's suffrage and their eligibility in federal elections. One of the last western countries, and indeed one of the last countries in the world to grant this elementary political right to half of its population, Switzerland had been the figurehead of conservatism, even of misogyny at the international level. It must, however, be recognized that a process of 'catch-up' has recently taken place. Soon after the introduction of women's suffrage, an entire series of changes made Switzerland into a country that conformed to the international standard in terms of equality between men and women. This catch-up was surprising not only because of its extent, but also, and perhaps especially, for its speed. Indeed, the transformations affected not only the division of political power but also many other domains, particularly the revision of laws, especially equality and family codes, the creation of government agencies responsible for gender equality and the introduction of a minimum 30 per cent quota for women in extraparliamentary commissions of the Confederation. Moreover, the speed of the achievements was exceptional for a political system known for its sluggish decision-making, especially where controversial issues are concerned.

While limited to the representation of women in the Swiss legislative assemblies, this chapter will analyze the catch-up process and will advance a number of explanations. The first section outlines the pattern of women's political representation since the 1970s, followed by consideration of a number of possible explanations including institutional variables intrinsic in the Swiss political system. In conclusion, the issue of female political participation will be highlighted within the context of more recent developments in contemporary Switzerland.

Swiss Catch-up – A Thirty-Year Process

If female representation more or less progressed everywhere during the three last decades, the Swiss case merits notice. At the dawn of the year 2000, women represented approximately a third of the Swiss government, a quarter of the lower house (23 per cent of the National Council) and a fifth of the upper house (19.6 per cent of the Council of States). These ratios, still far from equal or proportional to the Swiss female population still appear sizeable if one considers the fact that voting rights and electoral eligibility were not granted to women until 1971, just over thirty years ago. Compared with other European countries, Switzerland was ranked 11 of 21countries in terms of female representation with its first legislative election in 1971 and has more or less maintained this position (at 7th place in 1979, 12th in 1995 and 12th in 2000). Two other considerations tend to highlight Switzerland's progress. On the one hand, compared to Liechtenstein (four per cent women MPs in 2000), the last country in Europe to introduce women's suffrage, Switzerland has improved substantially. On the other hand, by its self-exclusion from the European Union, Switzerland did not directly benefit from the spill-over effects of egalitarian policies that were openly promoted by the EU institutions (European Communities 1998, pp.20-1).

Can Switzerland be considered a success in terms of women's representation? A thorough examination of the question suggests a rather inconclusive answer. To understand the dynamics of women's participation in politics more fully, it is necessary in the Swiss case to examine female representation at all levels: state (federal), regional (called cantons in Switzerland) and local (called communes).

Currently, the local (communal) parliaments are the most feminised at approximately 29.8 per cent female, whereas the regional (cantonal) parliaments are only 24.2 per cent female and the federal National Council is 26 per cent female. This pattern suggests the observation that female representation decreases as the level of political power increases. Furthermore, one must also note that the proportion of women elected at the national level decreases even more when one considers the Upper House (the Council of States), where the cantons are represented and which is only 23.9 per cent female (Table 12.1). Thus, the 'glass ceiling' in Switzerland still exists today and it becomes more pronounced as one advances towards the center of power.

If one considers female representation in the legislative assemblies over time, it becomes evident that even the modest proportions that have been reached today are the result of a gradual process of development.

Table 12.1 Women in Swiss parliaments (%), 1971-2003

Year	National Council	Council of States	Cantonal Parliaments	Local Parliaments
1971	5.0	2.3	7.2	-
1975	7.5	0.0	6.2	-
1979	10.5	6.5	8.6	14.2
1983	11.0	6.5	10.2	15.9
1987	14.5	10.9	12.3	18.1
1991	17.5	8.7	15.2	23.5
1995	21.5	17.4	22.0	27.3
1999	23.5	19.6	24.8	29.8
2003	26.0	23.9	24.2	-

Source: Swiss Office of Statistics, 1999, 2000 and 2004

Table 12.1 reveals a slow yet continuous progression at each electoral level, with variations in each case. At the level of communal (local) assemblies, a shift seems to have taken place at the end of the eighties, following which female representation exceeded a threshold of 20 per cent. A rather similar but later evolution took shape for the cantonal parliament. It is possible to detect three phases of development at this level, each approximately one decade in length. The first, from 1970 to 1979, registered less than 10 per cent female representation; the second, from 1980 to 1991, saw an improvement but without exceeding the 20 per cent limit. The largest increase in women's representation came during the third phase, from 1991 to 2003, although it still did not exceed 30 per cent. The pattern of women's representation in the federal National Council is rather similar, but within shorter, eight-year phases. The Council of States, even though it is elected by a majoritarian system and at different dates, seems to also follow this model of development since 1971. A feminisation of legislatures that varies inversely with the degree of power and that only progresses and converges gradually, the Swiss catch-up does not seem so unusual after all. In addition, averages of simultaneous progression at all political levels – communal, cantonal and federal – obscure the actual rates of representation. In effect, behind these percentages, one must detect many gaps in the feminisation process that may be partisan, regional, or demographic in nature. We will limit ourselves to the most significant of these.

To begin with, the proportion of women elected to the Swiss parliaments differs greatly along political lines. In general, one can say that feminisation is appreciable on the left of the political spectrum, modest in the center and insignificant on the right. In the 1999 national elections, for example, the partisan composition of the female contingent in the National Council was as follows: 55.4 per cent on the left (the Socialist and Ecological Parties), 36.1 per cent in the center (the Radical Democratic and Christian Democratic Parties) and 8.5 per cent on the right (the Swiss People's and the Liberal Parties). These variations are even more visible if one takes into account the electoral forces of the parties in question. Elected women formed two-thirds (67 per cent) of the Ecological delegation and two-fifths (39 per cent) of the Socialist delegation but they represented no more than one-fifth (21 per cent) of the Radical Democratic delegation or the Christian Democratic delegation (23 per cent) and less than one-tenth (seven per cent) of the Swiss People's delegation.

These differences in party attitudes and practices regarding women's representation are connected to a change in the electoral policy of parties in the early eighties (Ballmer-Cao, Bendix 1994, pp.130-132; Office fédéral de la Statistique 2000, p.7). Ideological (increased value of principles such as equality and pluralism), and strategic (partisan competition) imperatives led parties on the left to take an interest in the female electorate, promote the rise of women in the party and to address the question of inequality between the sexes. Gradually, this policy was reinforced by the progressive feminisation and political agendas of the leftist parties.

The implications of this are significant. Quantitatively speaking, one must note that the centrist and right-wing parties in Switzerland form a strong 'bourgeois' majority, while both the traditional and recently-formed parties on the left constitute a much weaker political force. As a result, the scope for an increase in women's electoral presence on the left is limited, given that left parties attract only 25 per cent or so of voter support. It is possible to thus observe a new aspect to the tension in the party system that reinforces the traditional polarization between left and right. A study of voting patterns of women and men in the National Council illustrates a rift between leftist women and bourgeois men (Ballmer-Cao, Schulz 1991, pp.86-7). Of course this double opposition hardly facilitates the legislative process associated with the central issue of gender equality. From the perspective of the political agenda, one ultimately observes the creation of a self-reinforcing dynamic around the question of gender: one-sided specialisation and monopolisation on the part of the left; relegation and corresponding disinterest on the part of the right that extends beyond the National Council and into the regional and local parliaments.

In addition to partisan variations it is necessary to consider differences at regional and local levels. In general, female representation increases according to the size of the constituencies and their degree of development. For example, the most populous and economically advanced regions tend to have the greatest influence over the election of candidates to the federal Popular House (National Council). This can be seen as an expression of an urban-rural divide in terms of progressive versus conservative political attitudes, yet it is more complex than this simple bi-polar explanation would suggest. Electoral mathematics, for example, function in such a way that the minimal proportion of the votes necessary to obtain a mandate is lower in the constituencies that have several seats, and cantons vary in seat size from one to 34, depending on population. Political psychology also plays a role: parties are more likely to feminise their lists when the number of available seats is sufficiently large. In addition, it is in the large electoral districts that left-wing parties are most active. A 1994 study shows for example that, of the 26 Swiss constituencies, 'the six largest electoral districts constituted 60 per cent of representatives in the Popular Assembly and elected 65 per cent of the female legislators between 1971-91' (Ballmer-Cao and Bendix, 1994, p.129).

At the regional level, the disparity in women's representation among the 26 cantonal parliaments is notable. The average, 24.8 per cent, masks very significant variations. Whereas certain groups hold proportions of 30 per cent and more, others have more modest numbers (i.e. less than 15 per cent). Apart from explanatory factors that are mathematical, psychological or ideological in nature, which we have already discussed at the national level, the same study of Ballmer-Cao and Bendix suggests that regional political culture can also play a certain role in the explanation of the differences between the cantons. Prior to the introduction of female suffrage at national level in 1971, ten cantons had already granted women voting rights. The authors regard this phenomenon as 'proof of an egalitarian sensibility' and write that 'thereafter one would expect that this predisposition would facilitate a collective shift towards egalitarianism, translated into concrete acts and integrated in the political culture of the canton' (1994, p.128).

In short, inequality constitutes a major characteristic of the female presence in the Swiss legislative assemblies. Explanatory factors include the accentuated urban-rural divide, strong regional cultural disparities and large partisan differences. But these variations are not the only problems hidden by averaged figures. In addition to discovering the proportion of women elected in the parliaments, we must explore who they are, their political careers, and the extent of their power.

Who are Elected and How?

In terms of the national parliament, it is clear that the likelihood of being elected has tended to increase for female candidates since 1971, the year in which females obtained the right to run for election. But the improvement was rather modest and the probability of winning a seat remained lesser for women than for men (Office fédéral de la Statistique 2000, pp.15-20). This raises the question of the profile most likely to enhance a woman's electoral opportunities. An in-depth investigation in the late-1980s examining female representatives after elections at all political levels highlighted their very privileged socio-economic status, including: 'a copious stock of education, comfortable material living conditions and a relatively good integration into the labour market'. This explanation did not account for social mobility models, (provided by the extended and immediate families) experience with participation (at the associative level in particular), or the more flexible standards of gender roles (within the couple). (Ballmer-Cao, Wenger 1989, p.133). In addition, it was found that socio-economic status increased with the degree of power obtained. Compared to women in the regional parliaments and especially to those in the local parliaments, women in the federal parliament come from even more privileged social backgrounds. It may seem odd that the authors of the study use the word 'elitism' to qualify this emerging group of political women (Ballmer-Cao, Wenger 1989 p.135). This term should not, however, be considered erroneous. Paradoxically, the privileged status of elected women actually reflects unequal opportunities for women to enter the political sphere. Only individuals with sufficient resources, male or female, possess such opportunities. The threshold for acquiring necessary capital, however, is obviously higher for the marginal groups than for established groups. In other words, even if elective offices are formally open to women, only the already privileged among them will in fact have the possibility to seek and gain electoral office.

A subsequent investigation limited to the federal Popular House yields even more precise details. Compared to elected men, elected women are commonly younger and better educated, but are also less 'brilliant' professionally and less 'conventional' matrimonially (Ballmer-Cao, Schulz 1991 pp.82-3). Indeed the comparison mentions on the one hand, the concentration of elected women coming from 'feminine' professions, their frequent career interruptions for 'private or family' reasons and the lower professional positions they obtained compared to their training level; and on the other hand, the significant number of 'single women, women married without children and unmarried or previously married women with children'. Thus, the study notes 'the simultaneous existence of elitist elements and residual elements of more traditional gender roles'. Also, 'the access of marginal groups to dominant groups does not necessarily imply the democratization of the selection of elites' (Ballmer-Cao, Schulz, 1991, p.83).

An examination of the work that women perform in the parliaments also shows the limits of female integration into the political system. Again, at the national, cantonal, and communal levels, there is a profound specialisation among female representatives regarding issues traditionally identified with women: family, culture, education, youth (Ballmer-Cao, Wenger, 1989, pp.22-7). Thus, one is confronted not only by a glass ceiling, but also by walls of glass that characterize a political realm that remains largely segregated. However, the question of whether these invisible partitions constitute a barrier or a springboard for women in politics remains unanswered. The same study reveals large differences in interpretation on this subject by elected females. While some women speak about 'constraint' or the 'prolongation of traditional distribution of political gender roles'. Others speak of their 'crucial role' and their 'uniquely feminine contributions'.

Though it can appear remarkable, the Swiss catch-up should be contextualised by other studies that reveal a more nuanced perspective. It is evident that the proportion of females elected varies inversely with the level of power they stand to gain. In addition, the slowness of the progression, party differences, disparities between the regions, inequalities between male and female candidates before and after the elections, also constitute a good set of indicators of the limits of power-sharing between men and women.

Obstacles and Opportunities for Female Representation

Even after providing a contextual background, the Swiss political catch-up still requires explanation. It is not only a question of locating the forces behind the overall positive assessment but also identifying the obstacles hindering progress.

To this end, the role of the women's movement, along with the contribution of Swiss federalism, direct democracy and the electoral system, will be examined for their part in shaping the conditions for women's electoral prospects.

The Women's Movement

Women's organisations played an essential role in the long fight for the women's suffrage. Furthermore, once voting rights were introduced in 1971, collaborations gradually developed among feminist groups, as well as between feminists and governmental bodies charged with instituting gender equality. Aided by the Swiss system of direct democracy, women were mobilized around topics like equal rights, abortion, matrimonial rights, maternal assurances, and others. The issue of women's lack of political representation was a focus for action and campaigning by women's groups, with some success. For example, in 1993, the non-election of a female candidate to the Swiss government provoked a massive protest by women, and led to the election of more women in the subsequent regional and local elections (Haas et al, 1993). Inside political parties, women were just as active. In addition to many support measures such as the creation of an election manual for women, offers of specific training for candidates, creation of female electoral commissions, several parties introduced quotas (from 30 per cent to 60 per cent) for party lists and/or leadership roles (Commission fédérale pour les questions féminines 1995, pp. 54-5).

Federalism

Compared to other federal states, Swiss federalism is distinguished by strong decentralization, which implies a weak central state and very autonomous cantons (member states) which influence female political opportunities. Thus, far from playing a leading role, the Swiss federal state is often satisfied to follow the cantons in the introduction of new laws or practices. This is the result of a federalism simultaneously 'disposed to experimentation' (Aubert 1978, pp. 218-9) and 'open to all', where regions are more or less free to equip themselves with their own capacities or programs that can serve as examples for other member states or for the federal government to follow. Women's suffrage was a test case, introduced in ten cantons before it was introduced at the federal level or in other cantons. This model of innovation, which is based on institutions mimicking each other horizontally has some advantages. On the one hand, it frees the political situation in certain 'avant-garde' cantons, previously sensitized to gender equality. On the other hand, it persuades the more suspicious cantons, providing them evidence in favour of the innovation in question. Rapid progression in the election of women in Switzerland is explained partly by these mechanisms. As we have already underlined, the modern cantons played a significant role after the introduction of women's voting rights in 1971 by supporting the female delegation in the parliaments. This driving effect then took hold in a number of cantons that were also predisposed to implementing a progressive policy (Ballmer-Cao, Bendix 1994, p.127). Behind this process, it is also necessary, of course, to recognize the role of female organisations. These vigilantly inform each other of what occurs elsewhere, making local obstacles public by contrasting them with accounts of progress in other places. They thus create for themselves windows of opportunity that are open to social actors interested in change. By its thorough decentralization, Swiss federalism makes the democratization of power possible. By fostering extreme institutional diversity, the Swiss system tends to multiply its political structures, in particular its representative bodies at the local and regional levels. This small country of seven million inhabitants has in the entire political system, approximately 1,000 executive and 7,500 legislative representatives; this does not include public and private functionaries involved with the administration, parties, trade unions, associations. The scale of representational opportunities is sufficiently large and diverse to satisfy the aspirations of the many individuals interested in a political career, including women as new arrivals and as a marginal group. Of course, the various offices do not all offer equal degrees of power or prestige, but still this system of 'non-centralization' (Linder, 1999, p.136) democratizes power, and at the same time, it brings it to the citizens, most importantly to women (Aubert, 1978, pp.216-7). Indeed, the literature largely reports feminine 'localism', that is to say, women's tendency to engage in local and communal politics (Pagnossin Aligisakis, 1991, pp.356-60; Fox, 1997, p.67, 113). In addition, political opportunities are more prevalent at the local level, which represents an attraction for women to enter politics. The empirical data in Switzerland show in particular a tendency to rapid feminisation in the cantonal and especially local parliaments following the universalisation of voting rights and eligibility in 1971 (Figure 12.1).

Though favourable to the growth of female representation in politics, Swiss federalism also contains barriers to this progression. We begin with regional disparities. If the 'laissez-faire' attitude at the federal level is a response to national diversity, its weakness is apparent at times in its wait-and-see policy and even in its outright abstention, for instance, federal tolerance towards the cantons Appenzell Rhodes-Intérieures, where women's suffrage was introduced two decades after it had been accepted at federal level. There is also the risk of a decline in the national average each time a modern canton elects fewer women.

Direct Democracy

Direct democracy, another distinctive feature of the Swiss political system, also plays a significant role in the Swiss catch-up. Previously, it was considered as a weapon against women because it gave men the power to delay female political integration (Fauré 1999 p.146). However, direct democracy is a complex instrument whose impact is difficult to measure. On the subject of women's suffrage, for example, there were 136 cantonal votes between 1919 and 1984 (Ballmer-Cao, 1999 p.161); indicating that direct democracy was a frightening veto power in the hands of men, the only ones entitled to vote. In addition, highlighting the role of the male electorate in preventing female citizens from voting should not conceal the responsibility of political elites (also male) who often used the ballot boxes to transform parliamentary reticence into popular rejection. At this point it is necessary to make two points about the opportunities for women's political participation opened by direct democracy. First, it is used by individuals and groups that are female and/or feminist to intervene in the political agenda and to position themselves within the public sphere. In this respect, the campaigns for women's suffrage were not only significant moments in Swiss politics in general, but also constituted extremely important arenas of 'presentation' for one's political career. Only eight months passed between the acceptance of women's suffrage at the ballot box in February 1971 (65.8 per cent voted yes) and the election in October of the same year of ten women to the federal Popular House, several of them former 'suffragettes'. Second, as we will later see, occasionally direct democracy can contribute directly in making progress for female representation in politics. Indeed, popular initiatives were launched to introduce gender quotas in various decision-making bodies. In this case, direct democracy lends itself to the possibility of advancing and legitimizing a controversial issue.

Electoral System

The electoral system also constitutes a factor influencing the access of women to decision-making bodies in Switzerland, though the impacts of the electoral system are not easily measured and debate is far from over (Nohlen, 1990, pp.283-309). However, Swiss diversity is not only characterized by its political structures but also by its procedures, in particular the selection of elites. Indeed, the Swiss electoral system is extremely 'fragmented'. It happens, for instance, that the same political body may be elected by two different formulas, or that the electoral system may simultaneously produce 'contrary' impacts that are typically identified with another electoral system. It is necessary to take into account, moreover, a large variety of polling methods within federal, cantonal or local levels and that many exceptions render attempts at generalization futile.

In terms of the relationship between the electoral system and female representation, comparison of various empirical studies seems to suggest a that proportional representation delivers a 'feminising' result (Mossuz-Lavau, Sineau, 1984 pp.59-79; Ballmer-Cao, Pagnossin-Aligisakis 1997 pp.142-4). In the Swiss case, a comparison between the two federal houses shows that the upper house (Council of States), elected by majority vote, is less feminised than the lower house (National Council) elected by a proportionality system (Ballmer-Cao, 1995, p.265). Indeed, the party list proportional system introduces at least two elements favourable to the election of the women. To begin, this method is practiced in multi-member districts (two seats or more), which lowers the threshold of votes necessary to gain a seat and encourages the parties to propose female candidates on their lists. It is also true that the proportion of female representatives gradually increases with the size of constituencies (Ballmer-Cao 1995, p.265-266). Second, the Swiss electoral law also allows preferential voting. Voters sensitive to female representation in politics have the possibility of modifying the list proposed by the parties and to feminise it as they choose. Such a practice is present among left-wing voters, who often prove more egalitarian than their parties (Ballmer-Cao, 1995, p.268). Thus, rapid progression of female representation in the federal Popular House may be explained in part by the contribution of the largest constituencies where left-wing parties are also very active.

Of course, the feminising effect of the proportional electoral system also has limits. The first of these is on the party level. In Switzerland as elsewhere, the rank-order of the candidates within the list remains significant: the positions at the top of the list appear to the voters as the preferred party candidates and this positioning gives the higher candidates an advantage over others on the party list. Not surprisingly, parties generally reserve these privileged positions for the candidates most likely to win. In addition, when the list is a long one, the visibility of higher-ranked candidates is more prominent than for their lower-ranked colleagues. These are significant considerations in large constituencies that, in theory, are more favourable to women's political opportunities, as they emphasise the dependence of candidate positioning on party decision-making.

The second limitation of the proportional Swiss system is at the level of the electorate insofar as preferential voting can be turned against women. Maurice Duverger noted in the mid-1950s that 'The development of female representation appears under certain conditions, and it is even more pronounced since the freedom of choice of the voter is reduced' (cited in Mossuz-Lavau, Sineau, 1984, p.77). One half-century later, his statement is still valid in the case of Switzerland. The rare data concerning modification of the party lists according to the sex of candidates show that voters use their freedom differently, depending on partisan sympathies. Whereas the left-wing electorate is more disposed to feminising party lists, the right-wing electorate tends to 'virilise' candidate choices (Ballmer-Cao, 1995, p.268). This behaviour has serious consequences for women political hopefuls. To begin, it accentuates the left-right polarisation on the issue of female political representation, which we have already noted, even more so since, on average, leftist lists offer a greater number of female candidates than ballots on the right. It also supports the status quo because the leaders of the parties, especially of the right-wing parties, have little reason to change their policy which relies on putting forward strong male candidates. Lastly, female candidacies are seldom encouraged, given that vote maximisation strategies in a fragmented party system rely on parties running high-profile males.

In summary, an extremely advanced federalism, generous popular rights and a liberal electoral system – these are three distinctive features of the Swiss political system that applied pressure to the catch-up process of shared political power between men and women. These factors are far from the only ones, and their impact is not always unidirectional. This explains, on the one hand, the speed of take-off, but on the other, the persistence of faults as well as the formation and maintenance of obstacles to women's political progression.

The International Context

Of course, a Swiss catch-up process is not carried out in isolation from other influences. The international context plays a significant role in particular. If the influence of international relations on the question of gender equality seems to be an established fact (Sapiro, 1981, Berkovitch, 1999), the accelerating effect of globalization also seems to exert an influence (Procacci, Rossilli, 1997; Reinalda, 1999). To postulate such a relation in the Swiss case nevertheless requires additional explanations, because this country sees itself as an exceptional example ('Sonderfall'), and consequently, its foreign policies hardly promote active integration.

Because of its doctrine of neutrality, Switzerland has historically remained apart from three of the largest or at least most visible international organisations, namely, the United Nations, the European Union and NATO (North Atlantic Treaty Organisation). Although in 2002 the Swiss electorate voted to join the UN, it has not to date voted to become a member of the other two international bodies. Nonetheless, Switzerland is economically, culturally and politically active on the international stage (Armingeon, 1996). It is precisely in this context that the link becomes visible, between the Swiss take-off on issues of equal rights between men and women (encompassing access to political power and decision-making), and the progress made in other Western countries and the efforts made by the international organisations.

The introduction in 1971 of women's suffrage in Switzerland coincided with the renewed debates on women's rights gaining political salience in liberal democracies elsewhere. This temporal coincidence leads Christine Fauré to contextualize the Swiss late suffrage and refer to feminism as an 'instituting movement' (Fauré, 1999, pp.148-51). Strikingly, international relations were used directly by women's organisations to bring attention to their issues. The ratification of the European Convention of Human Rights by Switzerland in 1969 in particular provided an occasion to highlight the deprivation of Swiss women of the most elementary political right. The extension of the vote to women in 1971 is the product of this campaign. There is additional evidence of the direct impact of the UN on the question of equality between men and women in Switzerland, without Switzerland's formal membership of the UN. Already following the first World Conference on Women organized by the United Nations in 1975, for example, Switzerland supported recommendations in favour of a political promotion of women, in particular by creating government agencies in charge of this issue or by inscribing gender equality into the federal constitution. The political arena was thereby widened considerably, the national and international levels taking turns to complete and reinforce one another. Even remaining apart from the European Union and the United Nations, Switzerland is nevertheless permeable to the policies followed by these organisations. The UN recommendations or the directives of the European Union indirectly constitute standards for compatibility. Thus, the formation of international regimes, particularly regarding gender equality, has also had an undeniable impact on non-member states such as Switzerland. Even when neither conventions nor formal treaties exist, the Swiss government is placed under moral pressure, all the more so more when civil society can utilise international points of reference from which to legitimise their claims. Therefore, although remarkable at first glance, the progression of female representation in Swiss politics was no miracle. On the contrary, it constituted a rather faithful reflection of Swiss society, of its values, its political system and its position in the world.

Conclusion

Would parity of the sexes be the logical outcome of the Swiss catch-up? Once again, the fault-lines in this process already highlighted invite consideration. Strong regional variations testify to the existence of pockets of resistance; left/right disparity tends to undermine competition between the parties for the promotion of women and to delegate the question to the left-wing minority; the variations in numbers and especially of electoral opportunities between male and female candidates show that neither the parties nor the voters treat men and women identically; the strong presence of female representatives coming from traditionally feminine domains strongly moderates the widespread idea that women's access to the parliaments implies shared power and integration in public spaces; great biographical differences between male and female elected representatives such as social background, civil status and professional position are also indicators of a public career marked by gender inequalities. Of course, as was underlined on several occasions, the Swiss political system has some potential to feminise decision-making offices. However, one must wonder if its feminising effects could be fully deployed in an environment where women's electoral boost from the first years of women's suffrage is disappearing, where competition between candidates is accentuated and partisan rivalry becomes more intense.

It is in this context that the quota issue finds relevance in Switzerland. Indeed, beginning in the 1990s, one finds a whole wave of proposals seeking to introduce gender/women's quotas at various levels of government and in a range of public decision-making institutions. These proposals were not successful due to a strong and effective opposition to the demands for gender equity. Nevertheless, the debate had the merit of putting the problem of power-sharing on the agenda and in the process illuminating a remarkable fact: even in a country reputed for its proportionalism, gender is less recognized as an important criteria for representation as compared with region, partisan tendency or language.

Chapter 13

Australia and New Zealand

Sandra Grey and Marian Sawer

Introduction

In the late 19th and early 20th centuries Australia and New Zealand were hailed as pioneers of women's political rights and supported suffrage struggles elsewhere, particularly in the 'home country'. In 1911 the wife of the Australian Prime Minister together with the wife of a former New Zealand Premier marched through the streets of London for women's suffrage. But early achievement of rights in the Antipodes did not guarantee the presence of women in parliament, even as Hansard reporters. It was not until the 1990s that the two countries began to regain a pioneering reputation, Australia for its femocrats and New Zealand for its women political leaders. The patterns of convergence and divergence between Australia and New Zealand over the last 110 years tells us much about the specific obstacles to women's political representation and the methods used to overcome those obstacles.

Westminster in the Antipodes

Australia and New Zealand share a common political inheritance as former British colonies or settler societies within the Westminster tradition of responsible parliamentary government. The colonial heritage is manifest in the presence of Governors-General in Australia and New Zealand (and state Governors in Australia) who represent the British monarch and act as the head of state. It is also manifest in the similarity of the countries' flags, which both feature the Union Jack and the Southern Cross.

The two Australasian nations share another tradition – that of social liberalism, the form of liberalism that was at its height at the time of Antipodean nation-building. The pioneering social legislation introduced by Australian and New Zealand liberal governments in the late 19th and early 20th centuries, including industrial arbitration and old-age pensions, earned them a reputation as social laboratories of the world. The commitment to equal opportunity helps explain the early attainment of political rights by women. The similarities are particularly clear when we look at the colonies where women first gained political rights, New Zealand and South Australia. The latter was the Australian colony most like New Zealand in terms of its protestant population, the strength of the 'social gospel' in the late 19th century and the absence of Irish Catholic or convict legacies.

In both Australia and New Zealand the early flowering of social liberalism was squeezed out by the consolidation of class-based politics in the early 20th century and the rise of political labour. Fairly stable two-party systems established themselves on the basis of the class divide between labour and non-labour and the associated divide between more collectivist or more individualist ideology. The labour parties (spelled differently in the two countries) were created as the political arm of the trade union movement, and affiliated trade unions continue to play an important role in their structure. Since the 1970s post-materialist parties such as the Greens have appeared in both countries and the increased use of proportional representation (PR) in Australia and its introduction for the 55 list seats of the New Zealand House of Representatives has encouraged the diversification of the party system and some modification of Westminster majoritarianism.

While the political inheritance of the two nations is similar, there are also significant differences. Australia has a Westminster parliamentary system complicated by federalism and a Constitutional division of power between national and sub-national levels of government. There are six States, which all came into being in 1901 on the basis of the former colonies and which have equal representation in the powerful Australian Senate (the first popularly elected upper house in the world). There are two self-governing Territories, the Australian Capital Territory and the Northern Territory, which do not have the same powers as the original States, but which have representation in both Senate and House of Representatives. Australian parliaments are generally bicameral, with strong upper houses, except in Queensland where the upper house was abolished in 1922 and in the Territories, which have unicameral legislative assemblies.

Australia has experimented with many different electoral systems and has specialised in forms of preferential voting – particularly the alternative vote, and the single transferable vote (STV). At the national level the STV form of PR has been used since 1949 for the Senate, with State or Territory-wide constituencies, while the House of Representatives is elected through the alternative vote and single-member constituencies (Sawer, 2001).

New Zealand has in the past been acclaimed as the purest example of the Westminster system of responsible parliamentary government, with a unitary political system, a weak appointed upper house (abolished in 1950) and an electoral system based on single-member electorates and simple plurality (first-past-the-post) voting – resulting in a two-party political system and single-party majority governments. All this changed in 1996 with the introduction of the mixed-member proportional (MMP) voting system resulting in the shift to a multi-party system and coalition governments. In 1992 and 1993 referendums were held in New Zealand on the electoral system. At these referendums the voters opted to change from the first-past-the-post electoral system to MMP. This move came about due to voter disillusionment with the untrammelled nature of executive power exercised by governments in a unicameral Westminster system. There had been almost ten years of drastic neo-liberal reform by both Labour and National governments, with what voters believed to be little regard for the views of the electorate.

From Rights to Representation

A common heritage may explain similarities in the time lines for the attainment of political rights by women. Australasian women campaigning for the vote in the late 19th century saw it as the key to increasing women's influence on national life, particularly in areas such as temperance and child protection (Lake, 1999; Grimshaw, 1987). The Woman's Christian Temperance Union, brought to Australasia from the United States in the 1880s, was a major player and its white ribbon was everywhere in the suffrage campaigns. New Zealand granted women the right to vote in 1893, South Australia the following year and in 1902 newly federated Australia became the first country to allow women both to vote and to stand for national parliament. On both sides of the Tasman, however, four decades went by before voting rights were converted into the presence of women in the national parliament. It was not until 1933 that the first woman elected to the New Zealand House of Representatives while the first two women to enter the Australian Federal parliament arrived in 1943. As we discuss below, this long gap was the price paid for earliness combined with failure of the major parties to nominate women candidates and women's distrust of the party system.

There are some early differences in the stories of women's political rights. Australian suffragists were able to exploit the window of opportunity provided by federation to achieve national political rights. South Australian delegates to the 1897-98 constitutional convention argued that South Australian voters (who included women) would not vote for federation if South Australian women were to lose their vote in federal elections. As the achievement of federation was dependent on the outcome of referendums in each colony, this political blackmail was successful. A new clause was inserted in the Constitution whereby no one who already had the vote would lose it. The resulting anomalies, and the desire for a uniform national franchise for the new nation, led to the swift passage of uniform suffrage legislation for the federal parliament, at least for non-Indigenous Australians. The right to stand for parliament had been tied to voting rights, paving the way for women candidates in the 1903 federal election.

An early trans-Tasman difference in voting rights was the treatment of Indigenous peoples. New Zealand was notable for not excluding Indigenous women from the franchise. The Maori Representation Act 1867 created four Maori seats in the House of Representatives for which adult Maori males could vote. Maori women won the vote along with Pakeha (white) women in 1893. In Australia, Indigenous voting rights for the federal parliament were not made uniform until 1962. Although Aboriginal women were not excluded when women's suffrage was granted in South Australia in 1894, at the federal level Aboriginal voting rights (where they existed) were gradually eroded due to racial attitudes of the time.

The final major difference, as can be seen in Table 13.1, was the lag between voting rights and the right to stand for the New Zealand House of Representatives. However, in five of Australia's six States there was also a lag between granting of women's suffrage and the right to stand for parliament. The early timing of womanhood suffrage in New Zealand and Australia, meant those fighting for this right did not think it possible to extend their claims to include the right to stand in parliament. It is only in South Australia (and, as noted, at the federal level) that women won the right to stand and the right to vote at the same time.

Table 13.1 Women's political rights and representation

	Australia	New Zealand
Votes for most women	1902	1893
Votes for all women	1962	1893
Women's right to stand	1902	1919
First women elected	1943	1933
First woman in cabinet	1949	1947
First woman party leader	1986	1993
First woman Prime Minister	none	1997
First woman speaker	1986	none
First woman Governor General	none	1990

Source: Authors' calculations

Since the arrival of the first women in parliament, New Zealand has had slightly higher female representation in national politics than Australia. The divergence in parliamentary representation increased in the 1990s and in April 2003 New Zealand ranked 15th in the world according to the Inter-Parliamentary Union's index of women's parliamentary representation while Australia ranked 23rd. However, once we aggregate Australia's federal, State and Territory parliaments, to cover the same spread of legislative powers exercised by New Zealand's unitary parliament, we find that the representation of women in the two countries is almost identical.

Table 13.2 Women's parliamentary representation in Australia and New Zealand, April 2003

Country	Party	Number of women	%
Australia*	Greens	8	47.1
	Australian Democrats	5	41.7
	Australian Labor Party	152	35.3
	Independent	11	25.0
	Liberal Party	51	21.9
	Country Liberal Party	2	16.7
	One Nation	1	16.7
	National Party	8	13.1
Total		*238*	*28.9*
New Zealand	Greens	4	44.4
	ACT NZ	4	44.4
	Labour	18	34.6
	National NZ	6	22.2
	United NZ	1	12.5
	NZ First	1	7.7
	Progressive Coalition	0	0.0
Total		*34*	*28.3*

* The aggregate of Australia's federal, State and Territory parliaments is used, to cover the same spread of legislative powers exercised by New Zealand's unitary parliament.

Source: Commonwealth of Australia Department of the Parliamentary Library and the New Zealand Electoral Commission

New Zealand women have, however, gained a definite edge in terms of political leadership at the national level. In 1989 Helen Clark was elected deputy leader of the Labour Party and in 1993 became the party's parliamentary leader. On the other side of politics, a party-room coup inside the National government in 1997 led to Jenny Shipley becoming the first woman Prime Minister of New Zealand. Two years later, Helen Clark defeated her to become the first elected woman Prime Minister. Women held 35 per cent of positions in Clark's new Cabinet, including that of Attorney-General. A woman was co-leader of the Greens, the party holding the balance of power in parliament at that time, and a second woman was appointed to be Governor General in 2000.

There have yet to be similar successes in Australia where the only political parties to have been led by women at the federal level so far have been the minor parties. Since its formation in 1977 five of the nine federal leaders of the Australian Democrats have been women. At the State and Territory level things have been somewhat better: since 1989 two women have been Labor Premiers, two have been Labor Chief Ministers and one has been a Liberal Chief Minister.

Obstacles to Representation

Why did it take forty years for women to arrive in parliament in Australasia and another fifty for women to 'arrive' in leadership roles? Why have New Zealand women done better in national legislatures than Australian women? On both the supply and demand side of women's political recruitment, we will attempt to compare the institutional and cultural factors in Australia and New Zealand affecting women's political representation and impact.

It is sometimes said that low numbers of women in parliament can be explained by women choosing to stay out of the political sphere. While candidate figures are not a pure indication of the willingness of women to stand, because of the gatekeeping role of political parties, they do tell us something. Between 1901 and 1939 only 25 women stood for Australia's federal parliament, meaning 99.3 per cent of candidates were male. The situation improved marginally over the next 30 years (until 1969), when only about 96 per cent of candidates were male. Similarly in New Zealand nearly 93 per cent of all candidates between 1946 and 1975 were male (Hill and Roberts, 1990, pp.64-7; Sawer and Simms, 1993, p.56).

Apart from the small number standing as candidates in both countries, another reason for the failure of women to be elected was the decision by many to remain outside the existing political parties, by choice as well as by necessity. In the period up to 1940 in Australia, 75 per cent of women candidates ran as Independents or for minor parties. This is a remarkable statistic cross-nationally (Sainsbury, 2001, p.73), particularly given high levels of stable party identification and the unlikely event that sex loyalty would prevail over party loyalty. However, those who had been involved in the suffrage movement had few illusions about the existing parties – the parties lacked principle and were created by men to protect men's interests. These women also believed in the power of the vote, and thought it would enable them to purify politics and achieve social reform without being corrupted by the party spirit.

Some women, however, stood for parliament immediately after being granted the right to do so. Four women stood in the 1903 federal elections in Australia, and the same number of women put themselves forward in the 1919 New Zealand general election. The experience of the early cohort of women political candidates was not particularly encouraging and attitudes about women's roles in society and their maternal responsibilities were an inhibiting factor. It was not acceptable for married women to work outside the home in the first part of the twentieth century and this was underpinned in both Australia and New Zealand by the 'family wage'. In both countries suffragists provided endless reassurances that they would not neglect home and family if given the vote, but questions of who would mind the baby and who would cook the dinner dogged the political ambitions of women. When the first woman was elected to an Australian parliament she was accused by opponents of heartlessly neglecting her husband and children, although she was 60 at the time and her youngest child was 30 (Cowan, 1978, p.162).

The priority given to women's role in the home made political candidacy difficult and ensured it was largely restricted to women who had already fulfilled the expected wifely and maternal roles. Before 1960, nine of the twelve women

MPs in Australia were married at the time they won their seats and they were all older women. In New Zealand before 1960 only one of the seven women elected to the House of Representatives was unmarried. While social disapproval may have lessened, the practical difficulties of juggling family and political career are still considerable. A 1994 survey of women politicians in Australian and New Zealand showed that the carer role impacted on the willingness of women to participate in national politics in both countries (Coopers and Lybrand, 1994, pp.11-14).

One way for the first generation of women parliamentarians to achieve acceptance was through the 'halo effect' of standing in place of a deceased husband or father. The first woman elected to the House of Representatives in New Zealand, Elizabeth McCombs, took the seat of her late husband. Her two earlier attempts to gain a place in parliament had been unsuccessful. Six out of 11 of New Zealand women elected prior to 1970 were following in the footsteps of political husbands or fathers. In Australia, of the first ten women elected to State parliaments between 1921 and 1939, five were political widows or daughters and another had a brother in parliament (Sawer and Simms, 1993, p.78). The first two women elected to the Australian House of Representatives were also political widows, including Dame Enid Lyons, widow of a former Prime Minister. Political parties were willing to play the sympathy card, seeing political widows and daughters as useful seat warmers until another candidate was in place. On the other hand, these women often had considerable political experience and had significant political careers of their own.

It was the arrival of the 'second wave' of the women's movement that led to a sudden jump in the number of women candidates in both countries. Several factors combined in the 1970s to enhance the willingness of women to enter politics, including increased participation in higher education; economic changes resulting in increased workforce participation; consciousness raising by the women's movement; and political mobilisation to achieve women's movement demands (Mayer, 1973; Aitken, 1980).

But to be elected, there also needed to be a change of heart by the political parties. Australia and New Zealand are no exception to the general rule that in the older democracies political parties are the main barrier to women's political representation (Lovenduski and Norris, 1993). Prior to World War II no major party in Australia fielded a woman candidate for the Senate, and only one was fielded for a winnable seat in the House of Representatives. Women generally lacked the backgrounds in law or business or, on the other hand, the years spent in the trade union movement, that would have made them identi-kit party candidates. Nor did they have the networks from the clubs and pubs. Prejudice again women candidates remained strong within the major political parties into the 1970s (Wilson, 1992, p.40). In fact New Zealand Labour women were driven to picket their own party in 1974 demanding women's issues be given greater priority, at the same time that ALP women were downing tea towels at party conferences to make policy instead.

In terms of differences, local government participation was more important in the careers of the early cohort of women MPs in New Zealand than was the case in Australia. Until the 1970s Australian local government was largely concerned with roads, rates and rubbish and did not have the education, health and housing responsibilities which attracted women into local government elsewhere (Sainsbury, 2001, p.74). Unions were also even less likely to provide a pathway to parliament for women in Australia than in New Zealand. The lack of these local government and union pathways is one part of the explanation for historical differences in the levels of women's parliamentary representation in the two nations.

The excuse made by the major political parties well into the 1970s for the failure to put women into parliament in the two countries was that women political candidates were vote losers. In fact their poor performance reflected the character of the seats they were allocated to contest (industrial seats for conservative women, blue-ribbon conservative seats for Labor women). When Senator Susan Ryan was appointed to the ALP front bench after the 1977 federal election she commissioned polling research showing the fallaciousness of received party wisdom that women were vote losers. It was not until 1990, however, that the first woman (a former State cabinet minister) was pre-selected to a safe seat in the Australian House of Representatives – a seat with a margin of at least five per cent. In New Zealand it was not until 1972, nearly forty years after the first woman took her place in parliament, that a woman was given a safe seat.

As happens in many democracies, smaller parties in Australia and New Zealand field a higher proportion of women candidates than do the major parties. For the most part such candidacies are of the altruistic flag-waving variety and there is much less competition for them than for the safe seats of major parties. When it looks as though a minor party has a real chance of electoral success, the proportion of women candidates tends to go down, a phenomenon observed in both countries.

Making Policy not Tea

Of the major political parties in Australasia, we would expect the Labour parties to be more committed to equality and more prepared to take robust measures to achieve it. Statistics show the New Zealand Labour Party achieving greater levels of female representation in parliament than the conservative National Party. This is in part due to the philosophies of the two parties. Throughout Labour's history in New Zealand the party has had an egalitarian philosophy which had made it ready (if somewhat reluctantly) to accept the place of women in the party (Wilson, 1992, p.42). The major party of the right in New Zealand, National, is more focussed on individualism than on collective action, making it less likely philosophically to take action to increase the number of women in parliament. The difference between New Zealand's major parties was clearly in evidence after the 1999 election, when over a third of Labour MPs but less than a quarter of Nationals MPs were women. On the party lists women had been allocated 40 per cent of the top twenty Labour positions but only 30 per cent of the top twenty National positions. Similarly, as we can see in Table 13.3, in Australia women constituted 33 per cent of federal Labor parliamentarians after the 2004 election, but only 20 per cent of Liberal parliamentarians.

Table 13.3 Women in the Australian House of Representatives, 1972-2004 (selected parties)

	Australian Labor Party			Liberal Party		
Year	Candidates	MPs	%	Candidates	MPs	%
1972	4	0	0.0	3	0	0.0
1975	6	0	0.0	3	0	0.0
1977	15	0	0.0	2	0	0.0
1980	23	3	5.9	5	0	0.0
1984	18	7	8.5	14	1	2.2
1987	26	8	9.3	12	1	2.3
1990	19	7	9.0	18	3	5.5
1993	26	9	11.3	21	4	8.1
1996	30	4	8.2	34	17	22.4
1998	51	16	23.9	31	15	23.4
2001	58	20	30.8	24	16	23.2
2004	46	20	33.3	23	15	20.0

Source: Sawer (2001), updated

Table 13.4 Women in the New Zealand House of Representatives, 1972-2002 (selected parties)

	Labour Party			National Party		
Year	Candidates	MPs	%	Candidates	MPs	%
1972	5	4	7.3	5	0	0.0
1975	6	2	6.2	5	2	3.6
1978	12	3	7.5	7	1	2.0
1981	11	6	14.0	11	2	4.3
1984	16	10	17.9	15	2	5.4
1987	23	11	19.3	10	3	7.5
1990	28	8	27.6	28	8	12.0
1993	33	14	31.1	19	6	12.0
1996	35	13	35.1	18	7	16.0
1999	51	17	34.0	24	9	23.1
2002	38	18	34.6	17	6	22.2

Source: McLeay (1993), Catt (1997) and New Zealand Electoral Commission

The record of New Zealand Labour relative to the Nationals has not always been due to the selection of greater numbers of women candidates, but to the pre-selection of women for safe seats from 1972 and their placement high on party lists from 1996 (Table 13.4).

A number of political events occurred in the late 1970s prompting New Zealand

Labour to select women as candidates in winnable seats. A new wave of feminists mobilised by the women's movement joined the party. They arrived just as Labour was forced to rethink its electoral strategy, following a devastating loss in the 1975 general election. The review examined, among other things, how the party could gain greater support from women voters. At the same time, the new post-materialist NZ Values Party fielded a significant number of women candidates (25 per cent), creating a 'contagion' effect (Hill and Roberts 1990, pp.63-8; Matland and Studlar, 1996, p.712).

Labour women also managed to secure important changes within the party. Two special places were reserved for women on the Council of the Labour Party and the Labour Women's Council was revived in 1975 as a formal part of the party structure with its own budget and paid women's organiser. Unlike the case in Australia, the Women's Council is elected by the women's conference, open to all women party members. These separate structures helped give women the leverage that resulted in the feminisation of the party (Wilson, 1992, p.48–9). Three different women held the position of party president in the decade from 1986 and by 1999 women formed the majority (52 per cent) of party members and 45 per cent of its main policy body. The combination of a party review, structures committed to women, placement of women within the party machinery, and the contagion effect resulted in women candidates receiving winnable seats in general elections from the late 1970s.

Much the same opportunity structure opened up in the ALP as in New Zealand Labour in the 1970s. There was an influx of feminists mobilised by the women's movement at the same time as the party undertook a major internal review, following federal electoral defeats in 1975 and 1977. Like its New Zealand counterpart, the ALP set out to overcome its image as a workingman's party, and allowed new women's structures to be created, such as a national labour women's conference. There were several structural and ideological barriers not found in New Zealand's Labour Party, however, and the outcomes were more mixed. The influence of Irish Catholicism was much greater than in New Zealand, together with the associated gender ideology and 'machine' politics (trading of rewards and political favours). Feminism was deemed to be a middle-class cause, disruptive of working class solidarity. Labor women made up a smaller proportion of party membership in Australia than in New Zealand and occupied fewer leadership roles. Historically there had been women's organisations within the party, but too often they were regarded as the 'catering division'. At the time of the arrival of the 'second-wave' of the women's movement in the 1970s and its impact on the party, women constituted only about 25 per cent of party membership and were virtually absent from decision-making levels (ALP, 1979).

The impetus for change came from outside the party system, and it was organisations such as Women's Electoral Lobby (WEL) that successfully pressured the ALP to take on women's policy in government. WEL members who joined the party also played an important role in moving it towards quotas, to overcome entrenched barriers to women.

Strategies for Change – A Hard Case

The feminists who entered the ALP in the 1970s used both new and revitalised women's structures to press for change. By 1981 they had persuaded the party to adopt a national affirmative action program, with a target of 30 per cent representation of women (mirroring estimated membership) at all levels of the party, including parliamentary parties, by the end of the decade. For a brief period all went well: a section on women was included for the first time in the party platform and a wide-ranging women's policy, including detailed legislative and machinery of government proposals, was taken to the 1983 election. The new Labor Prime Minister, Bob Hawke, declared: 'I have no doubt that our comprehensive policies for women and number of ALP women candidates were vital to our electoral successes' (quoted in Moore, 1986, p.46).

However, the same 1981 conference that adopted affirmative action also adopted rule changes that entrenched the role of formal factions within the ALP. The women who had worked together for affirmative action were now divided by factions and efforts to reach out to women in the community lapsed as energies turned inwards. Factional loyalty became the first prerequisite of a career in the ALP and the numbers men who headed the factions and made the deals within the party had little time for feminist niceties. A formal factional system, entrenched in the party structure, is one obstacle that New Zealand Labour women did not have to contend with. In the absence of other factions, the Labour Women's Council in New Zealand has itself been able to operate like a faction, obviating the need for quotas.

The results of voluntary affirmative action programs within the ALP remained patchy. After a new push, headed by women ex-premiers, Carmen Lawrence and Joan Kirner, and after prolonged factional negotiations, the ALP finally adopted a binding target at its 1994 national conference. Television cameras captured the jubilation of the women delegates. Women would be 35 per cent (again mirroring membership) of all candidates of parliamentary parties by 2002, with the sanction of the national executive reopening pre-selections. Even this was insufficient to overcome resistance within the party or the effects of factions. Some prominent women chose to exit the Queensland branch of the party in 1995 to create the Australian Women's Party. They argued that a hundred years of working inside the party had moved women no closer to equality. After some initial success the party faded away as have all previous attempts to create women's parties in Australia.

Other prominent women stayed within the party but embarked on a new organisational strategy. Led by Kirner and Lawrence, they set about creating a body independent of party control to provide assistance to Labor women candidates with feminist commitments. The Australian EMILY's List was launched in 1996, modelled on the body of the same name set up in the United States a decade before to raise campaign funds for pro-choice Democrat women. In each subsequent Australian election, EMILY's List-supported candidates have received financial assistance as well as campaign advice, mentoring, and personal support. EMILY's List is independent of the factions as well as of the party and operates under the slogan: 'When women support women, women win.' Its organisational independence was a continuing source of friction within the party, exacerbated by hostility of the Catholic-influenced Right over the abortion issue. The National Executive of the party subsequently resolved to create a rival Labor Women's Network controlled by the National Executive which appointed its office bearers (Sawer, 2000a).

Despite the continuing tensions, EMILY's List has been a high-profile success, claiming by mid 2003 to have helped 91 new women MPs into parliaments around Australia, including the first four Indigenous women in parliament. The election of a high-profile EMILY's List supporter, Jenny Macklin, as Deputy Leader of the federal ALP in 2002, and new policy commitments in areas such as paid maternity leave and childcare, led to hopes that the party would become more attractive to women in the electorate. Unlike the New Zealand Labour Party, which the New Zealand Election Studies show has consistently attracted more votes from women than from men since 1990, with the gender gap widening to nine points in 1999, the ALP has a recurrent shortfall in women's votes.

One of the catalysts for the formation of EMILY's List was the windscreen-wiper effect whereby women holding Labor marginals were swept out of parliament in the 1996 federal defeat of the party. In their place came a large cohort of Liberal Party women. Their success, which brought the number of Liberal women in the House of Representatives up from four to 17, has been partly attributed to a training and mentoring program set up for potential women candidates by the Liberal Women's Forum. However the increased turn to the right by the party in the 1990s, with the ascendancy of market liberalism over the equal opportunity emphasis of social liberalism, has seen no further gains.

At its initiation in 1944, the Liberal Party gave women a much more significant role in its structure than they had in the ALP. This was due to a hard bargain driven by the Australian Women's National League, the largest conservative political organisation in Australia between the wars. They agreed to merge their organisation into the new party in return for equal representation of women at all levels of the Victorian division of the party (up to State president), a lesser number of guaranteed positions in the New South Wales division, women's sections and a Federal Liberal Women's Committee represented on the Federal Executive. They have also constituted a much higher proportion of party membership than in the ALP and their strong organisational position enabled women to achieve a guaranteed position on Victorian Liberal Senate tickets from 1949. The adoption of affirmative action by the ALP in the 1970s and its eschewal by the Liberal party ('patronising to women') has seen the partisan balance reversed for most of the subsequent period.

Electoral Systems

The experience of both Australia and New Zealand supports international findings on the advantages of proportional representation (PR) for the representation of women and minorities (Rule and Zimmerman, 1994). Indeed women's organisations have pressed for PR in both countries since the 1890s for this very reason. With PR there is an incentive to present a balanced ticket that appeals to different sections of the community as well as satisfying different elements within the party. PR also makes it easier to introduce and implement quotas. In Australia, as in other countries, women have generally been better represented in chambers elected through PR than in those elected from single-member constituencies. The positive influence of PR is also seen in the sudden rise in the number of women in parliament when New Zealand moved to MMP. In the last first-past-the-post election 21.2 per cent of MPs elected were women, but in the 1996 MMP election in New Zealand 29.2 per cent of those elected, including minority and Indigenous women.

PR has helped to increase the proportion of women in Australian and New Zealand parliaments, but in Australia quotas are now blurring this effect. In the past there has generally been a higher proportion of women in the Senate and in State houses of parliament where PR is used. The ALP quotas adopted in 1994 are now changing this and women are no longer uniformly better represented in chambers using PR. Neither chamber of the Victorian parliament is currently elected using PR but after the 1999 State election women constituted 44 per cent of the new ALP Cabinet, a record high in Australia. Quotas have a greater effect than the electoral system in ensuring the election of women, however quotas are easier for parties to implement in PR systems.

New Zealand experience also confirms that PR is only one of the factors impacting on the number of women MPs. New Zealand used first-past-the-post voting and classical Westminster-style single-member constituencies until 1996. Despite this, by 1993 women occupied 21 per cent of seats in the New Zealand House of Representatives, a higher percentage than in any other national parliament elected from single-member constituencies. As already noted, the changeover to the MMP did result in a rise in the number of women in parliament after the 1996 election. Women gained only 15 per cent of constituency seats, but 45 per cent of list seats. However in 1999, the number of women in the New Zealand parliament rose by only one, with women gaining 23 per cent of constituency seats and 39 per cent of list seats.

One significant effect of PR is that minor parties are more likely to win places in parliament. This has several benefits for the representation of women. Firstly, women are generally better represented as candidates in smaller parties. Secondly, women are more likely to hold high level positions within such parties. In Australia PR has been essential to the success of the minor parties that have facilitated women's political leadership since the 1970s. In New Zealand, in order to have seats allocated in proportion to the votes gained, a party must secure at least five per cent of the votes or win one constituency seat. Under the STV systems used in Australia seats are determined by quotas derived from number of seats to be filled. In most cases the quota is higher than five per cent, but parties with much less than this in terms of primary votes can benefit from preference flows and end up gaining a seat.

Summarising the Evidence

The Australian and New Zealand cases highlight the importance of political parties in determining the access of women to parliament. The major factor we have identified that accounts for the divergence in the patterns of women's political history in Australia and New Zealand is the differing nature of the respective labour parties. The ALP, impelled by the organisational efforts of Labor women, has been addressing this problem through quotas, so the outcome in terms of representation of women and women's political leadership is becoming more like what has been achieved in New Zealand without quotas.

In addition to parties, electoral systems have had a significant effect in both countries on the representation of women in parliaments and in positions of political leadership. Australia has had more than a hundred years of experimentation with the STV version of PR, whereas in New Zealand PR has arrived only in the last decade. PR means broader social representation and an end to two-party domination. The impact of the electoral systems however is always mediated by the actions of political parties and their willingness to promote women candidates into safe positions.

A final factor has been the agency of women. From the early campaigns by suffragists, to more recent campaigns for affirmative action, women in Australia and New Zealand have seized upon any political opportunity to ensure the greater influence of women in public decision-making. In Australia, pressure from women's organisations outside the parties or independent of the parties (as well the influence of femocrats discussed below) has been particularly important. In New Zealand women have gained much from their organised presence within the Labour Party.

Changes to the structures and rules of political parties, moves to PR and quotas, and changes in attitudes towards women have all combined to increase the levels of women in Australian and New Zealand parliaments. The final question is whether women are making any difference to the political sphere now the numbers have risen beyond token levels.

Making a Difference

As more women enter national parliaments there is an expectation that they will impact upon politics in three distinct ways. Women are expected to change the political culture, the parliamentary agenda, and the policy outcomes (Dahlerup, 1988, pp.275-6; Norris, 1996, pp.93-101).

From the beginning it was hoped that women's political rights would serve to purify politics. However female politicians have found it more difficult to change the gladiatorial style of politics in Australia and New Zealand than to introduce new policy agendas (Broughton and Zetlin, 1996; Grey, 2002). In New Zealand the change to MMP and coalition government, coupled with the rise in women MPs, was expected to soften the gladiatorial style of politics. That this has not happened may be due to the number of MPs who have been in the New Zealand parliament for over four terms (12 years). These long-term MPs bring with them traits and habits from the old first-past-the-post parliaments and a level of social conservatism not found in young politicians (O'Regan, quoted in Grey 2002).

New Zealand women have impacted on the nature of the parliament as a workplace. Women politicians successfully campaigned to have a crèche set up in parliament and they have managed to get changes to sitting hours to make them more family-friendly. There are still no crèches in Australian parliaments and while there has been some success in introducing family-friendly sitting hours there has also been some back-sliding. While there is little evidence of women MPs 'civilising' the debating chambers, there have been changes in political agendas attributable to rising proportions of female politicians. In Australia there is evidence that when women move from a small to large minority, women's issues become more salient. An issue such as violence against women was raised three times as often in the Senate (elected by PR) than in the Australian House of Representatives in the period between 1981 and 1993 (Sawer, 2000b, p.369). In New Zealand a study of parliamentary debates has shown that 'women's issues' received greater attention once the proportion of women in the parliament reached a little over 14 per cent. (Grey, 2002). Evidence from New Zealand is in line with expectations found in critical mass literature that minorities will make a difference to the political agenda once they reach a level of about 15 per cent (Dahlerup, 1988). Critical mass literature also anticipates that women will make a difference to policy decisions and outcomes once they move from a token minority to a larger presence.

The impact on public policy agendas is evident in both Australia and New Zealand. In Australia women politicians from all parties except the rural-based National Party have supported the introduction of anti-discrimination and equal opportunity legislation, although such bipartisanship has become more difficult as the Liberal Party has moved further to the Right. Cross-party cooperation between women politicians has also been evident on a number of women's health issues, most notably abortion. One recent example was the joint work by all eleven women members (Labor, Liberal, Green and Independent) of the two houses of the Tasmanian parliament in December 2001 in drafting the private member's bill, brought forward by the woman health minister, to clarify the legal status of abortion in that State.

In New Zealand women have also been responsible for equal opportunities legislation and other women friendly legislation. The 1990 repeal of the Employment Equity Act by the National Government highlights, however, the importance of party ideology as well as the strength of women representatives. There were eleven women in the Labour government that passed the equity legislation, while there were only eight in the National Government that repealed the Act. The lack of women in the National Party, in combination with its individualistic ideology, contributed to the repeal of the legislation.

While the political traditions of Australia and New Zealand have encouraged activists to look to the state, there have been differences in women's movement strategies to achieve policy change. In Australia the less woman-friendly character of the ALP led women to put more energy into both separate institution-building outside the main political parties and feminist interventions in the bureaucracy. In New Zealand women found the political parties, and in particular the Labour Party, more welcoming. The centralised Westminster system of New Zealand may also have encouraged women to look to a major political party as the primary means for changing women's condition (McLeay, 1993, p.61; Curtin and Sawer, 1996, p.168).

In both countries the institutionalising of status of women committees (or women's caucuses) within parliamentary labour parties has been important in enhancing women's policy impact. Such caucuses foster solidarity and teamwork as well as identifying and promoting gender perspectives on policy. Australia's Federal Parliamentary Labor Party Status of Women Committee was created in 1981 and meets weekly when parliament is sitting. It reinforces femocrat monitoring of the gender impact of policy and has been singled out for its significance in bringing together women who would otherwise be divided from each other by factional loyalties (Broughton and Zetlin, 1996). The Labour Women's Caucus in the New Zealand parliament, which is closely linked to the Women's Council of the extra-parliamentary party, has also been an effective body in monitoring policy proposals for gender impact.

By contrast, the more individualistic style of conservative women MPs and the career-damaging effects of being feminist-identified, has meant a lack of interest in an equivalent body on the conservative side of politics in Australia. In New Zealand, however, once the numbers of National Party women MPs had reached eight, they decided to have regular and formalised women's caucus meetings (Shipley, 1993, p.99).

The increase in numbers of women in parliament has flowed through to a powerful presence on front benches, particularly in New Zealand. By 1999, as already noted, seven of the twenty members of Helen Clark's cabinet were women. Partisan ideology is also important when examining whether women are likely to make a difference. In both the New Zealand and Australian parliaments it has largely been labour women (together with women from post-materialist minor parties) who have been responsible for introducing feminist perspectives and issues such as violence against women into parliamentary debate. However women on both sides of the house have been more likely than their male colleagues to raise such issues. Interestingly, a study of Australian Senate debates over a 12-year period found that while Labor women Senators were most likely to raise these issues, male Labor Senators were least likely to raise them (Williamson, 2000).

One Australian achievement has been feminist intervention in the bureaucracy to ensure the needs of women are taken into consideration in public decision making. For a time in the 1980s Australia was a pace-setter in institutionalising recognition that no government activity could be assumed to be gender neutral in its effects. This meant location of women's policy machinery in central coordinating areas of government, where it would have access to all Cabinet submissions and Cabinet processes. It also meant introducing women's budget processes, a formal mechanism to ensure all budgetary proposals were analysed for gender impact. As well, femocrats also provided internal advocacy for a wide range of government funded women's services, often delivered by organisational hybrids that combined feminist collectivism with the compromises required by government accountability. In the 1990s Australia slipped back from its earlier leadership role, although one advantage of its federal political structure was that momentum could be sustained somewhere in the system. Moreover, intergovernmental relations can provide forums such as the Commonwealth/State Standing Committee of Women's Advisers (also attended by New Zealand) which enable sharing of 'best practice' and scope for policy learning.

Governmental women's policy machinery was not established in New Zealand until after the election of the Lange Labour government in 1984, and it took the form of a Ministry of Women's Affairs rather than following the Australian model (Sawer, 1998). The Ministry was a pioneering organisation both in its commitment to feminist ideas about process and its commitment ahead of the rest of government to biculturalism. New Zealand ministers and officials meet regularly with their Australian counterparts at ministerial and women's advisers' meetings. As in Australia, the 1990s saw a move away from the strongly feminist ideals of process seen earlier in the Ministry.

Conclusion

Both Australia and New Zealand are examples of countries where women are achieving parliamentary presence and political leadership just when the rise of neo-liberalism in conjunction with the mobility of international capital is making achievement of feminist policy outcomes increasingly difficult. The sustained attack on the welfare state from free-market think-tanks is also necessarily an attack on women as the major beneficiaries of the welfare state whether as users of services, as employees, recipients of income support or consumers protected by state regulation. In neo-liberal discourse, women are blamed for the growth of the state, for increased expenditure on community services and social security (and hence for higher taxes), and for labour market regulation in the interests of equal opportunity and equal pay. All these interventions, which might be seen as making states responsive to the needs of female as well as male citizens, are instead viewed as introducing rigidities and making countries uncompetitive in global markets.

These challenges are clearly on view in New Zealand, where Helen Clark's government has improved the level of pensions, increased the top level of income tax, engaged in some re-regulation of the labour market, introduced paid maternity leave and cut expensive defence items. Economic commentators are accusing her and her government of leading New Zealand down the path to economic oblivion. Cartoonists have also been unkind, depicting her husband (a university professor) as reduced to doing the vacuuming in a flowery apron.

On the other hand, Clark has been riding high in the opinion polls. The success or otherwise of her attempts to wind back some of New Zealand's neo-liberal experiment, in the interests of social justice and gender equity, will be watched extremely closely by aspirant women leaders in Australia.

Chapter 14

Spain

Celia Valiente, Luis Ramiro and Laura Morales

Introduction

In Western countries, the gender gap in political representation has been the object of increased attention by scholars, politicians and the public. In response to a growing expectation that women should be more fully represented in political life, some political parties have adopted internal mechanisms to increase the presence of women among the parliamentarian elite. In other instances, countries reformed their electoral laws in order to feminize the political elite. Spain is no exception to this pattern. Some Spanish parties have gender quotas and some legislative attempts to modify the electoral laws have been discussed (and up to now defeated) at the national and regional level.[1]

The aim of this chapter is three-fold: to test whether Spanish women are discriminated against while trying to enter the parliamentary elite, to examine demand-side explanations that maintain that women as a group do not have enough resources to obtain an egalitarian representation in elected institutions, and to study the differences (if any) between female and male members of the lower chamber of the Spanish parliament (the Chamber of Deputies, *Congreso de los Diputados*) with respect to their socio-economic characteristics and their parliamentary work. In assessing these three aspects of the elective process, we mainly analyse two types of empirical data: lists of candidates in the 2000 general elections; and information on female and male deputies in the 2000-2004 legislative term.

First, we offer a general overview of the Spanish political system and the situation and evolution of women's role in politics in Spain, and more specifically of female members of the Spanish parliament (MPs). Second, we review the (scant) literature on the under-representation of Spanish women in Parliament. Third, we use empirical data to test some demand-side and supply-side explanatory factors of women's unequal parliamentary representation in Spain. More concretely, we study whether it is possible to affirm that women are discriminated against while trying to become deputies; the potential impact of the size of the electoral district on women's chances to become MPs; and whether the lower education level of women (as a group) is an obstacle for them to be parliamentarians. Finally, we analyse the differences (if any) between female and male Spanish deputies concerning their socio-economic characteristics and their parliamentary work.

Politics and Women in Spain

From 1939 to 1975 Spain was governed by a right-wing authoritarian regime headed by General Franco. The current political system was formed during the transition to democracy initiated in 1975. This transition was characterized by the negotiation between reformist political forces from the dictatorship and the democratic opposition. The transition was formally symbolised by the public adoption of a democratic constitution in 1978. The King is the head of state but with few formal powers. Parliament is composed of two chambers: the lower chamber, the Congress of Deputies, and the upper chamber, the Senate. Members of the Congress of Deputies are elected by proportional representation under the D'Hondt system with closed lists. The 52 constituencies, based on provincial boundaries, vary in size from one to 34 members and return a total of 350 parliamentarians to the lower house. There is a three per cent minimum threshold for representation at the electoral district level. These characteristics of the electoral system imply that electoral results tend to favour big parties and parties with geographically concentrated support.

The Spanish political party system is a limited multi-party system with a low level of ideological polarisation (Linz and Montero, 1999). In general, three nation-wide political parties attract the majority of popular support, the centre-right Popular Party (*Partido Popular*, PP), the Spanish Socialist Workers' Party (*Partido Socialista Obrero Español*, PSOE) and United Left (*Izquierda Unida*, IU). Three regional parties play a pivotal role in forming parliamentary majorities, the Catalan centre-right coalition Convergence and Union (*Convergència i Unió*, CiU), the center-right Nationalist Basque Party (*Partido Nacionalista Vasco*, PNV) and the smaller Canary centre-right coalition Canary Coalition (*Coalición Canaria*, CC). During the 1993-96 and 1996-2000 parliamentary terms the regional parties CiU, CC and PNV supported the respective PSOE and PP minority governments. The CiU, the CC and the PNV have governed their respective regions for a long time. In post-authoritarian Spain a process of devolution of powers to the regions has produced a quasi-federal state.

For a short period between 1931 and the mid-1930s Spain was for the first time in its history governed by a democratic regime, known as the Second Republic. The Spanish Republican Constitution of 1931 was the first to establish the equal right of men and women to vote and to be elected in national elections (Montero, 1996), after a vivid and historical parliamentary debate that took place between the Radical deputy Clara Campoamor – in favour of female suffrage – and the Radical-Socialist deputy Victoria Kent who opposed it for tactical reasons. Before that, the suffrage movement in Spain had been rather weak in organisational terms, but had gradually introduced the issue of female suffrage into public debate. The first public vindication of female suffrage took place in 1854 (Fagoaga, 1985, 44ff) and it was not until 1883 that the first signs of suffragist collective action emerged (Fagoaga, 1985, 74ff). Nevertheless, during the 1920s the Spanish suffrage movement organised more effectively around their claims for voting rights, with the creation of several organisations such as the Spanish Women National Association (ANME), the Women Union of Spain (UME), the Crusade of Spanish

Women, and the Feminine Association for Civic Education (AFEC), and with a burst of public suffragist demonstrations in the streets seeking the vote for women (Fagoga, 1985, p.153).

During the Second Republic women entered parliament and held political office: thirteen women were elected as deputies in each of the three legislative terms, representing both left- and right-wing parties and another, the anarchist Federica Montseny, briefly served as a Minister of Public Health during the Civil War, thus becoming the first ever woman Minister. Unfortunately, women's political rights were to be short-lived. Women's right to participate in politics in Spain ended with the Civil War, fought between 1936 and 1939. Many women in the Republican zone joined the armed forces until the Republican government prohibited them from fighting at the front. After the end of the war, the dictatorship of General Franco attempted to send women back to the home and reinforced traditional gender roles in the family, society and politics. The only role women could exercise in the public sphere during the authoritarian regime was linked to the activities of the Women's Branch of the single official party, the *Sección Femenina*, which was responsible for the political indoctrination of women and the socialization of women in traditional roles (cooking, sewing, religious faith and practice) and charitable activities. However, some women continued to participate in politics within the underground organisations of the opposition political parties and illegal trade unions, and the modern feminist movement first appeared in the late 1960s, although it only really developed in organizational terms in the mid-1970s (Scanlon, 1990, Threlfall, 1996).

With the new 1978 constitution most but not all of the discriminatory laws introduced during the dictatorship were abolished and the constitution granted equal rights for men and women and full citizenship for the latter. With the restoration of democracy the presence of women began to increase in Parliament, public office-holding, and the political parties and trade unions (Instituto de la Mujer, 2003; Inter-Parliamentary Union, 2002). With regard to the Congress of Deputies, the proportion of female MPs rose throughout the whole democratic period, from six per cent in 1977 to 36 per cent in 2004. After the 2004 elections, the PSOE had the highest representation of female parliamentarians (46 per cent), followed by the PNV (29 per cent), the IU-IC (40 per cent), the PP (28 per cent), PNV (14 per cent) and the CiU (10 per cent). The percentage of women in the parliamentary groups of PP, PSOE, IU, CiU, and PNV has generally increased in the last three decades, and especially since 1989. This increase has been continuous in the cases of the PP and PSOE, and it has experienced some periodic reversions in the cases of IU, CiU and PNV due to their smaller parliamentary seat share (Table 14.1). In the Senate, the proportion of women has always been slightly lower than in the Congress of Deputies, and women senators held 25 per cent of the seats in the 2004-2008 Senate. In the 17 regional parliaments women have gradually increased their presence from an average of six per cent in 1983 to an average of 32 per cent in 2003 (Threlfall, 1996; Montero, 1996; Instituto de la Mujer, 2003), and reached 53 per cent in the regional parliament of Castilla-La Mancha in the regional elections of May 2003.

Table 14.1 Women MPs in Spanish Lower Chamber (%), 1977-2004

Election	Total	PSOE	AP-PP	PCE-IU	CiU	PNV
1977	6	8	6	15	0	0
1979	5	4	11	9	11	0
1982	5	7	1	0	0	12
1986	7	7	6	0	6	0
1989	14	17	9	12	6	0
1993	16	18	15	22	6	0
1996	22	28	14	33	25	20
2000	28	37	25	25	13	29
2004	36	46	28	40	10	14

Source: Authors' calculation from data in www.congreso.es. Percentages based on the number of women originally elected as MPs at the beginning of the term.

In addition to their representation in elective office, women are gradually finding their way into governmental office. By May 2004, 25 women had been appointed ministers. The first woman minister was Soledad Becerril, appointed in December 1981 with the centrist government of UCD headed by Leopoldo Calvo-Sotelo. She was in charge of the Ministry of Culture and remained in government for one year. The next women to be appointed ministers were the Socialists Matilde Fernández and Rosa Conde, Minister for Social Affairs and Government Spokesperson respectively, both of whom took office in 1988, six years after the first women minister had left office. The twelve Socialist governments (PSOE) in office between 1982 and 1996 included a total of five female ministers and a maximum of three in a single cabinet, and they were responsible for the Ministries of Social Affairs, Government Spokesperson, Culture, and Health and Consumption. The governments of the Popular Party (Partido Popular) between 1996 and 2004 have appointed a total of eleven female ministers and a maximum of five in a single cabinet. These female ministers have headed the Ministries of Justice; Agriculture, Fisheries and Food; the Environment; Education and Culture; Health and Consumption; Science and Technology; Public Administration, and Foreign Affairs. The 2004 government of Prime Minister José Luis Rodríguez Zapatero was the first ever gender parity government in Spain, with 50 per cent female ministres (eight out of 16) and the first to have a female first Vice-Prime Minister (María Teresa Fernández de la Vega). As a consequence, since the first democratic government of 1977 to the 2004 government, women's presence in governmental ministries went from 0 to 50 per cent.

Issues of representation have preoccupied the Spanish feminist movement for many years. The first democratic elections in four decades, in June 1977, raised expectations among many advocates of women's rights. Therefore, on 13 July 1977, at the first meeting of the Congress of Deputies, women's rights activists presented their manifesto in support of the 25 women elected to parliament, denounced the fact that there were so few elected, and asked the three feminist MPs to push the feminist agenda in Congress (Escario, Alberdi and López-Acotto,

1996, pp.270-2). Through these years, however, the feminist movement pursued an ambitious agenda that went far beyond issues of women's presence in politics. In the 1970s and through the 1980s, among the goals pursued were equality before the law, reproductive rights such as decriminalisation of the selling and advertising of contraceptives (achieved in 1978), a divorce law (obtained in 1981), legalisation of abortion (partially achieved in 1985), criminalisation of sexual violence, and equal employment policies. Since then, as many of the most pressing legal changes (divorce, contraception, violence) have been achieved, the issue of representation has taken up more of the agenda. Moreover, because the Spanish feminist movement in general has involved women within left-wing parties, it is not surprising that they have come to focus on matters of access to elected office, both within their parties and more generally (Jenson and Valiente, 2003). The Spanish feminist movement continues its campaigns on the increase of the presence of women in institutions (the so-called objective of 'parity democracy'). However, the success of this mobilisation will in part depend on party and electoral dynamics, many of them beyond the control of the women's movement.

Obstacles to Women's Political Participation in Spain

In comparison with research on female MPs undertaken in other advanced industrial countries, studies on Spanish women parliamentarians are still in an embryonic stage. Generally speaking, studies that explain how and why women reach political decision-making positions are less available in Spain than quantitative reports which map the modest presence of women in those positions. Due to the dearth of these studies, we can only offer some provisional conclusions. Since Spanish political parties are gatekeepers to legislative positions of power, research on legislative recruitment is intrinsically linked to the analysis of party candidate selection (Uriarte, 1997, p.58), with explanations emphasising the demand-side factors influencing female political participation (for example, García de León, 1994). In Spain, the number of women on electoral lists has been increasing over the last few decades in the majority of political parties. Nevertheless, women seldom occupy the leading positions on these lists (Ortiz, 1987, pp.129-39). Relegation to the bottom of electoral lists not only deprives women candidates of the possibility of gaining political office but it also excludes them from public view. Candidates who head the lists usually lead the electoral campaign in Spain. This is an excellent chance for candidates to gain experience as political leaders. Most female candidates cannot avail themselves of this opportunity (García de León, 1991, p.39).

An early study of women's political opportunities indicated that the proportion of women among the candidates with serious chances of winning a seat was higher in the leftist than in the conservative parties, and higher for parties with a small or no presence in the chamber (Barbadillo, Juste and Ramírez, 1990). Bearing in mind the time that has elapsed since these findings were first published, it would be interesting to test the conclusions of this study again. Echoing the experience of other European countries, it seems that the number of female candidates of any modern Spanish political party increases when the probability of obtaining votes diminishes. All parties now draw attention to the presence of women on their lists in an attempt to win votes (IMOP-Encuestas, 1999, pp.99-100). However, male politicians promote male candidates when the party has a real possibility of winning a seat in Parliament (García de León, 1996, pp.171-2). It has also been argued (but has not been empirically tested) that other things being equal, women have a higher probability of being elected as legislators in the larger constituencies (García de León, 1996, p.173). Later, we will put this hypothesis to the test.

The different degree of trust given to female and male candidates by voters has also been identified as an obstacle to a higher presence of women among the political class. Uriarte (1997, p.69) supports this argument referring to the results of a survey undertaken in 1986 by the Women's Institute showing that 47 percent of men and 40 percent of women trust male candidates more than female candidates.[2] This general indication of preference for male candidates is known to party leaders who in turn reflect this preference when composing their electoral lists.

The organisational culture of the parties also militates against a high presence of women in the legislative elite. In their investigations of party cultures Gaitán and Cáceres (1995) studied the image of women in the documents of the main political parties produced between 1977 and 1994. Women are presented in these documents as individuals who participate, mainly in the economic and social spheres. This is a very positive image, given the fact that the Francoist regime (1939–75) actively opposed the advancement of women's rights and status. However, the willingness of political parties to present positive images of women does not extend to political images. To the extent that the cultures of political parties are reflected in their documents, these are organisations whose political world is male.

The impact of party quotas on the representation of women has been successful. The Spanish case shows that when a quota is introduced in a party, the number of female legislators from that party elected in the subsequent election increases significantly. Moreover, although only left-wing parties have introduced quotas, their effect tends to spread to other parties who are pressured by their achievements. Conservative parties (which have no quota) increased the number of their female representatives after the introduction of the quota in left-wing parties (Uriarte, 1997, pp.69-70).

Supply-side explanations of the weak presence of women among the legislative elite have also been made but are more recent and scarce than demand-side approaches. For example, even if the level of education is in general the same for young women and men, this is not the case for the population of all ages. The difference in education is an impediment for women to run for parliamentary office, since this political activity usually correlates with a high level of education. Additionally, the supply of women decision-makers is seriously hampered by the difficulties of combining women's professional and family responsibilities (Uriarte 1999; Uriarte and Ruiz 1998 and 1999).

Also from the supply-side perspective it has been hypothesised (but not empirically proven) that women and men become members of political parties for different reasons. According to the literature, women tend to participate in politics in order to help others or change and improve society. Relatively few women engage in political party work in order to achieve prestige, professional upward mobility and economic privileges. These are precisely the reasons that induce some men to be politically active and to try to reach leadership positions in political parties (Vázquez, 1989, p.16). Again, it is imperative to test these propositions present in the literature.

In sum, most academic works on gender and the legislative elite show that on the whole women are discriminated against while trying to reach parliamentary office. According to these studies, the forms of discrimination are common to Spain and most advanced industrial countries. This evidence supports the demand-side explanation for the low presence of women in Parliament. However, recent studies also provide some evidence that corroborates the supply-side thesis. In contrast with the topic of gender and legislative recruitment, we know virtually nothing about the impact of Spanish female legislators. This is an area where research is badly needed.

Demand and Supply

One of the main goals of this chapter is to explore some of the theoretical hypotheses proposed by other scholars, and reviewed previously, for the Spanish case. We will thus approach the analyses of women's under-representation in the Spanish lower chamber by distinguishing between demand-side and supply-side explanations. First, we test two demand-side hypotheses: a) that parties, as gate-keepers to elected office, discriminate against women; and b) that some institutional characteristics, such as the small size of electoral districts, make it difficult for women to access the parliamentary elite. Second, we examine the supply-centred thesis that women's lower levels of education obstruct women's presence in the legislative elite.

Demand

One way to explore the adequacy of the proposition that parties act as gatekeepers to political office and discriminate against women for the Spanish case is to compare the levels of female membership in political parties and compare it with (i) the proportion of women in electoral lists, (ii) the proportion of women in electoral lists in 'safe' positions, and (iii) the proportion of women actually elected as MPs. The levels of female membership of political parties should be considered as the starting point of the analysis because it is mainly from party members that Spanish parties recruit their candidates. Any arguments about parties discriminating against women should, therefore, take into account the membership baseline within each party. We will do this by limiting the analysis to the general elections of 2000 and for the main five parties represented in the Congress of

Deputies. The results shown in Table 14.2 are revealing. When we take female party membership as the starting point, it would seem that none of the main Spanish parties substantially exclude or discriminate against women when it comes to the composition of electoral lists. On the contrary, we can see that PSOE and IU even favour them by granting women an over-representation in their lists when compared to the proportion of female members. However, the crucial aspect is not so much whether women are included in the lists but whether they make it to positions where they are likely to be elected. This provides the real test with regard to discrimination against women members.

Table 14.2 Women's access to the Spanish parliament, 2000

Party	% women Party members	% women on lists	% women in safe positions	% women MPs
PP	32.7	34.0	20.5	25.2
PSOE	28.0	46.9	37.6	36.8
IU	29.0	44.6	31.6	25.0
CiU	29.4	28.3	18.8	13.3
PNV	34.5	33.3	20.0	28.6

Source: Instituto de la Mujer, 2001; authors' calculations from B.O.E 15/02/2000 and from data held at www.congreso.es; party membership data from 2001. 'Safe' seats are defined as those seats won or held by parties in the 1996 general election.

In this case, the Socialists still appear to grant more favourable treatment to women than they might expect from their proportional party membership. The left-wing IU allocates more women in safe list positions in proportion to their party membership, while the centre-right parties PP, CiU and PNV clearly under-represent them. These latter parties seem to discriminate against their female party members when it comes to deciding rank-order in the electoral lists. Centre-right women party members have a harder time getting through to the positions which will make them likely to be elected. The main outcome of this candidate selection process is that only the PSOE has been able to get a higher percentage of elected female MPs than their female party membership would push them to do, reaching one-third of women MPs in their parliamentary group. The electoral setback of IU has prevented it from guaranteeing a fair representation of its women party members among its MPs. And, finally, the three main centre-right parties, especially CiU, are clearly not giving their female party members equal treatment with men.

Constituency size in Spanish general elections range from the single-member districts of the autonomous cities of Ceuta and Melilla to the large multimember districts of Madrid (34 MPs) and Barcelona (31 MPs). We examined the effect of district magnitude on women's representation in Spain by assessing if smaller electoral districts disadvantaged women in their efforts to gain a seat in parliament. The results shown in Table 14.3 would suggest that constituency size does not matter much for women's access to the lower house. Around 30 per cent of elected MPs are women regardless of the size of the electoral district. True, women are slightly under-represented in smaller districts, but this difference is clearly not substantial.

Table 14.3 Male and female MPs by constituency size, 2000

Constituency	Total	Men		Women	
Size	Seats	N	%	N	%
1-5 seats	116	84	72	32	28
6-8 seats	74	50	68	24	32
9-34 seats	160	108	68	52	32
Total	350	242	69	108	31

Source: Authors' calculations from www.congreso.es

On closer scrutiny we find that women MPs are elected in slightly larger districts of around 12.5 seats than men, who are elected in constituencies of around 11.6 seats, but the difference in the average constituency size where male and female MPs are elected is not statistically significant. Hence, our data do not support the conclusion that smaller electoral districts are a fundamental barrier for gender equality in political representation.

Supply

As we have seen in previous sections, an increasingly common argument is that women are still under-represented in political offices partly because they lack the resources needed to fully participate in political activities. In this sense, explanations which highlight the importance of resources argue that women are less able to supply what is needed to compete for and gain elective office. Resources can be of very different types: time, money, and skills. O aspect of skill is measured by educational attainment. It was traditionally argued that women's lower levels of education acted a barrier to their access to elective positions, since elective offices require skills that are usually enhanced by education. For this proposition to be valid two conditions must be present: a) that women are less educated than men, and b) that education acts as a relevant factor in the selection process of candidates.

Table 14.4 shows educational levels of men and women extracted from a national sample in 2002. These results give a somewhat nuanced picture of educational differences between men and women. On the one hand, women are more likely than men to have only basic educational qualifications, but on the other hand men and women are nowadays equal when it comes to university degrees and education. Given that more than 70 per cent of MPs have some kind of university education, we are able to argue that women are not really disadvantaged in terms of the educational skills required for parliamentary office (i.e. university qualifications). Thus, today, Spanish women have the educational skills necessary to gain elective positions, at least as much as Spanish men do.

Table 14.4 Education and gender in Spain (%)

Education	Total	Men	Women
Primary or less	51.7	46.7	56.6
Second level	29.7	33.6	26.0
Third level	18.0	18.9	17.0
DK/NA	0.6	0.8	0.4
Total	100.0	100.0	100.0

Source: Survey no. 2450 (CIS, 2002)

Let us turn now to the second condition: does education act as a relevant factor in the selection process of candidates? Answering this question is much more difficult than it was for the first condition. It is logical to expect that the acquisition of educational skills will have some kind of impact on these processes, however it is not possible to quantify with a degree of certainty to what extent it does. Hence, we will use an indirect method to check if this is the case. Also from survey data it is possible to get some kind of estimate of the educational differences between male and female party members. The 2002 survey revealed that women party members actually possess higher qualifications than their male counterparts. True, as we already know, women are less likely to become party members than men. However, those women who eventually become party members are more likely than male party members to have obtained university degrees. Therefore, if educational attainment was a determining factor in being selected as a candidate for parliament, women should be on electoral lists in a higher proportion to their membership. As we have seen in previous sections, this is not the case in Spain. Our data, thus suggest that a restricted access to resources, at least educational, is not what is preventing women from gaining access to elective offices in Spain. Nor are demand-side explanations particularly illuminating. Therefore we must conclude that other extraneous factors, such as political culture and traditional attitudes militate against women's selection as candidates.

Do Male MPs Differ from Female MPs?

We now analyse the socio-economic characteristics and parliamentary work of female and male deputies in order to assess the similarities and differences between political women and men in Spain. All data in this section refer to MPs in the Congress of Deputies for the 2000-2004 legislative term. There are few differences between this cohort of male and female MPs in age, education levels and occupational activity. The average age of female deputies, at 45.9 years, is five years younger than that of male deputies. Male and female MPs show similar levels of educational attainment, although women MPs are slightly more likely to have completed primary education only, and less likely to hold a doctoral degree. It is interesting to note, however, that 72 per cent of female and male deputies hold university degrees. There is also a similarity in the occupational profiles of female and male MPs. About one in three male and female MPs are drawn from middle-management, teaching and lecturing occupations. Another one-fifth (21.5 per cent) have backgrounds in the traditional professions (for example, lawyers, architects, medical practitioners), where men dominate, and administrative and service work which is more prevalent among female MPs. A very similar proportion of female (16 per cent) and male (17 per cent) MPs had been politicians or trade union representatives before entering parliament.

In contrast, differences in the marital status of female and male MPs are marked. Marital status is, as already noted in the literature, a differential trait of male and female MPs. Women are much more likely than men to be single (26 per cent), whereas Spanish male MPs are almost invariably married (80 per cent). Therefore, it seems that indeed the attention given by women to political and elective office-holding is not compatible with family obligations in Spain.

So far we have seen that female MPs do not greatly differ from their male counterparts in their socio-economic characteristics. They differed more in terms of marital status and age. However, the most recent international literature argues that while women MPs are becoming more similar to men in their socio-economic characteristics, they are still different with regard to their policy orientation and preferences (Berkman and O'Connor, 1993; Tamerius, 1995; Childs, 2001; Dodson, 2001; Swers, 2001). A related but different proposition states that not only their policy activities might be different but that when we get a more nuanced picture of women's parliamentary role we can still find important gender inequalities. We will see how far these observations can be applied to the Spanish case on the basis of data collected from all 350 Spanish MPs serving in the 2000-04 parliamentary term.

To analyse the potential existence of different policy priorities or preferences of women and men MPs, we examined the membership of female and male MPs to parliamentary commissions related to social policies.[3] A sharp difference was found between the proportion of women (78 per cent) and men (46 per cent) MPs who belong to parliamentary commissions related to social policies. The difference is so pronounced that it may indicate the existence of different preferences of female and male MPs regarding membership to specific types of commissions. It could also be hypothesised that women are welcome in these commissions but not in others. However, more research is needed to clarify the causes of this difference.

We have also analysed the access of women and men MPs to high parliamentary positions. In Table 14.5 we first show gender differences in membership of the main governing bodies of the Congress of Deputies: the Spokespeople Council (*Junta de Portavoces*), the Permanent Council (*Diputación Permanente*) and the Presidency (*Mesa del Congreso*).[4] The first two governing bodies are more important than the third one. As we can see, male MPs are over-represented in the more powerful governing bodies of the lower house, while female MPs are over-represented in the Presidency, the least relevant of all three. Almost eight per cent of men MPs but only about three per cent of female MPs belong to the Spokespeople Council. This difference would indicate that political elites have noticed that it is important in terms of the public image of parliament that women are represented in the governing bodies of the chamber, but that power structures are still heavily skewed in favour of men. Women are very welcome in symbolic positions, but when it gets to sharing real power things are somewhat different.

Table 14.5 Membership of the main governing bodies of the *Congreso* by gender

Governing bodies	Male MPs	Female MPs
Spokespeople Council	7.4	2.8*
Permanent Council	31.4	21.3**
Presidency	1.2	5.6***

Source: Own calculation from data in www.congreso.es. Percentages are column percentages and they do not add to 100 because not all MPs are members of these governing bodies. *** Difference statistically significant for $p \leq 0.01$. ** Difference statistically significant for $p \leq 0.05$. * Difference statistically significant for $p \leq 0.1$

A similar picture is portrayed by the analysis of the roles and positions gained by female MPs in some parliamentary commissions. In Table 14.6 we highlight gender differences for different positions within parliamentary committees according to a distinction between two types of committees and the degree of relevance of the position. First, we distinguish between two types of committees: type 1 includes the most 'relevant' committees; that is, those that deal with core issues or that assume legislative functions. These include the permanent legislative committees and the committees for the National Audit Office and the European Union. Type 2 committees are those without legislative functions and those related to non-core issues including the joint committees with the Senate for women's rights, the study of drug issues and for relations with the Ombudsman. On the other hand, we can distinguish between three broad types of positions within committees: directive positions, leadership positions, and plain membership. These three can also be graded within them as we do in Table 14.6.

If we take into account these two dimensions of power structures related to committee involvement we can distinguish a clearly gendered pattern. The most powerful positions in the more relevant committees (type 1 committees) are mostly filled in by men. Proof of this phenomenon is the presidency role in type 1 committees: men are almost three and one half times more likely to hold one of these positions than women are: almost seven per cent of the male MPs preside a type 1 committee while the percentage of female MPs in such a position is reduced to under two per cent. But there is also quite a substantive gap in the likelihood of becoming a spokesperson between male and female MPs: 26.6 per cent of men MPs but only 12 per cent of women MPs are spokespeople in type 1 committees. However, once we go down the ladder of 'relevance' of the position within each category, gender differences disappear or reverse. An even more gendered pattern appears when we consider type 2 committees. In this case, the reduced saliency of the issues dealt with in these groups have as the main consequence the clear over-representation of women in some positions.

Table 14.6 Roles in Spanish parliamentary committees by gender

Position	Type 1 Committees		Type 2 Committees	
	Male MPs	Female MPs	Male MPs	Female MPs
Presidency	6.6	1.9**	1.2	1.9 n.s
Vicepresidency	10.3	11.1 n.s	2.1	4.6 n.s
Secretary	11.2	12.0 n.s	0.8	1.9 n.s
Spokesperson	26.6	12.0***	3.3	6.5 n.s
Adjoint spokesperson	13.6	18.5 n.s	1.7	4.6*
Member	81.4	80.6 n.s	13.2	34.3***
Attendant	20.7	42.6***	2.5	6.5*

Source: Authors' calculations from data in www.congreso.es. Percentages do not add up to 100 because categories are not mutually exclusive. *** Difference statistically significant for $p \leq 0.01$. **Difference statistically significant for $p \leq 0.05$. *Difference statistically significant for $p \leq 0.1$ n.s statistically not significant for $p \leq 0.1$. A grey shading is given to the group (men or women) over-represented in each category if a statistically or substantively significant difference is present.

These results clearly support a less naïve vision of gender inequalities in parliamentary representation in Spain. Women are certainly gaining access to parliament, they are certainly similar to men in their social traits, they have improved their position within power structures, but nonetheless they are still far from sharing power with men on an equal basis. Not even those women that make it through to parliament are given the same opportunities and responsibilities given to men. Women MPs occupy less politically relevant positions.

Conclusion

The proportion of women among members of the Spanish Congress of Deputies has increased steadily since the transition to democracy to reach the current level of 36 percent. Nevertheless, the presence of women in the legislative elite is lower than their proportion of the general population. In this chapter we have shown that the socio-economic characteristics of women and men deputies are similar, with the exception of their marital status and (to a lesser extent) level of education. Women deputies are also slightly younger than men deputies.

Differences between female and male deputies are very marked concerning their parliamentary work: the percentage of women as members of parliamentary committees on social issues is higher than that of men. This difference may reflect a dissimilarity in the political preferences of women and men MPs, but it may also be the result of discrimination against women, who are relegated to these types of committees. Women are under-represented among those deputies who occupy positions in governing bodies of the lower chamber and among those that hold leading positions in the most important parliamentary committees. Men MPs are over-represented in the most important governing bodies of the Congress of Deputies (the Spokespeople Council and the Permanent Council). Male MPs significantly outnumber women MPs who occupy the main leading positions (president and spokesperson) of the most important parliamentary committees – the permanent legislative committees and the committees for the National Audit Office and for the European Union.

What are the causes of women's under-representation in the legislative elite? In this chapter we have tested demand-side and supply-side explanations. The proportion of women in safe positions in electoral lists for the 2000 general election was lower than that of female members of the party in the PP, the CiU and the PNV, equal in the IU, and higher in the PSOE. Hence, the demand-side thesis that affirms that parties discriminate against women while composing their electoral lists is partly confirmed in the case of the three centre-right parties, but not so for the two left-wing parties. To study whether this discrimination is due to the ideology of parties is beyond the scope of this chapter but may be a matter for future research. In addition, this chapter has tested (and rejected) another demand-side thesis: that small electoral districts are detrimental to women's presence among the legislative elite. Around 36 per cent of members of the Congress of Deputies are women regardless of the size of the electoral district where they were elected.

The supply-side hypotheses that women as a group have lower human capital, expressed in lower educational levels, and that this difference in education negatively affects women's chances to become MPs have also been tested and rejected in the Spanish case. Studying the Spanish population as a whole, we see that a very similar percentage of women and men have university degrees, while the proportion of individuals with university degrees is higher among female members of political parties than among male members.

The results of this chapter indicate the need to continue the study of women's under-representation in parliament in particular and in politics in general. The chapter highlights the need for further investigations into party selection practices, parliamentary culture and the legislative input of men and women in order to add to our understanding of women's contribution to the building of Spain's democracy. Efforts to increase the presence of women in the Spanish political elite are one of the goals of Spanish feminist groups and it is explicitly mentioned in the electoral platforms of the left-wing parties. In this regard, this issue will be present to some extent in future political debates. However, the possibilities for the advancement of democratic parity will depend on multiple factors, some of them beyond the control of the feminist movement. Therefore the future of women's political representation in Spain remains unpredictable.

Notes

[1] Electoral laws governing regional elections in Castilla-La Mancha and the Balearic Islands were amended in June 2002 to introduce a compulsory 50 per cent gender parity in party electoral lists. However, in September 2002, the national government challenged the constitutionality of this provision. Both laws were temporarily suspended and the May 2003 regional elections were conducted under the former regulations.

[2] The Eurobarometer of the 1994 European elections (study 41.1) showed that about 38 per cent of Spanish voters thought that the number of female candidates in party lists was very important in influencing their voting decisions. Only citizens of former East Germany indicated a higher level of support, suggesting that Spanish voters are highly sensitive to gender equality in political representation.

[3] The following commissions were viewed as dealing with social policies: Education; Culture and Sports; Social Policy and Employment; Health and Consumption; International Cooperation to Development; Joint Comittee with the Senate for Women's Rights; Joint Committee with the Senate for the Study of Drug Issues.

[4]We analysed full and substitute members of the Spokespeople Council. Regarding the Permanent Council we studied full members, deputy members and MPs with any directive role in the unit.

Chapter 15

Scandinavia

Jill M. Bystydzienski

Introduction

The Scandinavian countries – Norway, Sweden, Denmark, Finland and Iceland – have most of the world's highest female representations in their national parliaments. Particularly since the 1970s, the percentage of women in all five countries' parliaments increased significantly, reaching world record highs in the 1990s. This chapter first provides a comparative Scandinavian context for understanding why and how large numbers of women obtained parliamentary seats in this world region, and subsequently focuses on Norway as a specific case. It then discusses the significance of large numbers of women in Scandinavian parliaments and concludes with an assessment of challenges that still lie ahead.

Characteristics of the Nordic Political System

Each of the five Nordic countries has a unitary state and a unicameral parliamentary system which in this region had its origins during the Viking era. Already between the 8th and the 11th century, Viking men and women participated in the *thing*, 'the equivalent of law court and parliament', to hear cases of breach of laws and to make policies (Jonassen, 1983, p.34). However, only in the 19th century were multiparty systems and proportional representation instituted, and in the 20th century universal suffrage and preferential voting rules established, in Scandinavia (Elder, Thomas and Arter, 1982).

In the Nordic countries, the gatekeepers to parliaments are the political parties. With the exception of Iceland (where political parties began to form after World War I), parties were first established toward the end of the 19th century. Today, all candidates for election to parliament must be nominated by the political parties and placed on party lists. All the Scandinavian countries now have multiparty systems with anywhere between twelve to six different parties being represented at any given time, but often many more actively engaged in political activity. The political system is generally dominated by five parties arranged into two blocs: conservative, liberal, and agrarian parties on the right, and social democratic (labour) and socialist/communist parties on the left (Bystydzienski, 1995, p.22).

Although the specific electoral rules vary from country to country, Iceland, Sweden, Denmark, Finland, and Norway have all adopted some form of proportional representation (PR). Under this system, the existing parties develop lists of candidates for parliament which are then presented to voters. The proportion of members elected to parliament from each party reflects the proportion of votes given each party by the electorate. Under PR, more than one party representative from an electoral district can be elected, unlike under the single-member electoral system. The Nordic countries also combine PR with a system known as the 'preference vote'. Under the preference system, voters may change the order in which candidates appear on the ballot, and in some cases cross out or add names of candidates, or they can move candidates from one party list to another. All five countries use this system in local (municipal) elections, while only Denmark and Finland allow for preferential voting in parliamentary elections.

The combination of multiparty, PR, and preference voting structures in Scandinavia has been cited often as a primary reason for the high percentage of women in Nordic parliaments. The multiparty system works to the advantage of women because several parties compete for the same voters and once the presence of women on party election lists becomes recognized in terms of voter appeal, one party after another places women candidates on its list (Skjeie, 1991). The PR system emphasizes political party representation rather than election of individuals and aids minority representation. When more than one party representative has a chance to be elected, women and other under-represented groups are more likely to be placed on party lists than in 'winner take all' systems. A number of researchers have found a positive relationship between PR and women's opportunity for election (see, e.g., Bogdanor, 1984; Lovenduski and Norris, 1993; Rule, 1981). In addition, Rule and Shugart (1991), in a comparison of 23 political democracies, found that countries with systems of party lists with preference voting had the highest proportions of women in parliaments.

Women's Parliamentary Representation in Scandinavia

The Nordic countries have been characterised by an ideological dualism, comprising, on the one hand, ideals of justice and equality (Bergqvist *et al.*, 1999) and, on the other, practices and attitudes that treat and regard women as different from and inferior to men (Bystydzienski, 1995, pp.17-20). The tensions between these two ideological strands are particularly visible in the history of Scandinavian women's attempts to obtain political rights.

Nordic women's struggle for suffrage was an integral part of the first wave of women's movements in the 19th century. These movements emerged first in the urban areas among female intellectuals from the upper and middle classes, but eventually involved also women from the working and farming strata (Skard, 1987). These early movements found allies among male intellectuals, writers, politicians and social commentators who tended to champion the cause of any group that in their view had not received its rightful measure of equality and fair treatment (Jonassen, 1983, pp.128-9). But despite such support, it took many years for Scandinavian women to obtain the right to vote and to stand for public office. In the 1870s and 1880s, Nordic women established women's rights organisations and women's unions, and actively pressed for entry into the public political sphere (Skard, 1987). The Scandinavian nations granted women the right to vote earlier than other western countries. Finland adopted universal suffrage in 1906, Norway in 1913, Denmark and Iceland in 1915, and Sweden in 1919-1921 (Skard and Haavio-Mannila, 1985, p.38). In the parliamentary election of 1907 in Finland, women gained ten per cent of the seats. The percentage of women MPs increased to 12.5 in 1908, but then fluctuated between seven and 12 per cent until the 1950s (Bergqvist *et al.*, 1999, p.298). Norway, Denmark and Sweden were slower to attain double-digit percentages of women parliamentarians, while Iceland's percentages have been the lowest of all five countries (see Table 15.1) due to the small size of the Icelandic Parliament (only sixty members) combined with large numbers of electoral districts and political parties, as well as a system of direct primaries.

Table 15.1 Women MPs in five Scandinavian countries (%), 1910-2003

Year	Denmark	Finland	Iceland	Norway	Sweden
1910	0	9	0	0	0
1915	0	10	0	0	0
1920	3	10	1	0	0
1925	2	9	2	1	2
1930	3	7	1	1	1
1935	2	7	2	2	4
1940	2	8	2	1	5
1945	5	12	0	5	8
1950	8	15	4	5	10
1955	9	14	2	5	12
1960	10	14	3	7	13
1965	10	17	2	8	13
1970	11	22	2	9	15
1975	16	23	5	16	21
1980	24	26	5	24	28
1985	26	31	15	35	30
1990	33	32	21	36	38
1995	33	34	25	39	40
2000	37	37	35	36	43
2003	38	38	30	36	45

Source: Bergqvist et al., (1999, p. 298); Nordic Council of Ministers (2002, pp. 173-81). http://www.ipu.org/parline-e/parlinesearch.asp

Denmark and Finland were the first western nations to have women as members of cabinets. Nina Bang was Minister of Education in the Danish Social Democratic government from 1924 to 1926. Bang was the second female cabinet minister in the world, preceded only by Alexandra Kollontaj who was People's Commissar for Soviet

Social Affairs in 1917 (Skard and Haavio-Manila, 1985, p.78). Finland followed Denmark when Miina Sillanpaa became Minister of Social Affairs in the Social Democratic government in 1926; her tenure lasted twenty years (Begqvist *et al*., 1999, p.32). By the 1950s, four of the five Nordic governments (excluding Iceland) had established a system of appointing at least one female minister (Skard and Haavio-Mannila, 1985, p.78).

Since the 1970s, women's parliamentary representation in the Scandinavian countries has increased significantly. Along with growing female parliamentary representation, women's presence increased proportionately in government cabinets, at top and middle levels of ministries, and on public boards, committees, and councils of the Nordic corporate system. Women have constituted at least 40 per cent of the Norwegian Cabinet since 1986, Denmark has had 35 per cent women in the government since 1998, Finland 39 per cent since 1995, and Sweden by 1998 had 50 per cent women cabinet ministers (Bergqvist *et al*., 1999, pp.306-10). In Sweden, Denmark, and Norway, it has been the practice to alternate the minister and vice-minister in terms of gender, so that if a minister is male, the vice-minister is female, and vice-versa. Over time, the portfolios of female ministers have expanded to include not only social affairs, education, health and culture, but also areas that traditionally were not allocated to women such as industry and energy, finance, employment, transport, defense, and foreign affairs (Bergqvist *et al*., 1999, pp.306-10).

All five Scandinavian countries also have had a steady increase of women in the corporate sector. By the late1980s, Norway and Sweden had 32 and 23 per cent women respectively on their public boards, councils and committees, while in Denmark and Finland the figures were 15 and 13 per cent respectively (Halsaa, 1989, p.18). By the mid-1990s, four of the five countries (excluding Iceland) had close to 40 per cent women in such positions (Bergqvist *et al*., 1999, pp.40-1). However, the proportion of women chairing committees is substantially lower, around 20 per cent (Bergqvist *et al*., 1999, p.40). In recent years, Norway has had a female head of state, the President of Iceland for 16 years was a woman, and currently Finland has a woman Prime Minister.

Denmark, Finland and Sweden, as members of the European Union, are entitled to vote in elections for the European Parliament. The Parliament in its fifth session (1999-2004) had 626 members, with Denmark and Finland each contributing 16 members and Sweden 22. Six (37 per cent) of Denmark's MEPs, seven (43 per cent) of Finland's, and nine (40 per cent) of Sweden's, are women (Nordic Council of Ministers, 2002, pp.182-5).

From an international perspective, the above statistics indicate an atypical amount of female political representation and activity. However, numbers do not automatically translate into women's influence and decision-making (see Bystydzienski, 1995, Ch.5). Moreover, since the Scandinavian countries are not totally homogeneous, there are differences among the Nordic nations in the percentages of female parliamentary representation as well as in content of political activity (Bergqvist *et al*., 1999). While the women's movements in Scandinavian countries have been successful in significantly increasing female parliamentary representation, government structures have remained gendered, and whether the relatively large numbers of women have brought about substantial and meaningful change is still a matter of debate (Bystydzienski, 1995, pp. 100-13; Karvonen and Selle, 1995; Bergqvist *et al.*, 1999; Solheim, 2000). Although a number of obstacles to women's political equality have been lifted, significant barriers still remain.

Obstacles and Opportunities for Women in Parliamentary Politics

Even though historically there were more women in the Nordic parliaments, and women voted at higher rates, than in other western countries, until the 1950s, with the exception of Finland, the participation of women in parliamentary politics as candidates for office and the numbers of female MPs remained minimal. Women found obstacles to political involvement due to the persistence of traditional forms of sexism in the highly gendered institution of politics as well as the unequal demands placed on them by their family roles (Holter, 1970).

During the post-World War II period, Scandinavian countries experienced many social and economic changes. With urbanization and economic growth, these nations began to offer women greater educational and employment opportunities. With increased levels of education, more women sought paid employment and began to have fewer children. Women started to accumulate more political resources and increasingly demanded equal status with men. During this time also, Scandinavian government bureaucracies expanded greatly, including the public corporate sector and civil service. Nordic governments developed broad social policy aimed at preventing labour market failure as they sought to provide social benefits for all citizens. These benefits were made possible through the expansion of the public sector and growth of social services. The Nordic advanced 'institutional' welfare states (Knutsen, 1989), with their commitment to universalism and equality of opportunity and results, increasingly developed policies focused on health and family care which affected women more than men (Hernes, 1987). Women were drawn in large numbers into the state apparatus as clients, consumers, and employees. While women became increasingly dependent on state institutions, the state became more 'woman-friendly' (Hernes, 1987, p.15). Thus, the modern Nordic state emerged as a viable power base for women activists who by the late 1960s sought greater political representation.

It is important to note, however, that the above developments occurred at different rates and in somewhat different socio-political and economic contexts in the five Nordic countries. For example, in 1970, only 23 per cent of Norwegian women worked outside the home, while 53 per cent of Swedish women had paid jobs (Frones, 1996). The Nordic democracies and post-World War II expansion model thus requires modification to take account of circumstances of individual Scandinavian countries (Bergqvist *et al.*, 1999).

After World War II, the majority of the legal restrictions on women's activities in the Nordic nations were abolished. With the elimination of legal discrimination, many Scandinavians believed that the problems of sex inequality had been solved. However, during the 1950s and 1960s a critical sex-role debate took place in the Nordic countries (Skard, 1987). It became widely recognized that a striking disparity existed between the formal equality of the sexes and the everyday reality faced by women. Women fared much worse than men in all areas of life, especially in the spheres of paid employment where they were concentrated in jobs with low prestige and wages, with few chances for advancement, and in formal politics where their representation and participation were far from equal. Women continued to shoulder most of the responsibility for housework and child care, the possibilities of controlling reproduction were limited, and the number of child care centers were insufficient (Holter, 1970).

The sex-role debate stimulated the growth of a new wave of feminism in the beginning of the 1970s that began to systematically press for social change. The political involvement that sprang from the women's movements took various forms as it was embedded in the specific socio-economic context of each country (Karvonen and Selle, 1995). In Denmark, Iceland and Norway, a variety of independent women's groups flourished, while in Sweden and Finland there was relatively little new organisational activity, and the work for gender equality was largely accomplished through traditional political institutions and political women's organisations (Skard, 1987).

Due in large part to the pressure and actions of the women's movements, Scandinavian governments passed legislation aimed at equalizing the status of women and men. Women activists were able to take part in a universe of political discourse that was responsive to disadvantaged groups' struggle to obtain political power as well as to take advantage of widespread belief that governments exist to help groups that lack access to societal resources (see Bystydzienski, 1995, pp.27-30). The Icelandic Equality Act was adopted in 1976; Denmark passed its Equal Pay Act in 1976 and its Equal Treatment Act in 1978; Norway acquired its Equal Status Act in 1978; and Sweden obtained corresponding equality legislation in 1979. Finland passed its bill against sex discrimination in 1985 (Eduards, Halsaa and Skjeie, 1985, pp.145-7). The equality legislation in the five Nordic countries is very similar, being largely prohibitive. However, the Norwegian and Danish acts allow for positive discrimination in favor of women. The Norwegian Equal Status Act begins with a clause which states: 'This Act shall promote equal status between the sexes and aims particularly at improving the position of women' (Equal Status Ombud, 1989, p.2). The Act thus provides a legal framework for the introduction of quota systems and preferential treatment regulations that have benefited women (Halsaa, 1989, p.27).

Beginning in the late 1960s, a particularly effective strategy for increasing the numbers of female political representatives developed by women's movement organisations, especially in Norway, Denmark and Iceland, have been information campaigns waged before elections. Women activists began these campaigns by arranging unconventional demonstrations, capturing the interest of the mass media, and creating widespread and intensive public discussions and debates. The campaigns, which included pressuring political parties to nominate more women for election, resulted in a steady growth of women representatives in parliaments (see Table 15.1 above) as well as at other levels of governance. By the mid-1980s, four of the five Nordic countries had more than 25 per cent female representation in their parliaments, and by 2000 all had more than one-third women MPs.

A brief examination of the strategies used by women activists to increase female parliamentary representation in Norway and the question of whether women have made a difference in the Norwegian parliament, will illuminate some of the complexities of the efforts to achieve equal political representation in the Nordic region.

Strategies for Increasing Women's Parliamentary Representation in Norway

Despite favourable ideological conditions (widespread belief in equality and social justice; existence of social democratic and socialist parties) and the relatively open and participatory structure of the political system (multiple parties; proportional representation; preference voting rules) in 20th century Norway, the country's women did not achieve significant political representation until relatively recently (Bystydzienski, 1995). In a period of about a decade, between 1970 and 1980, the percentage of women in Norway's parliament (the Storting), and other elected political offices, tripled. While favourable conditions were in place for a long time, it was not until an especially strong phase of the women's movement mobilised more women to enter the formal political arena, and deployed specific strategies so they could become elected, that female representation increased significantly.

Norwegian women had organised as early as 1884 through the Norwegian Association for the Rights of Women, formed the National Council of Women of Norway in 1905, and created the Norwegian Women's Association in the 1950s. These established women's organisations were supplemented by new feminist organisations of the 1960s and 1970s which were more ideologically radical, class conscious, and structured through a loose network of small groups, the largest of which was the Women's Front (Dahlerup and Gulli, 1985, p.28). Women in both of these types of organisation formed coalitions and were able to identify issues of common interest including equal pay, abortion, rape and abuse, and pornography. They also agreed to work together to elect more women to Parliament and at the local level. Beginning with the 1967 local election, women's coalitions would come together before every election, develop information campaigns, and systematically work toward the election of more women.

Although the very first campaign for mobilization of women to run for public office was a local (municipal/county) election, campaigns soon developed before parliamentary elections as well. A particularly effective campaign took place before the 1977 parliamentary election. A coalition of about four hundred women from all political parties, most women's associations, and many new feminist groups, as well as women leaders from all sectors of Norwegian life, came together, united by their support for increased female representation. While there were areas of disagreement among the women (particularly on the issue of abortion), they were able to agree on three goals: that women occupy 50 per cent of all top positions in Norway, beginning with political leadership, that they be entitled to two extra years of education, and that women should have full economic independence. In order to achieve these goals, the coalition put pressure on the political parties to nominate more women and to place them high on party election lists, and established several committees to work on policy development in politics, education, the economy, the legal sphere, the arts, and religion, with a view to generally improving the status of women in Norwegian society (Bystydzienski, 1995, p.46).

As a specific tactic, members of the coalition who were involved in political parties, pressured party leaders for a sex quota of 40 per cent (i.e. that there should be at least 40 per cent of each sex within the parties at all levels and among candidates for election). They also contacted women in existing political positions and secured their overt and tacit support. And they used the media to promote the message that gender is a legitimate category for political representation.

To ensure that women's issues and interests be reflected in politics, the coalition of four hundred began to formulate a feminist political agenda. Many of the members of the coalition served on committees whose task was to develop policies dealing with women in specific areas of Norwegian life that could be put forth through the political parties by women whom they aimed to get elected as well as those who were already participating in the parties. The coalition remained active for a period of 18 months and the results of its efforts were impressive. After the 1977 campaign and election, the percentage of women representatives in the Storting increased from 16 to 24. In addition, women's issues and interests gained a permanent place on the party agendas. Discussions at party meetings dealing with discriminatory treatment of women and how it could be remedied became much more frequent in the late 1970s, and by the early 1980s all the parties (with the exception of the right wing Party of Progress), in one form or another, incorporated women's demands into their programs (Halsaa, 1989). In 1983, the Labour Party, the largest and most powerful of all the Norwegian parties, officially adopted the 40 per cent sex quota by including the quota in its constitution.

The campaigns continued throughout the 1980s and the 1990s, although they gradually began to lose the drive and intensity of the earlier actions. Many of the women who were engaged in these campaigns, and in the women's movement generally, entered political parties, unions, and the public corporate sector which led to a less vibrant movement and a corresponding decrease in the scope of pre-election campaigns. However, the campaigns did not cease, but rather became institutionalized as a cooperative endeavor between the government's Equal Status Council and autonomous women's groups. This institutionalization is not surprising, given the Norwegian government's role as equalizer of political power and a widespread belief in the legitimacy of women's claims to formal equality with men (Holter and Sorensen, 1984).

Beginning with the 1985 pre-election action, the Equal Status Council took the initiative to arrange a meeting for women's independent and political party organisations to discuss strategies, and provided office space for the campaign as well as funding (Halsaa, 1989, p.38). The council did this again at two-year intervals between 1987 and 2001, alternating between local/county and parliamentary elections.

Even though the numbers of activists involved in the campaigns had decreased over time, and by the early 1990s the Council provided, each time, pay for only one person who acted as coordinator, female political representation continued to rise steadily until 1995, levelling off somewhat in the last two parliamentary elections at 36 per cent (see Table 15.1).

Women's Influence in Parliamentary Politics in Norway

The activists who were involved in the campaigns to elect more women to Parliament in Norway assumed that women as a group had something different to bring to the public political sphere. While achieving equal representation was in itself a cause worth striving for, first the new feminists, and later other women as well as men, began to accept the idea that a more nearly equal ratio of women to men would result in a change in the content and form of politics.

Interviews conducted with Norwegian Members of Parliament in 1986 and in 1991 indicated that women and men politicians perceived several types of changes resulting from the increased female representation (Bystydzienski, 1995). Above all, the majority agreed that women had made the most difference in the types of issues they brought into discussions and debates, and to policy making. Issues that pertained to situations and conditions of life that touch women most directly, often referred to as 'soft issues', such as sexual reproduction, the care of children, the aged and the disabled, violence against women, pornography and prostitution, the unequal division of labour by sex, and lack of equal pay, were taken up by women parliamentarians and led to the development of policies and legislation aimed at improving the status and situation of women. This research and that of others (Skjeie, 1993; Halsaa, 1989) found that women parliamentarians in Norway raised and promoted women's issues more often than their male counterparts.

During the time that the numbers of Norwegian women parliamentarians increased significantly, important changes took place in policy and legislation related to issues of concern to women. Between 1977 and 1994, parental leave legislation was amended several times to gradually increase paid maternity leave from 12 to 32 weeks. A specific four-week paid leave was also provided only for fathers. In 1978, Norway adopted a law that allows for abortion on demand, and in 1979 a new provision was added to the Marketing Act prohibiting sex discrimination in advertising. By 1980, an amendment to the Names Act gave married women the option to use their family name and to give the mother's name to children, and in 1981 a new provision was added to the Equal Status Act requiring representation of both sexes on all public boards, commissions, and committees. In 1982, the Storting ratified several measures passed by trade unions regarding equal opportunities for women and equal treatment of women in the workplace. In 1986, when Gro Harlem Brundtland became Prime Minister, Parliament adopted an 'Action Plan to Promote Equal Status' and subsequently all the ministries developed their own action plans for promoting equality between the sexes. The Equal Status Act was strengthened in 1988 with a 40 per cent sex quota provision pertaining to the public sector (Equal Status Council, 1989). In the 1980s and 1990s, Parliament provided funding to municipalities for battered women's shelters and amended legal codes to allow for more effective prosecution of domestic violence and rape cases (Van der Ros, 1994). Many more changes and amendments were made to laws and provisions which recognized the discriminatory treatment of women and attempted to promote equality between the sexes.

While the above changes in legislation were not due solely to the entrance of more women politicians into Parliament, growing female representation did account for much of this development. The fact that many of the female MPs were active in the women's movement and took part in the pre-election campaigns meant that they were aware of women's issues and tended to promote them once they were elected.

Studies carried out in the other Scandinavian countries also show that female politicians to a greater extent than their male counterparts represent the interests of women. A survey of members of the Swedish Riksdag conducted in three different years (1985, 1988, and in 1995) found that more than half of women parliamentarians felt it was their duty to promote the interests and views of women as compared to less than ten per cent of men MPs (Wängnerud, 2000, p.75). The same study indicated that while 75 per cent of female members of parliament addressed issues of family policy, elder care, or health care in their election campaigns as well as once they were elected, only 44 per cent of male parliamentarians did the same (Wängnerud, 2000, p.81). A similar pattern was found in Finland (Sinkonnen and Haavio-Mannila, 1990, p.113) and in Denmark (Pedersen, 1989). However, it should be pointed out that all the studies also indicate that, in general, members of Nordic parliaments take up relatively few issues and proposals which concern the specific interests of women. Between five and ten per cent of all questions and proposals raised in Scandinavian parliaments during the years 1970-1984 dealt with such issues, although the vast majority were initiated by women MPs (Skard and Haavio-Mannila, 1985, p.76).

Other changes identified by parliamentarians in Norway as resulting from the increased female representation included: changes in political culture, that is beliefs about how politics should be conducted as well as norms of conduct; changes in political discourse or the language of politics; and changes in women's power especially in relation to the positions that women occupy in the national legislature and the resulting influence that they wield. Women and men MPs reported that the greater presence of women had created a more informal climate in meetings, led to politicians making shorter speeches, and promoted more openness to discussions of people's concrete experiences. Due to the introduction of women's issues, politicians have had to adopt a new vocabulary (usually imported from the women's movement) to discuss topics previously omitted or neglected such as sexual harassment, women's health, and violence against women (Bystydzienski, 1995, p.57-63).

As more women with diverse backgrounds and experiences began to enter the Norwegian Parliament, they were no longer relegated to the lower and less powerful positions, but were increasingly found on all standing committees and in leadership roles. For instance, in 1995, women chaired the Energy and Environment, Finance, Foreign Affairs, and Justice Committees and the leaders of the three largest and most influential parties in Parliament were women (Royal Norwegian Embassy, 1995, p.2). The scope of women's parliamentary activity also increased over time. While the proportion of speeches made by active women members in parliamentary discussions and debates was only 12 per cent between 1973-1977 and 20 per cent between 1977-1979 (Skard and Haavio-Mannila, 1985, p.71), by 1992, women MPs accounted for 38 per cent of all speeches (Skjeie, 1993, p.245).

While the above findings are impressive, they do not allow for the conclusion that Norway, or any of the other Nordic countries, has achieved gender equality in parliaments. Scandinavian women have yet to attain representational parity with men and it remains to be seen whether they will reach 50 per cent of parliamentary seats in the future. Moreover, as my research and that of others (Bergqvist *et al.*, 1999; Karvonen and Selle, 1995) indicates, even though women parliamentarians have brought women-specific issues into politics and have been able to influence certain legislation to reflect women's interests, the way in which Scandinavian parliaments continue to function does not make it easy for female politicians to promote women's interests effectively.

Prospects for Women's Full and Equal Participation in Nordic Parliaments

Despite the substantial increase in the percentages of female parliamentary representatives, Scandinavian parliaments have not changed their structures in a significant way. Party alignments continue to dominate policy formation even though some shifting of individual parties' positions from left-to-right and right-to-left has occurred in recent years (Shaffer, 1998). Thus, there is tremendous pressure on women parliamentarians to vote on issues according to party lines rather than as a gender-identified group (Skjeie, 1992; Wängnerud, 2000).

For example, in interviews with female and male parliamentarians in Norway it was found that while women were more likely than men to initiate discussion and legislation on issues like childcare and parental leave, when it came to specific policy preferences on such issues, the left-right party alignment was a better predictor than gender of where MPs would stand on these issues (Bystydzienski, 1995, pp.74-7). Thus, members of non-socialist parties tend to prefer providing government assistance to parents who take care of their own children, while left wing party members tend to favor collective approaches like child care centers. Moreover, even though Norwegian women parliamentarians have periodically formed cross-party coalitions to promote the passage of specific legislation, such alliances have seldom been successful as women MPs tend to be fragmented by party ideology (Bystydzienski, 1995, pp.77-9; Skjeie, 1992).

Research examining the role of women in parliamentary debates on childcare policy in Sweden, Finland and Iceland also found a low level of consensus among women parliamentarians regarding specific childcare provisions. Women from the non-socialist parties were more inclined to support parents' choice to use child care centers or to stay at home with children, while women from left parties regarded such proposals as undermining gender equality and reinforcing the traditional gendered division of labour (Bergqvist *et al.*, 1999, Ch. 8).

Another obstacle to women's equal participation is the gendered structure of parliaments. Parliaments are organisations which are not gender-neutral – rather, their structures and practices assume a male participant. Masculine assumptions are deeply ingrained in these institutions' norms, and their organisational processes reflect and reinforce societal gender arrangements and systems of inequality (Kelly and Duerst-Lahti, 1995; Acker, 1990; Bystydzienski, 1995, Ch. 6). Even though the significant numbers of women in Scandinavian parliaments have succeeded in making some changes, parliamentary politics in Nordic countries remains a masculine enterprise.

Divisions of labour and power by gender continue to exist in Nordic parliaments. In Norway, as in other Scandinavian countries, while women parliamentarians are no longer marginalized in the political hierarchy, they nevertheless are less likely than men to serve on the most important and influential parliamentary committees and to chair committees (Bergqvist *et al.*, 1999, p.40). Additionally, significantly more women than men MPs report feelings of powerlessness in terms of not being able to influence policy decisions (Bystydzienski, 1995, pp.87-8). Divisions by gender also exist in the types of issues women and men parliamentarians raise and promote, with women expected and more likely to address so called 'soft' or women's issues (even though women's issues usually constitute only about a quarter of all issues addresses by women MPs), while those issues advanced by men are generally perceived as universal or gender-neutral (Bystydzienski, 1995, p.87). Studies of parliamentary debates in Finland and Norway and election campaigns in Finland show that women still bear the sole responsibility for placing 'women's issues' on the political agenda; there is a striking lack of activity on the part of men in 'women's issues' (Karvonen, Djupsund and Carlson, 1995, p.372).

While men are to adhere to one set of standards regarding the appropriate conduct for politicians, women are to meet two sets of expectations: to both play by men's rules and to act according to norms governing traditional women's behavior (to be strong, assertive and decisive, but at the same time to be 'feminine', that is, not too aggressive or overbearing) (Bystydzienski, 1995, p.88). Unlike male politicians, who are expected to adhere to one set of rules that conflates their gender and political status, female parliamentarians are expected to act as both politicians and as women. For example, a study of Finish candidates running for parliamentary seats found that 'female campaigning ... created a dual image of softness accompanied with sufficient toughness' (Karvonen, Djupsund and Carlson, 1995, p.372). Such divisions are constantly re-created and tend to persist due to construction of images and symbols of politicians by the media, creation of gender identities by female politicians themselves, and male-female interaction that reinforces the masculine ideal of the politician, making it problematic for women to express themselves as women and as representatives of women's interests (Bystydzienski, 1995, p.95).

Like most other contemporary public institutions, government organisations, including the Nordic parliaments, are structured so that their members' primary commitment in terms of time and energy is to the organisation. When parliament is in session, MPs are expected to devote their total attention to its business and work hours are typically very long. Such arrangements fit more easily the social roles of men, but often pose difficulties for female politicians many of whom are faced with juggling family demands in addition to their political roles.

Scandinavian women MPs thus occupy an ambiguous and problematic position in relation to Nordic parliaments. They have made some significant inroads by gaining substantial representation and changing some aspects of the political culture and political agendas, policies and legislation, but the increasing numbers of women parliamentarians have not transformed political structures and ideals to reflect the realities and interests of both women and men.

Conclusion

By many indicators, women have achieved important gains at the national level of politics in the Scandinavian countries. All five countries have at least 30 per cent female representation in their parliaments and women no longer occupy the lowest positions within parliamentary hierarchies. With the exception of Iceland, women hold a high percentage (at least one-third) of seats in Nordic ruling cabinets, and their representation on the corporate boards, councils and committees that influence national political and economic policies is close to 40 per cent. Women parliamentarians have had substantial influence on the issues discussed, debated and legislated in parliaments, and have changed somewhat the culture of parliamentary politics.

The situation of Nordic women parliamentarians can be characterized as what Rosabeth Moss Kanter called 'the tilted group' (1977, p.115), that is, one where minority representation approaches 40 per cent and the minority becomes strong enough to influence the values and norms of the organisation. Kanter argued that an organisation will become 'balanced' when the ratio of minority to majority is closer to 50 per cent, or at the very least 40/60. Only in Sweden have women parliamentarians passed the 40 per cent mark. However, there is no guarantee that even a 50 per cent female representation will result in a truly gender-balanced parliament. Indeed, simply focusing on increasing numbers as a strategy for change neglects the complexities of gender integration (Bystydzienski, 1995, Ch. 5) and overlooks other factors such as intrusiveness by the under-represented group and occupational inappropriateness which create more of a threat to the dominant group than mere numbers (Yoder, 1991). There is evidence from other countries such as the United States and Australia that as the proportion of women increases in a legislative body, men become more verbally aggressive and controlling of the legislative process (Kathlene, 1994) and women representatives do not influence policies in a significant way (Grey, 2002).

The challenge for equal and full participation of women in Nordic parliaments that still remains is to transform parliamentary structures (systematic practices and power relationships) so that they are indeed balanced in that they reflect the experiences and interests of both women and men in all their diversity, and not advantage men over women. This will not happen until structural arrangements in politics combine both equal representation and the particularities of women's different and varied needs and circumstances (Armstrong, 2002). This may require, for example, that parliamentary structures become less hierarchical and more participatory so that all representatives, regardless of gender, have equal access to power and influence. The tension between equality and difference thus needs to be recognized and continually debated (Bergqvist *et al.*, 1999, p.289) by women and men parliamentarians as well as everyone else in society. Only out of such discussions and negotiations may more inclusive structures eventually emerge.

Chapter 16

The Netherlands

Monique Leyenaar

Introduction

Watching the party leaders campaigning for the parliamentary election of 15 May 2002, one is inclined to conclude that only men participate in politics in the Netherlands. Not one woman is present in the many televised debates with party leaders. No colourful distraction, only dark grey, dark blue and black suits, light shirts and suitable (not too flashy) ties. However, when one takes a closer look at the different lists of candidates for these parliamentary elections, one finds the names of women candidates in second place on these lists. With the exception of the party List Pim Fortuyn, so named after the leader and founder of the party, and the small religious parties, all other political parties placed a woman candidate second. The outgoing governing parties, PvdA, VVD and D66, nominated their women ministers, while the opposition parties selected their most known women parliamentarians for these slots. Women candidates were also found in other positions on the lists, with the progressive parties leading with 40-45 per cent women candidates and the Christian-Democratic and conservative parties following with 25-35 per cent.

So although the absence of women politicians on television during the 2002 election campaign consolidated the image of politics as a male monopoly, the electoral system ensures that the moment the votes are cast, women will enter the parliament in relatively large numbers. We therefore start this chapter with a short description of the electoral and party system of the Netherlands.

In the second section the evolution of women's representation in parliament is discussed. Legally women's representation of women began in 1917 when women were granted the right to stand for election, but in practice it took until the end of the 1970s before a substantial number of women participated in both government and in parliament. This section discusses the relevant players in getting more women into politics: women's organisations, political parties and the Dutch government. Obstacles to women's participation in parliament and strategies to overcome these barriers are discussed in the third section. Questions as to whether their presence has changed the political agenda and performance of the politicians are addressed in section four. The closing section deals with the future. Politics in the Netherlands is in turmoil as it is in many European countries. Many citizens are turning away from the traditional parties and new parties enter the political arena addressing more explicitly than ever before the issues of immigration and concerns about personal and collective safety. In the Netherlands the 2002 parliamentary elections led to a change in government: a right-wing government replaced a centre-left wing government. The emergence of new parties, both at the national and local level has resulted in a decline in the political representation of women. The new parties seem to be less convinced of the necessity of gender balanced candidate lists. The question is now whether the upward trend in women's political participation was after all not a trend, but a short upheaval. Can we really speak about a change in attitudes of political parties and government in terms of a greater sense of gender equality and a greater willingness to sharing power or is the relative high representation of women just a coincidence?

Political System

The Netherlands is a constitutional monarchy with a parliamentary system. Queen Beatrix as head of state, together with the cabinet ministers, constitutes the government. The parliament consists of two houses, the First Chamber (Upper House), which has 75 members who are indirectly elected by the members of the Provincial Councils, and the Second Chamber (Lower House) with 150 members elected through universal suffrage by all electors over the age of 18 years. Apart from these two houses of parliament, there are the local councils and the provincial councils whose members are also directly elected once every four years. In 2003 there were 12 provinces and 496 municipalities. The leader of the administration of both representative bodies, the Commissioner of State and the Mayor respectively are appointed to their posts by the cabinet.

Electoral System

The electoral system dates from 1917 when the system of proportional representation was introduced together with universal suffrage (in 1917 for men and in 1919 for women). The constitution requires an election every four years for the Second Chamber, after which the leader of the largest party is asked by the Queen to form a majority government together with other parties. However, since World War II it has become common practice for the Queen to appoint an informateur first, whose task is to inform the Queen about the viability of possible coalitions.

Parliamentary elections take place at least once every four years or when the government is dissolved. Seats are divided according to a system of proportional representation with party lists. At elections voters mark ballot papers containing the names of all candidates competing for seats, grouped by party. The number of seats a party acquires is proportional to its share of the vote. And since the whole of the country is treated as one single constituency, it is a very proportional system with a very low threshold for parliamentary representation. A candidate needs just 0.67 per cent of the vote to win a seat. The party specifies the order of the candidates on the party list, and this order determines in practice who gets returned to parliament. The same procedure applies to local and regional council elections. It happens only rarely that candidates who are placed in non-electable positions on the list are directly elected by preferential votes. In the parliamentary elections of January 2003, 80 per cent of the electorate voted for a list by giving their vote to the first candidate on the list. Two candidates were directly elected with preferential votes, one male and one female candidate. The woman was a candidate for the Christian Union Party and she was placed as number four on the list, while the party only collected votes for three seats. The other candidate was a former cabinet minister for the LPF.

Party System

The origins of the Dutch party system can be traced back to the mass emancipation movements of the second half of the 19th century. These movements were not only shaped by class conflict, as was the case in all European countries, but even more by religious distinctions between Calvinist, Catholic and Dutch Reformed segments of the population. The various emancipatory movements gave rise to political parties, but also to a wide array of other social institutions, organised along denominational and class lines. Political, social, cultural and some economic organisations were to a large extent based on the same cleavages in the population, resulting in the formation of relatively cohesive segments of society or subcultures for Catholics (the most numerous group), Protestants, Socialists, and 'Neutrals' (secular, liberal) groups. This system of 'Verzuiling' (pillarization) together with the strong religious overtones in politics are important when explaining women's (lack of) political involvement.

Three party groups have historically dominated Dutch politics: the Christian Democrats (Christen Democratisch Appel, CDA), the Labour Party (The Partij van de Arbeid, PvdA) and the Conservative-Liberal grouping consisting of the conservative liberal party Volkspartij voor Vrijheid en Democratie (VVD) and the left-liberal party Democraten 66 (D66). Apart from these parties, there are two left-wing parties, a green party, Groen Links, and the Socialist Party (Socialistische Partij). On the right of the spectrum two small orthodox parties are active, the Christen Unie (CU) and the Staatkundig Gereformeerde Partij (SGP). From 1917 until 1994 the Christian Democrats were always part of the coalition government, either with the VVD or the PvdA. In 1994 the 'purple cabinet' was formed consisting of the PvdA, VVD and D66, excluding the CDA.

In the run-up to the parliamentary elections of 2002 it became clear that relations between the three governing parties were tense and that the coalition was unlikely to last. The break up of the coalition was speeded up by the arrival of a new party Leefbaar Nederland (LN), formed by independent local councillors and others as a protest against the governing parties. This new party challenged the lack of transparent decision-making and government indecisiveness as well as the inability of the 'purple cabinet' to solve problems such as hospital waiting lists and growing crime rates. Furthermore, the LN placed the issue of immigrants and especially the question of their (lack of) integration in Dutch society high on the political agenda. The popularity of LN really increased with the selection of a party leader. Pim Fortuyn, a former professor in sociology and columnist came forward to take up this role. His flamboyant public performances, along with his open homosexuality and direct manner in dealing with the media made him a popular leader. However, his individualistic leadership style was also a drawback, as he was not willing to be bound by the strictures of party discipline. In February 2002 matters were brought to a head when the executive of LN dismissed Fortuyn as their leader. Fortuyn, by now convinced of his electoral attraction given his high poll ratings, founded his own party, Lijst Pim Fortuyn (LPF) and submitted a list of candidates for the election of May 2002. Fortuyn was murdered nine days before the parliamentary elections. The effects of all this on the election results are described by Andeweg and Irwin (2002, p. 99):

> This first murder of a political figure in 330 years sent a shockwave through the country and led to an unprecedented public display of mourning. Amidst accusations that by 'demonizing' Mr. Fortuyn the Left and the media had created a climate of opinion that made the assassination possible, the elections went ahead as scheduled on 15 May. Exit polls show that the murder changed the preference of 12 per cent of the voters. Some voters used the ballot box to send a message of condolence, but other voters, apparently fearful that polarization would destabilize the country, produced a last-minute swing towards the Christian Democrats.

As predicted by the polls, the coalition parties were severely beaten in the elections. The PvdA went from 26 per cent to 15 per cent (23 seats) the VVD from 25 to 16 per cent (24 seats) and D66 dropped from nine to five per cent (six seats). Voter support shifted to the opposition CDA and the new LPF. The CDA became the largest party with 29 per cent (43 seats). LPF received 17 per cent of the total vote and won 26 seats in parliament, making it the first time in history that a new party gained such a high level of support.

The arrival of LPF on the stage has shaken the Dutch party system. Its policies appeal to a significant section of the public harbouring a growing sense of powerlessness and loss of confidence in the government. The violent death of its leader served to reinforce its message as a populist party, appealing to the dissatisfaction among voters that became expressed at the general election. Politics had become too professional and politicians were too alienated from the citizens. Being interviewed by the media, government ministers or party leaders never seemed to give straight answers, nor were able to admit to failures. The straightforward way of communicating by Fortuyn, visible in the many televised debates during the campaign, was a welcome distraction from the somewhat arrogant attitude of the 'old' political male leaders.

However, the coalition government formed after the 2002 elections lasted only 87 days. Internal fights, especially among the politically inexperienced LPF ministers, caused the fall of the cabinet in October 2002. In the 2003 elections the LPF lost 18 of their 26 seats and the traditional parties again came to dominate. The consequences of all this for the representation of women will be discussed in the next sections.

Political Empowerment of Women

Political Rights

In 1917 the qualification 'male' was erased from Dutch election law. From that moment on women were allowed to stand for election. Two years later, in 1919, the law was changed again and women could also vote: they did so for the first time at the parliamentary election of 1922. The granting of these formal political rights did not happen overnight. Until 1887 there was no explicit constitutional prohibition barring women from voting. It was a woman, Aletta Jacobs, who pointed out the discrepancy between the Constitution and the actual practice. As a woman of independent means (she was the first woman to go to university and subsequently became a medical practitioner), she attempted to assert her voting rights. But even an appeal to the Higher Court did not help. The Higher Court ruled, that when the Constitution referred to an 'inhabitant of the Netherlands' it was referring to men, since 'otherwise this would have been explicitly stated'. Moreover it was argued, that, since the husband and father paid taxes for his wife and children, it was logical that women should not be allowed to vote. Rather conveniently, those women, such as widows and unmarried women, who also paid taxes, were not taken into account. The result of Jacobs' action was that in 1887, when the Constitution was renewed, the word 'male' was added to 'inhabitant of the Netherlands' (Jacobs, 1978, p.94). The publicity around this case raised interest in the issue of suffrage for women, and led to the establishment of several organisations and from 1890 onwards many women and men committed themselves to the cause of general suffrage. Public opinion was mobilised through demonstrations, articles in the newspapers while members of parliament were lobbied constantly on the issue.

Traditionally the religious parties criticized women's participation in the public sphere more so than the other large parties. For example, the parliamentary leader of the Christian Historian Union, a large religious party at that time, expressed in a parliamentary debate in 1916 his fear that women MPs would have a seductive influence on the voting behaviour of their male colleagues. He expressed the concern that if women were permitted to enter parliament, the possibility existed that male MPs would base their voting behaviour not on the nature of the issue at hand, but on the basis of their (intimate) feelings towards the women in the Chamber. But in the end all the Catholic MPs and a majority of the Protestant parliamentarians voted in favour of the bill introducing women's suffrage. This, however, was largely due to a deal that was made between the political parties. The socialist and liberal parties got general suffrage, while the religious parties got a favourable settlement of their fight for the establishment of independent and government funded Christian schools. An underlying reason for granting women the vote was the fear among a majority of MPs of a possible left-wing revolution as had occurred in 1918 in Germany. Since women were thought to be more conservative in their voting behaviour, the participation of women in politics was seen to be a stabilizing factor. A third reason the religious parties supported the change in the Constitution was their conviction that women were more likely to vote for the religious parties than for the liberal or socialist parties.

From Token to Player

The political empowerment of women in the Netherlands can be seen to evolve through four distinct phases. First, there are the pioneers, the women who entered parliament between 1917-1946. Then there are the tokens, the women MPs from 1946 until the mid-1970s. In the third period, from 1977-1990 we find the group representatives. And the 1990s may be characterized by the players.

During the first period women entered parliament only very slowly and their representation was never higher than seven per cent. The few women in the parliament at that time were very much part of an upper social echelon, often from an upper or upper-middle class family, with a university degree, unmarried, and childless. Mothers were, especially for the religious parties, not acceptable to the party elite making the nominations for parliament. The majority of the women MPs were lawyers or teachers before becoming parliamentarian. The fact that women in 1919 became important targets as potential voters did not mean that parties set up conscious policies to nominate women for political positions, despite the presence of women's wings in these parties.

The end of World War II renewed the demand for a greater representation of women. Active women in the parties made it clear that they would not accept the parties' lack of support for the participation of women. Although the representation of women did not rise above ten per cent, more parties felt obliged to nominate at least one woman not only to the parliamentary party, but also as government ministers: women as tokens. In seven of the eight cabinets formed between 1953 and 1972 there was always one woman holding the position of minister or junior minister. As in the first period, the parties regarded women as primarily homemakers and mothers, and preferred their female MPs to be unmarried and childless. Women were present within the parties and representative bodies based on a very restricted gender-identity. They were expected to defend and articulate women's interests, at that time defined as the interests of mothers and homemakers.

The mid-1970s mark a turning point in the political representation of women in the Netherlands. The Dutch political system had been confronted in the 1960s with developments such as depillarisation and secularisation, as well as with a growing demand for more political influence and a less paternalistic, more open, attitude on the part of the political elite. In the late 1960s women's groups were also emerging, pursuing equal rights for men and women. The combination of these demands for more participation and for equal rights turned out to be a strong catalyst in the fight for equal political representation. After the elections in 1977, for example, the percentage of women MPs increased from nine to 14, while four women junior ministers and one woman minister were appointed in the cabinet formed in that year. Compared to their colleagues in the previous periods, women MPs in the 1970s did not have to choose so often between motherhood and a political career. Although more likely to be single than their male colleagues, a majority of the women MPs nonetheless were married with children. Gender identity, seen in terms of a clear division between male and female MPs with regard to the issues they dealt with inside parliament, was again less strict in this period. Although the majority of women MPs were still more likely to sit on education, health and welfare committees, in this period women also occupied seats on committees on policing, defence, foreign affairs and finance (Leyenaar, 1989, p.171).

The upward trend of women's political representation continued in the 1990s and more women than ever were to be found in parliament and government. Various developments had a positive impact on the empowerment of women. For example the economical and social advancement of women in Dutch society played a significant part, especially as women in the Netherlands caught up with men in higher education and the majority of adult women became involved in paid employment. A greater availability of childcare made it easier for women to emerge from their private domains. More than ever it was now widely accepted that women might occupy political positions.

Another positive impact came from the formation of the 'purple cabinet', consisting of three parties, PvdA, D66 and VVD, in 1994 and in 1998. The Christian Democrats, who were ideologically positioned between D66 and VVD, were kept out of government, something that had not happened since 1917. The cabinet formed in 1994 headed by a Labour prime minister, consisted of four women out of 14 ministers and five women among the 12 junior ministerial appointments. Women were now in charge of the ministries of health, traffic, justice and infrastructure. After the elections of 1998, the coalition continued and again nine women were part of the government.

Nonetheless, gender differences in respect of socio-economic characteristics persist (Table 16.1). Although the average age of male and female MPs has converged, two-thirds of male MPs held a university qualification as compared with just over half of female MPs. Successful female candidates are overwhelmingly drawn from higher social backgrounds, while the social roots of male MPs, of whom half come from wealthier backgrounds, has remained consistent across the century. In terms of family circumstances, gender patterns have changed little over the century. Female politicians have an equal chance of being married or single, while the vast majority of their male colleagues are married. About half of women MPs are childless; very few of their male counterparts are childless.

Table 16.1 Social profile of Netherlands MPs, 1918-1986

	1918-46		1947-67		1968-77		1978-86	
Gender	M	F	M	F	M	F	M	F
High social background (%)	48	77	51	70	50	82	46	90
University degree (%)	45	54	52	45	59	54	64	53
Age at entry to parliament (yrs)	46	47	45	45	42	41	41	41
Unmarried (%)	0	50	4	53	8	37	7	44
No children (%)	0	83	0	56	7	59	8	48

Source: Leyenaar, 1989, pp. 142-52

The greater number of women MPs was certainly a result of changes in the outlook of selectors. Party leaders and policy makers were increasingly recognising that having more women in their midst was likely to be an asset for the organisation. Taking ideas from management and organisation studies, the selectors of political personnel assumed that having more women would bring about a different atmosphere and change in focus, in short, give a fresh perspective to politics. The overall attitude towards political integration of women in the 1990s and onwards was much more positive than that of two or three decades previously. Party leaders actively sought women candidates.

In addition to the political parties, another prime mover in the process of the empowerment of women has been the Dutch government. From the early 1980s there was an active government policy to increase women's participation in politics and public administration. Important policy instruments have been financial support, research and regulation and/or legislation. With regard to financial support, the government has subsidised many activities to get more women elected, initiated by women's groups or by parties. An example is the financial support the Ministry of Internal Affairs offered in 1987 to each political party represented in Parliament, under the condition the money had to be used for activities aiming to increase the number of women in the electoral bodies. All parties, with the exception of the SGP (an orthodox Calvinist party), accepted the money and most parties used the money to hire someone for three years to take charge of formulating affirmative action strategies. Two other orthodox parties, who do not subscribe to the governments' policies on gender equality, used the money for training (Leyenaar, 1993, p.226).

The Dutch government has also invested in gender equality by financing many research projects. The Ministry of Internal Affairs financed a large research project in 1983 that sought to explain the limited political representation of women. Every three or four years, this ministry as well as the Ministry of Social Affairs and the Ministry of Cultural Affairs and Education initiated research on the under-representation of women in politics. These projects have contributed to the development of policies aimed at enhancing the number of women participating in political decision-making.

The Netherlands government, contrary to the Belgian or French government, has always been reluctant to introduce legislation promoting the participation of women in electoral bodies. The main argument used against the introduction of legislation was the fact that it was seen to be unconstitutional, given the existence of non-discrimination laws and the autonomy of political parties. Instead of introducing legislation, the government decided in 1992 to take additional measures to raise the percentage of women in politics and public offices. In a specific policy programmeme submitted by the cabinet and accepted by the parliament, nineteen concrete measures were initiated ranging from the publication of yearly statistics on women in politics; half-yearly talks between the Minister of Internal Affairs and the leaders of the political parties on the progress in this matter; requesting the provincial commissioners (responsible for the nomination of mayors) to nominate at least 50 per cent qualified women candidates for mayor; to a regulation that for those external advisory bodies with less than 15 per cent women members, the nominating organisations may only nominate women candidates. Only when it was established that no qualified women were available could a male candidate be nominated (Ministerie van Binnenlandse Zaken, 1992). These concrete policy measures helped in convincing party leaders to nominate more women.

Exclusion from Politics

For a long time it was possible to explain the under representation of women in politics by distinguishing between individual and institutional barriers affecting the chances of women to become involved in political decision making. The first category addresses the extent to which individual characteristics favour political participation. For example, high levels of educational and professional experience, or coming from a 'politicised' family are advantages when pursuing a political career. On the other hand being married and having small children is a disadvantage to women who are striving to achieve a representative position. Institutional factors affecting the achievement of participation by women relate to the organisation of society, its norms and values, as well as to the political system itself. The lack of childcare facilities is an obstacle, but also the selection procedures used in political parties offer many obstacles for women.

Following women's footsteps in politics over time, it becomes clear that the relative weight of the different factors changes over time. In the early 20th century legal obstacles, like the ban on women's suffrage or of mothers in paid employment, were of great importance. Before and immediately after World War II, religion and the existing traditional gender ideology, as well as individual barriers such as the lack of educational and professional background, stopped women from gaining political power. At the beginning of the 21st century the selection process and selection criteria are the main obstacles, as well as a culture of politics that results in a personal choice of many women not to pursue a political career. These are three main explanations for the continuing under representation of women in representative bodies, and are discussed in more detail below.

Power and Selection

One of the main explanations of the persistent character of the under representation of women in politics is that getting many more women into decision-making involves a radical redistribution of power. Research has shown that people in power obviously do not like to give up their privileged positions. Many procedures for selecting and nominating political leaders are biased in ways that promote the continued tenure of groups, typically of men, that already hold positions of power. For example, what is typically valued most is to be well known within the party. A long party career brings the necessary reputation, as well as being valued as a sign of strong party affiliation, indicating that the candidate will be a trustworthy party representative. The most common route to a high-level position is through previous political positions. All parties view demonstrated political experience as the most crucial requirement for a potential candidate. Such selection criteria have a negative effect on women's chances of being selected. Taking into account the length of membership and the number of activities carried out by women within the parties, women often still have less experience than men.

Quality of Life

A second factor explaining women's lack of power is related to the importance of quality of life as an issue for women. Common features of senior political positions are the heavy demands of the job, 24-hour availability, the necessity for total dedication and the need for mobility. Meetings are an important part of a representative's job and often one is dependent on voluntary workers, which means that meetings have to be scheduled for evenings and weekends. However, being flexible is often problematic for women, since careful planning is the only way to combine work, care and politics. Another aspect is that for women other spheres of interests besides a (political) career, such as family, friends and local community, are just as important (De Gilder, 1998). The attention of women is often divided among these spheres, more so than for men. Socialization of men over 45 years has caused a more narrow orientation towards work and career and a lesser interest for these other spheres (Chodorow, 1978; Gilligan, 1982). The fact that women divide their time and attention between a career, family, friends and community stands in the way of a traditional linear career pattern. Research shows that men and women differ in the importance they attach to a high salary (more important for men) and to relevant and interesting work (more important for women) (Valian, 1998). Women are less inclined to make sacrifices in order to reach the top of the political ladder. It is not true that these women lack ambition or commitment, but more that they do not possess a clear career plan, that includes spending time on politics. Women see themselves as having more alternative possibilities at their disposal and therefore will not set everything aside for a political career. In politics and especially for the leadership positions, one has to be prepared to defend one's position, and strong women candidates often give in to pressure by the party leadership to step down in favour of a male candidate. This was the case in the leadership fight in 2002 in the German Christian Democratic Party, where Angela Merkl voluntary retreated in favour of Edmund Stoiber. During the 2002 parliamentary elections campaign, the second candidates on the lists of PvdA and VVD, both women, gave way to men placed lower on the lists. These men were thought by the party leadership to be more electorally attractive and they were given a prominent role in the campaign when the number one candidates of both parties (men) were attacked by the media.

Culture of Political Organisations

A third main reason for the lack of power of women is that the culture of organisations such as political parties and representative bodies does not coincide with the cultural norms and values of most women. Research has shown that in many organisations values such as independence, control, competition, rationality and objectivity are dominant, while there is less room for values and practices related to caring, emotionality, and closeness. Men and women differ in attitudes to decision-making: women are more focused on consensus and balance in communication and more democratically oriented, while men are more focused on competition and have a more autocratic orientation (Vianen, 1998). Many women politicians often do not feel at home in elected assemblies and experience isolation from the informal networks within a parliament. Apart from the time factor, the sense of exclusion experienced by women can be an underlying factor in their decision to leave their political position after one term, while men are more often inclined to stay on for another term (Castenmiller, 2002).

Does Gender Matter in Parliament?

It is now well established that a group becomes significant when it reaches a critical mass of 30-35 per cent of the arena to which it belongs (Kanter, 1977). One would expect therefore that women MPs in the 1990s and later have been able to put their own stamp on political decision-making. This, of course, touches upon the question of whether women MPs represent distinctive women's interests. We know from interviews with the pioneer women MPs that they, although unmarried themselves, took the attitude of 'housewife-politicians'. They mainly interested themselves in issues related to the family and children, as well as with educational matters (Pothuis-Smit, 1946). According to two interviews, one with a socialist woman MP and one with a woman MP from the CHU, the women in parliament addressed issues that their male colleagues would not have 'touched' and they dealt with these issues using 'a feminine perspective' (Pothuis-Smit, 1946, pp.157-8). The first woman in parliament, Suze Groeneweg, always pointed to the role of women when discussing policy issues. Her maiden speech on 7 November 1918 elaborated on the interests of the wives of the military and twice she submitted a proposal for legal arrangement of pregnancy leave and mother care. Further she stood for unmarried teachers who were being discriminated against in salary and she pleaded in favour of a ban on the selling of alcohol (Handelingen Tweede Kamer, 1918). In the second period, women MPs mainly dealt with issues related to motherhood. However, the fact that many of women legislators of that time had been active in women's organisations before entering parliament, made them also aware of other interests of women. An intriguing example is the fact that all female MPs, including those from the Protestant and Catholic parties, voted in favour of a motion proposed by a Labour woman MP stating that 'except when abuse is apparent, it is not in the State's remit to prohibit the work of married women'. With this motion, the attempts of the government to limit paid work of married women at times of unemployment were finally stopped. The motion passed with the narrow margin of 46 to 44, thanks to the support of the women from the confessional parties (Plantenga, 1998 p.56).

Between 1977 and 1990, the women's movement reached its peak in the Netherlands and promoted vigorous debates on issues such as the legalization of abortion and the equalizing of tax regulations. Some women MPs in that period were prominent participants in demonstrations and other activities organised by feminist groups. The majority however played the parliamentary game and voted according the party lines, even when, as feminists, they might well have voted differently. Women Labour MPs had particular difficulties with the strict application of party discipline (Visser, 1955, p.10). But many women MPs succeeded in expressing a feminist ideology. In 1978 a Parliamentary Standing Committee on Equality was formed, dealing with issues regarding the advancement of women in Dutch society. An even more clear-cut statement was the establishment in 1981 of the All Parties Women's Caucus. The main objective was to see whether women MPs of different political parties could be united on certain issues. They met every six weeks and participation was variable. The emphasis in this period was less on gender differences than on the premise that gender should no longer be grounds for differentiation. The women MPs viewed themselves in the first place as 'group-representatives' of the party group. In the second place, however, they also represented women by extending the parliamentary agenda through raising issues of great concern to women and by identifying themselves as women, for example in their all-women meetings.

In the 1990s and at the start of the 21st century the improvement of the social, economic and political position of women has a firm place on the political agenda. A majority of women MPs in this period still viewed the gendered division of labour as an important source of inequality and they kept on working in the parliament to change these gender roles. One important success of several women MPs has been the parliamentary approval of gender mainstreaming as a governmental approach to overcome the remaining barriers to gender equality: equality policy has to be integrated into all regular policy. Effects of this 'Plan of Action on Gender Mainstreaming' are that since 1999 all ministries have to determine and implement at least three concrete acts of emancipation, as well as specify in their budgets the amount of money allocated to gender equality (Ministerie van Sociale Zaken en Werkgelegenheid, 2002). At the same time, however, political identity has again become more important than gender identity. For example, the Parliamentary Standing Committee on Equality was abolished in 1994 as well as the All Party Women's Caucus. The Caucus ceased to exist in the 1990s when attendance steadily declined. We also see a growing number of young and highly educated women MPs, who themselves experienced no gender discrimination in education and in finding a job, and who do not see any problems for women as a group. They do not view themselves as women representing women, but as individual MPs representing their party.

This attitude is also visible in the parties. The women's section of the Labour Party decided to disband in 1995 and, since then, the party executive takes responsibility for the formulation and implementation of affirmative action strategies. At that time a specific training programme was started directed at scouting, recruiting and training of women and ethnic minority candidates. In 2000 this training programmeme was replaced by the PvdA Women's Network. The women's section of the VVD followed in the footsteps of the PvdA. In 2002 the section ceased to exist and a new Liberal Women's Network was established. The idea is not only to involve women party members but also women from outside the party and to create a large network of liberal women. Green Left started its Feminist Network in 1997. Femnet is not a critical lobby group, but 'an open network where Green Left members and supporters interested in gender issues can meet to discuss these issues' (Groen Links, 2003).

The network organisational structure seems to be a much looser structure with no statutes, rules or regulations, headed by a more or less flexible group of women. The choice for a network structure instead of a fully embedded women's section fits in with the shift of responsibility for gender equality from women party members to the party leadership as a whole. There appears to be no further need for a separate section to pressure a party leadership to deliver on gender equality.

Conclusion

By the beginning of the 21st century, women had become a force to be reckoned with in Dutch politics. Albeit at a very slow pace, the 'pioneers' and 'tokens' had been replaced by 'group representatives' and 'players'. Since 1977, the number of women involved in political decision-making has been increasing, reaching 37 per cent women MPs after the parliamentary elections of 2003. The sudden decrease of women's parliamentary representation after the 2002 parliamentary election to 33 per cent does not call this conclusion into question, since it can be attributed to one new (and now unsuccessful) party that gained 17 per cent of the seats and sent only three women (11per cent) to parliament. The parties on the left nominated around 50 per cent women candidates to eligible places on their lists, while CDA and VVD nominated around one third women candidates. And for the first time in history a woman standing for a small orthodox religious party was elected, not because she was placed high on the candidate list, but because of preferential votes. However, the fact that fewer women were elected in the local elections of 2002 and in the regional elections of 2003 shows us the importance of the 'goodwill' of party leaderships. Without an explicit plan and associated selection procedures, a balanced participation of women in the representative bodies is clearly difficult to achieve. Without these extra measures women still tend to lose fights over the allocation of power or even decide not to fight at all.

Today's women MPs differ from those elected in the previous century. They are much more diverse in background, while being married or having young children is no longer an obstacle to selection by the parties. In contrast to the situation in the previous century, there are no clear-cut women's issues on which to lobby, such as the ban on employment for married women or legalisation of abortion or the expansion of public childcare facilities. Women MPs can no longer be labelled as feminists, mothers or housewives according to the interests they stood for in parliament. In the 1990s, when women came to be a substantial group they changed the content of the political agenda. Issues such as childcare, sexual violence, combining paid and unpaid work are fully-fledged political issues these days. In the 21st century, gender differences in parliamentary behaviour are slowly disappearing. Male MPs are also dealing with so-called women's issues. Compared to the situation ten or twenty years ago, the women who now enter politics, especially at the national level, make a conscious decision to do so. They are welcomed and sought after, often finding a route into politics through new instruments of recruitment and new criteria for selection. The Labour Party, for instance, finds its potential candidates for the parliamentary party through advertisements in national newspapers. In the two parliamentary elections in 2002 and 2003 about 50 per cent of all applicants to these advertisements were women. Women are more inclined to put themselves forward when invited in such a transparent and open procedure. The fact that a lengthy party career is not seen as a necessary asset in order to become a serious candidate works in favour of women.

What can we conclude for the near future? Two important questions remain open. The first is whether the continuous decline in political party membership can be reversed if parties broaden their support base. A related issue is the general turmoil within the party system. We have seen that the arrival of new, conservative, parties on the political scene in the Netherlands lowers the chances for a future gender balance in both representative bodies and government. If this remains the case, then institutional guarantees, such as laws on the gender composition of lists of candidates, may also become necessary in the Netherlands. The second open question is whether in the future there will be enough women who are willing to play the political game. So far it is only at the local level that women are more reluctant than men to enter and continue with council work. The main reason is the double burden of work such a commitment entails: the combination of a job, politics and family with the number of evenings and weekends one has to spend in council or party activities. There has been no lack of women candidates for office at the national level. At this level, however, we see a reluctance of women to go for the highest-level political jobs: party leader, state commissioner, minister and prime minister. Genuinely gender – balanced political offices are therefore still a utopia.

Chapter 17

Conclusion

Yvonne Galligan and Manon Tremblay

Historically, winning the vote was a major milestone in women's political citizenship. Yet, the hope that obtaining the franchise would in turn lead to unproblematic and equal participation in power was not realised. As the chapters in this book show, in countries where women were granted early enfranchisement (Australia, Norway and Canada were among the first countries to give women the right to vote) the electoral outcomes were not more positive for women's representation than in countries where women's right to vote was delayed (Switzerland granted universal female franchise in 1971 while in South Africa black women got the vote in 1994). Although the chapters highlight many differences in the historical trajectory of women's political empowerment across established and emerging democracies, the barriers identified to women's full parliamentary representation are remarkably similar across all cases. In turn, the strategies used to overcome these obstacles also cover bear a close resemblance to one another. The chapters also underline the importance of feminist activism in generating support for an increased presence of women in parliament, and, once in parliament in some numbers, women MPs indicate an awareness of a responsibility to represent women's views and interests in addition to the interests of their geographical constituency. This final chapter draws together and compares the main chapter findings on the progress of women in sharing political power with men.

Obstacles

In much of the literature on women's political participation, the obstacles to women's equal political presence are generally seen as located in three distinct, yet inter-related, arenas: socio-cultural attitudes, women's individual capacity, and institutional political arrangements. The analysis of women's marginalisation from elected office in this book provides rich evidence that this typology is valid in a comparative context. One of the strongest themes emanating from the chapters is the complex interconnection between cultural attitudes towards gender social roles and the institutional conceptualisation of power as a gendered construct. In effect, the cases in this book repeatedly highlight the prevalence of a patriarchal, masculinist understanding of politics and power where men and male-centred perspectives dominate and which in turn assigns women to the sphere of the family and 'private' power. In many, if not all, cases, these gendered attitudes are influenced by deeply-embedded religious beliefs and social practices that endow power with a male-gendered preference. In Indonesia, prevailing traditional gender role stereotypes, buttressed by conservative Islamic teaching, were harnessed by the state for political ends – effectively conceptualising women as instruments for national development through their family role. This conjunction of social and religious conservatism acting to limit women's capacity as public and civic actors in an Islamic state is similar to state policy on women promoted in Ireland, Italy, France and other countries with strong Catholic traditions. Countries where social attitudes are largely shaped by secular norms and values (such as Britain, Canada, Hungary, and Croatia) share an understanding of politics as being a male-gendered arena similar to that of their religious-influenced counterparts. In secular cultures, however, religious conservatism is replaced by the hegemony of liberal individualism which reinforces rather than mitigates patriarchal views of politics through its emphasis on the meritocratic principle as the basis for political advancement. Even in countries where an egalitarian culture has had some fostering (Scandinavia), and where there is a substantial presence of women in parliamentary life (Netherlands), a societal debate on the patriarchal construction of public life not only continues, but is seen by women in these countries as an important issue to continue debating if women are to retain, and increase, their presence and influence in public decision-making.

Thus, generalised social norms that endow men with political power and confer a subordinate political citizenship on women are reflected in practices that inhibit women from sharing power with men. Again, across these chapters, authors raise similar circumscribing conditions of women's lives. Social expectations that women will undertake the bulk of home and family duties, which translates into a general absence of childcare and other family supports, inhibit women's opportunities for engaging in the political world. Limited access to individual financial resources – through low pay and long working hours or non-participation in paid work – reflect and compound social inhibitors to women's political engagement. As a consequence, the dominant understanding of politics, legislative politics in particular, as a masculine interest, is reinforced. The chapter on Africa reminds us that female disadvantage can have very deep roots, and the unequal access of women and girls to education acts against women when they seek to participate in political decision-making.

Given the construction of the public space as highly masculinised and reinforced through decades – indeed centuries – of social practice, it is not surprising to find that the political institutions underpinning democratic decision – making are also founded on a gendered perspective of social relations. Once again, the chapters in this book draw attention to the manner in which electoral systems and candidate selection processes interact with cultural perspectives on gender roles to marginalise and exclude women from electoral politics. Irrespective of whether the major exclusion points are the multiple mandates held by male representatives (France), the absence of formalised selection rules (Peru, UK), candidate rank-ordering practices that give preference to men (such as in Spain, Switzerland, Hungary, and Peru), an electoral system composed, either wholly or in significiant part, of plurality rules (France, Italy, UK, many African states, Canada and Switzerland), or other gendered practices, the outcome is virtually designed to ensure that women are under-represented in parliament. There are also examples of how a single political crisis can either advantage or disadvantage women. In the case of Italy, the corruption scandal that rocked the political system resulted in an exclusion of women in favour of well-established male non-political figures untainted by the crisis. In contrast, Peru's political corruption scandal opened opportunities for women to enter politics. One common thread of analysis reveals the power of incumbency. While given special attention in the chapters on Canada, Ireland, Australia and New Zealand and the UK, the importance of incumbent seat-holding runs through all chapters, and re-emphasises the gendered nature of legislative power and presence. Male incumbency strikes at the core of gendered power-sharing, and the quest by women for an equal sharing of the task of representation is a fundamental challenge to the male-gendered order of political power. It comes as no surprise to find that the strategies employed by women political activists to share power with men are strongly resisted.

Strategies

The full range of interventionist measures designed to increase women's parliamentary representation are on display in the chapters in this book. Ranging from public awareness campaigns (Scandinavia and Peru) to legislated quotas (Djibouti, France, Peru, Italy) and reserved seats for women in parliament (Sudan, Uganda, Tanzania), the results of gender-specific interventions show that equal opportunities in the political sphere is not a matter of merit alone, but of challenge to a male-gender bias entrenched in political practices. It is not surprising to find that candidate training by women's organisations and political parties is by far the most prevalent measure of support for women seeking parliamentary careers, as this strategy supports the empowerment of individual women and is generally tolerated in male-gendered political culture. The second most frequently employed strategy is that of voluntary party quotas, clearly evident in African and Scandinavian countries, Indonesia, and centre-left parties in Hungary, Spain, Australia and Ireland. In Canada and the UK, this voluntary quota is specifically directed towards gender balancing candidate slates. The motivations for the adoption of this strategy varies widely from case to case, but all have one factor in common – a realisation that supporting women's participation in politics helps to garner electoral support.

More vigorous forms of intervention in the political process do not find the same measure of tolerance as the strategies discussed above. Our cases show that the adoption of quota laws, such as enacted by France, is not widespread, and reserved seats for women in parliament are very much an exceptional occurrence. Thus, irrespective of geographical location, ideological composition of government, or of socio-economic stage of development, political systems across the world display resistance to direct interference in the 'rules of the game'. However, evidence for more modest and subtle adjustments to opportunities for women's political entry is sprinkled throughout the chapters in this book. One recurring feature in this regard is the work of women's non-governmental organisations in mobilising women to stand for elections, lobbying political parties to include more women candidates, and providing leadership training for women political aspirants. A second avenue of support for women's political representation is through the funding process. Dedicated campaign funds for women candidates are available in Canada and Australia, while restrictions on campaign spending (Canada, Ireland) seek to make entry to, and continuance in, political life a realistic ambition for motivated candidates of relatively modest means. In other instances (Netherlands), government support for political parties is partly dependent on the proportion of women candidates. Although not a widespread strategy, a party's gender behaviour can be influenced in cases where parties are reliant on public funding to support their activities. Finally, the electoral system structures the political landscape, exerting a strong influence on party selection strategies which in turn has important implications for women's parliamentary representation. Many chapters in this book refer to this important point (including Switzerland, Australia and New Zealand), with the case of Peru illustrating the vulnerability of women to electoral rule change, the case of the United Kingdom – specifically Scotland and Wales – showing how party commitment to gender equality combined with electoral rule changes can significantly improve women's political representation.

Ultimately, the range of supportive measures adopted in any country is shaped by the political context in which such measures are considered. Constitutional and law-making strategies are viable in the rule-bound political tradition of France, but sit less comfortably in the broad social democratic and equality-conscious cultures of Scandinavia where voluntary party measures are preferred. The reserved parliamentary seats for women in Tanzania, Rwanda and Sudan are possible in cultures where women have actively contributed to establishing the nation state and whose claim to representation in the political affairs of the emerging nation cannot be ignored by male leaders. Yet, reserved seats act to marginalise women politically, removing them from a constituency base, limiting their opportunities for building popular support, and restricting the significance of their political contributions. However, in the masculinist politics of Africa, women's political presence would be minimal, at best, without reserved seats. In a similar vein, 'top-up' seats, distributed according to overall party support, such as found in Hungary, Scotland and Wales, can be said to be a form of 'reserved' seat allocation. MPs holding top-up seats are also acutely conscious of their weaker legitimacy and seek to build a popular profile as a counterbalance. In general, few of the top-up list parliamentarians are women, which suggests that parties use these seats primarily to promote male political careers. In the case of top-up lists, there have been calls for parity between women and men in party seat distribution as a way of increasing women's political representation (Laver *et al.*, 1997). Indeed, the study of seat-holding by appointment, as top-up and reserved seats basically are, deserves greater comparative scrutiny to determine the patterns of representation, the motives for party gender allocation decisions and the opportunities and constraints placed on seat-holders as compared with MPs returned from constituencies.

Countries where liberal individualism is the dominant ideology indicate strongest resistance to the adoption of quotas, either as legally-binding requirements or as voluntary party commitments. In these cases, while some parties will adopt quotas, the contagion effect is limited and other parties in the political system do not feel compelled to follow that route. Many of the countries in this book fall into this category. In many of these instances we find widespread use of the softer interventionist measures – training programmes for women aspirants, awareness-raising among the electorate and NGO lobbying campaigns intended to convince political leaders of the significance of women's contribution to parliamentary decision – making. These strategies signify the masculinist bias of liberal democracy, where women's merit must be argued for to be (possibly or eventually) accepted. Here too, scholars must continue to ask difficult questions, exploring and revealing the male-ordered assumptions underlying much of the politics of liberal democracies around the world.

Making a Difference

The general evidence from the wide range of cases in this book suggests that there are grounds for holding the expectation that female MPs will be conscious of their gender as well as their political affiliation and constituency duties. It is also clear from these contributions that the capacity of elected women to represent women in society is circumscribed in all cases by their numerical representation in the governing parliamentary party, party discipline, the confluence of patriarchal norms and political ideology, the level of feminist consciousness among elected women and relations between elected women and women's organisations.

Where women have a significant presence of one-third or more MPs, as in the Netherlands, Scandinavia and the regional legislatures of Scotland and Wales in the United Kingdom, the effects of their participation are evident and substantial. In these parliaments, women's participation in legislative business is seen as a routine activity. Rather than being perceived as exotic additions to a predominantly male assembly, their numerical presence conveys the sense that participation in political leadership, debates and decision – making is the work of both women and men. Their proportional presence in legislative decision – making enables substantial gender-related agenda setting and the enactment of gender-sensitive policy reforms. Importantly, too, women in these legislatures comprise a significant presence in the ruling party or coalition, thereby having a direct link, if not actually responsible for, government policy – making.

Women MPs in parliaments with upwards of one-fifth female members (Africa, Switzerland, Spain, Australia and New Zealand) have a discernible impact on legislative policy priorities, in particular in raising anti-discrimination and equal opportunities issues, women's health and reproductive rights, and sexual violence against women. In some instances, such as Australia and New Zealand, women MPs work on a cross-party basis to advance gender equality initiatives. Their scope for action on women's concerns, is, however, limited by their numerical presence in a way that is not as evident in parliaments with more than one-third female representation.

For societies with one-fifth women MPs or less (Canada, Croatia, France, Hungary, Indonesia, Ireland, Italy, Peru and the UK) women's restricted parliamentary presence makes it more difficult to address women's concerns and secure support for political reforms on gender equality issues. In these cases, the work of individual women politicians, such as Kofifah in Indonesia and Lotti in Italy, is often drawn on to illustrate the nature and scope of women-centred reforms. It is evident that women MPs in these parliaments are more active in supporting women's issues than men, even though such issues are marginal to the political agenda. In these instances the women's movement often proves to be more influential in bringing about change, through lobbying and campaigning, than women MPs. Indeed, while many female MPs would consider that they make a difference in policy terms by supporting woman-friendly policy initiatives, their political contribution to gender equality, being less visible, is less recognised by women's groups.

Thus, on grounds of numerical representation alone, the above findings show that one cannot assume that elected women have similar opportunities for feminising the agenda and working practices of parliament. What our cases also show is that it is not only important for women to constitute a 'large minority', to borrow Dahlerup's phrase, in order to be in a position to impact on the legislative process; it is also important that they have a sense of gender identity in order to pursue issues relating to the social, economic and political positions of all women. It is also important that they win the support of male colleagues in introducing measures to foster these agendas. The experience of the Netherlands, Scotland and Scandinavia, where gender equality issues such as sexual violence, childcare and family-friendly work practices have a firm place in legislative concerns illustrates not just the power of numbers, but also the power of gender-aware female legislators, supported by sympathetic male colleagues. In these instances also, gender differences in parliamentary behaviour are decreasing and male MPs are representing women's issues. Yet, even in these three cases there are challenges emerging to dilute the feminisation of parliament. On the one hand, there is the issue of identity. A growing number of younger female MPs, confident in the ability of equal opportunity practices to prevent gender discrimination, are less critically aware of the gender bias in liberal democracy and see themselves as individual MPs representing their party. Thus, political identity, for a new generation of elected women, is shaped by the party they support, while feminism is a declining influence on their critical judgement. Ironically, this attachment to party perspective, unleavened by a gendered awareness of the construction of social and economic relations and undisturbed by the absence of a visible feminist political agenda, is very similar to the attitudes prevailing among female MPs in countries with low levels of female representation. In the former case, feminist concerns have been so successfully incorporated into mainstream politics that the liberal women's rights agenda is seen as largely fulfilled; in the latter case feminist issues, with occasional exceptions, have been so successfully blocked from political consideration it is as if they do not exist. In both cases, the outcome is similar – women MPs do not feel a responsibility to speak and act for women: they focus their representative functions exclusively around party identity.

The second major challenge facing parliaments with a significant female presence is in shaping the institutions and structures to reflect the diverse experiences of both women and men. Even in the Scandinavian experience, much remains to be done to bring about an equal sharing of power between women and men within the parliamentary framework. Legislatures are gendered institutions based on hierarchical, exclusionary power relations. Many of the chapters in this book implicitly or explicitly explore this dimension of inequality, and examples are discussed of modifications to the parliamentary structures designed to support more inclusive participation by all MPs. However, these initiatives are minor and appear to have a marginal (if symbolically important) effect on the masculinist norms of power underpinning legislative roles and tasks. This appears to be an area that calls for further dialogue critical reflection between female and male parliamentarians on how parliamentary practices exclude women's perspectives. For scholars such as Studlar and McAllister (2002) and Grey (2002), having a critical mass of women MPs is not the most important variable in feminising the content of parliamentary debates. Their point is elaborated on by Jill Bystydzienski who observes in her chapter on Scandinavian parliaments that political equality and inclusiveness at representational level is dependent on an ongoing debate around equality and difference among parliamentarians, women and men, as well as within society as a whole. For many of the parliaments represented in this book, this is a neglected issue, challenging as it does the male hegemony of parliamentary and societal power.

Networking among women parliamentarians and between elected women and women activists provide important opportunities for influencing the political agenda. Many of the cases in this book discuss the capacity of women's parliamentary caucuses and the combined efforts of women MPs and civil society activists in bringing women's issues to the fore of the political agenda in their respective countries. In the case of Peru, for example, the work of the congressional Commission on Women was complemented and supported by strongly-organised women's groups working to achieve gender equality.

The question of women representing women still remains an open one, however. At one level, there is tension for women MPs in assuming responsibility for different forms of representation – as a party and constituency representative, and as a spokesperson for women's interests. As many of the chapters point out, this tension is a very real one. Indeed, the mechanisms employed to bring more women into political life are indicators of the general view regarding women's representational role. Political elite tolerance of 'soft' measures to support women's representation suggests that recognition of customary representative roles for women MPs is prevalent. Elite acceptance – and even imposition – of more vigorous mechanisms such as quotas and reserved seats suggests that there is some acknowledgement within the political culture that female MPs can also be representatives for women. Of more fundamental interest to sharing power in parliamentary assemblies, however, is the question of whether sufficient women are willing to risk the uncertainty and demands of a political career in order to contribute to decision making. As parties lose their membership, selection strategies persist in discriminating against women, and as women's capacity to contribute to public life is constrained by norms that expect child and family care be undertaken primarily by women, there is justifiable cause for concern that in many countries women's representation will continue to be marginalised in parliaments. In countries where democratic practice is emerging or being renewed, the situation of parliamentary women is even more complex. Are women MPs in post-authoritarian regimes such as Peru, Indonesia and some African states contributing to the democratisation of their countries? Are women in post-communist societies such as

Hungary and Croatia complicit in the perpetuation of discrimination against women due to the discredited legacy of gender equality strategies such as quotas? What space is there in these newly democratising circumstances for the development of gender-aware politics and are women MPs sufficiently confident and aware to articulate this politics? Similar questions must be asked of female representatives in established democracies, and, given their more settled engagement with liberal democratic practices, their actions in fostering a gender-equal political culture requires particular scrutiny.

Bibliography

Acker, Joan (1990), 'Hierarchies, Jobs, Bodies: A Theory of Gendered Organisations', *Gender & Society*, Vol 4 (2), pp. 139-58.

Africa Online, *Gender Profiles: Tanzania* available at http://www.afrol.com/Categories/Women/profiles/tanzania_women.htm.

Africa Online (2003), *Women and Ruling Party Win Djibouti Elections*, available at http://www.afrol.com/News2003/dji002_poll_women.htm.

Ágh, Atilla and Kurtán, Sándor (eds) (2001), *Democratization and Europeanization in Hungary: The Second Parliament 1994-1998*, Hungarian Centre for Democracy Studies, Budapest.

Aitken, Judith (1980), 'Women in New Zealand Politics', in Howard R. Penniman (ed.) *New Zealand at the Polls: The General Election of 1978*, American Enterprise Institute, Washington DC.

Alfaro, Rosa María (1996), *Mundos de Renovación y Trabas Para la Acción Pública de la Mujer*, Asociaciones de Comunicadores Sociales Calandria, Lima.

Alfaro, Rosa María (1997), Modernidades Discursivas e Inequidades de Género: La Mujer Como Sujeto de Derechos en la Opinión Pública, Asociaciones de Comunicadores Sociales Calandria, Lima.

Alfaro, Rosa María (1998a), *La Política, Sí es Cosa de Mujeres*, Asociaciones de Comunicadores Sociales Calandria, Lima.

Alfaro, Rosa María (1998b), *Una Vida Cotidiana Sembrada de Conflictos: Opinión Pública e Igualdad de Género*, Asociaciones de Comunicadores Sociales Calandria, Lima.

Alincic, Mira (1999), 'Nekoliko Obiljezja Obiteljskog Zakona' (Some Characteristics of Family Law), *Zena*, available at http//www.pitagora.hr/zena-sch/Br. 1999 01/0 zakon.htm.

Alliance of Independent Unions of Croatia (Women's Section) and Transition to Democracy Women's Group (2000), *'Raspoznajmo, Izaberimo': Rezultati Analize Aktiviteta Zastupnica/ka Zastupnickog Doma Sabora, Saziv 1995/99*, (Let's Find Out, Let's Choose: Results of an Analysis of the Activity of Male and Female Representatives in the House of Representatives of the Sabor, 1995-1999 Sessions), Zenska grupa T.O.D. i Zenska sekcija SSSH, Zagreb.

ALP (Australian Labour Party) (1979), *National Committee of Inquiry Discussion Papers*, APSA, Adelaide.

Amongi, Betty Ongom (2002a), 'Engendering Legislation and Government Policies in Uganda: Tactics and Strategies of Uganda Women Parliamentarians', presented at the Third International Congress on Women Work & Health, Stockholm, Sweden, 2-5 June.

Amongi, Betty Ongom (2002b), 'Women in Politics Particularly the Legislative Process in Uganda', presented at the Eighth International Interdisciplinary Congress on Women, Makerere University, Kampala, Uganda, 21-26 July 21-26.

Andeweg, Rudy and Irwin, Galen (2002), *Governance and Politics of the Netherlands*, Palgrave Macmillan, Basingstoke.

Armingeon, Klaus (1996), 'Integriert und Isoliert: Die Schweiz im Prozess der Globalisierung', in Klaus Armingeon (ed.) *Der Nationalstaat am Ende des 20 Jahrhunderts*. Haupt, Bern, Stuttgart, Wien, pp. 7-20.

Armstrong, Chris (2002), 'Complex Equality: Beyond Equality and Difference', *Feminist Theory* Vol. 3(1), pp. 67-82.

Asia Pacific 50/50 Campaign, Report of the Jakarta Workshop, available at www.cld.org/50/5-.htm.

Aubert, Jean-François (1978), Exposé Des Institutions Politiques de la Suisse à Partir de Quelques Affaires Controversées, Payot, Lausanne.

Ballmer-Cao, Thanh-Huyen (1988), Le Conservatisme Politique Féminin en Suisse: Mythe ou Réalité?, Georg Editeur, Genève.

Ballmer-Cao, Thanh-Huyen (1995), 'Vingt-deux Ans de Suffrage Féminin en Suisse: Bilan et Perspectives', in Franca Cleis et al., (eds.), *Donne Oggi. Valori Femminili e Valori Maschili Nella Società*. Edizioni Casagrande, Bellinzona.

Ballmer-Cao, Thanh-Huyen (1998), 'Les Modes de Scrutin en Suisse et Leur Logique Intitutionnelle', paper presented at the Joint Conference organized by the French Association of Political Science and the Swiss Association of Political Science, Paris, 4-5 June.

Ballmer-Cao, Thanh-Huyen (1999), 'Suffrage, Séparation des Sphères et Démocratie', in Birgit Christensen (ed.), *Demokratie und Geschlecht*, Chronos, Zurich.

Ballmer-Cao, Thanh-Huyen and Wenger, Ruth (1989), *L'élite Politique Féminine en Suisse*, Seismo, Zurich.

Ballmer-Cao, Thanh-Huyen and Schulz, Patricia (1991), 'L'égalité des Sexes et le Parlement Fédéral (1971-89)', in Services du Parlement (ed.), *Parlement: Autorité Suprême de la Confédération?* Mélanges sur l'Assemblée Fédérale à L'occasion du 700e Anniversaire de la Confédération Suisse, Haupt, Berne.

Ballmer-Cao, Thanh-Huyen and Bendix, John (1994), 'Etudes de Quelques Déterminantes de la Représentation des Femmes dans les Assemblées Législatives Suisse', in Office Fédéral de la Statistique (ed.), *La Difficile Conquête du Mandat de Députée. Les Femmes et les Élections au Conseil National de 1971 à 1991*, OFS, Berne.

Ballmer-Cao, Thanh-Huyen and Pagnossin-Aligisakis, Elisabetta (1997), 'La Participation des Femmes à la Vie Politique. Analyse des Aspects Statistiques de l'Enquête Comparative Mondiale de 1996 Menée par l'Union Interparlementaire', in Union Inter-Parlementaire (ed.), *Hommes et Femmes en Politique. La Démocratie Inachevée. Etude Comparative Mondiale*. Série 'Rapports et documents' No 28, Genève.

Banks, Olive (1993), *The Politics of British Feminism 1918-1970*, Edward Elgar, Aldershot.

Barbadillo, Patricia, Juste, María G. and Ramírez, Ana (1990), 'La Mujer en el Congreso de los Diputados: Análisis de su Participación en las Candidaturas Electorales', *Revista Española de Investigaciones Sociológicas*, Vol. 52, pp. 101-35.

Bard, Christine (1995), Les filles de Marianne. Histoire des féminismes, 1919-1940, Fayard, Paris.

Barrio, Emilia (1996), Historia de las Transgresoras: La Transición de las Mujeres, Icaria, Barcelone.

Bashevkin, Sylvia B. (1982), 'Women's Participation in the Ontario Political Parties, 1971-1981', *Journal of Canadian Studies,* Vol. 17(2), pp. 44-54.

Bashevkin, Sylvia B. (1983a), 'Social Background and Political Experience: Gender Differences Among Ontario Provincial Party Elites, 1982', *Women's Studies Journal/Journal d'études sur la femme*, Vol. 9(1), pp. 1-12.

Bashevkin, Sylvia B. (1983b), 'The Dimensions of Underrepresentation', *Status of Women News*, April, pp. 16-17.

Bashevkin, Sylvia B. (1991), 'Women's Participation in Political Parties', in Kathy Megyery (ed), *Women in Canadian Politics: Toward Equity in Representation*, Dundern Press, Toronto, (Volume 6 of the Research Studies, Royal Commission on Electoral Reform and Party Financing) pp. 61-80.

Bashevkin, Sylvia B. (1993), *Women and Party Politics in English-Canada*, 2nd edn., Oxford University Press, Toronto.

Bergqvist, Christina et al. (eds.) (1999), *Equal Democracies? Gender and Politics in the Nordic Countries*, Scandinavian University Press, Oslo.
Berkman, Michael B. and O'Connor, Robert E. (1993), 'Do Women Legislators Matter? Female Legislators and State Abortion Policy', *American Politics Quarterly*, Vol. 21(1), pp. 102-24.
Berkovitch, Nitza (1999), 'The Emergence and Transformation of The International Women's Movement', in John Boli and George M. Thomas (eds.), *Constructing World Culture: International Nongovernmental Organizations Since 1875*, Stanford University Press, Stanford, pp. 100-26.
Bessell, Sharon (1998), 'The Politics of Children's Work in Indonesia: Child Labour in Domestic and Global Contexts', unpublished PhD Thesis, Monash University.
Birch, A.H. (1964), Representative and Responsible Government: An Essay on the British Constitution, Unwin University Books, London.
Blackburn, Susan (1994), 'Gender Interests and Indonesian Democracy', in David Bouchier and John Legge (eds.), *Democracy in Indonesia 1950s and 1990s*, Monash University, Clayton, pp. 168-81.
Blackburn, Susan (2001a), 'Gender Relations in Indonesia: What Women Want', in Lloyd Grayson and Shannon Smith (eds.), *Indonesia Today: Challenges of History*, ISEAS, Singapore, pp. 270-82.
Blackburn, Susan (2001b), 'Commentary', in Kathryn Robinson and Sharon Bessell (eds), *Women in Indonesia: Gender, Equity, and Development*, ISEAS, Singapore, pp. 78-98.
Blackburn, Susan and Bessell, Sharon (1997), 'Marriageable Age: Political Debate on Early Marriage in Twentieth Century Indonesia', *Indonesia*, Vol. 63, pp. 107-42.
Blondet, Cecilia (1998), *La Emergencia de las Mujeres en El Poder: Hay Cambios?*, Instituto de Estudios Peruanos, Lima.
Blondet, Cecilia (1999a), *Las Mujeres y la Política en la Década de Fujimori*, Instituto de Estudios Peruanos Lima.
Blondet, Cecilia, (1999b), Percepción Ciudadana Sobre la Participación Política de la Mujer. El Poder Político en la Mira de las Mujeres, Instituto de Estudios Peruanos, Lima.
Blondet, Cecilia (2002), El Encanto Del Dictador. Mujeres y Política en la Década de Fujimori, Instituto de Estudios Peruanos, Lima.
Bogdanor, Vernon (1984), *What is Proportional Representation?*, Basil Blackwell, Oxford.
Bourchier, David (2000), 'Habibie's Interregnum: Reformasi, Elections, Regionalism and the Struggle for Power', in Chris Manning and Peter van Dierman (eds.), *Indonesia in Transition: Social Aspects of Reformasi and Crisis*, ISEAS, Singapore, pp. 15-38.
Bradbury, Jonathan, Denver, David, Mitchell, James and Bennie, Lynn (2000), 'Devolution and Party Change: Candidate Selection for the 1999 Scottish Parliament and Welsh Assembly', *Journal of Legislative Studies*, Vol. 6(3), pp. 51-72.
Brand, Laurie (1998), Women, the State, and Political Liberalization: Middle Eastern and North African Experiences, Columbia University Press, New York.
Breitenbach, Esther and Mackay, Fiona (eds.) (2001), *Women and Contemporary Scottish Politics: An Anthology*, Polygon at Edinburgh, Edinburgh.
Breitenbach, Esther, Brown, Alice, Mackay, Fiona and Webb, Janett (2002), 'Introduction: The Changing Politics of Gender Equality', in Esther Breitenbach et al. (eds.), *The Changing Politics of Gender Equality in Britain*, Palgrave, Basingstoke, pp. 1-19.
Brock, Kathy (1997), 'Women and the Manitoba Legislature', in Jane Arscott and Linda Trimble (eds.), *In the Presence of Women: Representation in Canadian Governments*, Harcourt Brace and Company, Toronto, pp. 180-200.
Brodie, Janine (1985), *Women and Politics in Canada*, McGraw-Hill Ryerson, Toronto.
Brodie, M. Janine and Vickers, Jill (1981), 'The More Things Change: Women in the 1979 Federal Campaign', in Howard R. Penniman (ed.), *Canada at the Polls, 1979 and 1980: A Study of the General Elections*, Washington, American Enterprise Institute for Public

Policy Research, Washington, pp. 322-36.
Brodie, Janine (with Celia Chandler) (1991), 'Women and the Electoral Process in Canada', in Kathy Megyery (ed.), *Women in Canadian Politics: Toward Equity in Representation*, Dundern Press, Toronto, (Volume 6 of the Research Studies, Royal Commission on Electoral Reform and Party Financing), pp. 3-60.
Broughton, Sharon and Zetlin, Di (1996), 'Queensland ALP Women Parliamentarians: Women in Suits and Boys in Factions', *International Review of Women and Leadership*, Vol. 2(1), pp. 47-61.
Brown, Alice (1998), 'Deepening Democracy: Women and the Scottish Parliament', *Regional and Federal Studies*, Vol. 8(1), pp. 103-19.
Brown, Alice (1999), 'Taking their Place in the New House: Women and the Scottish Parliament', *Scottish Affairs*, Vol. 28, Summer, pp. 44-50.
Brown, Alice, Donaghy, Tahyna Barnett, Mackay, Fiona and Meehan, Elizabeth (2002), 'Women and Constitutional Change', *Parliamentary Affairs*, Vol. 55(1), pp. 71-84.
Budlender, Debbie et al. (1999), *Participation of Women in the Legislative Process*, European Union Parliamentary Support Programme Cape Town, South Africa.
Busby, Nicole and Macleod, Calum (2002), 'Maintaining a Balance: the Retention of Women MPs in Scotland', *Parliamentary Affairs*, Vol. 55(1), pp. 30-42.
Bystydzienski, Jill M. (1992), 'Influence of Women's Culture on Public Politics in Norway', in Jill M. Bystydzienski (ed.), *Women Transforming Politics*, Indiana University Press, Bloomington, Indiana, pp. 11-40.
Bystydzienski, Jill M. (1995), *Women in Electoral Politics: Lessons from Norway*, Praeger, Westport, Connecticut.
Calandria and Grupo Impulsor Nacional de Mujeres por la Igualdad Real (2000), *Buscando la Equidad en el Congreso. Encuesta Sobre Participacíon Política de la Mujer*, Asociacion de Comunicadores Sociales Calandria, Lima.
Cameron, Maxwell, and Mauceri, Philip (eds.), (1997), *The Peruvian Labyrinth*, Pennsylvania University Press, University Park, Penn.
Carbert, Louise (1997), 'Governing on "the Correct, the Compassionate, the Saskatchewan Side of the Border"', in Jane Arscott and Linda Trimble (eds.), *In the Presence of Women: Representation in Canadian Governments*, Harcourt Brace and Company, Toronto, pp. 154-79.
Caress, Stanley M. (1999), 'The Influence of Term Limits on the Electoral Success of Women', *Women and Politics*, Vol. 20(3), pp. 45-63.
Carroll, Susan J. (1994), *Women as Candidates in American Politics*, 2nd edn., Indiana University Press, Bloomington.
Carroll, Susan J. and Jenkins, Krista (2001), 'Unrealised Opportunity? Term Limits and the Representation of Women in State Legislatures', *Women and Politics*, Vol. 23(4), pp. 1-30.
Carty, R.K. and Erickson, Lynda (1991), 'Candidate Nomination in Canada's National Political Parties', in Herman Bakvis (ed.), *Canadian Political Parties: Leaders, Candidates and Organization*, Dundern Press, Toronto, pp. 97-189.
Castenmiller, P., Leyenaar, Monique, Niemoller, B, and Tjalma, H. (2002), *Afscheid van de Raad (Leaving the Council)*, SGBO, Den Haag.
Catt, Helena (1997), 'Women, Maori and Minorities: Microrepresentation and MMP', in Jonathon Boston et al. (eds.), *From Campaign to Coalition: the 1996 MMP Election*, Dunmore Press, Wellington, pp. 199-205.
Caul, Miki (1999),'Women's Representation in Parliament: the Role of Political Parties', *Party Politics*, Vol. 5(1), pp. 79-98.
Caul, Miki (2001), 'Political Parties and the Adoption of Candidate Gender Quotas: A Cross-National Analysis', *Journal of Politics*, Vol. 63(4), pp. 1214-29.
Cawthorne, Maya (1999), 'The Third Chimurenga', in Patricia McFadden (ed.), *Reflection*

on Gender Issues in Africa, Sapes Books, Harare, pp. 55-83.

Center for Legislative Development (2001), *Quota System*, UNDP-Asia Pacific Gender Equality Network, Philippines.

Central Intelligence Agency (2001), *The World Factbook 2001*, available at http://www.cia.gov/cia/publications/factbook/.

Chaney, Paul (2003), 'Increased Rights and Representation: Women and the Post-Devolution Equality Agenda in Wales', in Alexandra Dobrowolsky and Vivien Hart (eds.), *Women Making Constitutions: New Politics and Comparative Perspectives*, Palgrave, Basingstoke and New York, pp. 173-84.

Chaney, Paul and Fevre, Ralph (2002), The Equality Policies of the Government of the National Assembly for Wales and their Implementation: July 1999 to January 2002, Institute for Welsh Affairs, Cardiff.

Chaney, Paul, Mackay, Fiona and McAllister, Laura (2005 forthcoming), *Women and Contemporary Welsh Politics*, University of Wales Press, Cardiff.

Chazan, Naomi et al. (1999), *Politics and Society in Contemporary Africa*, Lynne Rienner Publishers, Boulder, Colorado.

Childs, Sarah (2001a), 'Attitudinally feminist? The New Labour Women MPs and the Substantive Representation of Women', *Politics*, Vol. 21(3), pp. 178-85.

Childs, Sarah (2001b), 'Reconsidering the Substantive Representation of Women', paper presented at seminar *Women in Parliament: Influencing Change?*, in Centre for Advancement of Women in Politics, Queen's University Belfast, 26-27 October.

Childs, Sarah (2002), 'Hitting the Target: Are Labour Women MPs "Acting for" Women?', in Karen Ross (ed.), *Women, Politics and Change*, Oxford University Press, Oxford, pp.143-53.

Childs, Sarah (2003), 'Concepts of Representation and the Passage of The Sex Discrimination (Election Candidates) Bill', *Journal of Legislative Studies*, Vol. 8(3), pp. 90-108.

Childs, Sarah (2004), New Labour's Women MPs: Women Representing Women, Routledge, London.

Chodorow, Nancy (1978), *The Reproduction of Mothering*, University of California Press, Berkeley.

Chubb, Basil (1963), '"Going about persecuting civil servants": the role of the Irish parliamentary representative', *Political Studies*, Vol. 11(3), pp. 272-86.

Coakley, John and Manning, Maurice (1998), 'The Senate Elections', in Michael Marsh and Paul Mitchell (eds.), *How Ireland Voted 1997*, Westview Press, Boulder, Col., pp. 195-214.

Collin, Françoise (1999), *Le Différend des Sexes*, Editions Pleins Feux, Paris.

Commission Fédérale pour les Questions Féminines (ed.) (1995), *Des Acquis – Mais Peu de Changement? La Situation des Femmes en Suisse*, CFQF, Berne.

Commission Fédérale pour les Questions Féminines (ed.) (1998a), Femmes Pouvoir Histoire. Evénements de l'Histoire des Femmes et de l'Égalité des Sexes en Suisse de 1948-1998, CFQF, Berne.

Commission Fédérale pour les Questions Féminines (ed.) (1998b), *Questions au Féminin*, CFQF, Berne.

Commission on Gender Equality (1999), *Review of the 1999 Elections from a Gender Perspective*, available at http://www.cge.org.za/publications/elections.htm.

Connelly, Alpha (1999), 'Women and the Constitution of Ireland' in Yvonne Galligan, Eilís Ward and Rick Wilford (eds.), *Contesting Politics, Women in Ireland, North and South*, Westview Press, Boulder, Colorado, pp. 18-37.

Conway, Margaret (2001), 'Women and Political Participation', *PS: Political Science and Politics*, Vol. 34(2), pp. 231-33.

Coopers and Lybrand (1994), *Women and Parliaments in Australia and New Zealand*, a discussion paper prepared for the Commonwealth-State Ministers Conference on the Status of Women, September.

Coote, Anne and Patullo, Polly (1990), *Power and Prejudice: Women and Politics*, Weidenfield and Nicolson, London.

Cotta, M. (1979), Classe Politica e Parlameto in Italia, 1946-76, il Mulino, Bologna.

Cowan, Peter (1978), *A Unique Position: A Biography of Edith Dircksey Cowan, 1861–1932,* University of Western Australia Press, Nedlands.

Cowell-Meyers, Kimberley (2002), 'Gender, Power and Peace: a Preliminary Look at Women in the Northern Ireland Assembly, *Women and Politics*, Vol. 23(3), pp. 55-88.

Cowell-Meyers, Kimberley (2003), *Women Legislators in Northern Ireland: Gender and Politics in the New Legislative Assembly*, Centre for the Advancement of Women in Politics, Occasional Paper No. 3, Queen's University Belfast, Belfast.

Craske, Nikki (1999), *Women and Politics in Latin America*, Rutgers University Press, New Brunswick NJ.

Crow, Barbara A. (1997), 'Relative Privilege? Reconsidering White Women's Participation in Municipal Politics', in Cathy J. Cohen, Kathleen B. Jones and Joan C. Tronto (eds.), *Women Transforming Politics: An Alternative Reader,* New York University Press, New York, pp. 435-46.

Cullen-Owens, Rosemary (1984), Smashing Times: a History of the Irish Women's Suffrage Movement 1889-1922, Attic Press, Dublin.

Currell, Melville (1974), *Political Women*, Croom Helm, London.

Curtin, Jennifer and Sawer, Marian (1996), 'Gender Equity in the Shrinking State: Women and the Great Experiment', in Francis G. Castles et al. (eds.), *The Great Experiment: Labour Parties and Public Policy Transformation in Australia and New Zealand,* Allen and Unwin, Sydney, pp. 149-69.

Dador, Jenny (2000), 'Alianzas Transversales Entre las Mujeres del Congreso: Una Experiencia Construida Desde la Sociedad Civil', unpublished paper, Lima, available at http://www.manuela.org.pe.

Dahlerup, Drude (1988), 'From a Small to a Large Minority: Women in Scandinavian Politics', *Scandinavian Political Studies,* Vol. 11(4), pp. 275-99.

Dahlerup, Drude (1994), 'Learning to Live with the State – State, Market, and Civil Society: Women's Need for State Intervention in East and West', *Women's Studies International Forum*, Vol. 17 (2-3), pp. 117-27.

Dahlerup, Drude, and Gulli, Brita (1985), 'Women's Organizations in the Nordic Countries: Lack of Force or Counterforce?', in Elina Haavio-Mannila et al. (eds.), *Unfinished Democracy: Women in Nordic Politics*, Pergamon Press, Oxford, pp. 6-36.

Darcy, Robert Welch, Susan and Clark, Janet (1987), *Women, Elections, and Representation*, Longman, New York and London.

Darcy, Robert, Welch, Susan and Clark, Janet (1994), *Women, Elections, and Representation*, 2nd ed., University of Nebraska Press, Lincoln.

Del Re, Alisa (1983), 'Verso l'Europa: Politiche Sociali, Donne e Stato in Italia Tra Produzione e Riproduzione', in Alisa Del Re (ed.), *Il Genere Delle Politiche Sociali in Europa* (1960-1990), CEDAM, Padova.

Del Re, Alisa (1999), *Donna in Politica*, FrancoAngeli, Milan.

Del Re, Alisa (ed.) (2004), *Quand le Donne Governano le Città*, FrancoAngeli, Milan.

Demichel, Francine (1996), 'A Parts Égales: Contribution au Débat sur la Parité', *Recueil Dalloz Sirey*, 12e Cahier- Chronique, pp. 95-7.

Denver, David (1988), 'Britain: Centralised Parties with Decentralised Selection' in Michael Gallagher and Michael Marsh (eds.), *Candidate Selection in Comparative Perspective: the Secret Garden of Politics*, 2nd edn., Sage, London, pp. 47-71.

Desserud, Don (1997), 'Women in New Brunswick Politics: Waiting for the Third Wave', in Jane Arscott and Linda Trimble (eds.), *In the Presence of Women: Representation in Canadian Governments*, Harcourt Brace and Company, Toronto, pp. 254-77.

Dobrowolsky, Alexandra Z. and Hart, Vivien (2003), *Women Making Constitutions: New Politics and Comparative Perspectives*, Palgrave Macmillan, Basingstoke and New York.

Dodson, Debra L. (2001), 'Acting for Women: Is What Legislators Say What They Do?', in Susan J. Carroll (ed.), *The Impact of Women in Public Office*, Indiana University Press, Bloomington and Indianapolis, pp. 225-42.

Dolan, Kathleen and Ford, Lynne E. (1995), 'Women in the State Legislatures: Feminist Identity and Legislative Behaviours', *American Politics Quarterly*, Vol. 23(1), pp. 96-106.

Donaghy, Tahyna Barnett (2003), *Mainstreaming: Northern Ireland's Participative-Democratic Approach*, Centre for the Advancement of Women in Politics, Occasional Paper No. 2, Queen's University Belfast, Belfast.

Eagle, Maria and Lovenduski, Joni (1998), *High Time or High Tide for Labour Women*?, Fabian pamphlet 585, Fabian Society, London.

Eberhardt, Eva, (2003), *Analysing Female Visibility: Hungary,* Report to European Commission as part of the Enlargement Gender and Governance (EGG) project, Queen's University Belfast, Belfast.

Eduards, Maud, Halsaa, Beatrice and Skjeie, Hege (1985), 'Equality: How Equal?', in Elina Haavio-Mannila et al. (eds.), *Unfinished Democracy: Women in Nordic Politics*, Pergamon Press, Oxford, pp. 134-59.

Elder, Neal, Thomas, Alastair H. and Arter, David (1982), The Consensual Democracies? The Government and Politics of the Scandinavian States, Martin Robertson, Oxford.

Elshtain, Jean Bethke (1992), 'The Power and Powerlessness of Women', in Gisela Bock and Susan James (eds.), *Beyond Equality and Difference. Citizenship, Feminist Politics and Female Subjectivity*, Routledge, London, pp.110-25.

Equal Status Council (1989), *Milestones in 150 Years' History of Norwegian Women*, Equal Status Council, Oslo.

Equal Status Ombud (1989), *The Norwegian Equal Status Act with Comments*, Engers Boktrykkeri, Otta.

Erickson, Lynda (1991), 'Women and Candidacies for the House of Commons', in Kathy Megyery (ed.), *Women in Canadian Politics: Toward Equity in Representation*, Dundern Press, Toronto, pp. 101-26 (Volume 6 of the Research Studies, Royal Commission on Electoral Reform and Party Financing).

Erickson, Lynda (1993), 'Making Her Way In: Women, Parties and Candidacies in Canada' in Joni Lovenduski and Pippa Norris (eds.), *Gender and Party Politics*, Sage, London, pp. 60-85.

Erickson, Lynda (1997), 'Canada' in Pippa Norris (ed.), *Passages to Power: Legislative Recruitment in Advanced Democracies*, Cambridge University Press, Cambridge, pp. 33-55.

Erickson, Lynda (1998), 'Entry to the Commons: Parties, Recruitment, and the Election of Women in 1993', in Manon Tremblay and Caroline Andrew (eds.), *Women and Political Representation in Canada*, University of Ottawa Press, Ottawa, pp. 219-55.

Erickson, Lynda and Carty, R.K. (1991), 'Parties and Candidate Selection in the 1988 Canadian General Election', *Canadian Journal of Political Science*, Vol. 24(2), pp. 331-49.

Escario, Pilar, Alberdi, Inés and López-Accotto, Ana I. (1996), *Lo Personal es Político : El Movimiento Feminista en la Transición*, Instituto de la Mujer, Madrid.

European Commission (1997), *Equal Opportunities for Men and Women in Europe? Special Report*, available at http://europa.eu.int/comm/public_opinion/.

European Commission (1998), *Equal Opportunities for Women and Men in the European*

Union, Annual Report 1997, Office for Official Publications of the European Communities, Luxembourg.

European Forum for Democracy and Solidarity (1995), *Status of Women in Eastern and Central Europe, Project Report*, European Forum for Democracy and Solidarity, Amsterdam.

Fagoaga, Concha (1985), La Voz y el Voto de las Mujeres: El Sufragismo en Espana 1877-1931, Icaria, Barcelona.

Fauré, Christine (1999), 'Sphère Privée et Espace Public: (In)égalité des Sexes et 150 Ans de Démocratie Moderne', in Birgit Christensen (ed.), *Demokratie und Geschlecht*, Chronos, Zurich, pp. 145-56.

Fealy, Greg (2001), 'Parties and Parliament: Serving Whose Interest?', in Lloyd Grayson and Shannon Smith (eds.), *Indonesia Today: Challenges of History*, ISEAS, Singapore, pp. 97-111.

Fearon, Kate (1999), Women's Work: The Story of the Northern Ireland Women's Coalition, Blackstaff Press, Belfast.

Feld, Val (2000), 'A New Start in Wales: How Devolution is Making a Difference', in Anne Coote (ed.), *New Gender Agenda*, IPPR, London, pp. 74-80.

Fisher, Mary Ellen (1998), 'From Tradition and Ideology to Elections and Competition – The Changing Status of Women in Romanian Politics', in Marilyn Rueschemeyer (ed.), *Women in the Politics of Postcommunist Eastern Europe*. M. E. Sharpe, New York, pp. 168-95.

Fornengo, Graziella and Guagadnini, Marila (1999), *Un Soffitto di Cristallo? Le Donne Nelle Posizioni Decisionali in Europa*, Fondazione Adriano Olivetti, Turin.

Foro-Mujer (1994), *Propuestas Políticas Desde las Mujeres*, Conferencia Política de Mujeres, Ediciones ForoMujer, Lima.

Foro-Mujer (1995), Propuestas Desde las Mujeres: Politicas Publicas, Foro-Mujer: Lima.

Foster, Annie (1993), 'Development and Women's Political Leadership: The Missing Link in Sub-Saharan Africa', *Fletcher Forum of World Affairs*, Vol. 17(2), pp. 101-16.

Fox, Richard Logan (1997), *Gender Dynamics in Congressional Elections*, Thousand Oaks and Sage, London and New Dehli.

Franco, Gloria Ángeles (1986), 'La Contribucion de la Mujer Española a la Política Contemporánea: de la Restauración a la Guerra Civil', in Rosa María Capel Martínez (ed.), *Mujer y Sociedad en España (1700-1975)*, Instituto de la Mujer, Madrid, pp. 239-63.

Freedman, Jane (2002), 'Women in the European Parliament', *Parliamentary Affairs*, Vol. 55(1), pp. 179-88.

Frones, Ivar (1996), 'Revolusjon Uten Oppror: Kjonn, Generasjon og Sociale Forandring i Norge pa 1980-tallet' (Revolution Without Unrest: Gender, Generation and Social Change in Norway in the 1980s), *Tidsskrift for Samfunnsforskning (Journal of Social Research)*, Vol. 37(2), pp. 71-86.

Gaitán, Juan A. and Cáceres, María D. (1995), 'La Mujer en el Discurso Político', *Revista Española de Investigaciones Sociológicas*, Vol. 69, pp. 125-47.

Gallagher, Michael (2003), 'Stability and Turmoil: Analysis of the Results', in Michael Gallagher, Michael Marsh and Paul Mitchell (eds), *How Ireland Voted 2002*, Palgrave Macmillan, Basingstoke, pp. 88-118.

Gallagher, Michael and Komito, Lee (1999), 'The Constituency Role of TDs', in John Coakley and Michael Gallagher (eds.), *Politics in the Republic of Ireland*, 3rd edn., Routledge, London, pp. 206-31.

Gallagher, Michael and Marsh, Michael (2002), Days of Blue Loyalty: the Politics of Membership of the Fine Gael Party, PSAI Press: Dublin.

Galligan, Yvonne (1998), Women and Politics in Contemporary Ireland: From the Margins to the Mainstream, Pinter, London.

Galligan, Yvonne (2003), 'Candidate Selection: More Democratic or More Centrally Controlled?', in Michael Gallagher, Michael Marsh and Paul Mitchell (eds.), *How Ireland Voted 2002*, Palgrave Macmillan, Basingstoke, pp. 37-56.

Galligan, Yvonne, Laver, Michael and Carney, Gemma (1999), 'The Effects of Candidate Gender on Voting in Ireland, 1997', *Irish Political Studies* 14, pp. 118-22.

Galligan, Yvonne, Ward, Eilís and Wilford, Rick (eds.) (1999), *Contesting Politics: Women in Ireland, North and South*, Westview Press, Boulder, Colorado.

Galligan, Yvonne, Knight, Kathleen and Nic Giolla Choille, Una (2000), 'Pathways to Power: Women in the Oireachtas 1919-2000', in Maedhb McNamara and Paschal Mooney, *Women in Parliament, Ireland: 1918-2000*, Wolfhound Press, Dublin, pp. 27-69.

García de León, María A. (1991), *Las Mujeres Políticas Españolas (Un Ensayo Sociológico)*, Dirección General de la Mujer de la Comunidad de Madrid, Madrid.

García de León, María A. (1994), *Élites Discriminadas (Sobre el Poder de las Mujeres)*, Anthropos, Barcelone.

García de León, María A. (1996), 'Las Élites Políticas Femeninas', in María A. García de Léon, Marisa García de Cortázar and Félix Ortega (eds.), *Sociología de las Mujeres Españolas*, Editorial Complutense, Madrid, pp. 163-86.

Gaspard, Françoise, Servan-Schreiber, Claude and Le Gall, Anne (1992), *Au Pouvoir, Citoyennes! Liberté, Egalité, Parité*, Seuil, Paris.

Geisler, Gisela (1995), 'Troubled Sisterhood: Women and Politics in Southern Africa', *African Affairs*, Vol. 94(377), pp. 545-78.

Gilder, D. de, Ellemers, N., van den Heuvel, H. and Blijleven, G. (1998), 'Arbeidssatisfactie, Commitment en Uitstroom: Overeenkomsten en Verschillen Tussen Mannen en Vrouwen' (Labour Satisfaction, Commitment and Turn-over: Similarities and Differences Between Men and Women), *Gedrag en Organisaties (Behaviour and Organisations)*, Vol. 11, pp. 25-35.

Gilligan, Carol (1982), *In a Different Voice*, Harvard University Press, Cambridge.

Gingras, Anne-Marie, Maillé, Chantal and Tardy, Évelyne (1989), *Sexes et Militantisme*, CIDIHCA, Montreal.

Glaurdic, Josip (2003), 'Croatia's Leap Towards Political Equality: Rules and Players', in Richard E. Matland and Kathleen A. Montgomery (eds.), *Women's Accession to Political Power in Post-Communist Europe*, Oxford University Press, Oxford, pp. 285-303.

Global Coalition for Africa (1998), *African Social and Economic Trends 1997/1998*, Global Coalition for Africa, Washington, D.C.

Goetz, Anne Marie (1998a), 'Women in Politics and Gender Equity in Policy: South Africa and Uganda', *Review of African Political Economy*, Vol. 76, pp. 241-62.

Goetz, Anne Marie (1998b), 'Fiddling with Democracy', in Mark Robinson and Gordon White (eds.), *The Democratic Developmental State: Politics and Institutional Design*, Oxford University Press, New York, pp. 245-79.

Gordon, April (1991), 'Economic Reform and African Women', *Transafrica Forum*, Vol. 8(2), pp. 21-41.

Government of Hungary (2000), The Fourth and Fifth Reports of Hungary to the UN Committee for Elimination of all Forms of Discrimination against Women, Ministry of Social and Family Affairs, Budapest.

Grey, Sandra (2002), 'Does Size Matter?: Critical Mass and New Zealand's Women MPs', *Parliamentary Affairs* Vol. 55(1), pp. 19-29.

Grimshaw, Patricia (1987), *Women's Suffrage in New Zealand*, 2nd edn., University of Auckland Press, Auckland.

Groen Links (2003), *Feministisch Netwerk* available at http://www.groenlinks.nl/partij/werkgroepen.

Guadagnini, Marila (2001), 'Gendering the Debate on Electoral Reform in Italy: a Difficult

Challenge', paper presented at Research Network on Gender Policy and the State (RNGS) seminar, Belfast, Northern Ireland, 6-8 December.

Haas, Esther, Heim, Dore, Mutter, Christa and Stibler, Linda (eds.), (1993), *Der Brunner-Effekt*, Limat Verlag, Zurich.

Halimi, Gisèle (1997), *La Nouvelle Cause des Femmes*, Gallimard, Paris.

Halsaa, Beatrice (1989), *Policies and Strategies on Women in Norway*, Oppland Regional College, Lillehammer.

Hancock, M. Donald, Conradt, David P., Peters, B. Guy, Safran, William, White, Stephen and Zariski, Raphael (2002), Politics in Europe: An Introduction to the Politics of the United Kingdom, France, Germany, Italy, Sweden, Russia, and the European Union, Palgrave Macmillan, Basingstoke.

Handelingen der Staten Generaal (1918-1939), *Tweede Kamer* (*Public Records of Parliament),* Den Haag.

Hardmeier, Sibylle (1997), Frühe Frauenstimmrechtsbewegung in der Schweiz (1890-1930). Argumente, Strategien, Netzwerk und Gegenbewegung, Chronos, Zurich.

Hazell, Robert (ed.) (2000), The State and the Nations: The First Year of Devolution in the United Kingdom, Imprint Academic, Thorverton.

Hernes, Helga Maria (1987), *Welfare State and Woman Power*, Norwegian University Press, Oslo.

Hernes, Helga Maria and Hanninen-Salmelin, Eva (1985), 'Women in the Corporate System', in Elina Haavio-Mannila et al (eds.), *Unfinished Democracy: Women in Nordic Politics*, Pergamon Press, Oxford, pp.106-33.

Hill, Roberta and Roberts, Nigel S. (1990), 'Success, Swing and Gender: The Performance of Women Candidates for Parliament in New Zealand, 1946-1987', *Politics,* Vol. 25(1), pp. 62-80.

Hills, Jill (1981), 'Candidates: the Impact of Gender', *Parliamentary Affairs*, Vol. 34, pp. 221-8.

Holliday, Ian (1999), 'Territorial Politics' in Ian Holliday, Andrew Gamble and Geraint Parry (eds.), *Fundamentals in British Politics*, Macmillan, Basingstoke, pp.119-41.

Holter, Harriet (1970), *Sex Roles and Social Structure*, Norwegian University Press, Oslo.

Holter, Harriet and Sorensen, Britte A. (1984), 'Norway', in Alice H. Cook, Val R. Lorwin, and Arlene Kaplan Daniels (eds.), *Women and Trade Unions in Eleven Industrialized Countries*, Temple University Press, Philadelphia, pp. 239-60.

Howard, Rhoda E. (1985), 'Women and the Crisis in Commonwealth Africa', *International Political Science Review*, Vol. 6(3), pp. 287-96.

Humarau, Beatrice (1996), 'Women on the Run', *World Press Review*, Vol. 43(2), pp. 38-9.

Hunter, Alfred A. and Denton, Margaret A. (1984), 'Do Female Candidates "Lose Votes"?', The Experience of Female Candidates in the 1979 and 1980 Canadian General Elections', *Canadian Review of Sociology and Anthropology*, Vol. 21(4), pp. 395-406.

IMOP-Encuestas (1999), *La Situación de la Mujer en la Toma de Decisiones*, Instituto de la Mujer, Madrid.

Instituto de la Mujer (2003), *Mujeres en Cifras*, available at http://www.mtas.es/mujer/mcifras.

Inter-Parliamentary Union (1989), *The Participation of Women in the Political and Parliamentary Decision-making Process*, Series 'Reports and Documents', No.16, IPU, Geneva.

Inter-Parliamentary Union (1992), *Women and Political Power*, Series 'Reports and Documents', No.19, IPU, Geneva.

Inter-Parliamentary Union (1994), *Plan of Action to Correct Present Imbalances in the Participation of Men and Women in Political Life*, adopted by the Inter-Parliamentary Council (Paris 26 March), Series 'Reports and Documents', No.22, IPU, Geneva.

Inter-Parliamentary Union (1995), *Women in Parliaments 1945-1995: a World Statistical Survey*, Series 'Reports and Documents', No. 23, IPU, Geneva.

Inter-Parliamentary Union (1997), *Democracy Still in the Making: a World Comparative Study*, Series 'Reports and Documents', No. 28, IPU, Geneva.

Inter-Parliamentary Union (1999), 'Women in National Parliaments' available at http://www.ipu.org/.

Inter-Parliamentary Union (2000), *Politics: Women's Insights*, IPU, Geneva.

Inter-Parliamentary Union (2000), *Women in Politics: 1945-2000* (information kit), IPU, Geneva.

Inter-Parliamentary Union (2002), *Women in National Parliaments: Situation as of 1 July 2002*, available at http://www.ipu.org/wmn-e/classif.htm.

Jacobs, Aletta (1978), *Herinneringen* (Memories), Sun Reprint, Nijmegen.

Jain, Devaki, (1996), *Panchayat Raj: Women Changing Governance*, UNDP Gender in Development Series, United National Development Programme, Monograph Series Number 5, available at http://www.sdnp.undp.org/gender/resources/mono5.html.

Jaquette, Jane (2001), 'Women and Democracy: Regional Differences and Contrasting Views', *Journal of Democracy*, Vol. 12(3), pp. 111-26.

Jayawardena, Kumari (1986), *Feminism and Nationalism in the Third World*, Zed Books, London.

Jenson, Jane and Sineau, Mariette (1994), 'The Same or Different? An Unending Dilemma for French Women', in Barbara J. Nelson and Najma Chowdhury (eds.), *Women and Politics Worldwide*, Yale University Press, New Haven, pp. 243-60.

Jenson, Jane and Valiente, Celia (2003), 'Comparing Two Movements for Gender Parity: France and Spain', in Lee Ann Banaszak, Karen Beckwith and Dieter Rucht (eds.), *Women's Movements Facing the Reconfigured State*, Cambridge University Press, New York, pp. 69-93.

Jónasdóttir, Anna G. (1988), 'On the Concept of Interest, Women's Interests and the Limitation of Interest Theory', in Kathleen B. Jones and Anna G. Jónasdóttir (eds.), *The Political Interests of Gender: Developing Theory and Research with a Feminist Face*, Sage, London, pp. 33-65.

Jonassen, Christian T. (1983), Value Systems and Personality in a Western Civilization: Norwegians in Europe and America, Ohio State University Press, Columbus.

Jones, Mark (1998), 'Gender, Quotas, Electoral Laws, and the Election of Women', *Comparative Political Studies*, Vol. 31(1), pp. 3-21.

Kahn, Kim Fridkin (1996), The Political Consequences of Being a Woman: How Stereotypes Influence the Conduct and Consequences of Political Campaigns, Columbia University Press, New York.

Kanter, Rosabeth Moss (1977), *Men and Women of the Corporation*, Basic Books, New York.

Kardos-Kaponyi, Elisabeth (1988), 'The Protection of Human Rights: the Main Principles and Instruments in Europe', *Transition, Competitiveness and Economic Growth*, Vol. 3, pp. 613-29.

Kardos-Kaponyi, Elisabeth (1995), 'The Consequences of Political, Social and Economic Changes for the Position of Women in Central and Eastern Europe', *BIGIS Papers*, No. 3, pp. 151-9.

Karl, Marilee (1995), *Women and Empowerment: Participation and Decision-making*, Zed Books, London and New Jersey.

Karvonen, Lauri, and Selle, Per (1995), *Women in Nordic Politics: Closing the Gap*, Dartmouth, Brookfield, VT.

Karvonen, Lauri, Djupsund, Goran, and Carlson, Tom (1995), 'Political Language', in Lauri Karvonen and Peter Selle (eds.), *Women in Nordic Politics: Closing the Gap*, Dartmouth, Brookfield, VT, pp. 343-79.

Kasapovic, Mirjana (1996), *Demokratska Tranzicija i Politicke Stranke* (Democratic Transition and Political Parties), Biblioteka Politicka misao, Zagreb.

Kasapovic, Mirjana (ed.), (2001), *Hrvatska Politika 1990–2000* (Croatian Politics 1990-2000), Biblioteka Politicka misao, Zagreb.

Kathlene, Lyn (1994), 'Power and Influence in State Legislative Policymaking: The Interaction of Gender and Position in Committee Hearing Debates', *American Political Science Review*, Vol. 88(3), pp. 560-76.

Kathlene, Lyn (1995), 'Alternative Views of Crime: Legislative Policymaking in Gendered Terms', *Journal of Politics*, Vol. 57(3), pp. 696-723.

Katyasungkana, Nursyahbani (2000), 'Exchanging Power or Changing Power: The Problem of Creating Democratic Institutions', in Chris Manning and Peter van Dierman (eds.), *Indonesia in Transition: Social Aspects of Reformasi and Crisis*, ISEAS, Singapore, pp. 259-68.

Kay, Barry J., Lambert, Ronald D., Brown, Steven D. and Curtis, James E. (1987), 'Gender and Political Activity in Canada, 1965-1984', *Canadian Journal of Political Science*, Vol. 20(4), pp. 851-63.

Kay, Barry J., Lambert, Ronald D., Brown, Steven D. and Curtis, James E. (1988), 'Feminist Consciousness and the Canadian Electorate: A Review of National Election Studies, 1965-1984', *Women and Politics*, Vol. 8(2), pp. 1-21.

Kelly, Rita Mae, and Duerst-Lahti, Georgia (eds.), (1995), *Gender Power, Governance and Leadership*, University of Michigan Press, Ann Arbor.

Kennedy, Fiachra, (2002), 'Abortion referendum 2002', *Irish Political Studies*, Vol. 17(1), pp. 114-28.

Kennelly, Brendan and Ward, Eilís (1993), 'The abortion referendums', in Michael Gallagher and Michael Laver (eds.), *How Ireland Voted 1992*, Folens and PSAI Press, Dublin and Limerick, pp. 115-34.

Kenworthy, Lane and Malami, Melissa (1999), 'Gender Inequality in Political Representation: A Worldwide Comparative Analysis', *Social Forces*, Vol. 78(1), pp. 235-69.

Khaxas, Elizabeth (2002), 'Taking Stock of the 50/50 Campaign', *Sister Namibia*, Vol. 14(1), pp. 10-11.

Killian, Bernadeta (1996), 'A Policy of Parliamentary "Special Seats" for Women in Tanzania: Its Effectiveness', *Ufahamu*, Vol. 24(2-3), pp. 21-31.

Klatzer, Elizabeth (2000), 'Un Caso de Excepción: Las Mujeres en la Política y la Administración Pública Peruana', *El Proceso Social en el Perú: Investigaciones Sobre Sociedad, Promoción y Desarrollo*, PromPerú and Universidad del Pacífico, Lima, pp. 216-232.

Knezevic, Djurdja (1997), 'The Disappearance of Women from Public Life – Paradoxes of Democratic Changes in Eastern Europe', in Women's Infoteka (ed.), *Governments Without Women or the Long March*, Zenska Infoteka, Zagreb, pp. 18-40.

Knutsen, Ole (1989), 'The Priorities and Post-Materialist Values in the Nordic Countries: A Five Nation Comparison', *Scandinavian Political Studies*, Vol. 12(3) pp. 221-43.

Koncz, Katalin (1995a), 'Women in Policy: The Hungarian Case' paper presented at V World Congress for Central and East European Studies, Warsaw, 6-11 August.

Koncz, Katalin (1995b), 'The Position of Hungarian Women in the Process of Regime Change', in Barbara Lobodzinska (ed.), *Family, Women, and Employment in Central-Eastern Europe*, Greenwood Press, London, pp. 139-48.

Koncz, Katalin (2000), 'The Social Position of Women in Hungary in New Democracy and Market Economy', paper presented at Women's World Forum, Queen Sofia Centre for the Study of Violence, Valencia, 23-25 November.

Koncz, Katalin (2001), 'The Persistent Problem of Employed Women: How to Combine

Paid Work with Household Duties, *Society and Economy*, Vol. 23(1-2), pp. 171-93.

Krashinsky, Michael and Milne, William J. (1983), 'Some Evidence on the Effect of Incumbency in Ontario Provincial Elections', *Canadian Journal of Political Science*, Vol. 16(3), pp. 489-500.

Krashinsky, Michael and Milne, William J. (1985), 'Additional Evidence on the Effect of Incumbency in Canadian Elections', *Canadian Journal of Political Science*, Vol. 18(1), pp. 155-65.

Krashinsky, Michael and Milne, William J. (1986), 'The Effect of Incumbency in the 1984 Federal and 1985 Ontario Elections', *Canadian Journal of Political Science*, Vol. 19(2), pp. 337-43.

Kriesi, Hanspeter (1995), *Le Système Politique Suisse*, Economica, Paris.

Krupavičius, Algis and Matonytė, Irmina (2003), 'Women in Lithuanian Politics: From Nomenklatura Selection to Representation', in Richard E. Matland and Kathleen A. Montgomery (eds), *Women's Access to Political Power in Post-Communist Europe*, Oxford University Press, Oxford, pp. 81-104.

KSH, (2001), *Nők és Férfiak Magyarországon, 2000, Statisztikai zsebkönyv*, (Women and Men in Hungary, 2000, Statistical Manual), Ministry of Social and Family Affairs, Budapest.

Lake, Marilyn (1999), Getting Equal: The History of Australian Feminism, Allen and Unwin, Sydney.

Laver, Michael, Leyenaar, Monique, Galligan, Yvonne and Niemöller, Kees (1997), *Electoral Systems: the Gender Effect*, European Commission, Luxembourg.

Lawless, Jennifer and Fox, Richard (1999), 'Women Candidates in Kenya: Political Socialization and Representation', *Women and Politics*, Vol. 20(4), pp. 49-76.

Leinert Novosel, Smiljana (1990), *Zene – Politicka Manjina* (Women – A Political Minority), Radnicke novine, Zagreb.

Leinert Novosel, Smiljana (1999), *Zena na Pragu 21. Stoljeca Izmedu – Majcinstva i Profesije* (Women at the Turn of the 21st Century – Between Motherhood and Profession), Zenska grupa TOD i EDAC, Zagreb.

Levitsky, Steven, and Way, Lucan (2002), 'The Rise of Competitive Authoritarianism', *Journal of Democracy*, Vol. 13, pp. 51-65.

Leyenaar, Monique (1989), *De Geschade Heerlijkheid: Politiek Gedrag van Vrouwen en Mannen in Nederland, 1918-1988,* (The Strained Delicacy: Political Behavior of Women and Men in the Netherlands, 1918-1988), SDU, Den Haag

Leyenaar, Monique (1993), 'A Battle for Power, Selecting Women as Candidates in the Netherlands', in Joni Lovenduski and Pippa Norris (eds.), *Gender and Party Politics*, Sage, London, pp.205-30.

Linder, Wolf (1999), Schweizerische Demokratie. Institutionen, Prozesse, Perspektiven, Haupt: Bern.

Linz, Juan J. and Montero, José Ramón (1999), *The Party Systems of Spain: Old Cleavages and New Challenges*, Working Paper 138, Instituto Juan March, Madrid.

Lovenduski, Joni (1993), 'Introduction: the Dynamics of Gender and Party', in Joni Lovenduski and Pippa Norris (eds.), *Gender and Party Politics*, Sage, London, pp. 1-15.

Lovenduski, Joni (1996), 'Sex, Gender and British politics', *Parliamentary Affairs*, Vol 49(1), pp. 1-16.

Lovenduski, Joni (1999), 'Sexing Political Behaviour in Britain', in Sylvia Walby (ed.), *New Agendas for Women*, Macmillan, Basingstoke, pp. 190-209.

Lovenduski, Joni and Norris, Pippa (1989), 'Selecting Women Candidates: Obstacles to the Feminisation of the House of Commons', *European Journal of Political Research,* Vol. 17(3), pp. 533-62.

Lovenduski, Joni and Norris, Pippa (eds.), (1993), *Gender and Party Politics*, Sage, London.

Lovenduski, Joni and Randall, Vicky (1993), *Contemporary Feminist Politics: Women and Power in Britain*, Oxford University Press, Oxford.

Lovenduski, Joni and Norris, Pippa (2003), 'Women and Westminster: the Politics of Presence', *Political Studies*, Vol. 51(1), pp. 84-102.

MacGregor, Karen (2000), 'The Politics of Empowerment: Women in Parliament', *Indicator SA*, Vol. 16(3), pp. 26-33.

MacIntyre, Angus (2001), 'Middle Way Leadership in Indonesia: Sukarno and Abdurrahman Wahid Compared', in Lloyd Grayson and Shannon Smith (eds.), *Indonesia Today: Challenges of History*, ISEAS, Singapore, pp. 85-96.

MacIvor, Heather (1996), *Women and Politics in Canada*, Broadview Press, Peterborough.

MacIvor, Heather (2003), 'Women and the Canadian Electoral System', in Manon Tremblay and Linda Trimble (eds.), *Women and Electoral Politics in Canada*, Oxford University Press, Don Mills, pp. 22-36.

Mackay, Fiona (2001), Love and Politics: Women Politicians and the Ethics of Care, Continuum, London.

Mackay, Fiona (2003), 'Women and the 2003 Elections: Keeping Up the Momentum', *Scottish Affairs*, Vol. 44 (Summer), pp. 74-80.

Mackay, Fiona, Meyers, Fiona and Brown, Alice (2001), 'Making a Difference? Women and the Scottish Parliament – a Preliminary Analysis', paper presented at the ESRC seminar *Women in Parliament: Influencing Change?*, Centre for Advancement of Women in Politics, Queen's University Belfast, Belfast, October 26-27.

Mackay, Fiona, Meehan, Elizabeth, Donaghy, Tahyna Barnett, and Brown, Alice (2002), 'Women and Constitutional Change in Scotland, Wales and Northern Ireland', *Australasian Parliamentary Review*, Vol. 17 (2), pp. 35-54.

Mackay, Fiona, Myers, Fiona, and Brown, Alice (2003), 'Towards a New Politics? Women and the Constitutional Change in Scotland' in Alexandra Dobrowolsky and Vivien Hart (eds.), *Women Making Constitutions: New Politics and Comparative Perspectives*, Palgrave, Basingstoke and New York, pp. 84-98.

Mactaggart, Fiona (2000), 'Women in Parliament: Their contribution to Labour's First 1000 days', available at
www.fabian-society.org.uk/publications/extracts/womeninparliament.html

Maillé, Chantal (1990a), Les Québécoises et la Conquête du Pouvoir Politique, Saint-Martin, Montreal.

Maillé, Chantal (1990b), *Primed for Power: Women in Canadian Politics*, Canadian Advisory Council on the Status of Women, Ottawa.

Marques-Pereira, Bérengère (2001), 'Enjeux et Écueils de la Représentation Politique des Femmes', in Bérengère Marques-Pereira and P. Nolasco (eds.), *La Représentation Politique des Femmes en Amérique Latine*, GELA-IS et L'Harmattan, Bruxelles, pp. 7-16

Matland, Richard E. (1998), 'Enhancing Women's Political Participation: Legislative Recruitment and Electoral Systems', in Azza Karam (ed.), *Women in Parliament: Beyond Numbers*, International Institute for Democracy and Electoral Assistance-IDEA, Stockholm, pp. 65-88.

Matland, Richard E. and Studlar, Donald T. (1996), 'The Contagion of Women Candidates in Single-Member District and Proportional Representation Electoral Systems: Canada and Norway', *Journal of Politics,* Vol. 58(3), pp. 707-33.

Matland, Richard E. and Kathleen A. Montgomery (2003), 'Recruiting Women to National Legislatures: A General Framework with Applications to Post-Communist Democracies', in Richard E. Matland and Kathleen A. Montgomery (eds.), *Women's Access to Political Power in Post-Communist Europe*, Oxford University Press, Oxford, pp. 19-42.

Matland, Richard E and Montgomery, Kathleen A. (eds.) (2003), *Women's Access to Political Power in Post-Communist Europe*, Oxford University Press, Oxford.

Mayer, Henry (1973), 'Women in Politics' in Henry Mayer (ed.), *Labor to Power*, Angus and Robertson, Sydney, pp. 169-197.

Mayer, Nonna and Sineau, Mariette (2002), 'France: The National Front' in Helga Amesberger and Brigitte Halbmayr (eds.), *Rechtsextreme Parteien – Eine Mögliche Heimat für Frauen?*, Leske und Budrich, Opladen, pp. 61-112.

McBeth, John (1999), 'Political Update', in Geoff Forrester (ed.), *Post Soeharto Indonesia: Renewal or Chaos*?, Crawford House Publishing, Bathurst, pp. 21-32.

McClintock, Cynthia, and Lowenthal, Abraham (eds.), (1983), *The Peruvian Experiment Reconsidered*, Princeton University Press, Princeton, NJ.

McCullum, Janet, (1993), *Women in the House: Members of Parliament in New Zealand*, Cape Catley Press, New Zealand.

McDonald, Ronnie, Alexander, Morag and Sutherland, L. (2001), 'Networking for Equality and a Scottish Parliament: the Women's Co-ordination Group and Organisational Alliances', in Esther Breitenbach and Fiona Mackay (eds.), *Women and Contemporary Scottish Politics*, Polygon at Edinburgh, Edinburgh, pp. 231-40.

McLeay, Elizabeth (1993), 'Women and the Problem of Parliamentary Representation: A Comparative Perspective', in Helena Catt and Elizabeth McLeay (eds) *Women and Politics in New Zealand*, Victoria University Press, Wellington, pp. 40-62 .

Means, Ingrunn Nordeval (1972), 'Women in Local Politics: The Norwegian Experience', *Canadian Journal of Political Science*, Vol. 5(3), pp. 365-88.

Mény, Yves (1999), *Le Système Politique Français*, (4e édition) Montchrestien, Paris.

Merino, Beatriz, (1997), Matrimonio y Violación: El Debate del Artículo 178 del Código Penal Peruano, Manuela Ramos and UNICEF, Lima.

Meznaric, Silva and Ule, Mirjana (1998), 'Women in Croatia and Slovenia: A Case of Delayed Modernization', in Marilyn Rueschemeyer (ed.), *Women in the Politics of Post-Communist Eastern Europe*, M. E. Sharpe, New York, pp. 153-70.

Milidrag Šmid, Jagoda and Kokanovic, M. (1999), 'Polozaj Zena u Zakonima RH' ('The Position of Woman in the Laws of the Republic of Croatia'), Zenska sekcija SSSH, Zagreb.

Milner, Henry (1997), 'The Case for Proportional Representation', *Policy Options*, Vol. 18(9), pp. 6-9.

Milner, Henry (1999), 'The Case for Proportional Representation in Canada', in Henry Milner (ed.), *Making Every Vote Count: Reassessing Canada's Electoral System*, Broadview Press, Peterborough, pp. 37-49.

Ministerie van Binnenlandse Zaken (1992), *Kabinetsstandpunt Vrouwen in Politiek en Openbaar Bestuur* (Cabinet Decision on Women in Politics and Public Administration), Ministerie van Binnenlandse Zaken, (Ministry of Internal Affairs), Den Haag.

Ministerie van Sociale Zaken en Werkgelegenheid (2002), *Netherlands Interdepartmental Plan of Action and Final Report on Gender Mainstreaming*, Ministerie van SZW (Ministry of Social Affairs and Employment), Den Haag.

Montero, Jesús M. (1996), *Mujeres Públicas: La Segunda Representación*, Fundación Dolores Ibárruri, Madrid.

Montgomery, Kathleen and Ilonszki, Gabriella (2003), 'Weak Mobilisation, Hidden Majoritarianism and Resurgence of the Right: a Recipe for Female Under-representation in Hungary', in Richard E. Matland and Kathleen A. Montgomery (eds.), *Women's Access to Political Power in Post-Communist Europe*, Oxford University Press, Oxford, pp. 105-29.

Moore, Kate (1985), 'Gains for Women in the ALP', in Marian Sawer (ed.), *Program for Change: Affirmative Action in Australia*, Allen and Unwin, Sydney, pp. 33-50.

Morna, Colleen Lowe (1999), *Women's Political Participation in SADC*, available at http://www.idea.int/ideas_work/22_s_africa/elections_7_womens_participation.htm.

Moshi, Lioba (1998), 'Foreword', in Marianne Bloch, Josephine A. Beoku-Betts and B. Robert Tabachnick (eds.), *Women and Education in Sub-Saharan Africa: Power, Opportunities, and Constraints*, Lynne Rienner, Boulder, Colorado, pp. ix-xii.

Mossuz-Lavau Janine (1991), *Women and Men of Europe Today; Attitudes Toward Europe and Politics*, Supplement to Eurobarometre 31A, no. 35, Commission of the European Communities, Brussels.

Mossuz-Lavau, Janine, Mariette Sineau (1984). La Situation des Femmes dans la Vie Politique en Europe. Partie II: Les Femmes dans le Personnel Politique en Europe, Conseil de l'Europe, Strasbourg.

Movimiento Manuela Ramos (1995-1998), *Servicio de Información a Congresistas*, Newsletter, from No. 01, July 1995, to No. 24, April-June 1998, Movimiento Manuela Ramos, Lima.

Movimiento Manuela Ramos, (1996), *El Sistema de Cuotas*, Movimiento Mamuela Ramos, Lima.

Mujer y Politica (2000), *Las Mujeres en el Nuevo Congreso: Han Funcionado las Quotas?*, El Comercio, Lima, supplement, 26 August.

Nadia, Ita (1996), 'The Political Role of Women's NGOs', in Rustam Ibrahim (ed.), *The Indonesian NGO Agenda*, CESDA-LP3ES, Jakarta pp. 239-43.

Namibian Women's Manifesto Network (2002), *50-50 Women and Men in Government-Get the Balance Right!*, Sister Namibia, Windhoek, Namibia.

Nation Reporter (1998), *Prejudices, Illiteracy and Lack of Finance Failed Women Candidates*, available at http://www/kenyaelections.com/html.

National Assembly of Malawi and UNESCO (1996), Report of the Working Group to Enhance Women's Representation and Promote the Consideration of Gender Issues within Parliaments in Southern Africa, Mangochi, Malawi, available at http://unesdoc.unesco.org/images/0011/001159/115947eo.pdf.

National Women's Council of Ireland (2002), Irish Politics Jobs for the Boys! Recommendations on Increasing the Number of Women in Decision-making, National Women's Council of Ireland, Dublin.

Nelson, Barbara J. and Chowdhury, Najma (eds.) (1994), *Women and Politics Worldwide*, Yale University Press, New Haven.

New Zealand Select Committee on Women's Rights (1975), *The Role of Women in New Zealand Society*, Government Printer, Wellington.

Noerdin, Edriana (2002), 'Customary Institutions: Syariah Law and the Marginalisation of Indonesian Women', in Kathryn Robinson and Sharon Bessell (eds.), *Women in Indonesia: Gender, Equity and Development*, ISEAS, Singapore pp. 179-86.

Nohlen, Dieter (1990), *Wahlrecht und Parteiensystem*, Leske Verlag und Budrich GMbH, Opladen.

Nordic Council of Ministers (2002), *Nordic Statistical Yearbook*, Nordic Statistical Secretariat, Copenhagen.

Norris, Pippa (1985), 'Women's Legislative Participation in Western Europe', *West European Politics*, Vol. 8(4), pp. 90-101.

Norris, Pippa (1987), Politics and Sexual Equality: The Comparative Position of Women in Western Democracies, Rienner, Boulder, Colorado.

Norris, Pippa (1993), 'Conclusions: Comparing Legislative Recruitment', in Joni Lovenduski and Pippa Norris (eds.), *Gender and Party Politics*, Sage, London, pp. 309-30.

Norris, Pippa (1996), 'Women Politicians: Transforming Westminster?', *Parliamentary Affairs*, 49(1), pp. 89-102.

Norris, Pippa, (1996), 'Legislative Recruitment', in Lawrence LeDuc, Richard G.Niemi and Pippa Norris (eds.), *Comparing Democracies: Elections and Voting in Comparative*

Perspective, Sage, London, pp.184-216.

Norris, Pippa (1997), 'Procesos de Reclutamiento Legislativo: Una Perspectiva Comparada', in Edurne Uriarte and Arantxa Elizondo (eds.), *Mujeres y Politica: Análisis y Práctica,* Ariel, Barcelona, pp. 149-81.

Norris, Pippa (ed.), (1997), *Women, Media and Politics*, Oxford University Press, New York.

Norris, Pippa (2000), 'Women's Representation and Electoral Systems', in Richard Rose (ed.), *The International Encyclopaedia of Elections*, CQ Press, Washington DC, pp. 348-51.

Norris, Pippa and Lovenduski, Joni (1989), 'Pathways to Parliament', *Talking Politics*, Vol. 1(3), pp. 90-94.

Norris, Pippa, Carty, R. J., Erickson, Lynda, Lovenduski, Joni and Simms, Marian (1990), 'Party Selectorates in Australia, Britain and Canada: Prolegomena for Research in the 1990s', *Journal of Commonwealth & Comparative Politics*, Vol. 28(2), pp. 219-45.

Norris, Pippa, Vallance, Elizabeth and Lovenduski, Joni (1992), 'Do Candidates Make a Difference?: Gender, Race, Ideology and Incumbency', *Parliamentary Affairs*, Vol. 45(4), pp. 496-517.

Norris, Pippa and Lovenduski, Joni (1995), *Political Recruitment: Gender, Race and Class in the British Parliament*, Cambridge University Press, Cambridge.

Norris, Pippa and Inglehart, Ronald (2001), 'Women and Democracy: Cultural Obstacles to Equal Representation', *Journal of Democracy*, Vol. 12(3), pp. 126-40.

Nzomo, Maria (1993), 'The Gender Dimension of Democratization in Kenya: Some International Linkages', *Alternatives*, Vol. 18, pp. 61-73.

O'Donovan, Orla and Ward, Eilís (1999), 'Networks of Women's Groups in the Republic of Ireland', in Yvonne Galligan, Eilís Ward and Rick Wilford (eds.), *Contesting Politics, Women in Ireland, North and South*, Westview Press, Boulder, Colorado, pp. 90-108.

Oakes, Ann and Elizabeth Almquist (1993), 'Women in National Legislatures', *Population Research and Policy Review*, Vol. 12, pp. 71-81.

Ochwada, Hannington (1997), 'Politics and Gender Relations in Kenya: A Historical Perspective', *African Development,* Vol. 22(1), pp. 123-39.

Oey Gardiner, Mayling (2001), 'And the Winner is... Indonesian Women in Public Life', in Kathryn Robinson and Sharon Bessell (eds.), *Women in Indonesia: Gender, Equity and Development*, ISEAS, Singapore, pp. 100-112.

Office Fédéral de la Statistique (1999), Les Élections au Conseil National de 1999: L'évolution du Paysage Politique Depuis 1971, OFS, Neuchâtel.

Office Fédéral de la Statistique (2000), *Les Femmes et les Élections au Conseil National de 1999*, OFS, Neuchâtel.

Office Fédéral de la Statistique (2004), *Les Femmes et les Élections au Conseil National de 2003*, OFS, Neuchâtel.

Ortiz, Carmen (1987), La Participación de las Mujeres en la Democracia (1976-1986), Instituto de la Mujer, Madrid.

Otunga, Ruth (1997), 'Gender Differentiation and the Role of Culture in Tertiary Level Education: Implications for Employment Opportunities and Environmental Utilization by Women in Kenya', *UFAHAMU*, Vol. 25(2), pp. 42-53.

Pagnossin Aligisakis, Elisabetta (1991), 'Les Rôles Social et Politique des Femmes: Quels Changements?', in Anna Melich (ed.), *Les Valeurs des Suisses*, Peter Lang, Berne, pp. 337-88.

Parawansa, Kofifah Indar (2001), 'Institution Building: An Effort to Improve Indonesian Women's Role and Status', in Kathryn Robinson and Sharon Bessell (eds.), *Women in Indonesia: Gender, Equity and Development*, ISEAS, Singapore, pp. 68-77.

Parlement Européen (1997), *Incidences Variables des Systèmes Électoraux sur la*

Représentation Politique des Femmes. Direction Générale des Etudes, Série Droit des femmes W-10, Luxembourg.

Parpart, Jane L. (1988), 'Women and State', in Donald Rothchild and Naomi Chazan (eds.), *The Precarious Balance: State and Society in Africa*, Westview Press, Boulder, Colorado, pp. 208-30.

Pateman, Carole (1988), *The Sexual Contract*, Polity Press, Cambridge.

Paxton, Pamela (1997), 'Women in National Legislatures: A Cross-National Analysis', *Social Science Research*, Vol. 26(4), pp. 442-64.

Pedersen, Mogens (1989), *Dansk Politik i 1980'erne* (Danish Politics in the 1980s), Samfunvidenskabeligt Forlag, Copenhagen.

Pejanovic, S. (1984), *Društvena Jednakost i Emancipacija Zene* (Social Equality and the Emancipation of Woman), Prosvetni pregled, Beograd.

Pelletier, Réjean (2000), 'Constitution et Fédéralisme', in Manon Tremblay, Réjean Pelletier and Marcel R. Pelletier (eds.), *Le Parlementarisme Canadien*, Presses de l'Université Laval, Sainte-Foy, pp. 47-87.

Pelletier, Réjean and Manon Tremblay (1992), 'Les Femmes sont-elles Candidates dans des Circonscriptions Perdues d'Avance? De l'examen d'une Croyance', *Canadian Journal of Political Science*, Vol. 25(2), pp. 249-67.

Perrigo, Sarah (1996), 'Women and Change in the Labour Party', *Parliamentary Affairs*, Vol. 49(1), pp. 116-129.

Phillips, Anne (1995), *The Politics of Presence*, Oxford University Press, Oxford.

Picq, Françoise (2002), 'Parité: La Nouvelle Exception Française', *Modern and Contemporary France*, Vol. 10(1), pp. 13-23.

Pitkin, Hannah (1967), *The Concept of Representation*, University of California Press, Berkeley.

Plantenga, Janneke (1998), 'Double Lives: Labour Market Participation, Citizenship and Gender', in Jet Bussemaker and Rian Voet (eds.), *Gender, Participation and Citizenship in the Netherlands*, Ashgate, Aldershot, pp.51-64.

Platzdasch, Bernard (2000), 'Islamic Reaction to a Female President', in Chris Manning and Peter van Dierman (eds.), *Indonesia in Transition: Social Aspects of Reformasi and Crisis*, ISEAS, Singapore, pp. 336-49.

Pringle, Rosemary, and Watson, Sophie (1992), '"Women's Interests" and the Poststructuralist State', in Michelle Barrett and Anne Phillips (eds.), *Destabilizing Theory: Contemporary Feminist Debates*, Polity Press, London, pp. 57-73.

Procacci, Giovanna, Rossilli, Maria Grazia (1997), 'La Construction de l'Égalité dans l'Action des Organisations Internationales', in Christine Fauré (ed.), *Encyclopédie Politique et Historique des Femmes*, Puf, Paris, pp. 827-59.

Promujer (1998), *Poder Político con Perfume de Mujer. Las Cuotas en el Perú*, Manuela Ramos and Instituto de Estudios Peruanos, Lima. *Translation.*

Promujer (2000), *El Cuarto Femenino*, Vol. 2 (7) and Vol. 2(8).

Promujer (2001), *El Cuarto Femenino*, Vol. 3 (10).

Pugh, Martin (1992), Women and the Women's Movement in Britain 1914-1959, Macmillan, Basingstoke.

Puwar, Nirmal (2004), *Space Invaders: Race, Gender and Bodies Out of Place*, Berg Publishers, Oxford and New York.

Rai, Shirin M. (1994), 'Gender and Democratization: Or What Does Democracy Mean for Women in the Third World?', *Democratization*, Vol. 1(2), pp. 209-28.

Randall, Vicky and Smyth, Alpha (1987), 'Bishops and Bailiwicks: Obstacles to Women's Political Participation', *Economic and Social Review*, Vol. 18(3), pp. 189-214.

Rees, Teresa (2002), 'The Politics of "Mainstreaming" Gender Equality', in Esther Breitenbach et al. (eds.) *The Changing Politics of Gender Equality in Britain*, Palgrave, Basingstoke, pp. 45-69.

Reinalda, Bob (1997), '*Dea ex Machina* or the Interplay Between National and International Policymaking', in Frances Gardiner (ed.), *Sex Equality Policy in Western Europe*, Routledge, London/New York, pp. 197-215.

Reingold, Beth (2000), Representing Women: Sex, Gender and Legislative Behaviour in Arizona and California, The University of North Carolina Press, Chapel Hill.

Reynolds, Andrew (1999), 'Women in the Legislatures and Executives of the World: Knocking at the Highest Glass Ceiling', *World Politics*, Vol. 51(4), pp. 547-72.

Reynolds, Andrew and Reilly, Ben (1997), *The International IDEA Handbook of Electoral Systems Design*, International Institute for Democracy and Electoral Assistance Stockholm.

Richtman, Auguštin, D. (1980), *Moc Zene u Patrijarhalnoj Suvremenoj Kulturi* (The Power of Woman in the Contemporary Patriarchal Culture), Zena, Zagreb.

Roberts, Kenneth (1995), 'Neoliberalism and the Transformation of Populism in Latin America: The Peruvian Case', *World Politics*, Vol. 48 (October), pp. 82-116.

Rodriguez, Victoria (ed.) (1998), *Women's Participation in Mexican Political Life*, Westview Press, Boulder, Colorado.

Rokkan, Stein and Urwin, Derek W. (eds), (1982), The Politics of Territorial Identity: Studies in European Regionalism, Sage, London.

Ross, Karen (2002), 'Women's Place in "Male" Space: Gender and Effect in Parliamentary Contexts', *Parliamentary Affairs*, Vol. 55(1), pp. 189-201.

Roulston, Carmel (1999), 'Inclusive Others: The Northern Ireland Women's Coalition in the Peace Process', *Scottish Affairs*, No. 26 (Winter), pp. 1-13.

Royal Norwegian Embassy (1995), 'New Norwegian Government', *News of Norway*, Vol. 2, p. 2.

Ruiz, Antonia María (2002), *Mecanismos del Cambio Ideológico e Introducción de Políticas de Género en Partidos Conservadores: El Caso de AP-PP en España en Perspectiva Comparada,* Ph.D. thesis, Institituto Juan March, Madrid.

Rule, Wilma (1981), 'Why Women Don't Run: The Critical Factors in Women's Legislative Recruitment', *Western Political Quarterly*, Vol. 34(2), pp. 60-77.

Rule, Wilma (1987), 'Electoral Systems, Contextual Factors and Women's Opportunity for Election to Parliament in Twenty-Three Democracies', *Western Political Quarterly*, Vol. 40(3), pp. 477-98.

Rule, Wilma (1992), 'Multimember Legislative Districts: Minority and Anglo Women's and Men's Recruitment Opportunity', in Wilma Rule and Joseph F. Zimmerman (eds.), *United States Electoral Systems: Their Impact on Women and Minorities*, Preager, New York, pp. 57-72.

Rule, Wilma (1994), 'Women's Underrepresentation and Electoral Systems', *PS: Political Science and Politics*, Vol. 27(4), pp. 689-92.

Rule, Wilma, (1994), 'Parliaments of, by, and for the People: Except for Women?', in Wilma Rule and Joseph Zimmerman (eds.), *Electoral Systems in Comparative Perspective. Their Impact on Women and Minorities.* Westport: Greenwood Press, pp. 15-30.

Rule, Wilma and Norris, Pippa (1992), 'Women's Underrepresentation in Congress: Is the Electoral System the Culprit?', in Wilma Rule and Joseph F. Zimmerman (eds.), *United States Electoral Systems: Their Impact on Women and Minorities*, Preager, New York, pp. 41-54.

Rule, Wilma and Shugart, Matthew S. (1991), 'Electing Women's Representatives to Parliament: The Preference Vote Factor', paper presented at the International Political Science Association World Congress, Buenos Aires, Argentina.

Russell, Meg (2000), *Women's Representation in UK Politics: What Can Be Done Within The Law?,* The Constitution Unit, University College, London.

Russell, Meg (2003) 'Women in Elected Office in the UK 1992-2002: Struggles, Achievements and Possible Sea-change', in Alexandra Dobrowolsky and Vivien Hart (eds.), *Women Making Constitutions: New Politics and Comparative Perspectives*, Palgrave, Basingstoke, pp. 68-83.

Russell, Meg, Mackay, Fiona and McAllister, Laura (2002), 'Women's Representation in the Scottish Parliament and National Assembly for Wales: Party Dynamics for Achieving Critical Mass', *Journal of Legislative Studies*, Vol. 8(2), pp. 49-76.

SADC Gender Monitor (1999), *Thirty Percent Women in Power by 2005*, available at http://www.sardc.net/widsaa/sgm/1999/sgm_ch3.html.

Sadli, Saparinah (2001), 'Feminism in Indonesia in an International Context', in Kathryn Robinson and Sharon Bessell (eds.), *Women in Indonesia: Gender, Equity and Development*, ISEAS, Singapore, pp. 80-91.

Sainsbury, Diane (1993), 'The Politics of Increased Women's Representation: the Swedish Case', in Joni Lovenduski and Pippa Norris (eds.), *Gender and Party Politics*, Sage, London, pp. 263-90.

Sainsbury, Diane (2001), 'Rights Without Seats: The Puzzle of Women's Legislative Recruitment in Australia', in Marian Sawer (ed.), *Elections, Full, Free and Fair*, Federation Press, Sydney, pp. 63-77.

Sapiro, Virginia (1981), 'When are Interests Interesting? The Problem of Political Representation of Women', *American Political Science Review*, Vol. 75, pp. 701-16.

Sawer, Marian (1997), 'Mirroring the Nation? Electoral Systems and the Representation of Women', *Current Affairs Bulletin*, Vol 73(5), pp. 8-12.

Sawer, Marian (1998), 'Femocrats and Ecorats: Women's Policy Machinery in Australia, Canada and New Zealand', in Carol Miller and Shahra Razavi (eds.), *Missionaries and Mandarins: Feminist Engagement with Development Institutions,* Intermediate Technology Publications, London, pp. 112-37.

Sawer, Marian (2000a), 'Parliamentary Representation of Women: From Discourses of Justice to Strategies of Accountability', *International Political Science Review,* Vol. 21 (4), pp. 361-80.

Sawer, Marian (2000b), 'A Question of Heartland', in John Warhurst and Andrew Parkin (eds.), *The Machine: Labor Confronts the Future*, Allen and Unwin, Sydney, pp. 264-80.

Sawer, Marian (2001), 'Women and Government in Australia', in *Year Book Australia 2001*, Australian Bureau of Statistics, (CAT No. 1301.0), Canberra, pp. 72-89.

Sawer, Marian (2002), 'The Representation of Women in Australia: Meaning and Make-believe, in Karen Ross (ed.), *Women, Politics and Change*, Oxford University Press, Oxford, pp. 5-18.

Sawer, Marian and Simms, Marian (1993), *A Woman's Place: Women and Politics in Australia,* 2nd edn, Allen and Unwin, Sydney.

Sayers, Anthony M. (1999), Parties, Candidates, and Constituency Campaigns in Canadian Elections, UBC Press, Vancouver.

Scanlon, Geraldine M. (1990), 'El Movimentio Feminista en España, 1900-1985: Logros y Dificultades', in Judith Astellara (ed.), *Participación Política de las Mujeres,* CIS/Siglo XXI, Madrid, pp. 83-100.

Scannell, Yvonne (1988), 'The Constitution and the Role of Women', in Brian Farrell (ed.), *De Valera's Constitution and Ours*, Gill and Macmillan, Dublin, pp. 123-36.

Sen, Krishna (2001), 'The Mega Factor in Indonesian Politics: A New President or a New Kind of Presidency?', in Katherine Robinson and Sharon Bessell (eds.), *Women in Indonesia: Gender, Equity and Development*, ISEAS, Singapore, pp. 13-27.

Shaffer, William R. (1998), *Politics, Parties and Parliaments*, Ohio State University Press, Columbus.

Sharpe, Sydney (1994), The Gilded Ghetto: Women and Political Power in Canada, Harper Collins, Toronto.

Shepherd-Robinson, Laura and Lovenduski, Joni (2002), *Women and Candidate Selection in British Political Parties*, Fawcett, London.

Shipley, Jenny (1993), 'House Work', in Arthur Baysting, Dyan Campbell and Margaret Dagg (eds.), *Making Policy Not Tea: Women in Parliament*, Oxford University Press, Auckland, pp. 97-99.

Shvedova, Nadezdha (1998), 'Obstacles to Women's Participation in Parliament', in Azza Karam (ed.), *Women in Parliament: Beyond Numbers*, IDEA, Stockholm, available at http://www.idea.int/publications'wip/upload/1_Shvedova.pdf.

Siaroff, Alan (2000), 'Women's Representation in Legislatures and Cabinets in Industrial Democracies', *International Political Science Review*, Vol. 21(2), pp. 197-215.

Šiber, Ivan (1993), 'Structuring the Croatian Party Scene', *Politicka misao*, Vol. 30(2), pp. 111-29.

Šiber, Ivan (2001), 'Politicko Ponašanje Biraca u Izborima 1990 – 2000', (Political Behaviour of Voters in Elections, 1990—2000), in Mirjana Kasapovic (ed.), *Hrvatska Politika 1990 – 2000,* Biblioteka Politicka misao, Zagreb.

Sineau Mariette (1994), 'Law and Democracy', in Georges Duby and Michelle Perrot (eds.), *A History of Women*, The Belknap Press of Harvard University Press, Cambridge, pp. 497-525.

Sineau Mariette (2001), Profession: Femme Politique - Sexe et Pouvoir Sous la Cinquième République, Presses de Sciences Po, Paris.

Sinkonnen, Sirkka, and Haavio-Mannila, Elina (1990), 'The Impact of Women MPs and the Women's Movement on Political Agenda Building in Finland', Paper presented at the International Political Science Association World Congress, Stockholm, Sweden.

Sinnott, Richard (1999), 'The Electoral System', in John Coakley and Michael Gallagher (eds.), *Politics in the Republic of Ireland*, 3rd edn., Routledge, London, pp. 123-36.

Skard, Torild (1987), 'Women in the Political Life of the Nordic Countries', in Torild Skard (ed.), *Women in Contemporary Scandinavia*, Norwegian University Press, Oslo, pp. 639-55.

Skard, Torild and Haavio-Mannila, Elina (1985), 'Women in Parliament', in Elina Haavio-Manila et al. (eds.), *Unfinished Democracy: Women in Nordic Politics*, Pegamon Press, Oxford, pp. 51-80.

Skejeie, Hege (1993), 'Ending the Male Political Hegemony: The Norwegian Experience', in Joni Lovenduski and Pippa Norris (eds.), *Gender and Party Politics*, Sage, London, pp. 231-62.

Skjeie, Hege (1991), 'The Rhetoric of Difference: On Women's Inclusion into Political Elites', *Politics & Society*, Vol. 19(2), pp. 233-63.

Skjeie, Hege (1992), *Den Politiske Betydningen av Kjonn* (The Political Meaning of Gender), Institute for Social Research, Oslo.

Sklevicky, Lydia (1996), *Konji, Zene, Ratovi* (Horses, Women, Wars), Zenska Infoteka, Zagreb.

Social Watch (2001), *Report: Tanzania*, available at
http://www.socwatch.org.uy/2000/eng/nationalreports/tanzania_eng.htm.

Solheim, Bruce Olav (2000), On Top of the World: Women's Political Leadership in Scandinavia and Beyond, Greenwood Press, Westport, CT.

South Africa Parliament Joint Standing Committee on the Improvement of the Quality of Life & Status of Women (1999), *Employment: Second Annual Report, January 1998-March 1999*, available at http://womensnet.org.za/parliament/employment.html.

South African Gender Commission available at http://home.online.no/~sa-emb/government_gender_commission.html.

Squires, Judith and Wickham Jones, Mark (2001), *Women in Parliament: A Comparative Analysis*, Equal Opportunities Commission, Manchester.

Squires, Judith (1999), *Gender and Political Theory*, Polity Press, Cambridge.
Stephenson, MaryAnn (1997), *Fawcett Survey of Women MPs*, Fawcett Society, London.
Stocker, Monika and Bachmann, Edith (eds.), (1991), *Frauensession; Session des Femmes; Sessione delle Donne*, eFeF, Zurich.
Street, Maryan (1996), 'Politics and the Atypical: What Do Women Bring to MMP and What Opportunities Does MMP Offer Women?', in Su Olsson and Nicole Stirton (eds.), *Women and Leadership: Power and Practice International Conference 1996*, Massey University, Palmerston North, pp. 451-56.
Studlar, Donley T. and Matland, Richard E. (1994), 'The Growth of Women's Representation in the Canadian House of Commons and the Election of 1984: A Reappraisal', *Canadian Journal of Political Science*, Vol. 27(1), pp. 53-79.
Studlar, Donley T. and Matland, Richard E. (1996), 'The Dynamics of Women's Representation in the Canadian Provinces: 1975-1994', *Canadian Journal of Political Science*, Vol. 29(2), pp. 269-93.
Studlar, Donley T., and Moncrief, Gary F. (1997), 'The Recruitment of Women Cabinet Ministers in the Canadian Provinces', *Governance: An International Journal of Policy and Administration*, Vol. 10(1), pp. 67-81.
Sullivan, Norma (1994), Masters and Managers: A Study of Gender Relations in Urban Java, St Leonards, Allen and Unwin.
Suryakusuma, Julia I. (1996), 'The State and Sexuality in New Order Indonesia', in Laurie J. Sears (ed.), *Fantisizing the Feminine in Indonesia*, Durham, Duke University Press, pp. 92-119.
Swers, Michele (2001), 'Understanding the Policy Impact of Electing Women: Evidence from Research on Congress and State Legislatures', *PS: Political Science and Politics*, Vol. 34(2), pp. 217-20.
Tamerius, Karin L (1995), 'Sex, Gender and Leadership in the Representation of Women', in Rita Mae Kelly and Georgina Duerst-Lahti (eds.), *Gender Power, Leadership and Governance*, Ann Arbor, University of Michigan Press, pp. 93-112.
Tardy, Évelyne et al. (1982), La Politique: Un Monde d'Hommes ? Une Étude sur les Mairesses au Québec, Hurtubise HMH, Montreal.
Tardy, Évelyne, Tremblay, Manon and Legault, Ginette (1997), *Maires et Mairesses. Les Femmes et la Politique Municipale*, Liber, Montreal.
Temu, Fortunata and Kassim, Sherbanu (2001), *Women and Elections in Tanzania,* available at
http://tanzania.fes-international.de/Activities/Docs/womenandelections.html.
Thomas, Sue (1991), 'The Impact of Women on State Legislative Policies, *Journal of Politics*, Vol. 53(4), pp. 958-76.
Thomas, Sue (1994), *How Women Legislate*, Oxford University Press, New York.
Threlfall, Monica (1996), 'Feminist Politics and Social Change in Spain', in Monica Threlfall (ed.), *Mapping the Women's Movement*, London, Verso, pp. 115-51.
Tóth, Andrea (1995), 'Lehet-e Egy Fiúból Miniszterelnök? A Nök Részvételének Változásai az Európai Országok Döntéshozatalában' (Can a Boy Become Prime Minister? Changes of Women's Participation in the Decision-making Processes in Europe), in *Info-társadalomtudomány* (INFO Social Science, Scholarly Quarterly) Vol. 32, pp. 47-56.
Transparencia, (2000), *Datos Electorales,* Vol.1(23).
Transparencia, (2001) *Datos Electorales*, Vol.2 (1).
Tremblay, Manon (1993), 'Political Party, Political Philosophy and Feminism: A Case Study of the Female and Male Candidates in the 1989 Québec General Election', *Canadian Journal of Political Science*, Vol. 26(3), pp. 507-22.
Tremblay, Manon (1995), 'Les Femmes, des Candidates Moins Performantes Que les Hommes? Une Analyse des Votes Obtenus par les Candidates et Candidats du Québec à

Une Élection Fédérale Canadienne, 1945-1993', *International Journal of Canadian Studies*, Vol. 11, Spring, pp. 59-81.

Tremblay, Manon (1996), 'Conscience de Genre et Représentation Politique des Femmes', *Politique et Sociétés*, Vol. 29, pp. 93-137.

Tremblay, Manon (1998), 'Do Female MPs Substantively Represent Women? A Study of Legislative Behaviour in Canada's 35th Parliament', *Canadian Journal of Political Science*, Vol. 31(3), pp. 435-65.

Tremblay, Manon (1999), *Des Femmes au Parlement: Une Stratégie Féministe?*, Remue-ménage, Montreal.

Tremblay, Manon (2001), 'La Parité Femmes/Hommes en Politique: Un Élément de Réforme des Institutions Politiques Canadiennes?', *Journal of Canadian Studies*, Vol. 35(4), pp.40-59.

Tremblay, Manon (2002a), 'L'élection Fédérale de 2000: Qu'est-il donc Arrivé Aux Candidates?', *Politique et Sociétés*, Vol. 21(1), pp. 89-109.

Tremblay, Manon (2002b), 'Québec Women in Politics: Reappraisal', in Veronica Strong-Boag, Mona Gleason, and Adele Perry (eds.), *Rethinking Canada: The Promise of Women's History*, Oxford University Press, Toronto, pp. 375-93.

Tremblay, Manon and Boivin, Guylaine (1991), 'La Question de l'Avortement Au Parlement Canadien: de l'Importance du Genre dans l'Orientation des Débats', *Revue Juridique La Femme et le Droit*, Vol. 4(2), pp. 459-76.

Tremblay, Manon and Pelletier, Réjean (1993), 'Les Femmes et la Représentation Politique Vues par des Députées et Députés du Québec', *Recherches Féministes*, Vol. 6(2), pp. 89-114.

Tremblay, Manon and Pelletier, Réjean (1995), *Que Font-Elles en Politique?*, Presses de l'Université Laval, Sainte-Foy.

Tremblay, Manon and Pelletier, Réjean (2001), 'More Women Constituency Party Presidents: A Strategy for Increasing the Number of Women Candidates in Canada?', *Party Politics*, Vol. 7(2), pp. 157-90.

Tremblay, Manon, Pelletier, Réjean and Pelletier, Marcel R. (2000), *Le Parlementarisme Canadien*, Presses de l'Université Laval, Sainte-Foy.

Trench, Alan (ed.) (2001), The State of the Nations 2001: The Second Year of Devolution in the United Kingdom, Imprint Academic, Thorverton.

Trimble, Linda (1993), 'A Few Good Women: Female Legislators in Alberta, 1972-1991', in Catherine A. Cavanaugh and Randi R. Warne (eds.), *Standing on New Ground: Women in Alberta*, Calgary, University of Alberta Press, pp. 87-118.

Trimble, Linda (1997), 'Feminist Politics in the Alberta Legislature, 1972-1994', in Jane Arscott and Linda Trimble (eds.), *In the Presence of Women: Representation in Canadian Governments*, Harcourt Brace and Company, Toronto, pp. 128-53.

Tripp, Aili Mari (2001), 'Women and Democracy: The New Political Activism in Africa', *Journal of Democracy*, Vol. 12 (3), pp. 141-55.

Tripp, Aili Mari (2000), *Women and Politics in Uganda*, University of Wisconsin Press, Madison, Wisconsin.

Tripp, Ali Mari (2001), 'Women and Democracy: The New Political Activism in Africa', Journal of Democracy, Vol. 12(3), pp. 141-55.

Tuesta Soldevilla, Fernando (ed.) (1999), *El Juego Político. Fujimori, la Oposición y las Reglas*, Fundación Friedrich Ebert, Lima.

Ufomata, Titi (1998), 'Linguistic Images, Socialization and Gender in Education', *Africa Development*, Vol. 23(3-4), pp. 61-75.

Uhlaner, Carole Jane and Schlozman, Kay Lehman (1986), 'Candidate Gender and Congressional Campaign Receipts', *Journal of Politics*, Vol. 48(1), pp. 30-50.

UNICEF (1999), *Women in Transition – a Summary*, UNICEF, Florence.

United Nations (1992), Women in Politics and Decision-making in the Late Twentieth Century – A United Nations Study, Centre for Social Development and Humanitarian Affairs, New York.
United Nations (2000), General Assembly Plenary Twenty-Third Special Session, *Press Release*, 9 June, http://www.unhchr/huricane/.
United Nations Development Program (1999), Gender in Transition: Five Years of UNDP Projects in Eastern and Central Europe and CIS, UNDP, New York.
United Nations Development Program (2002), *Human Development Report 2002*, Oxford University Press, New York.
United Nations Development Program (2003), *Human Development Report 2003*, Oxford University Press, New York.
United Nations Educational, Scientific and Cultural Organization (1999), *UNESCO Statistical Yearbook 1999*, available at http://www.uis.unesco.org/en/stats/statistics/yearbook/.
Uriarte, Edurne (1997), 'Las Mujeres en las Elites Politicas', in Edurne Uriarte and Arantxa Elizondo (eds.), *Mujeres en Politica: Analisis y Practica*, Ariel, Barcelona, pp. 53-75.
Uriarte, Edurne (1999), 'El Acceso de las Mujeres a las Elites Politicas el Caso Español', in Margarita Ortega, Cristina Sanchez and Celia Valiente (eds.), *Genero y Ciudadania: Revisiones Desde el Ambito Privado*, Universidad Autonoma de Madrid, Madrid, pp. 341-65.
Uriarte, Edurne and Ruiz, Cristina (1998), 'Mujeres y Hombres en las Elites Políticas Españolas: Diferencias o Similitudes?', *Revista Española de Investigaciones Sociológicas*, Vol. 88, pp. 207-32.
Valian,Virginia (1998), *Why So Slow? The Advancement of Women,* MIT Press, Cambridge.
Vallance, Elizabeth (1979), *Women in the House*, Athlone Press, London.
Van der Ros, Janneke (1994), 'The State and Women: A Troubled Relationship in Norway', in Barbara J. Nelson and Najma Chowdhury (eds.), *Women and Politics Worldwide*, Yale University Press, New Haven, pp. 528-43.
Van Donk, Mirjam and Maceba, Maletsatsi (1999), 'Women at the Crossroads: Women in Governance', *Agenda*, Vol. 40, pp. 18-22.
Vargas, Virginia (2000), 'Las Trampas de la Representación de las Mujeres en el Gobierno de Fujimori', *Texto y Pretexto*, Vol. 1(1), pp. 1-8.
Vargas, Virginia, and Olea, Cecilia (1997), 'El Movimiento Feminista y el Estado: Los Avatares de Una Agenda Propia', paper presented at the Conference *El Movimiento Feminista y el Estado: Los Avatares de Una Agenda Propia*, CEDEP, Lima, September.
Vargas, Virginia. (2001), 'Mujeres por la Democracia. Los Conjuros Contra la Tentación de la Igualdad en Clave Autoritaria. Una Reflexión Político Personal', *Cuestión de Estado*, Vol. 27/28 (special edition), pp. 104-7.
Vázquez, Matilde (1989), 'Espagne: Étude de Cas National', paper presented at the Expert Group meeting on Equality in Political Participation and Decision-making, Vienna, 18-22 September.
Vianen, Annelies van and Fischer, Agneta (1998) 'Sexeverschillen in Voorkeuren Voor een "Mannelijke" organisatiecultuur' (Sex Differences in Preferences for a "Masculine" Culture of Organizations), *Gedrag en Organisatie* (Behavior and Organisations), Vol.11(5), pp. 249-64.
Vickers, Jill (1978), 'Where Are the Women in Canadian Politics?', *Atlantis: A Women's Studies Journal/Journal d'études sur la Femme*, Vol. 3(2), pp. 40-51.
Vickers, Jill McCalla and Brodie, M. Janine (1981), 'Canada', in Joni Lovenduski and Jill Hills (eds.), *The Politics of the Second Electorate: Women and Public Participation*, London, Routledge and Kegan Paul, pp. 52-79.
Villar, Eliana (1994), *Por Mérito Propio: Mujer y Política*, Centro de la Mujer Peruana Flora Tristan, Lima.

Visser, A. (1985), 'Aanpassen of Dwarsliggen' (To Adapt or to be Controversial), *Opzij* (Aside), Vol.13 (10), pp. 8-14.

Wahlke, John C., Eulau, Heinz, Buchanan, William and Ferguson, LeRoy C. (1962), *The Legislative System*, Wiley, New York.

Walter, Natasha (1998), *The New Feminism,* Little, Brown and Comp., London.

Wängnerud, Lena (2000), 'Testing the Politics of Presence: Women's Representation in the Swedish Riksdag', *Scandinavian Political Studies*, 23(1), pp. 67-91.

Ward, Lucy (2000), 'Learning From the "Babe" Experience: How the Finest Hour Became a Fiasco' in Anna Coote (ed.) *New Gender Agenda*, IPPR, London, pp. 23-32.

Ward, Margaret (2000), The Northern Ireland Assembly and Women: Assessing the Gender Deficit, Democratic Dialogue, Belfast.

Ward, Margaret (2001), 'Gender in Transition? Social and Political Transformation in Northern Ireland', paper presented at the University of Ulster Transitional Justice Seminar Series, Belfast, 2 November.

Waylen, Georgina (1994), 'Women and Democratization: Conceptualizing Gender Relations in Transition Politics', *World Politics*, 46 (3), pp. 327-54.

Waylen, Georgina (1996), *Gender in Third World Politics*, Lynne Rienner Publishers, Boulder, Colorado.

Williamson, Myffanwy (2000), Do Women Make a Difference? Testing For Critical Mass in the Australian Senate and the New Zealand Parliament, Research School of Social Sciences, Australian National University, Canberra.

Wilson, Margaret (1992), 'Women and the Labour Party', in Margaret Clark (ed.), *The Labour Party after 75 Years*, Victoria University of Wellington, Wellington, pp. 35-49.

Women in Development-Southern Africa Awareness (2000), *Women in Politics and Decision-Making*, Issue No. 22, available at http://www.sardc.net/widsaa/gadexchange/2001/Iss22/.

Women's Net (undated), *An Introduction to National Parliament's Committee on the Status of Women*, available at http://womensnet.org.za/parliament/mission.htm.

World Bank (2001), *World Development Indicators 2001*, World Bank, Washington, D.C.

Yoder, Janice D. (1991), 'Rethinking Tokenism: Looking Beyond Numbers', *Gender and Society*, Vol. 5(2), pp. 178-92.

Yoon, Mi Yung (2001a), 'Democratization and Women's Legislative Representation in Sub-Saharan Africa', *Democratization*, Vol. 8(2), pp. 169-90.

Yoon, Mi Yung, (2001b). 'Explaining Women's Legislative Representation in Sub-Saharan Africa', paper presented at the Annual Meeting of the Southern Political Science Association, Atlanta, Georgia, 8-11 November.

Young, Lisa (1991), 'Legislative Turnover and the Election of Women to the Canadian House of Commons', in Kathy Megyery (ed.), *Women in Canadian Politics: Toward Equity in Representation*, Dundern Press, Toronto, pp. 81-100.

Young, Lisa (2000), *Feminists and Party Politics,* UBC Press, Vancouver.

Young, Lisa (2002), 'Going Mainstream? The Women's Movement and Political Parties in Canada and the US', in Joanna Everitt and Brenda O'Neill (eds.), *Citizen Politics: Research and Theory in Canadian Political Behaviour*, Oxford University Press, Don Mills, pp. 413-25.

Young, Lisa (2003), 'Can Feminists Transform Party Politics? The Canadian Experience', in Manon Tremblay and Linda Trimble (eds.), *Women and Electoral Politics in Canada*, Oxford University Press, Don Mills, pp. 76-90.

Zaborszky, Dorothy (1987), 'Feminist Politics: The Feminist Party of Canada', *Women's Studies International Forum*, Vol. 10(6), pp. 613-21.

Zakošek, Nenad (1991), 'Polarizacijske Strukture, Obrasci Politickih Uvjerenja i Hrvatski Izbori 1990', (Polarization Structures, Patterns of Political Convictions and the Croatian

Elections of 1990) in Ivan Grdešic, M.Kasapović, Ivan Šiber and Nenad Zakošek (eds.), *Hrvatska u izborima '90*, Naprijed, Zagreb, pp. 131-87.

Zakošek, Nenad (1994), 'Struktura i Dinamika Hrvatskoga Politickog Sustava', (Structural Dynamic of the Croatian Political System), *Revija za Sociologiju*, Vol. XXV (1–2), pp. 23-40.

Index

For Product Safety Concerns and Information please contact our EU representative GPSR@taylorandfrancis.com
Taylor & Francis Verlag GmbH, Kaufingerstraße 24, 80331 München, Germany

www.ingramcontent.com/pod-product-compliance
Lightning Source LLC
Chambersburg PA
CBHW070610270326
41926CB00013B/2493
9781138276437